Eighth Edition

W9-CCD-374

Contemporary Urban Planning

JOHN M. LEVY

Virginia Polytechnic Institute and State University

PEARSON

Prentice Hall

Upper Saddle River, New Jersey 07458

Library of Congress Cataloging-in-Publication Data

Levy, John M.
    Contemporary urban planning/John M. Levy.—8th ed.
        p. cm.
    Includes bibliographical references and index.
    ISBN-13: 978-0-13-602545-0 (alk. paper)
    ISBN-10: 0-13-602545-5 (alk. paper)
    1. City planning—United States.   2. Urban policy—United States.   3. Urbanization—
United States.   4. Sociology, Urban—United States.   I. Title.
HT167.L38 2009
307.1'2160973—dc22

                                                                                    2008001680

Executive Editor: Dickson Musslewhite
Associate Editor: Rob DeGeorge
Editorial Assistant: Synamin Ballatt
Director of Marketing: Brandy Dawson
Senior Marketing Manager: Kate Mitchell
Marketing Assistant: Jennifer Lang
Senior Managing Editor: Mary Carnis
Production Liaison: Debra Wechsler
Project Manager: Shiny Rajesh, Integra
Copy Editor: Martha Williams
Operations Supervisor: Mary Ann Gloriande

Director, Image Resource Center: Melinda
    Patelli
Manager, Rights and Permissions: Zina Arabia
Manager, Visual Research: Beth Brenzel
**Manager, Cover Visual Research &
    Permissions:** Karen Sanatar
Image Permission Coordinator: Ang'john Ferreri
Cover Art Design: Jayne Conte
Cover Design: Maureen Eide
Cover Image: Robert Spencer/The New York
    Times

This book was set in 10/12 Palatino by Integra and was printed by R.R. Donnelley & Sons, Inc.
The cover was printed by R.R. Donnelley & Sons, Inc.

Credits and acknowledgments borrowed from other sources and reproduced, with permission,
in this textbook appear on page 422.

Pearson Education Ltd.
Pearson Education Singapore, Pte. Ltd.
Pearson Education Canada, Ltd.
Pearson Education–Japan

Pearson Education Australia PTY, Limited
Pearson Education North Asia Ltd.
Pearson Educación de Mexico, S.A. de C.V.
Pearson Education Malaysia Pte. Ltd.

10 9 8 7 6 5 4 3 2 1
ISBN-13: 978-0-13-602545-0
ISBN-10:   0-13-602545-5

Contents

Preface ix
Acknowledgments xi

PART 1 THE BACKGROUND AND DEVELOPMENT OF CONTEMPORARY PLANNING

1 An Overview 1
The Need for Planning 1
The Specific Concerns of Planning 3
Who Are the Planners? 4
Professional Organizations 5
Satisfactions and Discontents 6
Useful Abilities 7
The Plan of This Book 7
Note 8

2 The Urbanization of America 9
Urbanization in the Nineteenth Century 9
Urban Trends in the Twentieth Century 16
A Look Ahead 26
Summary 28
Notes 29
Selected Bibliography 30

3 The History of Planning: Part I 31
Colonial America 32
Limited Means and Growing Problems 34

The Pressure for Reform   35
The Birth of Modern City Planning   42
The Public Control of Private Property   44
The Emergence of Regional and State Planning   49
Grander Visions   52
Summary   55
Notes   56
Selected Bibliography   57

4   The History of Planning: Part II   58
Planning and the Great Depression   59
The Postwar Period   61
Summary   70
Notes   71
Selected Bibliography   71

**PART 2   THE STRUCTURE AND PRACTICE
OF CONTEMPORARY PLANNING** _____

5   The Legal Basis of Planning   72
The Constitutional Framework   72
Public Control over Private Property   74
The Fight over Eminent Domain   85
State-Enabling Legislation   87
The Federal Role   89
Summary   91
Notes   92
Selected Bibliography   92

6   Planning and Politics   93
Why Is Planning Political?   93
Planners and Power   95
The Fragmentation of Power   96
Styles of Planning   99
How Planning Agencies Are Organized   102
Summary   105
Notes   106
Selected Bibliography   106

7 The Social Issues   108

The Social Issues in Planning for Housing   109
Other Issues   118
Who Does Social Planning?   122
Summary   122
Notes   122
Selected Bibliography   123

8 The Comprehensive Plan   124

The Goals of Comprehensive Planning   124
The Comprehensive Planning Process   126
How Effective Are Comprehensive Plans?   133
Summary   134
Notes   135
Selected Bibliography   136

9 The Tools of Land-Use Planning   137

Public Capital Investment   137
Land-Use Controls   140
Combining Capital Investment and Land-Use Controls   164
Forces Beyond Local Control   166
Summary   168
Notes   168
Selected Bibliography   170

PART 3   FIELDS OF PLANNING

10 Urban Design   171

What Is Urban Design?   173
The Urban Design Process   180
What Is Good Urban Design?   182
Replanning Suburbia: The Neotraditionalists   188
Edge City   193
Visions of the City of the Future   197
Coming to Terms with the Automobile   200
Summary   201
Notes   202
Selected Bibliography   203

11   Urban Renewal and Community Development   204

Urban Renewal   205
Community Development   213
The Housing Question   217
Planning for Housing   219
Summary   222
Notes   223
Selected Bibliography   224

12   Transportation Planning   225

Recent Trends in Urban Transportation   225
Paying for Transportation   227
Transportation Planning and Land Use   228
The Transportation Planning Process   230
Changes in the Federal Role   238
Fine-Tuning the System   239
The Growing Role of Tolls and Privatization   240
Smart Highways, Intelligent Vehicles, and
    New Machines   243
Summary   245
Notes   246
Selected Bibliography   247

13   Economic Development Planning   248

Historic Roots   249
Perspectives on Local Economic Development   250
State Economic Development Efforts   254
Local Economic Development Programs   257
Summary   264
Notes   264
Selected Bibliography   265

14   Growth Management, Smart Growth, and Sustainable Development   266

The Origins of Growth Management   267
Winners and Losers in Growth Management   269
A Sampling of Local Growth Management Programs   271
State-Level Growth Management   274
Growth Management—Pro or Con?   278
The Challenge of Smart Growth   279

Planning for Sustainability   282
Summary   286
Notes   289
Selected Bibliography   290

15   Environmental and Energy Planning   291
The Environmental Planning Problem   291
Environmental Progress at the National Level   292
The Question of Global Climate Change   293
The Intergovernment Context of Environmental
    Planning   301
Economic and Political Issues in Environmental
    Planning   306
Local Environmental Planning   310
An Example of Environmental Planning   313
Energy Planning   316
Summary   319
Notes   320
Selected Bibliography   321

16   Planning for Metropolitan Regions   322
The Political Problem   322
A Brief History of Metropolitan Area Planning   324
Minneapolis–St. Paul: A Tale of Two Cities   328
The Port Authority of New York and New Jersey   331
The Atlanta Regional Commission   336
Summary   339
Notes   339
Selected Bibliography   340

PART 4   LARGER QUESTIONS

17   National Planning in the United States   341
Is There National Planning in the United States?   341
The Pattern of Land Settlement   342
Establishing the Rail Network   343
Water and the West   345
Systematic Regional Planning   349
The Interstate Highway System   351
Financing the Suburbs   355

Land Management   357
Summary   359
Notes   359
Selected Bibliography   360

18   Planning in Other Nations   361
Planning in Western Europe   361
Planning in Eastern Europe   387
Planning in the Third World   393
A Look Ahead   397
Summary   399
Notes   400
Selected Bibliography   401

19   Planning Theory   402
Is Theory Necessary?   402
A Distinction Between Public and Private Planning   403
The Process of Planning   404
Advocacy Planning   411
Planning from Right and Left   412
Summary   419
Notes   420
Selected Bibliography   421

Illustration Credits   422
Index   423

Preface

The term *Planning* is a very general one. There are city and town planners and also corporate planners. The Pentagon employs numerous military planners. The launching of a space shuttle is the culmination of a tremendously complex and sophisticated planning process. Wealthy individuals who prefer to leave as much as possible of their wealth to their heirs and as little as possible to the Internal Revenue Service employ the services of estate planners. And so on.

Planning in its generic meaning, then, is a ubiquitous activity. Cutting across all types of planning is a certain common denominator. All have in common a conscious effort to define systematically and think through a problem to improve the quality of decision making. The planning discussed in this book represents a very small part of the total planning activity in the United States. Specifically, this book focuses on public planning at the substate level, that which is done by and for cities, counties, towns, and other units of local governments. We will also examine, much more briefly, planning for metropolitan regions, the states, and the question of national planning. This edition also contains a chapter which surveys planning in a number of other nations.

The reader who has at least sampled other books on planning will notice that this book has some particular emphases, specifically on politics, economics, ideology, law, and the question of who benefits and who loses by particular decisions. These emphases stem from my experience as a working planner. I entered planning in 1969 with a background in economics and journalism but with no specific training in planning. In my ignorance of the field, I assumed that if engineers planned bridges and architects planned buildings, then city and town planners planned cities and towns in an essentially similar way. In effect, I thought of planning as engineering or architecture writ large.

It did not take me long to learn that planning is a highly political activity. Not only is it immersed in politics, but also it is inseparable from the law. The ultimate arbiter of many a planning dispute is the court. And for every case that comes to court, some dozens of planning decisions have been conditioned by what the participants in the process think would be the decision if the matter were to come to court.

Planning decisions often involve large sums of money. In some cases large sums of public money are involved in the form of capital investments. But even when little in the way of public expenditure is involved, planning decisions can deliver large benefits to some and large losses to others. Thus to understand planning, one must understand something of the economic and financial issues at stake.

The study of planning quickly takes one into ideology. Planning issues and controversy inevitably raise questions about the proper role of government and the line between public needs and private rights. What properly is to be a matter of political decision, and what properly should be left to the market? Planning can raise issues that are not easily resolved. Planners are a fairly idealistic lot and often enter the field to serve the public interest. After immersion in a few public controversies, the beginning planner may wonder whether there *is* such a thing as the public interest. For if there is, there ought to be some general agreement among the public on what it is. But one can spend a long time in some areas of planning without seeing a single instance of this agreement.

In this book I have tried to convey something of the reality of planning practice and something of what goes on under the surface of events. I hope that the reader will not find this reality disillusioning, for planning in an open and a democratic society cannot be smooth and simple. Planning as it is—involved in political controversy, hedged about by the trends of judicial decisions, inextricably tied to economic questions, and connected to issues of ideology—is far more interesting than it would be if it were simply architecture or engineering writ large.

The book contains a certain amount of material on history and technology because the issues that planning focuses on are largely ones that political, social, and economic change bring to the forefront. For example, it can be argued that one of the biggest influences on American cities in the 1960s and 1970s was the massive acceleration in the mechanization of agriculture that began after the end of World War II. That event, the result of both economic and technological forces, set in motion a huge migration of population. The effects of this migration are still being felt in America's cities. I hope the book will help readers make some connections of that sort and develop the habit of looking for other such connections on their own.

The best and most effective planners are those with good peripheral vision—those who not only have mastered the technical side of planning but also understand the relationships between planning issues and the major forces in the society around them. I have endeavored to write a text consistent with that view.

ACKNOWLEDGMENTS

It is not possible to thank everyone who assisted in the writing of a book. However, I would like to express gratitude to three of my former colleagues in the Department of Urban Affairs and Planning, Larz Anderson, C. David Loeks, and Robert Stuart, for reviewing and making helpful suggestions on earlier drafts of this book. Various editions of this book have been reviewed by Mirle Rabinowitz Bussell, Carissa Schively, and Sujata Shetty. I am grateful to all of them.

For ten years before I became an academic, I was employed in various capacities by the Westchester County, New York, Department of Planning, where I had a fine opportunity to learn some of the realities of planning. I am thus indebted to a number of my former colleagues there, in particular Commissioner Peter Q. Eschweiler and Planning Board Chairman Dr. William Cassella. When all is said and done, however, the viewpoints expressed here and any mistakes made are my own.

John M. Levy

To Lucie, Rachel, Bernie, Kara, and Christopher

CHAPTER 1

An Overview

THE NEED FOR PLANNING

Perhaps the first question that has to be answered in a book about planning is simply "why do we need planning?" The need for planning comes down to two words, *interconnectedness* and *complexity*. If there were few of us and the technologies by which we lived were relatively simple, there would be little need for planning as described in this book. We could each go our own way and would gain little from common planning efforts. However, the fact is that we are numerous enough and our technologies complicated enough that this is not the case.

Consider a simple illustration of interconnectedness, the use of a few acres of urban land. The amount and character of development on that land will determine the amount of traffic it generates. Developing it with single-family houses will produce a different traffic flow than developing it with apartments, which will generate a different traffic flow than developing it with apartments, which will generate a different traffic flow than developing it with a neighborhood shopping center. Thus a land development decision is a traffic decision as well. That, potentially, affects everyone in the area. How much of the site is paved, and even what material is used for paving, affects how fast rainwater runs off from the property. Runoff may affect flooding and stream flow conditions miles downstream from the property. The types and quantities of commercial or residential activity on the property may affect air quality, noise levels, water quality, and the visual and social qualities of the area.

Decisions about the residential uses of land will affect housing prices, rents, and vacancies—in short, who can live in the community. Those decisions, in turn, will have effects on the economy of the community and the demands that are placed on the community for educational, social, and other services.

The land-use decisions made by a community shape its very character—what it is like to walk through, what it is like to drive through, who lives in it, what kinds of jobs and businesses exist in it, how well the natural environment survives, and whether the community is an attractive one or an ugly one. In some cases such decisions may directly affect human life and health, for example, whether traffic patterns are safe or hazardous.

Land-use decisions affect the fiscal health of the community. Every property that is developed burdens the community with obligations such as education, police and fire protection, recreational services, and social services. Conversely, every development contributes, directly or indirectly, to municipal revenues through property taxes, sales taxes, or charges and fees. Thus the pattern of land development will affect how heavily the community must tax its residents and the level of public services the community can provide.

The land in question may be privately owned, in which case public control is exercised through a regulatory process. It may be owned publicly, in which case direct public investment will determine its use. But in either case there is a distinct public interest in what happens on the land. To generalize, it is the fact of interconnectedness, whether we are discussing land use or other questions, which helps to justify public planning efforts.

Complexity is the condition that justifies planning as a separate profession and as a separate activity of government. If all of the sorts of relationships suggested were simple, they could be dealt with simply and informally. If the community were tiny, perhaps direct negotiations between private parties would suffice. If the community were somewhat larger, perhaps the relationships could easily be dealt with along with the general flow of municipal business. But the complexity of a modern community renders such simple and direct approaches inadequate.

The complexity of the community also means that many things that in a simpler place could be done privately must be done publicly. In an agricultural area with a population of perhaps a few dozen people per square mile, water supply and waste disposal are handled on site by the individual household. No common decision making or investment is necessary. In a large metropolitan area, these functions are likely to involve systems that span many communities and may involve billions of dollars of capital investment. Comparable comments could be made about transportation, education, public safety, recreation, and the like.

Thus in the thousands of communities in the United States, planning is a formalized and distinct process of government. In relatively small communities, the planning function may be lodged in an unpaid part-time planning board with the technical work done by a planning consultant. In larger communities, the planning function is generally located within a planning department. Depending on community size, that department may have a staff ranging from one person to several hundred individuals. In a very small department, the planner(s) may be a jack-of-all-trades handling land-use questions one day, capital budgeting another day, and economic development a third day. In a larger agency, there may be considerable specialization of labor. One section of the agency may specialize in zoning issues, another in master planning, a third in planning-related research, another in environmental issues, and so on.

THE SPECIFIC CONCERNS OF PLANNING

What might a community seek to achieve through planning? In a growing community, planners might be concerned with shaping the pattern of growth to achieve a sensible and attractive land-use pattern. That concern means avoiding both oppressively dense development or overly scattered and fragmentary development. It means encouraging a pattern of development that gives residents ready access to recreational, cultural, school, shopping, and other facilities. It means having a street pattern that is convenient to use and through which traffic flows without excessive congestion. It means separating incompatible land uses and activities, for example, high-intensity commercial activity from residential areas. In a modern planned community, it might mean providing a system of pathways so that pedestrian and bicycle traffic is separated from automobile traffic.

The community's planners will also be concerned with the location of public facilities like schools and social service centers, both for the convenience of the people served and for reinforcing the development of a desirable land-use pattern. If the community anticipates or desires significant industrial or commercial development, its planners will be concerned with seeing that sufficient conveniently located blocks of land are available and that they are served with adequate roads, water, and sewer facilities.

In an older community that is not growing and that does not anticipate growth, planners may be concerned primarily with preserving or improving that which now exists. Thus planners may focus on measures to preserve the quality of the housing stock. In many communities planners will also be concerned with housing cost questions, specifically, how to provide housing for the community's lower-income residents. In many older communities planners devote much effort to preserving historic buildings and other landmarks. If the community is concerned (as many are) about the health of its downtown, planners may be involved in implementing street improvements and other changes designed to help downtown businesses compete successfully with establishments in outlying areas.

In a community that faces a serious unemployment problem or that sees its property tax base as being inadequate, economic development may be a major task of the planners. Much of their effort may be devoted to creating conditions that encourage existing industry to remain and expand and new firms to locate within the community.

In recent years much planning effort has focused on environmental issues: how to guide and manage development to minimize environmental damage. For example, a planner might be concerned with evaluating the relative environmental merits and financial costs of landfill disposal versus incineration for a municipality's solid wastes and then with helping to select the best site.

Planners employed by regional planning organizations may be concerned with improving the regionwide road network, with acquiring or developing land for a regionwide park and open space system, or with improving regionwide sewage disposal and water systems. They will also be concerned with encouraging coordination between the planning efforts of the various municipalities in the region to avoid duplication of capital facilities and interference effects (for example, community A siting its landfill operation at a point where it borders a residential area in community B).

This is far from a complete listing. It is simply meant to give some feeling for the range of planning issues.

WHO ARE THE PLANNERS?

Planners come from a variety of backgrounds. The single most common educational background is formal training in planning, most often a master's degree, either a Masters of City Planning (MCP) or a Masters of Urban and Regional Planning (MURP). But the field, and particularly larger agencies and consultants, absorbs people with many other backgrounds. Agencies that are large enough to have a separate research operation are likely to hire people with training in economics or statistics. Agencies that do transportation planning are likely to hire people with training in civil engineering and, particularly, transportation engineering. Large agencies often do a substantial amount of data handling and are likely to have on staff a few people with backgrounds in programming and data processing. Agencies that do significant amounts of environmental planning are likely to hire people with backgrounds in biology, chemistry, environmental science, and remote sensing. Planning inevitably involves mapping and spatially organized data, so that geographers and cartographers find their way into the profession. Planning involves many issues of law, particularly in regard to land use and environmental considerations. Thus many attorneys and people with joint training in law and planning have entered the field. In fact, several universities have joint four-year law and planning degree programs.

The majority of planners are employed by government. Of these, the larger share are employed by local governments, that is, by cities, towns, counties, and other substate jurisdictions. Smaller numbers are employed by state governments, by intergovernment organizations like councils of governments (COGs), and by a variety of authorities and special-purpose agencies. Some planners are employed by the federal government, particularly in departments like Housing and Urban Development (HUD), which fund and regulate planning-related activities of local governments. Most planners employed by government are civil servants, but a certain number are political appointees chosen outside the civil service process. Over the years many planners have found their way into municipal administration, where the sort of "big picture" view that planning tends to develop seems to be useful.

A substantial minority of all planners are employed within the private sector of the economy. Many work for planning consultants and in that capacity serve both government and a variety of private clients. A certain number of planners are employed directly by private organizations like land developers and corporations with substantial real property holdings. Some planners work for particular groups in society that feel they need the planners' skills to make their own case in the public forum. These may be neighborhood or community groups, environmental organizations, and citizens' groups of one type or another.

PROFESSIONAL ORGANIZATIONS

The most important national organization of planners in the United States is the American Planning Association (APA). In addition to the national organization there are state chapters and many hundreds of local chapters. The national organization publishes two magazines. *The Journal of the American Planning Association (JAPA)* which comes out quarterly is the more scholarly of the two. It provides articles on current research and theoretical issues in planning and, from time to time, on the history of planning. The APA also publishes *Planning* which comes out 11 times a year. It is the trade magazine of the profession in the United States. If you want to keep up with what is happening in planning—names, places, programs, controversies, court cases, and the like—it is the best available source. In addition to these two periodicals, the APA, through its Planning Advisory Service (PAS), publishes numerous technical, how-to-do-it reports for the practicing planner.

The work of the planner takes place within a complex legal framework and it is strongly affected by public funding, for one of the biggest, if not the biggest, shaper of the pattern of development is public capital investment. The APA thus lobbies Congress and, at times, state legislatures on a wide variety of matters, some instances of which are discussed latter in this book. It is, more than any other organization, the voice of planners in Congress and the state legislatures. Because the law is not only what is passed by legislative bodies, but also the precedents established in litigation, the APA takes positions on court cases and from time to time files *amicus curea* (friend of the court) briefs in cases involving land-use controls, environmental regulations, eminent domain, and other matters relevant to the practice of planning.

A second national organization is the American Institute of Certified Planners (AICP). This organization certifies planners. The planner who satisfies the organization's professional experience requirements and passes a written exam is certified and can put the letters AICP after his or her name. There are some planning jobs that require AICP certification and the certification may carry a certain weight with the user of planning services. For example, a municipality that purchases the services of a planning consultant may be reassured that the consultant or the consultant's personnel are AICP certified.

SATISFACTIONS AND DISCONTENTS

Planning is both anticipatory and reactive. At times planning will be devoted to anticipating and developing responses to problems that have not yet presented themselves. At other times planning will be devoted to responding to problems that are here and demand solutions. In either case, planning is about trying to serve that elusive and controversial but very important item known as "the public interest." It can be a profoundly satisfying field when one feels that one has succeeded in making a contribution to the public good. Because much of planning is concerned with the physical environment, the planner can often have the satisfaction of seeing the results of his or her efforts on the ground.

However, the field can also be frustrating, for planners are basically advisors. Sometimes they are heeded and sometimes they are not. And sometimes the planner's brainchild gets more than a little altered during that long trip from drawing board to reality. In general, it is not a good field for someone with a short time horizon or very low frustration tolerance. It is also not a good field for someone who cannot tolerate ambiguity, for many issues that appear black or white at a distance have the dismaying quality of becoming gray as one gets close to them. The field can present the thoughtful practitioner with ethical ambiguities. For example, both the APA and AICP have professional codes of ethics which enjoin the planner both to serve the public interest and also to render loyal and diligent service to his or her client. Many a planner has wrestled with the question of what to do when, in his or her view, the public interest and client loyalty are at odds with each other.

USEFUL ABILITIES

Of course, the planner needs to have the appropriate knowledge and skill for the particular task at hand, and that can vary considerably from one job to another. One needs different knowledge and skills for doing urban design than, say, for modeling traffic flow. However, there are some basic abilities that are highly important across the whole spectrum of planning.

One basic skill, which is probably not very teachable, is just being able to understand the political environment around oneself. Planning and politics are intimately related, and people who rise in planning generally have political smarts.

Planning is ultimately about persuasion. Good plans that are poorly expressed and poorly presented, generally end up on the shelf under a layer of dust.[1] Therefore the ability to speak well in public—to express an idea cogently and also to respond well to questions and criticism—is extremely important. The planner who cannot do this, if he or she stays in planning, will end up working for the planner who can.

The ability to write well is also extremely important. The planner doesn't need great literary gifts, but it is important to be able to explain things clearly and in a user-friendly way. In both writing and speaking it is important to be able to come in at the right altitude. One doesn't want to write or talk over the audiences' heads or befuddle them with technical jargon. But one doesn't want to come in too low and insult their intelligence either. In short, political smarts and good communication skills are important across the entire profession.

THE PLAN OF THIS BOOK

The main body of the book begins with a chapter (Chapter 2) on the history of urbanization of the United States. To a large extent, the history of planning in the United States is a series of responses to problems that have flowed from the process of urbanization. Thus that chapter serves as background for the rest of the book. Chapters 3 and 4 trace the history of planning in the United States in the historical context established by Chapter 2.

Planning is conditioned and limited by the law and takes place within a political process. Ultimately, planning is a political act. In Part II, Chapters 5 and 6 establish the legal and political framework in which planning takes place. All important planning decisions have social implications.

They deliver gains to some and losses to some, and they often get to the root of questions about what we consider to be a good and a just society. Chapter 7 lays out some of the main social issues in planning. The concept of the community master plan or comprehensive plan occupies a central place in the development of planning, and the development and implementation of such a plan is often a major task of the planning agency. Chapter 8 presents the comprehensive planning process. Chapter 9 follows with a presentation on the tools of land-use planning to give the reader a feeling for how the community can implement the comprehensive plan.

Part III of the book, from Chapter 10, "Urban Design," to Chapter 16, "Planning for Metropolitan Regions," covers a variety of fields in contemporary planning practice. If the book is used as the text for a short course, the instructor might select among these chapters on the basis of student interest. Once the material in Parts I and II has been assimilated, each chapter in Part III will stand on its own.

Part IV provides a larger view. Chapter 17, "National Planning in the United States," addresses the extent to which we have had de facto national planning. If the course has a purely local focus, it can readily be omitted. If there is time to include it, the chapter will help to place local planning in a historic and national context.

Chapter 18, "Planning in Other Nations," provides sketches of planning elsewhere with a view to expanding the reader's perspective on United States practice—to suggest that the way planning is practiced in the United States is only one of many possible ways, and to highlight the way a society's basic institutions and ideology shape planning practice.

Chapter 19, "Planning Theory," serves as a wrap-up and expansion of many ideas suggested earlier in the book. It contains two major components: a discussion of planning as a process and a discussion of the relationship of planning and political ideology. It is left to the end so that the reader can approach it with some background and thus be able to put some meat on the bare theoretical and ideological bones.

NOTE

1. For a good presentation on these and related matters, see Michael P. Brooks, *Planning Theory for Practitioners*, Planners Press, American Planning Association, Chicago, 2002, chaps. 12 and 13.

CHAPTER 2

The Urbanization of America

The history of planning in the United States is largely one of response to urbanization and the problems it has brought. To understand that history, it is necessary to have some sense of the main currents of U.S. urban history. This chapter will emphasize economic, technological, and demographic trends, for these, over the long term, have far more effect than discrete events like elections.

There is something of a break in the trend of U.S. urbanization around the end of the nineteenth century. For convenience, then, we will divide the discussion into two parts: an account of urbanization in the nineteenth century and another from the beginning of the twentieth century to the present.

URBANIZATION IN THE NINETEENTH CENTURY

In the year 1800 the urbanized population of the United States was roughly 300,000, and the total population was 5 million. Thus perhaps 6 percent of the U.S. population lived in urbanized areas. By 1900 the U.S. urbanized population was 30 million, and the total population was 76 million. Approximately 40 percent of the population lived in urbanized areas.[1] From 1800 to 1900 the U.S. population increased by a factor of 15, an annual compounded rate of about 2.4 percent. However, urban populations increased by a factor of 100, an annual compounded rate of about 5 percent. In 1800 the largest city in the United States, New York, had a population of well under 100,000. By 1900 its population was over 3 million.

The Forces Behind Urban Growth

One force behind urban growth was simply national population growth. The U.S. rate of natural increase (births minus deaths) was extremely rapid and was augmented by immigration, particularly after the inauguration of transatlantic steam service in the 1840s. But these facts do not answer the question of why urban growth proceeded so much more rapidly than did total population growth.

Part of the explanation was a side effect of the industrial revolution. As agricultural machinery made farmers more productive, workers were freed to take other employment, much of it in the cities. In 1800 perhaps 85 to 90 percent of the U.S. labor force was engaged in farming. By 1880 that figure was down to about 50 percent.

Another consequence of the industrial revolution was the shift from cottage industries to factory production, creating the need for mass labor forces at specific points. That, in turn, created the need for massed housing nearby. The growth of large-scale manufacturing also brought into being the modern corporation, with a large administrative force concentrated at a single point. Finally, factory production and the enormous increase in consumer goods it created brought into being the department store, which also concentrated a large labor force at a single point.

The growth of large cities was also promoted by the development of low-cost transportation. The coming of railroad and steamboat technology around 1830 gave cities a long reach into their hinterlands to obtain raw materials and agricultural products and also to market the products they produced. In the absence of such transportation, cities would necessarily be small, for the market areas that sustained their commercial and manufacturing sectors would have been small.

The rapid settling of the country and the opening of new lands demanded the creation in short order of a system of cities to perform the commercial and manufacturing processes that the new industrial technology was making possible. Thus a number of U.S. cities such as New York and Chicago grew at spectacular rates. Writing in 1899, Adna Weber noted,

> In a new country the rapid growth of cities is both natural and necessary, for no efficient industrial organization of a new settlement is possible without industrial centers to carry on the necessary work of assembling and distributing goods. A Mississippi Valley empire rising suddenly into being without its Chicago and its smaller centers of distribution is almost inconceivable to the nineteenth-century economist. That America is the "land of mushroom cities" is therefore not at all surprising.[2]

Although the four forces noted—population growth, increased agricultural productivity, factory production, and low-cost transportation—are sufficient to explain the rapid growth of urban populations, they do not entirely explain the form of nineteenth-century cities.

Urban Concentration and Density

The distinguishing feature of many nineteenth-century cities was concentration and density. As the century progressed, the more gracious and open pattern of the colonial city disappeared. The spaces between buildings vanished, and buildings grew higher. Streets became increasingly congested, and the natural world was replaced by a none-too-attractive human-made world.

Population densities that have never again been seen in the United States were built up in the late nineteenth and very early twentieth centuries. For example, Manhattan island in 1900 had about 2.2 million residents on 22 square miles for an average density of 100,000 people per square mile. In the most densely populated part of the island, the Lower East Side, densities in some wards were several times that high.[3] By 2000, Manhattan's population had fallen to slightly over 1.5 million, a drop of approximately 700,000.

What made nineteenth-century cities so concentrated? Much of the answer lies in the transportation technology of the age. At the opening of the nineteenth century, water transportation was cheap, and land transportation was expensive. The ton/mile cost of transporting freight by canal boat was about one-tenth that of transporting it by horse and wagon. The cost of transporting freight by sailing vessel was still lower than for canal boat. One effect of these cost differences was to favor the growth of port cities.[4] But another effect was to concentrate economic activity in those areas of the city with direct water access. Since most people got to work by walking, concentration of workplaces inevitably meant concentration of residences as well.

The coming of railroad technology beginning in the 1820s continued the concentrating effect. Over long distances railroad ton/mile rates were a very small fraction of the ton/mile rates for horse and wagon. Thus rail-served sites permitted manufacturers and wholesalers very large cost savings. But achieving these savings meant tremendous concentrations around rail terminals and sidings.

In port cities an ideal industrial location was one between rail lines and docks. The remains of such a configuration can be seen on the Lower West Side of Manhattan today. Old loft buildings once occupied by manufacturers lie immediately to the east of the Hudson shore and up against the former rail lines that connected Manhattan to the rest of the nation. Today the rail lines are gone, and cargo handling has ceased along the Manhattan waterfront. But in the nineteenth century, the port was busy, and lower Manhattan was a major manufacturing and goods-handling center. Goods could move between Europe and the Midwest through

Manhattan and make all but a few hundred yards of the trip entirely by lost-cost modes.

The desirability of rail- and water-served sites made centrally located land very valuable. That feature, in turn, caused the builders of industrial, commercial, and residential structures to use the minimum amount of land for a given amount of structure. Manufacturing and commercial uses were located in multistory loft buildings constructed side to side. For residences the same desire to crowd a maximum amount of structure on a given amount of land led to the tenement, with conditions of crowding that seem appalling by modern standards.

> The residence of the worker in New York City and other large industrial cities in 1850 was frequently the "railroad flat," a walk-up structure that was generally 5 to 7 stories high, 25 feet wide and 75 feet long on a 25 by 100 foot lot. Constructed solidly in rows across entire block faces, these units had four apartments on each floor surrounding a common staircase. The rooms in these apartments were constructed in tandem, with just one room in each apartment provided with a window or two for light and air. No sanitary facilities or water supply were provided for in these structures. The small rear yard contained a multi-seat outhouse and often a well, resulting in deplorable conditions of sanitation and public health.[5]

Thus a population of well over 100 people might be housed on a plot not much more than one-twentieth of an acre in size.

Several other features of emerging nineteenth-century technology also contributed to very dense patterns of development. In contrast to a modern factory, where power to run individual pieces of machinery is supplied electrically, power was generally supplied by a steam engine and transmitted through a system of belts, pulleys, and shafts. The distance that power could be sent in this manner was limited, thus further contributing to the use of compact loft buildings with transmission belts taking power from one floor to another. Shortly after the end of the Civil War, there emerged two other technologies that contributed to higher urban densities: the elevator and steel-frame construction. Together they made the sky-scraper economically and structurally possible.

For most of the nineteenth century, cities became both more populous and more dense. Industry was concentrated in cities and, most often, in the more central areas. There is some evidence that in the post–Civil War period, not only did manufacturing become more urbanized, but also it grew faster in the larger cities. In 1899 Adna Weber noted,

> In 1860 the annual production of manufacturers per capita was $60 for the United States as a whole, $193.50 for 10 cities having a population of 50,000 or more, $424 for 10 cities under 50,000, and $44 for the rural districts. Thus per capita production was at that time largest in the smaller cities. In 1890, however, the per capita product of manufacturers was $455 in the 28 great

Tenements on New York's Lower East Side (left) at the end of the nineteenth century. Note the narrow building width and side-by-side construction. The four windows across the building front represent two narrow apartments side by side. Behind them are two more apartments whose windows open onto the rear yard. Photos like that of the men's sleeping quarters (below) in a New York tenement about 1905 helped to put housing conditions on the top of the reformers' agenda.

cities, $335 in 137 cities of 20,000–100,000 population, and $58 for the remainder of the country. The superiority of the smaller cities in 1860 had in 1890 given way to that of the great.[6]

Congestion had more than just aesthetic or psychological consequences. In an age before treatment of water supplies, before modern sewage disposal, and before antibiotics—an age when communicable diseases were the major threat to health—the congestion of the city exacted a huge cost in death and illness. In fact, for much of the nineteenth century, most large cities experienced natural decrease (more deaths than births). They grew only because of in-migration. The situation was well understood at the time, and decongestion of the city was a major goal of reform-minded citizens and planners.

> Few municipalities have planned intelligently for this rapid urban growth. Buildings have been crowded upon land and people have been crowded within buildings. Urban living has become in many ways inconvenient, unsafe and unhealthful. . . . Transit facilities fail to develop much in advance of demonstrable need, so the population becomes crowded within a limited area. . . . It becomes used to living a life quite divorced from nature. The responsibilities of homeownership are felt only by a few. The sense of citizenship and the sense of moral responsibility for evils suffered by neighbors become weak.
>
> In the interests of both hygiene and public morality, the cottage home is much to be preferred to the tenement dwelling. . . . Tuberculosis is responsible for nearly one-tenth of all deaths in the United States. . . . The tubercule bacillus can live for weeks outside the human body in a sunless, damp room, hall or cellar. The tenement house may thus at once reduce vitality, through absence of sunlight and fresh air, and may provide abundant opportunity for transmission of prevalent and dangerous diseases.[7]

This widely held view helped to shape the agenda and direction of the planning profession in the nineteenth and early twentieth centuries.

The Beginnings of Decentralization

Late in the nineteenth century, the first forces for decentralization appeared on the urban scene. These forces have grown in strength to the present time. By the 1880s electric motor and power transmission technology had advanced far enough to make possible the electric streetcar. Faster and cheaper than the horse-drawn trolleys it supplanted, the electric streetcar was a powerful decentralizing force. In a few years the effective radius of the city was doubled. Three miles, a distance the average person can comfortably walk in an hour, had been something of a limit for the population that worked in the urban core. With the streetcar, tendrils of urban growth extended from the city, and the process of suburbanization was begun. In an aptly entitled book, *Streetcar Suburbs,* Warner describes how in a few years the streetcar effectively doubled the radius of Boston and converted the old "walking city" into a modern metropolis.[8] The decentralizing power of rail-based transportation was not lost on the more prophetic writers of the times. In 1902 H. G. Wells wrote,

> Many of our railway-begotten giants are destined to such a process of dissection and diffusion as to amount almost to obliteration. . . . The social history of the middle and later thirds of the nineteenth century . . . has been the history of a gigantic rush of population into the magic radius—for most people—of four miles, to suffer there physical and moral disaster . . . far more appalling than any pestilence that ever swept the world. . . . But new forces . . . may finally be equal to the complete reduction of all our present congestions. . . . What will be the forces acting upon the prosperous household? The passion for nature. . . . and that craving for a little private imperium are the chief centrifugal inducements. The city will diffuse itself until it has taken many of the characteristics of what is now country. . . . We may call . . . these coming town provinces "urban regions."[9]

Wells was writing about England, but the same forces of national population growth, the growth of manufacturing, and urbanization were operative in the United States.

In common with most nineteenth- and early twentieth-century reformers, Wells viewed the congestion of the city as a profound evil and the coming decentralization as an obviously desirable event. To the nineteenth-century reformer, what we now contemptuously refer to as "urban sprawl" or, sometimes, "suburban sprawl" would have looked like an improvement almost too good to be imagined.

By the end of the nineteenth century, manufacturing was beginning to decentralize though it was still a predominantly urban phenomenon. In larger urban areas, firms began to move out along rail lines toward the suburbs. These more suburban locations (many of which have since become urban with continued growth) offered lower land costs, often lower taxes, and the advantages of being able to locate heavy machinery on ground level rather than higher up. To some extent, the decentralizing of population by the streetcar provided the labor force for suburbanizing industry.

Population densities (people per square mile) at the center grew more slowly or actually began to decline, while population densities many miles out from the center increased rapidly.[10] The graph in Figure 2–1 shows the population density of Milwaukee as a function of distance from the city center over the period 1880 to 1963. From 1880 to 1920, population density continued to increase at the center, but in percentage terms the growth in the periphery was much more rapid. From 1920 to 1963, population density in the center fell drastically while growth in the periphery continued at a rapid pace. In fact, in 1963, population density in the center was actually lower than it had been in 1880, in spite of the fact that the total population of the metropolitan area was vastly larger.

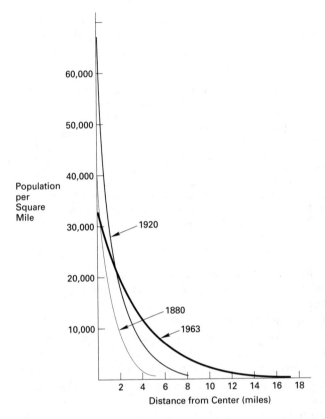

FIGURE 2–1 Population density at various distances from the center, Milwaukee 1880 to 1963. Note that the density gradient fell during the entire period and that from 1920 to 1963 the density at the center fell by about 50 percent.

Source: Plotted from data in Edwin S. Mills, *Studies in the Structure of the Urban Economy,* Johns Hopkins University Press, Baltimore, 1972.

There appear to be two main reasons for the change in population distribution in the last years of the nineteenth century. One, we noted, was the emergence of the streetcar. In a few metropolitan areas, steam railroads also stimulated some long-distance commuting. A more general cause of decentralization was simply the rise in incomes. People were able to spend more on land, more on transportation, and more on housing to escape the slums and tenements. Then, too, rising productivity permitted the shortening of working hours, which in turn permitted additional time to be spent on travel.

URBAN TRENDS IN THE TWENTIETH CENTURY _____

Just as nineteenth-century technology proved to be centralizing and to promote very great population densities, twentieth-century technology proved to be exactly the reverse. One decentralizing technology after another appeared on the scene, a process that continues to the present time.

For perhaps roughly the first half of the twentieth century, technology favored decentralization within metropolitan areas but did not favor smaller over larger areas. Thus many large metropolitan areas grew rapidly, usually with the major share of growth occurring in their suburban areas.

Figure 2–2 shows the redistribution of population across the twentieth century. The figure is based on standard U.S. Bureau of the Census categories. Any point in the nation is located either in a metropolitan or in a nonmetropolitan area. Within metropolitan areas any point is located either in a *central city*, usually a place with a population of 50,000 or more, or in what the U.S. Bureau of the Census refers to as the "part outside" and what is referred to more casually as the *suburbs*. The distinction between central city and suburb is based on jurisdictional lines and does not necessarily correspond to what you would see on the ground. There may be many areas in the "part outside" that are urban in character; and, conversely, many parts of the central city may have a lower-density, suburban character. Across the century, the U.S. Bureau of the Census has designated new central cities and new metropolitan areas, and existing metropolitan areas have grown as new counties have been added on their peripheries. Thus the picture presented by Figure 2–2 is only a rough abstraction of a very complex situation. Nonetheless, it correctly depicts a very massive change.

Note how the suburban portion of the total population began to grow very rapidly from the first postwar census (1950) and continued to grow rapidly through the 2000 census. In fact, by the 2000 census, the suburban population of the United States was as large as the nonmetropolitan and central city populations combined.

For population, the big decentralizing force was the automobile. Its speed and flexibility of route and schedule were preconditions for large-scale suburbanization. The first vehicles appeared in the 1890s, but their numbers grew slowly, reaching about 5 million by 1915. About this time, mass production of Henry Ford's Model T began, and the number of autos in the United States increased rapidly, reaching about 25 million by 1930. It is no coincidence that the first great period of suburbanization in the United States began in the 1920s.

The truck bore very much the same relationship to retailing, wholesaling, and light manufacturing as did the automobile to population. It permitted wide-scale decentralization by freeing firms from the necessity of being near rail lines. Retailers could follow their customers, and manufactures could follow the labor force, with far more freedom than would have been possible a few years earlier. The decentralization of wholesaling followed naturally from the decentralization of retailing, which in turn followed naturally from the decentralization of population.

Other forces also accelerated the process of suburbanization. Improved telephone communications made possible some decentralization of economic activity by reducing the need for face-to-face contact. The development of

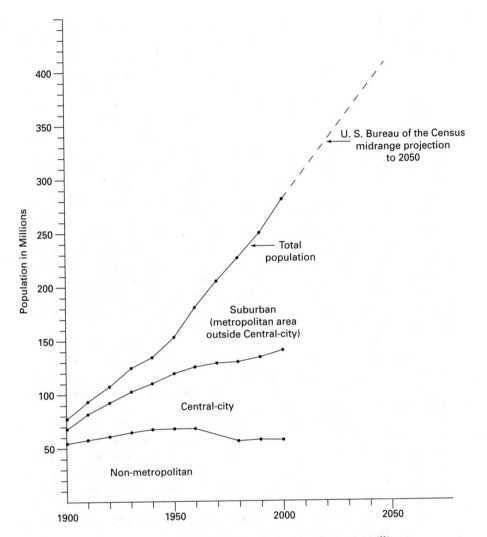

FIGURE 2–2 U.S. population 1900 to 2000 by place of residence, in millions.

Sources: For 1950 and earlier, Donald J. Bogue, *Population Growth in Standard Metropolitan Areas 1900–1950*, Housing and Home Finance Agency, Washington, DC, pp. 11 and 13. For 1960 and subsequent years, the *Statistical Abstract of the United States*, 112th and earlier editions, and direct communication with the Population Division, Bureau of the Census.

Note: The figures for 1900 through 1940 are estimated for 1950 Standard Metropolitan Statistical Area (SMSA) boundaries. From 1950 on, with each decennial census some SMSAs get larger as additional counties are added to them and some new SMSAs come into being as a function of population growth. Thus the trend lines up through 1940 and those after 1940 are not done on the same basis and are not entirely comparable.

motion pictures and commercial radio broke the monopoly of central places on entertainment and thus increased the relative attractiveness of outlying residential areas. The invention of the limited-access highway in the 1920s proved also to be decentralizing. The first limited-access divided highway in the United States, and possibly the world, was the Bronx River Parkway in Westchester County, New York, completed in 1926. Parkways were originally envisioned as giving the urban middle class, with its newly acquired automobiles, access to the countryside. Their unanticipated, but more profound, effect was to make it easier to live in suburbia while working in the central city.

Surburbanization proceeded at a moderate pace during the 1920s and then slowed somewhat during the Great Depression of the 1930s. America's participation in World War II between 1941 and 1945 represented a brief break in the suburbanizing process. Residential construction, other than for war workers, was halted; civilian automobile production was suspended; and gasoline was rationed. When the war ended, the country entered into a sustained suburban housing boom. In the first decade or so after the war, part of the force behind suburbanization came from accumulated demand from the low construction years between 1930 and 1945. But the process continued unabated for many years beyond the period that could be explained by pent-up demand from the 1930s and 1940s.

The Rush to the Suburbs

The forces behind this sustained growth of the suburbs were numerous. Mortgage finance was readily available on attractive terms (see Chapter 18). Employment was high, and incomes were rising rapidly. The nation thus had more wealth to spend on land development, on housing, and on the additional personal transportation that suburbanization required. Automobile ownership rose from 25 million in 1945 to about 40 million in 1950, to 62 million in 1960, 89 million in 1970, 122 million in 1980, and 134 million in 1990. At the end of World War II, there was one automobile for every five Americans. By 1990 there was one automobile for every 1.9 Americans. After 1990, the statistics for the number of automobiles registered in the United States stabilized, but only because so many people switched to vans and SUVs, which are classified as light trucks rather than automobiles.

Paralleling the increase in automobile ownership was a great expansion of the nation's highway system. Shortly after World War II there began a major surge of highway building by the states, powerfully encouraged by federal subsidies. Practical commuting distances increased, and suburban residence for city workers became much more feasible. Then the National Defense Highway Act of 1956 funded the beginning of the interstate highway system. The suburbanizing effect of the interstate highway system on both population and economic activity was enormous. This matter is discussed in detail in Chapter 18.

Decentralization has also been promoted by improvements in electronic communications. Long-distance direct dialing, common carrier links between computers, closed-circuit television, e-mail, and fax all reduce the need for face-to-face communication. Having the capacity for interaction at a distance does not cause decentralization, but it permits it if economic or social forces favor it. For example, stock and commodity brokerages involve a tremendous amount of communication. In fact, they involve little physical movement of anything other than paper. Several decades ago such activities were inevitably bound to a few downtowns because of the need for face-to-face communications. This arrangement is no longer necessary. In the 1970s New York City, desperate for revenues, decided that a "stock transfer tax" would be a good revenue raiser, given all the transfer activity that occurred on Wall Street. City officials were surprised and distressed when a sizable piece of the brokerage industry threatened to move across the Hudson River to Jersey City, and the stock transfer tax idea was quickly dropped. It was recently developed electronic communications that gave the brokerage industry that option. In many industries like brokerage and insurance, which still maintain a large central-city presence for the highest interaction activities, much "back office" work like data processing has moved to the suburbs, to nonmetropolitan American, and overseas. In the first years of this century much concern has been expressed about the outsourcing to lower-wage nations of all sorts of white-collar work including computer programming, income tax preparation, legal work, call center operations, analysis of X-rays and other medical diagnostic images, and the like. What has made all these outward moves possible is low-cost instantaneous transmission of words and data. In its way the microchip may be proving to be as powerful an agent of deconcentration as was the automobile.

The baby boom, a phenomenon that began in the late 1940s, peaked in 1957, and lasted into the mid-1960s, further fueled the suburban housing boom. The increase in births a generation later, the so called "echo" of the baby boom, added force to the suburbanizing trend toward the end of the twentieth century. The attraction of the suburbs for couples in the family-formation stage of life is an enormous decentralizing force.

Regional Trends

The period from the end of World War II to the present has also seen major changes in the regional distribution of population as shown in Table 2–1. The movement from "frostbelt" to "sunbelt" has been driven by many forces, some of which are the same as those that powered the movement from city to suburb.

One overriding force has simply been the growth in real per capita income. As people become more affluent, they are able to give more weight to their preferences and less weight to pure economic necessity. That trend has clearly favored warmer climates and places with superior natural amenities. The increase in average life span coupled with a younger retirement age

TABLE 2–1 Regional population, 1950–2000 (in thousands)

Region[a]	1950	1960	1970	1980	1990	2000	Percentage Change 1990–2000
Northeast	39,478	44,678	49,061	49,139	50,976	53,610	5.2
New England	9,314	10,509	11,848	12,348	13,197	13,983	6.0
Mid-Atlantic	30,164	34,168	37,213	36,788	37,779	39,672	5.0
North-central	44,461	51,619	56,589	58,854	60,225	64,429	7.0
East North-central	30,399	36,225	40,262	41,670	42,414	45,155	6.5
West North-central	14,061	15,394	16,327	17,184	17,811	19,274	8.2
South	47,197	54,973	62,812	75,349	86,916	100,237	15.3
South Atlantic	21,182	25,972	30,678	36,943	44,421	51,769	16.5
East South-central	11,477	12,050	12,808	14,663	15,347	17,023	11.0
West South-central	14,538	16,951	19,326	23,743	27,148	31,445	15.8
West	20,190	28,053	34,838	43,165	54,060	63,198	16.9
Mountain	5,075	6,855	8,289	11,368	14,035	18,172	29.5
Pacific	15,115	21,198	26,549	31,797	40,025	45,026	12.5

[a]These regions are standard U.S. Bureau of the Census groupings, as follows: New England: Maine, New Hampshire, Vermont, Massachusetts, Rhode Island, Connecticut; Mid-Atlantic: New York, New Jersey, Pennsylvania; East North-central: Ohio, Indiana, Illinois, Michigan, Wisconsin; West North-central: Minnesota, Iowa, Missouri, North Dakota, South Dakota, Nebraska, Kansas; South Atlantic: Delaware, Maryland, District of Columbia, Virginia, West Virginia, North Carolina, South Carolina, Georgia, Florida; East South-central: Kentucky, Tennessee, Alabama, Mississippi; West South-central: Arkansas, Louisiana, Oklahoma, Texas; Mountain: Montana, Idaho, Wyoming, Colorado, New Mexico, Arizona, Utah, Nevada; Pacific: Washington, Oregon, California, Alaska, Hawaii.

Source: U.S. Bureau of the Census, Census of the Population, 1950, 1960, 1970, 1980, 1990. Year 2000 figures from U.S. Bureau of the Census Web site, www.census.gov.

has increased the number of people who receive "mailbox income" (Social Security, pensions, and the like) and are thus free to live where they like. Many of these people have migrated southward. The interstate highway system and electronic communications have made many southern and southwestern locations much more accessible than they previously were. The development of air conditioning has made many parts of the south, especially the deep south, far more attractive than it once was.

One trend the state figures in Table 2–1 do not capture has been the coastward movement of population. By the end of the twentieth century one-half of the U.S. population lived within 50 miles of a coast. One reason for this is the attractiveness of coastal areas both for scenic and recreational reasons and also, in some cases, more moderate climate. Again, it is affluence and "mailbox income" that facilitate this trend.

The Age of Central-City Shrinkage

As Figure 2–2 indicates, the decades after World War II saw metropolitan areas grow rapidly in absolute terms and also as a percentage of total population. Within metropolitan areas most growth occurred outside the central cities. However, the picture is a mixed one. Much growth occurred in a number of western central cities. Some of this was genuine urban growth. But in many western cities, the city limits extend well beyond the urbanized area. Therefore, much growth that is suburban in character occurs within the city boundaries and appears as part of the central-city total. Then, too, if the city is not surrounded by incorporated municipalities that resist annexation, the city may grow substantially in land area. This was and is the case for many western cities.

In the older and larger cities in the east and north central parts of the nation, the general rule was shrinkage. Cities were usually surrounded by other municipalities, so that growth by annexation was difficult or impossible. Then, too, high population densities and a preautomobile street pattern made it difficult to compete with the surrounding suburbs for residents and jobs. From 1950 to 2000, the population of Buffalo shrank from 580,000 to 293,000, St. Louis from 857,000 to 348,000, Cleveland from 915,000 to 478,000, Chicago from 3,621,000 to 2,896,000, Boston from 810,000 to 589,000, Pittsburgh from 677,000 to 335,000, and Philadelphia from 2,072,000 to 1,518,000. New York City, an exception, grew slightly from 7,891,000 to 8,008,000 for reasons discussed subsequently.[11]

The population losses in many older cities are also related to the regional trends noted before. The city in a lagging region is, all other things being equal, more likely to lose population because the market for the goods and services it produces is not growing, nor is there increasing population pressure on it from surrounding areas. Thus for cities like Cleveland or Buffalo, internal forces predisposing to population and job loss were augmented by regional trends. Conversely, sunbelt cities like Fort Myers, Dallas, Houston, or Phoenix grew rapidly, in part because they are situated in growing regions. Central-city population losses were, as one would expect, paralleled by employment losses. Manufacturing jobs continued to move to suburban and exurban locations, drawn by lower land costs, often lower wages, and the availability of large blocks of land that facilitated the building of single-story plants. As suburban populations grew, their buying power necessarily drew both retailers and the wholesalers who serve them out of the city. The growth of the suburban labor force also pulled many business services and headquarters operations out of downtown and into the suburbs, for there is no greater determinant of business location than the availability of labor. Because of the decentralization of employment, there is now much more cross-commuting (commuting from suburb to suburb) than there is commuting from suburb to central city. The day when many suburbs served largely as bedroom communities for the central city is now several decades behind us.

Cities and the Poor

As many central cities lost population and employment, their populations also became poorer relative to that of the nation as a whole. In the 1950s, central cities had somewhat less than their proportionate share of the nation's poor. By the 1980s, they had more than twice their proportionate share.

One reason for the urbanization of poverty was simply selective migration. It was, by and large, the city's more prosperous residents who had the income to make the move to the suburbs, often at the same time making the switch from being renters to being homeowners. Another reason was the suburbanization of jobs and thus of income. These factors are closely related. Many firms followed their workers out to the suburbs or beyond. Conversely, many residents of the central city followed their employers out of the central city. Still another factor, and a very important one, was the extremely rapid mechanization of agriculture and the huge increase in agricultural productivity (output per worker) that occurred after World War II. In 1945, the year World War II ended, U.S. farm employment was 10 million, and the U.S. farm population was 25 million. By 1970, farm employment was under 4 million, and total farm population was under 10 million. This decrease occurred despite the fact that the U.S. population had grown from 140 million to 203 million. The agricultural labor force had shrunk by more than half was able to feed an additional 63 million people and produce a considerable surplus for export. Since 1970, the decline in farm employment and population has continued, but at a slower pace. By 1990, the agricultural labor force was down to 2.5 million, and the total farm population to 4.6 million.

The effect of this increase in agricultural productivity was to force enormous numbers of farmers off the land and set in motion a great

internal migration toward the cities. For the most part, the more prosperous farmers were the ones who could mechanize, acquire more land,
and stay in farming. It was the poorer farmers who were rendered surplus
and had little choice but to head for the cities. A displaced rural and small
town population, much of it without nonagricultural job skills, poured into
many of the nation's central cities during the 1950s, 1960s, and early 1970s.
Unfortunately, this was the very time that the central cities were losing
large amounts of manufacturing and goods-handling work, the kind of
employment that might have sustained many of these rural-to-urban
migrants. Thus in some ways the situation for these internal migrants was
more difficult than that which had faced the wave of European immigrants
who had arrived in the late nineteenth and early twentieth century. Though
social services were not nearly as good at the turn of the century as they
were five decades later, the European immigrants of that earlier time were
arriving when urban labor markets were expanding and before automation
and other modern technologies were decimating the demand for relatively
low-skilled manual labor.

   Today we take it for granted that in the older and more run-down
sections of most central cities, the population will be largely black or other
minority. This was not always the case. This situation, too, results largely
from the mechanization of agriculture. In, say, 1940, most U.S. blacks lived
in the states of the old Confederacy and were a largely rural and small-
town population. The mechanization of agriculture and the concurrent
increases in agricultural productivity hit black farmers especially hard
because they were often the poorest of the poor. Many were tenant farmers
or sharecroppers rather than owners of the land that they farmed. If the
farmer who owned the land could cut costs by replacing manual labor with
machinery, the tenant farmers had no choice but to move.[12] And that move,
more often than not, was to the central cities. Thus to the problems that
any large, rapid rural-to-urban migration would create were added a host
of other problems relating to racial discrimination, the legacy of three
centuries of slavery, and some decades of Jim Crow.[13]

Trends in the 1990s

The 2000 census showed a general continuation of the trends described
for the post–World War II period as a whole, with some minor variations
(see Table 2–1). For a great many older cities in the northeast and the north
central regions of the nation, population declined from 1990 to 2000, but
often at a slower rate than previously. This trend suggested to some that a
lower limit was being approached and that some reversal might be just
over the horizon. It seemed possible that population, traffic growth, and
rising land and housing costs in the surrounding suburbs might be deflect-
ing some growth back toward older urban centers. Just as the demography
of the baby boom favored the suburbs, today's population mix with higher

percentages of single adults and couples without children may mean more people who favor central-city residence.

A Few Exceptions

In the last decade for which we have full counts of the population, 1990 to 2000, a few older cities managed to swim against the tide and began to grow again. Most prominent among these was New York City. For most of the post–World War II period the city had experienced slow population decline. But from 1990 to 2000 the city's population grew by over 9 percent, from 7.3 million to 8.1 million, and estimates made since the year 2000 strongly suggest that growth is continuing. The New York City Planning Department now projects a population of at least 9 million by 2025.

To the visitor who has known the city for some time, some changes in the city are obvious. Manhattan seems more prosperous, glitzier, and pricier than ever. There is much new construction. The city has a very international tone. Walk in the streets, ride the subway, or sit in restaurant and you cannot avoid hearing a multiplicity of languages. Crime is down and the streets are safer. Though it is impossible to quantify or prove, in the opinion of many New Yorkers and periodic visitors to the city the general level of civility is higher than a few decades ago. Real estate prices, a key indicator of demand for residence in the city, are way up. The average price for a condominium or co-op apartment in Manhattan now is over $1 million. Prices in the other four boroughs are lower but still high and rising. Residents of single-family areas fight to prevent their neighborhoods from being redeveloped with high-rises.

What is behind the turnaround? One big factor is immigration. Like most other big cities, New York for years has experienced a steady out-migration of native-born residents, but unlike most other big cities, it has made up that loss through immigration. Its population at the end of the 1990s was 36 percent foreign-born, lagging behind only Los Angeles and Miami among other large American cities.

The growth of world trade has favored the city for the city has been able to capture a considerable amount of the office activity associated with that trade. The loss of manufacturing employment that has devastated many urban economies in the United States hit New York less hard than many other places because the city had long since lost most of its heavy industry and much light manufacturing as well.

The growth of the financial sector of the U.S. economy in recent years has also favored the city in recent years, for the city has always had sub-stantially more than its proportionate share of U.S. financial employment. In recent years finance has become increasingly international and New York's international character and coastal location have helped it to profit from that particular trend within a trend as well.

From 1990 to 2000 Miami grew slowly in population and current estimates suggest that trend is continuing and perhaps accelerating. Again immigration is a key factor. So, too, has been a growth of international trade and international finance.

Chicago, after several decades of population loss, grew by about 4 percent from 1990 to 2000 though post-2000 estimates suggest that the growth may have leveled off. Clearly, the spurt from 1990 to 2000 was a function of immigration. Chicago has traditionally been, and continues to be, one of the largest receivers of immigrants among U.S. cities.

To generalize, it appears that those big, older cities that have been able to swim against the tide and grow or at least not lose population are those that, in one way or another, have been able to benefit from that commonly used, but not precise term, *globalization*.[14]

Trends in Rapidly Growing Region

In many parts of southeastern United States, where overall population growth was rapid, a mixed pattern was observed. Some cities and inner suburbs gained population and acquired a more solidly urban character. At the same time, there was a great deal of leapfrog suburban development, often along the path of the interstate highways:

> . . . many suburbs simply detached themselves from an old-fashioned central anchor and became, in effect, suburbs without urbs, free-floating patches of population density tethered loosely to interstate highways.[15]

In many parts of the western United States, urban and suburban population densities rose without the leapfrogging observed in the south. Los Angeles, despite its reputation for sprawl, now has a higher population density at its center and for several dozen miles out than does the Washington, D.C., metropolitan area. A major reason for the difference is that of water supply. In the southeastern part of the United States, rainfall is plentiful, and water supply is not a major problem. Development is thus not constrained by water-supply problems. In the drier climate of the west, and particularly the southwest, water supply is a major constraint to development. Major metropolitan areas rely on water from distant sources, and significant development is limited to areas that have municipal utility service. The result is contiguous development without leapfrogging.

A LOOK AHEAD

In the year 2000, shortly before the results of the 2000 census became available, the U.S. Bureau of the Census made a series of population projections for the United States out to the year 2100.[16] Figure 2–2 shows one part of this series, the middle range projection out to the year 2050. If this projection proves to be accurate, the population of the United States will grow by somewhat over 100 million in the next half-century. About three-fifths of this increase will result from net immigration (moves in – moves out) to the United States and two-fifths from natural increase (births – deaths).

The middle range projection assumes continuation of the U.S. fertility rate in the 2.1 range, continuation of immigration in the one million per year range, and continued slow increases in life expectancy. Whether these assumptions will prove to be correct remains to be seen. If they do, what might we expect? As shown in Figure 2–2, the nonmetropolitan population of the United States has remained relatively constant across the last century. Decline in the nation's farm population, a result of increases in agricultural productivity, has been roughly matched by increases in the nonagricultural population of nonmetropolitan America. In principle, there is lots of room for substantial population growth in parts of nonmetropolitan America that are distant from metropolitan areas. And given modern transportation and electronic communications, such growth seems feasible. However, up to now, most nonmetropolitan growth has been in areas that are peripheral to metropolitan areas and that ultimately become parts of metropolitan areas. Nonmetropolitan growth is no longer tied to agriculture, and often places close to metropolitan areas offer more amenities than do more remote locations. Despite modern communications, high-tech industry has shown little tendency to locate far away from major metropolitan areas. Massive nonmetropolitan population growth in the coming decades, though entirely possible, seems unlikely.

Central-city growth in the last decades has been relatively modest. It has been a combination of three factors:

1. Growth in some cities, particularly in the western United States.
2. Shrinkage in many older large cities, particularly in the northeast and north central regions of the nation.
3. The emergence of new central cities as smaller cities passed the 50,000 population mark and were then classified as central cities by the U.S. Bureau of the Census.

A major acceleration growth in central-city populations is certainly possible but seems unlikely at this time. All of the forces that shifted the locus of growth from central city to suburb are still in place. Motor vehicle ownership per capita grew rapidly through the last decade of the twentieth century and continues to do so, communications and computer technology continue to advance rapidly, and real per capita income continues to rise.

The future of energy costs is a wild card. Very large increases in energy costs over a sustained period of time might possibly favor central locations because mass transit is often more fuel efficient on a passenger-mile basis than is the automobile. That could direct some growth back into central cities. But that ball might also bounce in another direction. Possibly higher energy costs would favor scattered mixed-use development where travel costs would be reduced not by changing the mode of transportation but by shortening the average trip length (see Chapter 10). It is also possible that fuel costs might go up considerably but that increases in fuel efficiency—changing from SUVs and large cars to hybrid subcompacts and the like—would allow people to continue driving much as they do now without major increases in the cost of driving.

On balance, it seems likely that the mass of population growth in the next few decades will occur in metropolitan areas but outside the central city—in what the U.S. Bureau of the Census refers to as the "part outside" or what is commonly and casually referred to as "the suburbs." Planners whose focus is *growth management*, or what is now often termed *smart growth*, need not fear any shortage of work or absence of controversy (see Chapter 14).

SUMMARY

The forces that produced a hundredfold increase in urban population in the United States between 1800 and 1900 included national population growth, increased agricultural productivity, the growth of factory production, and the development of low-cost modes of transportation. The nature of nineteenth-century transportation contributed to an extremely dense pattern of urban development.

In the late nineteenth century, the first signs of suburbanization became visible as the electric streetcar began expanding the old "walking city." In the twentieth century, automotive transportation, electronic communications, and increased income promoted massive suburbanization of population and economic activity, which continue to the present time.

We noted the slowdown of central-city population growth in the decades after World War II and declines in the population of many of the largest cities, particularly inland industrial cities such as Cleveland and St. Louis. But at the same time that central-city growth slowed, the total population of metropolitan areas continues to grow rapidly.

In the post–World War II period, central cities have grown poorer relative both to the suburbs and to nonmetropolitan areas. The selective out-migration of more prosperous households and the loss of employment to suburbs, nonmetropolitan areas, and overseas competitors have contributed to this trend. Another factor was the migration to the cities of a large, generally poor population pushed off the land by the rapid mechanization of agriculture in the decades after World War II.

NOTES

1. For urban data going back many decades, see *Historical Statistics of the United States*, U.S. Bureau of the Census, Department of Commerce, Washington, DC.
2. Adna Weber, *The Growth of Cities in the Nineteenth Century*, The Macmillan Company, New York, 1899. Reprinted by Cornell University Press, Ithaca, NY, 1963, p. 20.
3. Ibid., p. 460.
4. For discussion of the relationship between transportation costs and the growth of cities in the late eighteenth and early nineteenth centuries, see Alan Pred, *City Systems in Advanced Economies*, John Wiley, New York, 1977.
5. Frank S. So et al., eds., *The Practice of Local Government Planning*, International City Managers Association, Washington, DC, 1979, p. 27.
6. Weber, *Growth of Cities*, p. 208.
7. James Ford, "Residential and Industrial Decentralization," in *City Planning*, 2nd ed., John Nolen, ed., D. Appleton & Co., New York, 1929, pp. 334 and 335. The first edition was printed in 1916, and the article appears to have been written between 1910 and 1916.
8. Sam Bass Warner, *Streetcar Suburbs: A Process of Growth in Boston*, Atheneum, New York, 1968.
9. H.G. Wells, *Anticipation: The Reaction of Mechanical and Scientific Progress on Human Life and Thought*, Harper & Row, London, 1902, quoted in *Post Industrial America: Metropolitan Decline and Inter-Regional Job Shifts*, George Sternlieb and James W. Hughes, eds., Rutgers University Center for Urban Policy Research, New Brunswick, NJ, 1975, p. 176.
10. For a discussion of population density gradients, see John M. Levy, *Urban and Metropolitan Economics*, McGraw-Hill Book Co., New York, 1985, pp. 24–26.
11. Figures for 1950 are from the *Statistical Abstract of the United States*, Figures for 2000 are from the U.S. Bureau of the Census Web site www.census.gov.
12. For a vivid description of the impact of mechanization on black tenant farmers in the production of cotton in the immediate post–World War II period, see Nicholas Lemann, *The Promised Land: The Great Black Migration and How It Changed America*, Alfred A. Knopf, New York, 1991, pp. 5–6.
13. For an exposition of the view that much of our present problem with poverty, family breakup, and crime in central cities results from lack of job opportunities, see the work of William J. Wilson, most recently *When Work Disappears*, Alfred A. Knopf, New York, 1997. For a somewhat different perspective, see Robert D. Waldinger, *Still the Promised City?*, Harvard University Press, Cambridge, MA, 1996.
14. Kevin Phillips, American Theocracy: The Peril of Radical Religion Oil and Borrowed Money in the Twenty First Century, Viking, New York, 2006. The term is in very widespread use but does not have a precise, commonly agreed upon definition. In a general way it refers to the increasing interrelationship and interdependence among nations due to, but not entirely limited to, the increase in world trade as a percentage of total world output, increasing travel and migration between nations, the increasing importance of multinational corporations, the increasing international flows of of capital and increasing interaction between capital markets in different nations, and the increasing amount of communication of all sorts across national boundaries.
15. David Firestone, "The New-Look Suburbs: Denser or More Far-Flung," *The New York Times*, April 17, 2001, p. A1.
16. These projections, released in January 2000, can be seen on the bureau's Web site www.census.gov. Go to *projections*, then *national*, and then *summary tables*. The projection was made before the results of the 2000 census were available and was based on forecasts of the 2000 population. These forecasts were lower than the total measured in the 2000 census. Had the projections been done after the 2000 results were available, the 2050 middle series figure, 403 million, would have been several million higher. A projection is a set of calculations based on a set of assumptions. In that sense, a projection cannot be wrong unless there is a mistake in the mathematics. The assumptions, however, may prove to be either correct or incorrect, and thus the projected result may be either close to or distant from reality. A forecast, on the other hand, is an estimate of what will actually happen. Thus, unlike a projection, a forecast can

be either right or wrong. In addition to the middle series projection shown in Figure 2–2, the projections made by the U.S. Bureau of the Census also include a low-series figure of 313 million, a high-series figure of 578 million, and a zero international immigration figure of 328 million, all for the year 2050. As these figures suggest, different assumptions about fertility, mortality, and immigration can produce very different results.

SELECTED BIBLIOGRAPHY

CALLOW, ALEXANDER B., *American Urban History,* Oxford University Press, 1973.

GLAAB, CHARLES N., and BROWN, THEODORE A., *A History of Urban America.* The Macmillan Company, New York, 1973.

MCKELVEY, BLAKE, *The Urbanization of America,* Rutgers University Press, New Brunswick, NJ, 1963.

WEBER, ADNA, *The Growth of Cities in the Nineteenth Century,* first printed in 1899, reprinted by Cornell University Press, Ithaca, NY, 1967.

CHAPTER 3

The History of Planning: Part I

The history of city and town planning, in its full sense, goes back many centuries. The logical and orderly arrangement of streets and public spaces in Roman towns, for instance, indicates the existence of a high level of city planning before the birth of Christ. However, since the focus of this book is present-day planning, we do not present a full history of the subject. This chapter begins with a brief note on the prerevolutionary period in the United States and proceeds through the first great age of suburbanization, the 1920s. The following chapter picks up the story from the start of the Great Depression and carries it through to the present time.

The focus of this chapter, as of the book as a whole, is on events in the United States. However, the chapter does contain some discussion of planning in Europe as well, for the development of planning in the United States was and is closely tied to events across the ocean. In fact, today the American planner who observes the practice of planning in Europe—whether by visiting new towns in Scandinavia, France, or the Netherlands; by observing the preservation of historic districts in any one of a number of countries; or simply by observing the sensitivity and wisdom with which the Swiss have treated a beautiful but potentially fragile natural heritage—will realize that there is still much that we can learn from the Europeans.

Up to now planning in the United States and in Europe has had much more influence on other parts of the world than has the rest of the world had on Europe and the United States. For example, some thousands of Third World students have studied planning in the United States and Europe whereas there has been little if any flow of students in the opposite direction. But that unbalanced flow of influence may change in the decades to come. At present there is a tremendous amount of modern urban planning activity in the Third

World, particularly in those nations that have experienced the most rapid economic growth. This includes much work in existing cities, the planning of numerous new towns, the planning of modern public transportation systems, and the planning of highways to accommodate the very rapid increase in automobile ownership now taking place. Inevitably, we in the West will begin learning from non-Western experience, both from successes and from failures.

COLONIAL AMERICA

Prior to the American Revolution, municipalities had strong powers to control the use of land and thus shape their own form. These powers came out of a European tradition that treated the town or village as an independent corporation, which might own, control, or dispose of most of the land within its boundaries. Many U.S. communities started as grants to individuals or groups, which then, by virtue of the grant, had the power to dispose of land within their borders. Communities had broad powers to control economic activities within their borders. For example, municipal governments frequently had the power to decide whether an individual was to be allowed to practice a particular trade or to set up a business. Thus colonial towns had formidable powers to shape their pattern of development. In that preindustrial age, they also faced weaker growth pressures than was later to be the case.

Today one can see the results of prerevolutionary town planning in many communities where subsequent growth pressures were not so overwhelming as to sweep away all traces of earlier times.[1] Prerevolutionary planning survives well in parts of New England away from major metropolitan areas, including much of New Hampshire and Vermont as well as parts of Maine, western Massachusetts, and parts of Connecticut and Rhode Island. In fact, much of the charm of these areas comes from the fact that so much of the past does survive. The urban pattern that characterizes such towns—the town square, the reasonable amounts of space between buildings, the simple rectangular street pattern—are all legacies of the town planning of the period. The regular pattern of development and the open areas in Savannah are also an example of prerevolutionary town planning. The land for the city was a grant to a single individual, James Oglethorpe, who as grantee had the power to plan and to impose an orderly and a gracious pattern on subsequent development.

The Revolution changed much of this. A certain amount of disorder was one price to be paid for political and personal freedom—a small price for what was gained, but still a price. Quite obviously, the Revolution ended the practice of creating municipalities through the mechanism of royal grants to individuals. More important, it placed the bulk of political power in the hands of the states, and it made substate units of government "creatures of the state," possessing only those powers granted them by

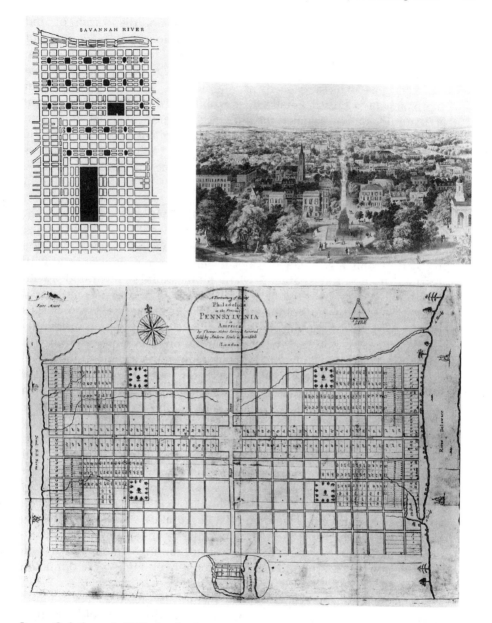

James Oglethorpe's 1733 plan for Savannah (top left) and the gracious and open results from an 1855 drawing (top right). William Penn's 1682 plan for Philadelphia is shown at bottom. In both plans, note the symmetry, the differentiation between primary and secondary streets, and the provision of public open space.

the states. Municipal powers to control the use and disposition of land were thus greatly diminished. The Constitution contains numerous safeguards for the rights of private property. (See, for example, the quotation from the Fifth Amendment in Chapter 5.) The protection of private property rights limits the capacity of a municipality to control development on privately owned land. Finally, the Revolution ushered in a very different set of attitudes that weakened the influence of hierarchy, social status, and authority; strengthened the claims of individualism; and enhanced the prestige of entrepreneurial activity. That general change in consciousness favored a more freewheeling and less orderly process of development.[2]

LIMITED MEANS AND GROWING PROBLEMS

The reductions in the powers of municipalities occasioned by the Revolution preceded by only a very few decades the emergence of enormous growth pressures discussed in Chapter 2. Many municipalities grew rapidly, with little public control over the pattern of growth. In most cases municipal planning was in the hands of the commercial elite of the city.[3] Planning thus often focused on the commercial heart of the city and ignored residential areas, particularly the less than prosperous ones. Often, planning was concentrated on steps that would facilitate the commercial and industrial growth of the city, such as inducing a railroad to extend a branch line to the city or improving the docks and the waterfront. Street patterns were often laid out in such a manner as to facilitate land subdivision and speculation.

The rectangular "gridiron" pattern became commonplace for exactly these reasons. It was easy to lay out, and it facilitated subdivision and speculation. More imaginative plans and plans adapted to particular terrain and topographic features were relatively rare. As land values rose with the growth of urban populations, pressures on remaining open space increased. Few municipalities were willing to accept the costs of acquiring land to protect it from development. Rapid growth, a strong regard for the sanctity of private property, the lure of quick profits from land development and speculation, and a feeling that promoting commercial growth was the number one function of municipal government were dominant motifs of the early-nineteenth-century urban scene.

There were a few exceptions to the picture just presented. For example, L'Enfant's plan for Washington, D.C., was a unified vision of how street pattern, public spaces, and structures should form a grand design. And the motivation behind it was essentially civic, not commercial. In Savannah, Georgia, Oglethorpe's original plan continued to guide the development of the city into the mid-nineteenth century. A number of the public squares shown in the figure on page 33 still remain. But more often than not, the forces of growth ran rampant over plans made in the prerevolutionary period.

For example, William Penn's plan for Philadelphia, formulated in the 1680s, called for a system of broad streets, public open spaces, and setbacks around individual structures. But the growth pressures that began in the late eighteenth century simply overwhelmed the plan. The side yard setbacks disappeared as houses were built wall to wall in block-long rows. Alleys were cut through blocks from one face to the other and then filled with row housing. Many of the public open spaces disappeared into commercial or residential use. There was no shortage of gracious and attractive city plans in eighteenth-century America, but most of them, like Philadelphia's, did not survive the growth pressures of the nineteenth century. By and large, Calvin Coolidge's famous aphorism, "the business of America is business," though uttered a century later, described early-nineteenth-century urban America quite well.

THE PRESSURE FOR REFORM

As urban populations and the density of urban development increased, pressures for reform mounted. U.S. planning history and tradition to a large extent mirror concern with the problems arising from urban growth. Over the years these problems have included sanitation and public health, the disappearance of urban open space, housing quality and overcrowding, the ugliness and grimness of the nineteenth-century industrial city, traffic congestion, and the problem of providing urban populations with adequate mobility. In recent years planning effort has also been directed to problems of urban unemployment, to urban fiscal problems, to a variety of issues that might be lumped under the heading of social justice, and to issues of environmental preservation and quality. And this listing is far from complete.

Sanitary Reform

In the mid-nineteenth century, sanitary conditions in most cities were appalling by modern standards. Human wastes were generally disposed of on-site in a backyard septic tank or cesspool—a situation that is acceptable at low population densities but a major menace to public health at high densities. The menace was compounded by the fact that most water for household use came from wells and streams. Thus contamination of drinking water sources was common. In an age before antibiotics and vaccinations, waterborne diseases like cholera and typhoid fever were major killers. So, too, were insect-borne diseases like malaria, yellow fever, and typhus. The mechanics of disease transmission were not known in the mid-1800s, for understanding of the relationship between bacteria and disease was still several decades in the future. However, it was widely understood that environments with large amounts of decaying material or stagnant water bred disease, perhaps because of "vapors" given off by putrefying materials or perhaps for some other reason.

Sewers, where they existed, served not to carry away organic wastes but to carry off storm water and prevent flooding. Very often they were constructed large enough for a man to go inside to make repairs. Water flow was too slow and too intermittent to carry off wastes, and so sewers themselves often became "elongated cesspools."[4]

Clearly the situation cried for reform. About 1840 a simple but very important invention that promised to be the agent of reform was made in England. This was the "water carriage" sewer. The insight behind the invention was remarkably simple. If a sewer pipe was made with a relatively small diameter and with a cross section somewhat like an egg sliced through the long way and provided with a sufficient source of water, it would essentially be self-cleansing. The water velocity would be sufficient to carry off animal carcasses, fecal matter, and so on. In this case, household wastes, instead of being dumped in on-site cesspools, could be piped into a common sewer and transported for miles before being released into the environment. The prospect for improvement in public health was enormous.

But building a water carriage sewer system for a city required planning on a major scale. Since the system was operated by gravity, the topography of the city had to be taken into account in the layout of streets. Because the system depended on a necessary volume of flow, streets had to be built with crowns so that rainwater would be diverted into the sewer. Deciding where to install sewer lines meant that some data on population distribution and present health conditions were needed. The "sanitary survey" of the late nineteenth century—a mapping of houses, cases of contagious disease, and presence of outhouses and cesspools and the like—was perhaps the first systematic data collection and mapping effort to be seen in many cities. The amount of planning required to provide sewers to a city did not constitute a comprehensive planning effort. But it did require that at least one aspect of the city be considered as a whole.

Planning for adequate waste disposal was only a part of the larger goal of a generally healthful environment. It was understood that dark, damp, crowded places were associated with higher rates of disease and death. Thus a more complete planning effort would include provision of open space, consideration of sunlight and ventilation, and some contractual arrangements (see Chapter 9) to prevent excessive density of development. In densely developed urban areas, little could be done about these latter considerations. Providing sewers was largely a matter of fitting, however it could be done, a system to an existing pattern of development. However, in developing new areas, a more comprehensive approach could be taken.

Sanitation and Integrated Design. Frederick Law Olmsted, probably the outstanding U.S. planner/urban designer of the second half of the nineteenth century, designed a number of new communities in which all these elements were part of an integrated design. The design was carefully keyed to the contour of the land for adequate drainage of both sewage and storm water. The location of swampy areas, brooks, streams, and other physical features was taken into account for health as well as aesthetic reasons. For example, it was known that malaria, which was widespread in the United States in the mid-nineteenth century, was somehow associated with swampy and poorly drained areas. Thus design that was sensitive to drainage patterns could minimize the incidence of the disease. The fact that it did so because it eliminated the breeding area for malaria-carrying mosquitoes was not to be understood for several more decades, but the beneficial effect could be achieved nonetheless. The location of open spaces and plantings was also considered for their effects on the adequacy of light and ventilation. In fact, in Olmsted's mind, planning was largely to be judged by the extent to which it reduced disease. Sunlight, good air circulation, and an adequate amount of vegetation were, in his view, the most effective preventives of disease.

Urban Open Space

The interest in sanitation dovetailed with another preoccupation of nineteenth-century planners, the provision of urban parkland. In an analogy that was used at the time, just as good ventilation would make a house a healthier house, so too would parkland serve to ventilate a city. Many splendid examples of municipal park design date from the mid-nineteenth century. New York's Central Park, designed by Frederick Law Olmsted and Calvin Vaux in 1857, furnished inspiration for parks in many other cities. The park covers a rectangle in Manhattan roughly two-and-one-half miles long by one-half mile wide. Bordered on all sides by dense urban development, it provides the Manhattanite with a beautifully landscaped piece of countryside in town. Across the East River in Brooklyn is a much less well-known but equally fine piece of Olmsted's design work, Prospect Park. A splendid system of meadows, wooded areas, connecting paths, and two artificial lakes provides an idyllic relief from mile upon mile of dense urbanization. In the case of both parks, as was true for the parks of many other cities, there is no doubt that had these areas not been acquired for public use, they would have soon been covered with a dense carpeting of residences, stores, and other commercial activities. Other examples of Olmsted's work in park design can be seen today in Buffalo, Chicago, Montreal, Detroit, Boston, Bridgeport, Rochester, Knoxville, and Louisville.

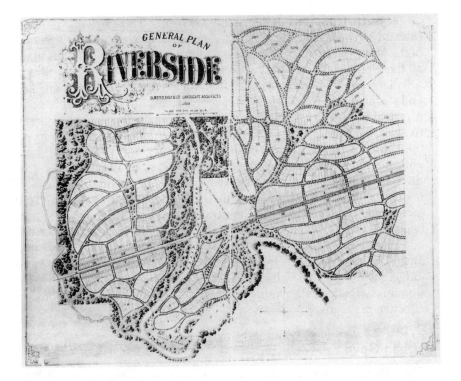

Riverside, a Chicago suburb, was planned by Frederick Law Olmsted and Calvin Vaux shortly after the Civil War. The curvilinear street pattern, close attention to fitting the street pattern to the topography, preservation of green areas, and separation of traffic from local traffic are all commonly used design techniques today.

Housing Reform

A major item on the agenda of nineteenth-century urban reformers was the condition of housing for the urban poor.[5] The issue of housing for those who do not have enough income to obtain on the private market what society deems to be adequate housing has been on the planning agenda ever since. In the nineteenth century, housing reform largely took the form of pressing for legislation that mandated minimum standards for housing quality.

In New York City the first legislation regulating tenement construction was passed in 1867, and other legislation followed at intervals thereafter. The city's 1901 Tenement House Act is considered a landmark in this tradition. It cut lot coverage back to 70 percent and required a separate bathroom for each apartment, courtyards (for light and ventilation) whose width was determined by building height, and improved fire safety measures. It also set up a Tenement House Commission, with a staff of inspectors and enforcement powers. By 1920 at least forty other cities had enacted building codes backed by some enforcement machinery.[6]

Although much was accomplished through housing regulation, we must also note what was not done. Housing reform in the United States took a conservative direction. The more far-reaching housing policies that had been adopted in some European countries were rejected here, much to the disappointment of the more radical reformers. In Europe much public money was invested in building housing for workers of modest means. Municipal governments often played the roles of landowner, developer, and financier. Local and national governments took the view that it was a responsibility of government to provide adequate housing at acceptable cost. The sort of policy that appealed to the more radical housing reformers was exemplified by the city of Ulm, Germany. The city acquired 1,400 acres of suburban land, planned the area, built housing, and sold it at cost to working-class families. The city also subsidized the building of cooperative apartments along with related community facilities.[7] But the view that prevailed in the United States was that housing is to be provided by the market and that the most government should do is to regulate the market. Government was not to be a landowner, a developer, or a source of housing capital. Even Lawrence Veiller, the moving force behind the 1901 Tenement House Act, believed that only local government should concern itself with housing and that such concern should be limited to regulatory matters and general planning issues such as street layout. He opposed the idea that public monies should be spent on housing.

The United States subsequently did move toward public housing and housing subsidies (see Chapter 4) but, in contrast to Great Britain, Germany, France, the Netherlands, and other European nations, has never gone very far in that direction. The great majority of Americans live in housing that has been built for profit by the private market. Whether the United States would have been wise to follow the European approach is arguable. What the divergence between them does clearly indicate, however, is that one cannot separate major planning questions from matters of political ideology. The European approach, regardless of its technical merits or demerits, looked too much like socialism to be accepted in the United States.

The Tradition of Municipal Improvement

Another part of the planning tradition that emerged in the second half of the nineteenth century might loosely be called municipal improvement. Its origins are generally traced to the founding of an improvement society in Stockbridge, Massachusetts, in 1853.[8] The civic improvement movement grew rapidly, at first largely in New England and then nationally. In 1900 the National League of Improvement Associations was founded, to be supplanted two years later by the American League for Civic Improvement. The agenda for the hundreds of civic improvement organizations included diverse items like tree plantings, antibill-board campaigns, paving of streets and sidewalks, provision of drinking fountains and public baths, provision of parks and recreational facilities, and numerous other public matters. The movement initiated a tradition of public concern with planning issues and helped build a climate of opinion that was receptive to municipal and regional planning, and it continues in force to the present.

The Municipal Art Movement

Toward the end of the nineteenth century, there formed an interest in municipal aesthetics that is generally referred to as municipal or civic art. A fusion of art, architecture, and planning, it attempted to transcend the mere utilitarianism of the late nineteenth-century city and to make it a place of beauty as well. Though later criticized for attending to the cosmetic aspects of urban life rather than the most pressing problems, the movement had a strong component of idealism.

> The darkness rolls away, and the buildings that have been shadows stand forth distinctly in the grey air. The tall facades glow as the sun rises; their windows shine as topaz; their pennants of steam, tugging flutteringly from high chimneys, are changed to silvery plumes. Whatever was dingy, coarse, and ugly, is either transformed or hidden in shadow. The streets, bathed in the fresh morning light, fairly sparkle, their pavements from upper windows appearing smooth and clean. There seems to be a new city for the work of a new day. . . . There are born a new dream and a new hope. And of such is the impulse to civic art.

Distinguishing between "civic art" and "art" in its usual meaning, the same writer stated,

> It is municipal first of all. If men seek it they seek it not for art's sake, but for the city's; they are first citizens and then, in their own way, artists jealous of the city's looks because they are citizens. . . . they so band themselves together and so commission sculptors, painters, artists, and landscape designers for the glorifying of civic art—not just because it is art, but because it is civic.[9]

The results of the movement are still visible all over America in the form of arches, fountains, statues, and other works of urban design and decoration. The inspiration for the movement came largely from Europe. One has only to look at the photographic plates of Robinson's classic work to see his inspiration: St. Paul's and the Thames embankment in London, the Arc de Triomphe in Paris, and other public areas in European cities. The motivation to catch up with the Europeans stemmed in part from the economic growth of nineteenth-century America, for it was wealth and leisure that gave us the feeling that we could afford that which was not purely functional.

The City Beautiful Movement

The City Beautiful movement brought together the ideas of municipal art, civic improvement, and landscape design. The event that is generally considered to mark the beginning of the movement is the 1893 Columbian Exposition in Chicago. Intended to celebrate the four-hundredth anniversary of the discovery of America, though it opened a year later, it had been the object of a major competition between a number of cities.

Designed by Daniel Burnham, possibly the most prominent architect and urban designer of the day, and Frederick Law Olmsted Jr. (the son of the designer of Central Park), the fairgrounds presented the visitor with a carefully integrated combination of landscaped areas, promenades, exposition halls, and other buildings. By the time the exposition closed, some 26 million people had seen it. By itself, the exposition opened the nation's eyes to what the planner, the architect, and the landscape architect, working in concert, could do.

> In this "White City" of almost 700 acres Chicagoans and millions of visitors, accustomed to urban ugliness, saw for the first time a splendid example of civic design and beauty in the classic pattern and on a grand scale, and they liked it. Indeed it marked the beginning in this country of orderly arrangement of extensive buildings and grounds.[10]

One effect of the exposition was to set off a wave of a particular type of planning activity in American cities. Plans coming out of the City Beautiful movement tended to focus on those things over which municipal government had clear control—streets, municipal art, public buildings, and public spaces. The results can be seen today in dozens of cities, particularly in civic centers, municipal buildings, and the like. Probably the best-known example of City Beautiful planning is the Mall and its immediate surroundings in Washington, D.C. The carefully designed vistas, the symmetry and axial layout (i.e., the Washington Monument placed at one end of the reflecting pool and the Lincoln Memorial at the other end), the formality, the classicism, and the scale and magnificence of the whole conception are hallmarks of the City Beautiful–era design. The City Beautiful movement obviously has close links to the municipal art movement, and to argue about whether a particular turn-of-the-century city hall and adjacent public spaces are products of one movement rather than the other is unimportant. Perhaps what distinguishes the two movements is more a matter of scale than intent. The municipal art movement tended to focus on particular points in the city: an arch, a plaza, a traffic circle, a fountain. The City Beautiful movement sought to create or remake a part of the city: a civic center, a boulevard, a parkway.

Two examples of the fruits of the municipal art–City Beautiful movement three-quarters of a century later. Above, Grand Army Plaza in Brooklyn, New York, and, below, the Pulitzer Fountain at Fifty-ninth Street and Fifth Avenue in Manhattan.

THE BIRTH OF MODERN CITY PLANNING

The single most important offshoot of the City Beautiful movement, as far as the development of an American planning tradition is concerned, was the *Plan of Chicago*. Interest in citywide planning, particularly within the business community, had been growing since the exposition. In 1906 the Merchants Club, essentially a chamber of commerce, commissioned Daniel Burnham to develop a plan. The work of planning was funded by the Commercial Club, another business organization, with $85,000, and the finished plan was presented to the city as a gift in 1909. The plan was remarkable for its scope. It laid out a system of radial and circumferential highways, some extending as far as 60 miles from the city center. Thus in its transportation elements it was a regional as well as a city plan. It laid out an integrated public transportation system and suggested the unification of rail freight terminals. Chicago's Union Station is one outgrowth of the plan. Within the city, extensive plans for street widening and overpasses at critical points were suggested. A system of parks and wildlife preserves both within and proximate to the city was suggested.

In a remarkable act of foresight, the plan's sponsors appreciated that the political and public relations side of planning was just as important as the technical side and set about fostering the public will to accomplish the plan. The original plan was a lavishly printed and expensive document that could have only a limited circulation. To make the concept of the plan known to the populace at large, a summary version was printed with private funds and given to every property owner in the city and to every renter who paid more than $25 per month. Shortly thereafter a version of the plan was done as a textbook and widely used in the eighth grade of the city schools. Not only did this reach many students as they were about to leave school—for many students ended their education with primary school at that time—but the plan also found its way into many households by this route. The plan was also promoted by means of illustrated lectures, a popular form of entertainment in that preelectronic age, and also by a short motion picture, *A Tale of One City*.

The Columbian Fountain at the 1893 Columbian Exposition in Chicago.

The city responded with the creation of a Planning Commission charged with the responsibility for carrying out the plan. As a strategy, the planners decided that one concrete accomplishment was needed to demonstrate that the plan was not simply an idle dream. The particular project was to carry Twelfth Street across the railroad yards south of the Loop on a viaduct and thus facilitate the flow of traffic within the city's downtown. When this was accomplished, skepticism about the practicality of the plan was greatly reduced, and one project after another was funded by bond issues. By 1931 close to $300 million had been raised by bond issues and special assessments to finance various elements of the plan. Robert L. Wrigley Jr., lists the following as some of its accomplishments:

> . . . The doubled decked Wacker Drive and several large bridges were major improvements along the main stem of the Chicago River. . . . The South Branch of the Chicago River was straightened, and harbor facilities were enlarged in the downtown area and at Lake Calumet. The famous Navy Pier was built far out into Lake Michigan. Now land was slowly built up as the Lake was pushed back and over 20 miles of lake-front park and beaches resulted. . . . And within these lake-front parks notable museums and other institutions were developed, much as Burnham and his associates had suggested. The outlying forest preserves were vastly extended until by 1933 they included 32,400 acres.[11]

By its very impressiveness, both as a document and as real accomplishment, the Plan of Chicago defined for a long time the planner's and perhaps also the informed citizen's view of what a plan should be. In particular, a plan should be comprehensive, and it should have a relatively long time horizon. The plan was to be effectuated largely through public capital investment on publicly owned land. Support by the citizenry was essential to provide the political will for making the necessary investment.

Some modern concepts of planning were absent from the Plan of Chicago. Among these were a concern with social issues, the notion of frequent plan revision and updating, and the view that the public should participate in the making of the plan rather than just receive and approve it as a finished document. The plan has sometimes been criticized for its emphasis on land and structures and its slighting of social issues. But judging the plan by the standards of a later day is not entirely fair. As a product of its time, it is a remarkable accomplishment.

THE PUBLIC CONTROL OF PRIVATE PROPERTY

The reader may have noticed that all the elements discussed in connection with the Plan of Chicago essentially pertained to public land, whether it was actually in public ownership at the time or was to be acquired at some later time. This focus on public-owned land was not accidental, for at the turn of the century, the public had little control over the uses to which privately owned land might be put.

One important part of the history of planning has been the evolution of public control over privately owned land. Beginning in the very late nineteenth century, a series of laws and court cases began to establish the right of local government to control the use of land that it did not own. The capacity of government to zone land for different uses was fairly well established by 1920 or so, though the definitive Supreme Court decision did not come until a few years later. The zoning process is one in which a municipal government can exercise control over the density with which land is developed, the types of uses permitted, and the physical configuration (heights of buildings, setbacks from property lines, etc.) of development. Typically, the community is divided into a number of zones displayed on a zoning map, and the permitted uses, densities, and design for each zone are specified in the zoning ordinance. The zoning process, as well as some related types of land-use controls, is described in detail in Chapter 9.

The Rush to Zone

The 1920s saw zoning ordinances appear across the nation with remarkable speed. The causes are not difficult to see. The legal precedents had been or were being established, and a very complex but legally defensible zoning ordinance enacted in New York City in 1916 gave some notion of what might be done. Automobile ownership was climbing at roughly 2 million vehicles per year. Within built-up areas, congestion, particularly in commercial districts, was mounting. Beyond that, widespread automobile ownership was promoting a vast wave of suburbanization. One way to control congestion in commercial areas and prevent the invasion of residential areas by commercial development was through zoning. To many communities, both in older areas and on the suburbanizing fringe, the power to zone looked like the best way to protect what was desirable in the status quo against the vagaries of rapid economic and social change. Perhaps a single-family neighborhood was threatened with invasion by filling stations, used car lots, and hamburger stands. Zoning it so that only single-family houses could be built seemed like an effective and a costless way to protect it from the undesirable side effects of progress.

Then, as now, zoning was not only a tool of planning and a technique for shaping the future, but also a device for defense of an existing order. And though no court would accept this as a legitimate purpose of zoning, the act of zoning might raise property values. Zone a pasture on the edge of town for manufacturing, and dreams of a prosperous retirement would glimmer in the eyes of the farmer who owned it. In fact, overzoning for commerce and industry was one of the hallmarks of the early age of zoning. For—aside from the pleas of expectant property owners—what municipality did not need more jobs for its people and more tax dollars for its coffers?

As we shall see, most planners regard zoning as only one aspect of planning and, particularly, as one tool for implementing the master plan. In the early 1920s, zoning often preceded planning and, in the minds of many, became almost synonymous with planning (a confusion that is much less common but not unheard of today). That view is not terribly surprising. A new technique with apparently substantial power to alter events had appeared on the scene, and it would take a while before its limits and its potential for abuse would become evident.

In 1921 it was estimated that there were 48 municipalities with a combined population of 11 million that had zoning. By 1923 the figures had risen to 218 municipalities and 22 million people.[12] The move toward zoning was further accelerated in 1924 when the U.S. Department of Commerce headed by Herbert Hoover came out with a model state zoning enabling act. Drafted by Edward M. Bassett, the attorney who had drawn up New York City's zoning ordinance a few years earlier, the Standard Enabling Act encouraged many states to adopt their own enabling acts. These acts, which specifically authorized local zoning laws, encouraged many more municipalities to enact zoning laws because it reassured them that their new laws would be able to withstand court challenge.

The Growth of Community Master Planning

Although the single most important trend in planning in the 1920s was the spread and acceptance of land-use controls, other events were occurring as well. In city after city, planning was institutionalized with the establishment of a planning commission. In some cases commissions had paid staffs that did the actual plan-making. More frequently, plans and zoning ordinances were drawn up by planning consultants. Roughly two dozen planning consultant firms were active in the United States in the 1920s.

Community plans of the period typically covered the following.[13]

> Land use (often considered synonymous with zoning)
> Street pattern
> Transit
> Rail (and where appropriate, water) transportation
> Public recreation
> Civic art

The goals of these plans typically included a number of items. One was an orderly and attractive pattern of land use. Related to this was avoiding the juxtaposition of incompatible land uses, for example, a factory in a residential area. Another goal was achieving a well-functioning system for both private and public transportation. Still another was to achieve an adequate system of parks and recreational areas. Goals of municipal beautification and attractive design for public spaces, for example, the area around the city hall, were common. Safeguarding property values and making the community attractive for business were very common general motivations behind the more specific goals already noted. The imprint of the City Beautiful movement and the Plan of Chicago are clear.

By modern standards these plans were less than complete. They neglected housing, except in the sense that zoning specified what housing types were permissible in the various zones. They generally neglected to plan for public capital investments, which in the view of most contemporary planners are often more powerful shapers of land use than are land-use controls. Citizen participation as we know it today was still beyond the horizon. Then, too, many planners of the time thought of the plan as something to be laid down once and then followed, much as an architect's drawings are to be followed as the building is erected. A more modern view, as we shall see, is that the plan is to be periodically monitored and revised as events take development in directions not anticipated in the plan or as community goals change.

But these limitations having been noted, it must be said that the typical plan for the 1920s was a major step forward in comprehensiveness from the focus on public places and public spaces that dominated the City Beautiful movement of a decade or two earlier. It covered the entire municipality, and it addressed a number of matters of municipality-wide concern.

As is the case today, most planning took place in established places where the planner worked within the constraints inherited from earlier periods. But a certain number of planners did have the ultimate design opportunity, the chance to plan a community de novo. Mariemont near Cincinnati; Palos Verdes in California; Longview, Washington; Chicopee, Massachusetts; Kingsport, Tennessee; Venice, Florida; and Radburn, New Jersey, are among the new communities planned in this period. Some, like Mariemont, were essentially residential and very often ended as expensive residences for the upper-middle class. Others, like Chicopee, were developed as industrial towns and contained places of employment and residences for the working class as well. Some were completed in the 1920s, and some were stopped short of full development by events beyond the planners' control.

For example, Radburn, New Jersey, billed as a suburb "for the motor age," was roughly half-built when the Great Depression began. It was never completed and today stands surrounded by conventional post–World War II suburban development. But the part that was completed is, in the eyes of many, a fine residential area. Planners and students of urban design still make field trips to Radburn. Large blocks of internal open space, a system of internal pathways, and a street pattern that keeps the automobile from intruding make it a very attractive living environment. House prices are high, vacancies are low, waiting lists are long, and many residents seem to take special pride in being Radburnites. By that ultimate arbiter, the marketplace, it is a very successful community. In general, many of the communities planned in the 1920s have stood the test of time quite well. When the planners had a clean slate, they often did very well. The more difficult feat was, and still is, to do well in an existing community, where the planner is stuck with the decisions (and mistakes) of the past and must confront a sea of special interests and local politics.

Master plan for Radburn, New Jersey, done in the 1920s, at left. At lower right is a detail for a court showing the separation of vehicular from pedestrian traffic. The housefronts face the walkway on the periphery of the block with vehicular access from the center roadway at the rear of the houses. That general plan has since been used in many planned communities. At lower left is an internal pathway for pedestrian use.

THE EMERGENCE OF REGIONAL AND STATE PLANNING _____

The 1920s also saw a growing interest in planning for an entire urban region, an idea that had been foreshadowed by the Burnham Plan of Chicago. Suburbanization and the emergence of widespread automobile ownership rapidly made city boundaries obsolete as the functional city—the economic and social city—often sprawled across dozens of political jurisdictions.

Perhaps the most comprehensive regional plan was one drawn up for the New York City region. The area then contained a population of 10 million, since grown to over 18 million. The plan covered 5,528 square miles, of which only 300 were New York City itself. The remainder consisted of nearby counties in New York State, Fairfield County in Connecticut, and about 2,000 square miles in adjacent parts of New Jersey.

The plan was drawn up by a nonprofit, nongovernment group, the Committee on a Regional Plan, which later metamorphosed into the Regional Plan Association (RPA), a group that exists to the present time. Funding for the plan, roughly $500,000, was provided by a philanthropy, the Russell Sage foundation.[14] The committee had no political power or status whatsoever. Thus whatever influence it had came purely from the force of its ideas and whatever public and political support those ideas could garner. Yet over the years the plan has had considerable effect on the physical shape of the region. Not only did it help guide the development of the New York region, but also it served as a model for many other metropolitan area planning efforts in decades to come.

The first task of the planners was simply to define the region. The criteria they used, which are still hard to improve upon, were described in this way: (1) "they [the region's boundaries] embraced an area within which the population can and does travel in a reasonable time from home to place of work"; (2) "they included the large outlying recreational areas within easy reach of the metropolitan center"; (3) "they followed the boundaries of cities and counties at the periphery"; and (4) "they had regard to the physical characteristics, such as watersheds and waterways."[15]

The transportation sections covered highway, rail, water, and perhaps surprisingly for the period, air transportation. The highway portions envisioned a complex of radial and circumferential routes, many of which have since been built. In a few cases routes that were envisioned originally as rail routes have subsequently been built as highways. By modern standards the plan was perhaps overly focused on physical features and capital investment and underemphasized some social and economic issues. But it was still a remarkable document in that it provided a unified vision of a three-state region containing hundreds of separate municipalities.

Regional plans appeared in numerous other parts of the country during the 1920s. John Nolen, a prominent planner and landscape architect, in 1929 listed about fifteen.[16] Many, like the plan for the New York region, were entirely private ventures. For example, the Tri-State District plan for the Philadelphia area (parts of Pennsylvania, New Jersey, and Delaware) was paid for by private subscription. Others, such as that done by the Boston Metropolitan Planning Commission, an official organization created by legislative act, were publicly funded. In several cases large counties engaged in regional planning even though the planning took place within a single political jurisdiction. On the East Coast, Westchester County, New York, with an area of about 450 square miles, engaged in extensive regional planning activity through the mechanism of the county parks commission. The results of that effort are visible today in the form of parkways and a splendid county park system of some 15,000 acres. On the West Coast, the largest county effort was Los Angeles County, with an area of about 4,000 square miles. Unlike the other regional plans of the era, it included a county zoning plan, believed to be the first in the United States.

In all cases other than counties, regional planning efforts had to be carried out in the face of the fact that there is no appropriate political entity corresponding to an urban region. Thus there is inevitably a question of where the political power to carry out the plan will be found. Intergovernment agreements may create some political basis for carrying out the plan. In some cases public authorities, which have some of the powers of government, have been created. Perhaps the best known of these is the Port Authority of New York and New Jersey, which has built or operated bridges, tunnels, port facilities, bus terminals, and airports and which has played a substantial role in shaping the New York region. But as a generality, the weakness in regional planning efforts was and is the mismatch between the nature of the tasks and the fragmentation of the underlying political structure. In the 1960s Robert Wood wrote a book on the New York region, with its complex of city, town, village, and county governments as well as numerous school districts, sewer districts, and other quasi-government organizations.[17] The book's title, *1400 Governments*, states in a phrase the essence of the problem.

The 1920s also saw the beginnings of state planning efforts. Statewide planning is bedeviled by a problem that is somewhat the opposite of the regional planning problem. The region is a natural unit that lacks an appropriate political structure. The state is the opposite, a political structure whose boundaries do not define a "natural" planning unit. Most states have boundaries that do not conform to any geographic, economic, or social reality. For example, New York State, which was the first state to attempt a statewide planning effort, extends from Montauk Point on Long Island, roughly due south of Rhode Island, to the shores of Lake Erie. The residents have little in the way of common interests other than that they are subject to the same state government. The state of Colorado has a natural break where the Rockies rise up out of the Great Plains. The eastern part, in a topographic and an economic sense, is part of the Great Plains. But the western part of the state, in an economic and a topographic sense, is part of the Rockies. The state's rectangular borders bear no relationship to these realities. Comparable comments can be made for most states. Yet despite these problems, a number of states have made substantial strides in statewide planning, particularly with regard to environmental and growth management issues, as will be seen in subsequent chapters.

Transportation plans done for the New York Regional Plan in the 1920s. A large part of what was planned has subsequently been built, though some of the transit links have been built as highways. The highway map (left) covers about 10,000 square miles, and the transit map (below) about 2,500 square miles.

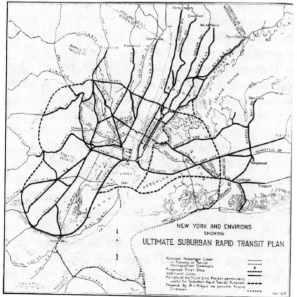

GRANDER VISIONS

The history of planning so far recounted is a largely pragmatic one, that of a profession seeking to solve problems within the existing urban framework. But there has also been within the profession a minority with much grander ambitions—one that seeks not simply improvement of the existing pattern but also a major restructuring of the form of human settlement. Although the issues change, the tension between those who see planning as an activity that optimizes development under the existing rules and those who hold a more radical view, who see the proper role of planning as rewriting the rules, is one of the central themes of planning history.[18]

Perhaps the most influential of all reformers and visionaries was the Englishman Ebenezer Howard. A court stenographer by profession, Howard conceived a vision of the city of the future and of a system of such cities. He set it forth in a short and very simply written book, *Garden Cities of Tomorrow*, published in 1902.[19] Howard observed the congestion and pollution of the late-nineteenth-century London and concluded that hope for the future lay in diverting population growth to new urban centers. People moved from the countryside to the congestion of the city for compelling economic and social reasons, but they paid a great price. The solution to the problem was to create new towns ("garden cities" in his terminology), which would offer the economic and social advantages of the city combined with the tranquillity, healthful environment, and closeness to nature that had been lost in the nineteenth-century city.

Howard proposed the following general design. The total development would have an area of about 6,000 acres (there are 640 acres in a square mile). The urbanized area itself would have an area of about 1,000 acres and be laid out in a circle about 1½ miles in diameter. A garden and a grouping of public buildings would constitute the core and would be accessible by radial boulevards. The core would be ringed by residential areas divided into neighborhoods by the boulevards. The residential ring would, in turn, be ringed by commercial and industrial establishments. The commercial and industrial ring would be enclosed in a circular rail spur, which would connect the city to other garden cities and to the central city of the region. Around the urban area would be agricultural and institutional uses. The dimensions of the city would be such that any resident would be within a few minutes' walk of both the city core and the places of work on the periphery. Yet he or she would live in an area from which industrial uses and heavy traffic were excluded.

The city, by virtue of quick rail access, would have close economic links to other cities, but it would have enough economic activity within its boundaries so that the great majority of its residents would not have to commute. Total population in the city would be about 30,000, and there might be another 2,000 or so people in the 5,000 acres surrounding the city. In the words of Lewis Mumford, perhaps the best known U.S. writer on architecture and urbanization, the garden city as conceived by Howard was more than just a bucolic retreat.

> [It should]. . . be large enough to sustain a varied industrial, commercial, and social life. It should not be solely an industrial hive, solely an overgrown market, or solely a dormitory; instead, all these and many other functions, including rural ones, should be contained in a new kind of urbanization to which he applied the slightly misleading name of garden city. Howard had no thought of a return to the "simple life" or to a more primitive economy; on the contrary, he was seeking higher levels of both production and living. He believed that a city should be big enough to achieve social cooperation of a complex kind based on the necessary division of labor, but not so big as to frustrate these functions—as the big city tended to do even when viewed solely as an economic unit.[20]

Howard perceived that no matter how well designed and well balanced the garden city might be, it could not exist in isolation. He envisioned a system of cities, all at a modest scale, as shown schematically in the accompanying illustrations. As Mumford characterized Howard's view,

> . . . a city, no matter how well balanced, can never be completely self-contained. He pointed out that in a group of garden cities united by rapid transportation each would have facilities and resources that would supplement those of the others; so grouped, these "social cities" would in fact be the functional equivalent of the congested metropolis.[21]

Howard, as did many other nineteenth-century reformers and planners, saw the fragmented private ownership of land as an impediment to good urban form because each property owner would be motivated to develop his or her land as intensely as possible and with no regard to its effect on the rest of the community. Thus one feature of his plan was common ownership of land, with profits from land development reverting to the municipal treasury.

The plan is a remarkable mixture of vision and practicality. Howard was a doer and an organizer as well as a visionary. In 1903 a company he organized purchased a site of 3,818 acres 35 miles from the center of London and proceeded to build the Garden City of Letchworth. Writing about it in 1945, F. J. Osborn stated,

> For Letchworth was, and remains, a faithful fulfillment of Howard's essential ideas. It has today a wide range of prosperous industries, it is a town of homes and gardens with ample spaces and a spirited community life, virtually all its people find employment locally, it is girdled by an inviolate agricultural belt, and the principles of single ownership, limited profit, and the earmarking of any surplus revenue for the benefit of the town have been fully maintained.[22]

A second planned community in the greater London area, Welwyn Garden City, was begun by Howard in 1919 with quite successful results.

Ultimately, Howard's work influenced urban development in dozens if not hundreds of communities from Radburn in the United States to Chandigarh in India. Radburn is very much an outgrowth of the garden city movement, as are Columbia, Maryland, and Reston, Virginia. In western Europe numerous new communities were built after World War II to deal with a desperate shortage of housing resulting from the low rates of construction during the Great Depression and the destruction of housing during the war. These communities, too, are an outgrowth or extension of Howard's garden city vision.

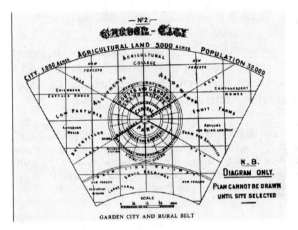

GARDEN CITY AND RURAL BELT

The plan for the entire 6,000 acres is shown at the upper left. Note the radial routes dividing the city into sectors and the circumferential rail line. One sector is shown at the lower left. Note the Grand Avenue and school. At the lower right is a schematic illustration of the system of garden cities. Replace the intermunicipal railway with a modern beltway and the garden cities with suburban subcenters like Tyson's Corner, Virginia, and the design looks relatively modern.

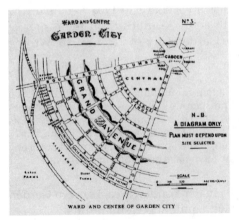

WARD AND CENTRE OF GARDEN CITY

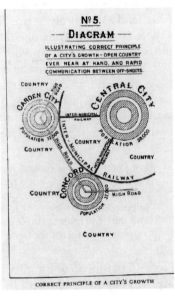

CORRECT PRINCIPLE OF A CITY'S GROWTH

In the last two decades of the twentieth century neotraditional design, also referred to as the new urbanism, became one of the most discussed trends in planning and urban design in the United States (see Chapter 10). It clearly draws much of its inspiration from Howard's work as its proponents readily acknowledge. In recent years there has been a spate of new town planning in a number of Third World countries. There, too, Howard's garden city concept has had an influence, albeit with some modern twists that Howard could not have anticipated. For example, the new town of Putrajaya, located near Kuala Lumpur, Malaysia, in an area that the Malaysian government is seeking to develop as a IT (information technology) oriented development center, bills itself as "the country's first intelligent garden city," a reference to its hoped for economic success in the field of information technology.[23] Both its own design and its relationship to the larger city of Kuala Lumpur suggest a Howardian influence.

SUMMARY

This chapter covered the history of planning in the United States from the colonial period to the end of the 1920s and the onset of the Great Depression. The Constitution made no direct mention of substate units of government. Thus municipalities became "creatures of the state," exercising only those powers granted them by the states. The Constitution also expanded the rights of individuals with regard to property rights and due process. The combined effect was to reduce greatly the power of municipalities to control the use and development of land within their boundaries. Early-nineteenth-century urban growth thus often occurred with a minimum of planning and public control. The crowding, ugliness, and haphazard development of many nineteenth-century cities gave birth to a series of reform movements, which shape to the present day much of the agenda of planning in the United States.

Among the movements discussed were sanitary reform, the movement to secure urban open space, the movement for housing reform, the municipal improvement movement, the municipal art movement, and the City Beautiful movement. The Columbian Exposition of 1893, which brought to millions of visitors a vision of what urban design and planning could accomplish, is often considered to mark the birth of the City Beautiful movement. The 1909 Plan of Chicago marked the beginning of the age of modern city planning and shaped the ideas of planners, politicians, and citizens about what a comprehensive plan should be and how it should be implemented.

The tradition of public control of the use of privately owned land evolved slowly, in part because of constitutional questions involved in the "taking" issue. However, roughly by the time of World War I, the right of local governments to exercise substantial control over the use of private property was reasonably well established. Post–World War I suburbanization, facilitated by a rapid expansion in automobile ownership, propelled hundreds of communities into zoning and master planning. The same period also saw the beginnings of regional planning as the automobile dispersed jobs and residences, creating vast urban regions.

NOTES

1. For a detailed account of prerevolutionary planning, see John W. Reps, *The Making of Urban America*, Princeton University Press, Princeton, NJ, 1965.
2. For an exposition of this change, see Gordon S. Wood, *The Radicalism of the American Revolution*, Vintage Books, Random House, New York, 1991.
3. For a discussion of urban government in the United States during the nineteenth century, see Charles N. Glanb and A. Theodore Brown, *A History of Urban America*, 2nd ed., Macmillan Publishing Company, New York, 1976.
4. See John A. Peterson, "The Impact of Sanitary Reform upon American Urban Planning," in *Introduction to Planning History in the United States*, Donald A. Krueckeberg, ed., Rutgers University Center for Urban Policy Research, New Brunswick, NJ, 1983, pp. 13–39.
5. For an example of reformist literature on urban housing and living conditions in the nineteenth century, see Jacob Riis, *How the Other Half Lives: Studies Among the Tenements of New York*, Dover, NY, 1971. First published by Scribner & Sons, New York, 1890.
6. Blake McKelvey, *The Urbanization of America*, Rutgers University Press, New Brunswick, NJ, 1963, p. 120.
7. Mel Scott, *American City Planning Since 1890*, University of California Press, Berkeley, 1971, p. 131.
8. For an account of the civic improvement movement, see John A. Peterson, "The City Beautiful Movement: Forgotten Origins and Lost Meanings," in Krueckeberg, *Planning History*.
9. Charles Mulford Robinson, *Modern Civic Art or The City Made Beautiful*, 4th ed., G. P. Putnam's Sons, New York

and London, 1917, p. 1. First edition published in 1903.
10. Robert L. Wrigley Jr., "The Plan of Chicago," in Krueckeberg, *Planning History*, p. 58.
11. Ibid., p. 70.
12. Scott, *American City Planning*, p. 194.
13. Ibid., p. 228.
14. Ibid., p. 261.
15. *Regional Plan of New York and Its Environs*, vol. 1, Committee on the Regional Plan of New York and Its Environs, William F. Fell Co., Printers, Philadelphia, 1929, p. 133.
16. For a contemporary description of regional planning efforts in the 1920s, see John Nolen, "Regional Planning," in *City Planning*, 2nd ed., John Nolen, ed., D. Appleton & Co., New York, 1929, pp. 472–495.
17. Robert C. Wood, *1400 Governments: The Political Economy of the New York Metropolitan Region*, Harvard University Press, Cambridge, MA, 1961. By *quasi-government* is meant a public body having some of the powers of government. For example, a school district has the power to collect taxes and to issue tax-exempt bonds.
18. See William H. Wilson, "Moles and Skylarks," in Krueckeberg, *Planning History*, pp. 88–121. Reprinted from William H. Wilson, *Coming of Age: Urban America 1915–1945*, John Wiley, New York, 1974.
19. Ebenezer Howard, *Tomorrow: A Peaceful Path to Real Reform* in 1988; republished with revisions as *Garden Cities of Tomorrow* in 1902; reissued by MIT Press, Cambridge, MA, 1970.
20. Lewis Mumford, "The Ideal Form of the Modern City," in *The Lewis Mumford Reader*, Donald L. Miller, ed., Random House, New York, 1986, p. 166.

21. Ibid., p. 169.
22. Howard, *Tomorrow*, p. 13.
23. The easiest way to get an idea of the development is to Google Putrajaya and also Cyberjaya, another new town being developed in proximity to Kuala Lumpur. They are in an area that the government of Malaysia has designated as an information technology (IT) corridor as part of the national economic development strategy.

SELECTED BIBLIOGRAPHY

See Selected Bibliography, Chapter 4.

The History of Planning: Part II

This chapter covers a nearly eight-decade period from the beginning of the Great Depression to the present time. The Depression years stand as an isolated decade sandwiched between the prosperous 1920s and the beginning of World War II. The period from the end of the war to the present is very different. Although marked by enormous social, political, and technological changes, it is a more or less continuous period. The 1930s was a period in which capitalism functioned very poorly and in which the enemy abroad, fascism, was on the political right. In the postwar period, capitalism in the United States, by and large, functioned well, and the enemy abroad, communism, was on the political left. Our former enemies had been defeated and were now our allies. Our former ally was now our mortal enemy. Then, in a series of remarkable events beginning in 1989, the Soviet empire in Eastern Europe and then the Soviet Union itself broke up, and the Cold War appeared to be over. These events will affect the background against which planning issues are decided well into the twenty-first century.

One theme of this book is that one cannot understand the history of planning by itself. One must see planning in a historic and an ideological context. This brief contrast between the 1930s and the postwar era is here to remind the reader to view the last eight decades of planning history against a changing ideological background. Whether the conflict referred to as the "war on terror" will have a major effect on planning remains to be seen.

PLANNING AND THE GREAT DEPRESSION

The 1930s was a peculiar time in the history of planning. It awakened great optimism about planning, and indeed, several new areas of planning were opened up. Yet on balance, for those who had great hopes for planning, this time was something of a disappointment. To those planners who would wish to see the scope of planning greatly enlarged—and this does not include all planners—the Depression years still have the bittersweet taste of a tantalizing opportunity nearly grasped. What happened?

The country began to slide into depression with the stock market crash of 1929, and economic conditions gradually worsened for the next several years. By the time President Franklin D. Roosevelt was inaugurated in March 1933, the unemployment rate was in the 25 percent range, and the cash value of goods and services produced had fallen by almost half since 1929. The fact that the free enterprise system was clearly malfunctioning and was unable to connect idle workers with idle machinery created an intellectual climate that favored planning in a way that the prosperous 1920s had not.

Planning is an ambiguous term. It may include everything from the most minor control over land use in a small town to Soviet-style centralized economic planning. But political moods and movements can be intellectually fuzzy. In general, the economic distress and disillusion of the Great Depression tended to favor more *planning*, whatever the word might mean.

There was relatively little consensus about what ought to be planned or by what principles. Within the Roosevelt administration there was a wide ideological spectrum. Roosevelt himself was not a radical. He was a pragmatist who would adjust and tune the system as required but who had no agenda for large-scale restructuring. Some in his administration, such as the secretary of the interior, Harold Ickes, were relatively conservative. Others, like Rexford Tugwell and Henry Wallace, who were well to Roosevelt's left, favored major change and a major shift of economic power from private to public hands.

Apart from the administration there was a Congress that, although much more willing to experiment than it had been in better times, was hardly radical. Finally, there was the Supreme Court, then a relatively conservative body, which in modern terms might be described as "strict constructionist."[1] The Court turned out to be a major limitation on the amount of social and economic experimentation in which the national government might engage.

A number of planning initiatives began during the Great Depression.[2] Some persist to the present time. Others have sunk without leaving much trace.[3] One initiative that lasted was the federal funding of local and state planning efforts. Federal funding was provided for planning staffs, both as a job-creation measure and as a commitment to planning. Numerous communities used federal funds to build and staff planning departments, to develop maps and databases, and to formulate plans, including many community master plans. In the slow-growing, fiscally strained environment of the 1930s, many plans simply sat on the shelf. But the federal funding did help build the size and technical competence of the profession.

Federal funding and increased state interest in planning accelerated a trend that had begun in the late 1920s, namely, the creation of state planning agencies. By 1936 every state except one had a state planning board. The focus of these boards varied greatly. In many, particularly those in which agriculture was a dominant part of the economy, the focus was on conservation and farmland preservation. In others the primary focus was on urban issues, including housing quality, sewage treatment, water pollution, the provision of adequate recreational facilities, public finance, and urban governance. Much of the work of state planning agencies focused simply on finding the facts, whether that meant mapping areas of soil erosion in a rural area or studying public finance and the structure of government in a metropolitan area.

The federal government moved into the provision of low-cost housing, an area in which it has remained in one way or another ever since. The motivation was twofold. First was the obvious goal of improving the housing of the poor. The second goal was expansion of construction as a way of stimulating the economy. At first the federal government built public housing directly. Then a Supreme Court decision forced a change in the program, and the federal government switched to providing financial support, both capital and operating, for local public housing authorities. There are today somewhat over 1 million units of public housing in the United States and several million units of privately owned but publicly subsidized units. That public presence in the housing market had its origins in the Great Depression.

In the mid-1930s, the Resettlement Administration embarked on a program of new town-building. The program lost favor with Congress after a time and was discontinued in 1938. However, three new communities, Greenbelt, Maryland; Green Hills, Ohio; and Greendale, Wisconsin, were constructed.

The housing initiative of the federal government that had the most far-reaching effects was not one that fell in the realm of planning but rather in the realm of finance. That was the provision of mortgage insurance by the Federal Housing Administration (FHA) noted briefly in Chapter 2 and discussed in more detail in Chapter 18. Few, if any, acts of the federal government have had more effect on the pattern of settlement than did FHA mortgage insurance.

The conceptual basis for Urban Renewal was also a Depression-era development. Economists and others within the federal government foresaw the difficulty that central cities would have in competing with suburban areas for development capital, largely because of differences in site-acquisition costs (see Chapter 11). The solution proposed was the City Realty Corporation, an organization that would use federal subsidy monies plus the power of eminent domain to produce marketable development sites at below cost.[4] World War II swept the City Realty Corporation off the national agenda, but the idea, under a different name, became one of the bases of the Housing Act of 1949, which established Urban Renewal.

Still another Depression-era initiative was the first planning for what was to become the interstate highway system. World War II shelved the idea for a time, but it reappeared as the National Defense Highway Act of 1956. This initiated the building of the interstate highway system, the largest single construction project in U.S. history.

The Depression also saw the creation of the National Resources Planning Board (NRPB) under the leadership of Rexford Tugwell, a member of FDR's so-called "brain trust." Though the board never fulfilled the dreams of those who favored the major move to the left, it did do a certain amount of useful work. One contribution was the support of local and state planning efforts. Another was the making of an inventory of natural resources on a national scale. In the conflicting political currents of the time, noted earlier, the board did not make much of a mark on the nation and in 1943 was dissolved by Congress. The war and national preoccupation with war-related matters was one cause of its demise. Another cause was that any organization that seeks to plan on a broad canvas will naturally step on toes and make enemies.

Whether the NRPB's dissolution is a cause for sorrow or rejoicing is largely a matter of ideology. From the left its dissolution looks like a major missed opportunity. From the right its dissolution looks like a slaying of the socialist monster in its crib before it could grow to maturity and do any damage.

Finally, the Depression era saw the start of a number of regional planning efforts, the best known of which was the Tennessee Valley Authority (TVA). Established in 1933 to provide a combined approach to flood control, power generation, and natural resource conservation, the TVA was planned on a major scale. Dams that served for flood control also produced power, which facilitated rural electrification and brought industry into the valley. The creation of lakes behind dams naturally led the agency into recreation planning. Among those who favored a much larger role for government, the TVA occasioned much enthusiasm as a prototype for what large-scale regional planning could accomplish.

Other regional initiatives included the New England Regional Commission, the Colorado River Basin Compact, and the Pacific Northwest Regional Planning Commission. The latter two ultimately resulted in the construction of the Boulder, Bonneville, and Grand Coulee dams.

THE POSTWAR PERIOD

World War II provided a sharp break with the Depression and Depression-era issues. The conversion to a war economy quickly ended the unemployment of the 1930s, and political and military events abroad shifted the nation's political focus from internal to external. From the end of the war to this writing, the country followed a generally successful economic course. It is true that there have been several recessions and several brief inflationary episodes, but on the whole, the U.S. economy has flourished. There was thus much less willingness to contemplate radical changes than there had been during the Depression. Perhaps this unwillingness was just a matter of heeding that bit of folk wisdom, "If it ain't broke, don't fix it." Then, too, the success of capitalist economies in Western Europe and Japan, and North America contrasted with the poor performance of centrally planned economies in the Soviet Union and Eastern Europe, militated against major moves toward national planning.

Postwar planning initiatives thus took place in a relatively conservative framework. Where possible, they involved a heavy reliance on private initiative and private capital. Typically, the major planning initiatives also involved a combination of federal, state, and local effort. A share of the funding and some legislative guidelines were provided by the federal government, but much of the initiative, detailed planning, and implementation came from state and local governments. As discussed in Chapter 18, planning in many European nations in the 1980s and 1990s came to resemble the American model much more than it had in the early postwar period, partly for some of the same ideological reasons and partly for economic reasons.

The Expansion of Municipal Planning

The postwar period saw a large expansion of planning activity at the city, town, and country level. The causes of this expansion were numerous. The prosperity of the postwar period gave municipal governments more funds to spend on planning. The satisfaction of private wants with the growth of the postwar economy naturally turned people's attention to public needs. It is easier to be concerned about the quality of one's community when one is well fed, well housed, and financially secure than when one is not. Postwar suburbanization, as it did after World War I, stimulated planning activity in thousands of suburban cities and towns by thrusting on them the problems of growth. The difference was that this time there was no Depression to cut short the suburbanization process. The growth of local planning activity was also powerfully stimulated by the federal government. Federal grants, Urban Renewal, and other programs discussed in this chapter stimulated the expansion of planning agencies. Beyond that, federal funds were made available to local agencies for general planning purposes under section 701 of the Housing Act of 1954 and subsequent legislation.

Urban Renewal

The first major initiative to appear after the war was Urban Renewal or, as it was called in its early days, Urban Redevelopment. The difficulties that cities faced in competing with suburban areas for investment capital had been perceived during the later years of the Depression. In the Housing Act of 1949, Congress set up the mechanism by which cities might be enabled to compete more effectively with outlying areas. At the time, the biggest need of the cities appeared to be for investment in housing, both to clear away many acres of slum housing and also to alleviate severe housing shortages resulting from low rates of construction during the Great Depression and World War II. Thus Urban Renewal started as a slum clearance and housing program. It soon added a major commercial thrust as well. By the time the program was ended in 1973, some $13 billion of federal funds had been expended. Several billions more were spent in projects that were in the pipeline at that time and were subsequently completed. Adjusted for inflation, expenditures on Urban Renewal probably totaled in the range of $100 billion in today's dollars. A great deal had been accomplished, but there were also very high human costs in the form of neighborhood disruption and the forced relocation of hundreds of thousands of households. The program is discussed in detail in Chapter 11.

The Age of Highway Planning

Another major theme of the postwar period was highway planning and highway building. The period after the war witnessed an enormous amount of suburbanization accompanied by massive increases in automobile ownership, as noted in Chapter 2. Coincident with the suburbanization of population was the suburbanization of economic activity. As a consequence of the changing distribution of economic activity, there was also a significant increase in the importance of truck transportation relative to rail transportation in the carriage of both intra- and intermetropolitan freight. Because of these pressures, one metropolitan region after another moved into large-scale highway planning. The first and possibly best known of these was the Chicago Area Transportation Study (CATS).

The postwar period also saw the building of the interstate highway system, which, measured in physical terms, is the largest engineering project in the history of the nation. The idea, as noted, is of Depression-era vintage, but work did not begin until after the passage of the National Defense Highway Act of 1956. Most of the system was constructed in the 1960s and 1970s. By the end of the 1980s, only a few links remained to be completed. The system, about 40,000 miles in length, has been a major force in reshaping the nation, largely, one suspects, in ways unanticipated by its planners. The transportation planning process is described in Chapter 12, and the interstate highway system is discussed in more detail in Chapter 17.

Environmental Planning

Environmental planning, a term that would have been virtually unrecognizable 40 years ago, emerged as a field at the end of the 1960s. Its emergence can be traced to two separate background forces. First, with the growth of population and prosperity, humanity had acquired more ability to damage the environment. More people, more kilowatt hours of electricity generated, more vehicle miles driven, more acres covered with paving and structures—all meant that the natural environment was at greater risk. Second, and more important according to some, were changes in what we produced and the way we produced it. Around 1940 there began a revolution in the types of materials we produced and used. Up to that time most of our materials were naturally occurring substances, though often processed and modified in some way. Since then we have increasingly relied on substances that have never before existed, which often have some degree of toxicity, and for which natural pathways of degradation do not exist. For example, in a very influential book, *Silent Spring,* Rachel Carson argued that DDT (a compound that had been known for some decades but came into use only about the time of World War II) was entering the food chain, with all sorts of dire consequences both to the ecosystem in general and to humans—who eat fairly high up on the food chain—in particular.[5] Barry Commoner in *The Closing Circle* (a title whose ominous ring fit the tone of the book well) cited a long list of changes in products and processes with adverse environmental consequences; for example, pesticides, chemical rather than natural fertilizers, and the increasing use of plastics like polyethylene for which natural degradative pathways do not exist.[6]

By the end of the 1960s, mounting concern with the effect of our impact on the environment resulted in the passage of the National Environmental Policy Act (NEPA), which created the Environmental Protection Agency (EPA). The act also required the filing of an environmental impact statement (EIS) for a project involving substantial amounts of federal funding, a stipulation that more than any other single event brought the field of environmental planning into being. Simply complying with the requirement that an EIS accompany a request for federal funding created employment for large numbers of environmental planners. In the following years many states passed laws analogous to NEPA, often referred to as "little NEPA" acts. Congress passed numerous other pieces of environmental legislation such as the Clean Air Act and the Toxic Substances Control Act. In each case, the studies and planning required to comply with the requirements of the law expanded the field of environmental planning. Increasing consciousness of environmental issues has also prompted agencies doing traditional land-use planning to consider environmental aspects that a few years ago were often ignored in the planning process. The subject is pursued further in Chapter 15.

For a time a subfield of environmental planning—energy planning— flourished. After the rise in oil prices following the Arab-Israeli War of

1973, there was much interest in reducing U.S. energy consumption. One path to that goal appeared to be community energy planning. For example, a community design that reduced the length of the average work or shopping trip would reduce automotive fuel consumption. A community land-use pattern that could be served by public transportation would be more fuel efficient than one that could be served only by private transportation. Planning for these and other measures made up the substance of energy planning. Interest in the field was strong until the early 1980s. At that time the real cost (dollar cost adjusted for inflation) of oil began to decline and with that interest in energy planning faded until some time after the events of 9/11. However, by late 2007 crude oil prices had climbed to almost $100 a barrel (44 gallons). Those prices, combined with a widespread perception that instability in the Middle East makes "energy independence" important for political and national security reasons, have put energy planning back on the national agenda.

Growth Control and Growth Management

In the 1960s growth control and growth management emerged as a distinct area of planning and also as an area of legal and moral controversy. Two separate trends in the postwar period combined to create this field. The first was the growth of population and the movement of population from central cities into suburban and exurban areas. Many communities felt themselves threatened by growth and thus saw a need to develop a means to prevent growth entirely or to limit and control it. The second factor was the growing environmental consciousness of the 1960s. Concern with the natural environment in general easily translated into concern with the natural environment of a particular city or town or county and furnished motivation and rationale for local growth-control efforts. One movement of the 1960s, spawned by global environmental concerns, was zero population growth (ZPG), whose slogan for would-be parents was "stop at two."[7] Concern with population control at the global or national level spilled over into concern with population control at the local level.

The growth-control movement raised legal and moral issues that have not been easy to resolve. In fact, there is now a substantial record of litigation pertaining to the subject. One question at issue is exactly what rights communities have to exclude potential residents. The subject is pursued in Chapter 14.

The Growth of Statewide Planning

Beginning in the late 1960s, the nation began to witness an increase in statewide planning efforts. This development was closely related to growing concern over environmental issues. In general, state planning efforts do not supersede local planning efforts but rather add another layer of control. State planning may address a variety of environmental or growth management goals that, because they transcend municipal boundary lines, cannot be adequately handled at the local level. A number of state planning processes are described in Chapter 14.

Economic Development Planning

In the period immediately after World War II, it was generally thought that the economic function of government was simply to ensure that the national economy functioned well. Specifically, the main problem was to employ suitable fiscal and monetary policies to maintain a high level of employment and a reasonable degree of cyclical stability. To the extent that there was poverty stemming from unemployment, the way out was thought to be economic growth in order to bring more people into the workforce and exert upward pressure on wages.

After a time, however, it became apparent that prosperous as the nation was, there were parts of the country in which poverty and unemployment were rampant. The first geographic area so recognized was the Appalachian region, sandwiched between the much more prosperous East Coast and the then thriving Midwest. The terms *pockets of poverty* and *structural unemployment* came into use.

At the beginning of the 1960s, the federal government began to fund local economic development programs through a series of agencies and programs discussed in Chapter 14. Briefly, its intention was to promote by means of planning and subsidies the flow of capital into distressed areas. Initially, most of the federal effort regarding structural unemployment had a rural and small-town focus, for in the early 1960s that was where the problem was most acute. Gradually, with the urbanization of poverty discussed in Chapter 2, the focus of these efforts became more urban.

For reasons of political ideology the Reagan administration was opposed to such programs, and the federal government largely withdrew from the field during the 1980s. Neither in the presidency of George H. W. Bush, nor in the two terms of Bill Clinton, nor in the presidency of George W. Bush was there an attempt to restore the federal role. However, thousands of local governments still pour much effort and billions of dollars into economic development. The structural unemployment issue is one of the prime motivations for such efforts. The other major motivation is property tax relief, a point discussed in Chapter 9. The property tax relief motivation was greatly strengthened in the late 1970s by increasing citizen resistance to further increases in local taxes, as exemplified by California's Proposition 13. For municipal governments trapped between citizen resistance to taxation on the one hand and rising costs of providing services on the other, expansion of the tax base through economic development seemed like the best way out. If anything, interplace economic competition grew more intense during the 1990s, and economic development planning was one of the growth areas in planning.

Planning for Smart Growth

In the mid-1990s, Maryland invented the term *smart growth* to describe its anti-sprawl state development plan. Within a few years, the term became one of the most, if not the most, commonly used planning terms in the United States. Closely allied with older ideas about growth management, smart growth was touted as the latest and most important answer to the problem of sprawl. With the U.S. population growing at somewhat more than 3 million people per year, and with most of that growth going into suburban areas, traffic congestion and other problems associated with sprawl were becoming daily more important to the public and to the planners who serve that public. Sprawl and smart growth are discussed in Chapter 14.

Planning and Public Safety

The need for safety was an important force behind the evolution of cities. The city was a more defensible place than an isolated settlement in the countryside. Several centuries ago, technology began to change that picture. When cannon first appeared in Europe in the late fifteenth century, city walls began to lose their protective value. In the twentieth century, the invention of the airplane converted cities from places of safety into huge targets, as World War II made unmistakably clear. In the early years after World War II, the existence of the Soviet Union armed with nuclear weapons made U.S. cities look like a major military liability. Many thought that the more densely urbanized we were, the more we invited nuclear attack and also the less able we would be to survive a nuclear attack.

Urban planners and federal officials began to discuss the question of whether promoting a more scattered pattern of development would be in the national interest.[8] However, this line of thought never gathered enough adherents to have a major effect on the U.S. pattern of development, though it may have affected the location of some defense facilities and the commercial and residential development associated with them. One reason that the United States did not adopt a policy of intentional dispersion was that very large numbers of people in this country believed that nuclear war between the United States and the Soviet Union simply would not occur. The key acronym was MAD (Mutual Assured Destruction), and the key assumption was that the leadership of the Soviet Union, though reprehensible in many ways, was cautious and sane. As the Cold War waned and détente grew, concern with the security implications of the pattern of development gradually evaporated. In looking back, it is clear that those who placed their faith in MAD were correct.

The events of September 11, 2001, placed the relationship between the pattern of settlement and safety back on the planners' agenda. No terrorist attack could approach the destructiveness of a nuclear exchange, but on the other hand, such an attack had happened, and the destruction it caused was still massive. Unlike the leadership of the Soviet Union, the leadership of al Qaeda was not cautious, and to most Americans, it also did not seem to be entirely sane. It was instantly clear to Americans that terrorism was not something that happened just in distant places like Israel or Sri Lanka or Kashmir. From 9/11 forward, Americans would have to contend with the possibility of terrorism at home.

Security concerns are now showing up in a variety of small ways in building design, site design, and the way that buildings and public spaces are operated. Shatterproof glass and stronger construction are now appearing in some new, larger structures. Barriers that make it impossible to bring a motor vehicle close to a building are now becoming commonplace in some urban areas. The new landscaping for the Washington Monument leaves the basic appearance of the monument site unaltered but surrounds the monument at some distance with walkways that have low walls sufficient to stop a truck from getting close to the monument.

How much effect the threat of terrorism will have on urban form in the long term will largely depend on how the "war on terror" progresses and whether there are further terrorist acts in the United States. If Americans feel relatively safe from terrorism, the long-term effects of 9/11 on U.S. cities may be small. To the extent that fear of terrorism does affect urban form, the overall effect is likely to be a dispersing one. Measures to keep traffic and parked vehicles away from buildings and, generally, to achieve safety through distance will necessarily be easier to implement and less costly in low-density environs. Such measures will be hardest, or in some cases impossible, to implement in densely built-up areas like lower and mid-town Manhattan or downtown Chicago.

How much the fear of terrorism will affect that unique symbol of urban development, the skyscraper, also remains to be seen. The first skyscraper to be built since 9/11 in the area of the World Trade Center, 7 World Trade Center, has a concrete rather than a steel core, extra fireproofing, pressurized staircases (to keep smoke out), and many other safety features, all of which should be reassuring to tenants but which also push up the cost of construction considerably.[9] Freedom Tower, the first building to be put up on the site itself will have all of these and many other safety features as well. The cost of constructing a square foot of net leasable space in a skyscraper was very high even before these additional costs. Its construction is financially feasible because it commands high rents. And, generally speaking, higher floors command higher rents. The key question, then, will be one of psychology. Will firms shrug off the risks and continue to pay top rents for prestige and better views? Or will fear and caution cause the market for skyscraper floor space to soften up and discourage further construction?

Planning for Natural Catastrophe

Natural disasters have always been with us and the history of many cities has been altered by floods, earthquakes, and other catastrophic events. But Hurricane Katrina of 2005 was of such a scale that it focused the minds of many people on the subject to an extent that had not been the case before. In looking back, it seems clear that Katrina presented us with a situation that calls for large-scale catastrophe planning—both what to do about the one that did occur and what to do about the possibility of recurrence. Though, in total, Katrina did more damage outside of New Orleans, the damage was greater there than in any other single location so we might focus there for a moment. A comprehensive planning approach for New Orleans might start with some very basic hydrologic considerations. What, if anything, is to be done about the Mississippi delta? If nothing is done, a combination of subsidence and the washing away of soil in the delta will render the city more and more flood prone and raise very serious questions about its long-term prospects. Multibillion dollar engineering projects to change the hydrodynamics of the delta are another option. Improving the system of levees, but not attempting to change the overall hydrodynamics of the delta, is another option. The choice of whether to write off part of the city and let it revert to a more natural state or to try to reconstruct the entire city are both options, in part depending upon the previous choices. The economic effect upon the entire region around New Orleans of major changes in the size of the city need to be considered. Much of the agricultural output of the American Midwest passes through the Mississippi on its way to other parts of America and the rest of the world. So what happens to the Port of New Orleans has ramifications far beyond New Orleans or the state of Louisiana.

There are a mass of social planning issues involving poverty, housing, and education. There are questions about whether more good will be done for poorer people by putting money into fixing the environment where they live or by spending money directly on them which, in some cases, may mean helping them move out of the area in which they live to places where jobs and housing are more available. In short, it is not hard to envision a huge planning effort that involves all levels of government from the federal government down and many nongovernmental parties as well. In fact, it is not hard to envision that planning for New Orleans might be folded into a larger planning effort that encompasses much of the Gulf Coast. So far, that has not happened.

To anticipate a theme that recurs through this book, what does and does not happen in planning cannot be understood without reference to politics. And, rightly or wrongly, in part depending on one's political and ideological preferences, that kind of approach to the aftermath of Katrina and the possibility of future Katrinas was just not in the cards politically. Whether it will be someday remains to be seen. Chapter 17 might give the reader a few thoughts on what such planning might look like.

SUMMARY

This chapter noted the increased interest in planning during the Great Depression, in part as a result of the poor performance of American capitalism during this period. Though the hopes of those such as Rexford Tugwell, who favored a major swing toward national planning, were disappointed, some planning initiatives that lasted well into the postwar period did have their origins in the 1930s.

Urban Renewal and the interstate highway system were conceived during the Great Depression, though not enacted into law and funded until after the war. Federal subsidization of housing and federal financial support of local planning efforts began during the Great Depression. Statewide planning, seen to a limited extent in the 1920s, became widespread during the Great Depression. World War II quickly ended the unemployment of the Depression years and shifted the nation's political focus from internal to international affairs.

The political climate of the postwar period was very different from that of the Great Depression, and there was little support for national planning. In fact, the National Resources Planning Board had been abolished during World War II and was never reconstituted. Nonetheless, there was a major expansion of planning activity, in large measure fueled by federal grants and pushed forward by national legislation. Among new or expanded activities were Urban Renewal, highway planning (including planning for the interstate highway system), environmental planning, community development, planning for growth management, and local economic development planning. In recent years, the question of *smart growth* has come to the fore as increasing numbers of people become concerned about the question of sprawl driven by continuing population growth.

Among the forces behind the increase in planning activity were the growth in population and wealth, the rapid suburbanization and increased automobile ownership that followed World War II, the weakened competitive position of many central cities vis-á-vis the suburbs, and increasing concern with the effects of human activity on the natural environment.

NOTES

1. Meaning a relatively literal interpretation of the Constitution based on the "original intent" of its authors and relatively little willingness to define new individual rights or new obligations of government that are not clearly implied by the wording of the Constitution. The reader who wants to pursue the debate over whether the Constitution should be interpreted strictly or flexibly might see Robert Bork, *The Tempting of America: The Political Seduction of the Law*, Free Press, New York, 1990.

2. For a general account of the New Deal, see William E. Leuchtenburg, *Franklin Delano Roosevelt and the New Deal*, Harper & Row, New York, 1963; or Arthur M. Schlesinger, *The Coming of the New Deal*, Houghton Mifflin, Boston, 1958.

3. For a general account of Depression-era planning initiatives, see Mel Scott, *American City Planning Since 1890*, University of California Press, Berkeley, 1965, chap. 5.

4. Guy Geer and Alvin Hansen, "Urban Redevelopment and Housing," a pamphlet published by the National Planning Association, 1941. For additional references to Urban Renewal, see Chapter 11.

5. Rachel Carson, *Silent Spring*, Houghton Mifflin, Boston, 1962. (Note: DDT was subsequently banned in the United States but is in use in parts of the Third World.)

6. Barry Commoner, *The Closing Circle*, Alfred A. Knopf, New York, 1971.

7. For a statement of the ZPG view, which was widely read and quoted at the time, see Paul Ehrlich, *The Population Bomb*, Ballantine Books, New York, 1971.

8. Michael Quinn Dudley, "Sprawl as Strategy: Planners Face the Bomb," *Journal of Planning Education and Research*, vol. 21, no. 1, Fall 2001, pp. 52–63.

9. David B. Caruso, Associated Press, September 7, 2006.

SELECTED BIBLIOGRAPHY

HALL, PETER, *Cities of Tomorrow*, Blackwell, London, updated edition, 1996.

KRUECKEBERG, DONALD, A., ED., *Introduction to Planning History in the United States*, Rutgers University Center for Urban Policy Research, New Brunswick, NJ, 1983.

REPS, JOHN W., *The Making of Urban America*, Princeton University Press, Princeton, NJ, 1965.

SCOTT, MEL, *American City Planning Since 1890*, University of California Press, Berkeley, 1965.

NOTE: For references to particular fields of planning mentioned in this chapter, see the Selected Bibliography for the chapter that treats that field in detail.

CHAPTER 5

The Legal Basis
of Planning

Planning, as discussed in this book, is an activity of government. It involves the exercise of powers vested in the government and the expenditure of public funds. It is limited by, among other things, the limitations of the powers of government. In this chapter we describe the legal framework and the legal limitations within which local and state governments act. In Chapter 6 we turn to the political framework.

THE CONSTITUTIONAL FRAMEWORK

The Constitution, although it has much to say about which powers and responsibilities are assigned to the federal government and which powers and responsibilities are delegated to state governments, is silent on the issue of how the powers of government are to be divided between state and substate units of government. In fact, a literal reading of the Constitution gives no indication that there are to be substate units of government at all: Words like *city, town, township, village, parish,* or *county* are totally absent. (The word *district* is mentioned, though its meaning is not entirely clear.)

As a result, it was understood from very early in the history of the United States that substate units of government derive all of their powers from the state or, in a phrase that came into use some years later, are "creatures of the state." This understanding, which was articulated in a strict manner by Judge John F. Dillion in 1868, has become known as Dillon's rule.[1] Briefly, the rule is that a substate unit of government has only those powers expressly granted to it by the state, or those powers that are directly and unarguably implied by those powers expressly granted it by the state.

In the years after the Dillon decision, a number of states modified their constitutions with *home rule* provisions or passed *home rule* legislation. In these states, substate governments have any power that is not forbidden them by the state and not in conflict with the state constitution or other state legislation. Thus all states can be classified as either Dillion rule states or as home rule states.[2] The central point, however, is that regardless of whether the state is a Dillon rule state or a home rule state, the powers of substate governments come from the state. This is equally the case under the only-those-powers-directly-permitted Dillion's rule form or under the those-powers-not-forbidden under the home rule form.

Obviously a state government cannot assign to a substate government powers that it itself does not have. But of those that it has, some will be assigned to substate units of government. In general, the structure of local governments and the powers and responsibilities of local governments are specified in charters, state enabling laws, and state constitutions.

Powers and Limitations

Just as state governments grant powers to local governments, they also can and do impose obligations on them. Local governments are also guided and limited in their actions by rights guaranteed individuals by the U.S. Constitution or by state constitutions. When there is disagreement over issues of individual rights or the extent of government power, the ultimate arbiter is the court system. Local planning efforts are thus limited by what the courts will allow or what local officials, property owners, and other concerned parties believe the courts might allow were the issue at hand put to a legal test. In many cases, local planning efforts are also influenced by what the courts require local governments to do.

Early planning efforts such as the Plan of Chicago often took place in the absence of any specific planning framework. In the Chicago case, the plan was formulated by a group that had no legal mandate or authority and that, in essence, delivered the plan as a gift to the city. The plan was implemented by the city through exercise of the normal powers of government. Specifically, the city used its powers to levy taxes and to issue bonds to raise funds, which were used to finance projects called for in the plan. The power of the city to enter into contracts was used to acquire properties in voluntary transactions. Where that did not avail, the city's powers of eminent domain were used to acquire property through condemnation.

The power of *eminent domain* is important and deserves a brief explanation. The phrase means that government has the right to take property for public purposes. The building of roads, for example, generally involves taking of private property for the right of way. When government takes property, it must compensate the owner for the value of what is taken. If agreement cannot be reached between government and property owner, the matter goes to court. After hearing expert testimony, the court then determines the value of the loss imposed on the property owner by the act of taking. That value, the condemnation award, must then be paid to the property owner by the government. The eminent domain process is an example of the exercise of government power subject to limitation by the constitutional rights of individuals. Specifically, the "taking" clause of the Fifth Amendment states, " . . . nor shall private property be taken for public use, without just compensation"—hence the necessity for the condemnation award. The Fourteenth Amendment states that no person shall be deprived of "life, liberty, *or property* without due process of law"—hence the requirement for a judicial procedure should voluntary agreement not be reached. The Fourth Amendment guarantees "the right of the people to be secure in their persons, houses, papers and effects against *unreasonable* searches and seizures." Thus the taking of property for a trivial purpose would not be sustainable in court.

PUBLIC CONTROL OVER PRIVATE PROPERTY

Public control over the use of private property is a very different matter from the public taking (with "just compensation") of private property. The evolution, over several decades, of the right of government to exercise some control over the use of privately owned property is one of the central stories in the history of modern planning. Were local governments unable to exercise control over the use of privately owned land, the practice of planning in the United States would be vastly different and more limited.

Public control of the use of private property involves the imposition of uncompensated losses on property owners. This point requires a word of explanation. Consider someone who owns a building lot in a downtown area. Market forces such as the demand for office space and the cost of construction create a situation in which the most profitable use for the site is a 12-story office building. If the municipality, however, limits the height of structures on the site to 6 stories, the difference in profit between the 12- and the 6-story building is a loss imposed on the owner of the site. This principle is true whether the owner would develop the site, sell the site to another party who would develop it, or lease the site to someone else who would build on it. In the first case the owner would take the loss directly in the form of reduced operating profits. In the latter two cases the loss would be manifest as a lower selling price or lower rental fee for the site.

The land-use control technique that has evolved over the years, zoning (see Chapter 9 for details), does exactly what is alluded to. It limits the uses to which land can be put. If the most profitable use is not among the permitted uses, a loss is necessarily imposed on the owner. However, no compensation need be paid to the owner, nor is a judicial procedure required for the community to exercise control and thereby impose the loss. The community's zoning law stands unless the property owner brings a successful lawsuit against the community. This capacity to obtain the benefits of limiting an owner's use of his or her property without having to pay compensation clearly accounts for the popularity of zoning. The community obtains partial rights of ownership—some control over the use of the property—without having to go to the expense of becoming an owner. Note that this is very different from taking with compensation under *eminent domain*. In that case, the municipality does become the owner of the property.

Given the apparent conflict between such community powers and constitutional guarantees regarding property rights—most particularly the requirement for "just compensation" in the "taking" clause of the Fifth Amendment—it is not surprising that it took many years and many court cases to establish the zoning rights of communities. Even today the legal structure of zoning is still evolving, and many an attorney earns his or her living in zoning-related litigation and negotiation. Some on the political right view all zoning as fundamentally illegitimate because it represents an uncompensated taking and hence a violation of constitutionally guaranteed property rights.[3]

The legitimacy of zoning rests on the legal concept of the *police power*. That perhaps misleading term refers to the right of the community to regulate the activities of private parties to protect the interests of the public. Very often a phrase like *health, safety, and public welfare* will be used to indicate the range of public interests that may be safeguarded through exercise of the police power. Thus a law that limited the height of buildings so that they not cast the street below into a permanent shadow might be justified as an exercise in the police power. So, too, might a law that prevented certain industrial or commercial operations in a residential neighborhood. So, too, might laws that prevented property owners from developing their lands so intensely that undue congestion resulted in nearby streets.

The rights of the community under the concept of the police power and the rights of the property owner under constitutional and other safeguards push in opposite directions. Exactly where the equilibrium point is located is a matter to be decided by the courts. The question of how much and for what purposes government can take some of the value of privately owned property, as in the building height example, is generally referred to as the "taking issue" and is the subject of a very large literature.[4] The question of what regulatory actions do or do not constitute a "taking" is crucial because if it is determined that a "taking" has occurred, then the Fifth Amendment of the Constitution requires that payment be made to the property owner. If no "taking" has been made, then no compensation is required.

The process by which municipalities acquired some control over the use of private land began in the late nineteenth century. It typically started with the passage of legislation that limited the use of, and hence "took" some of the value of, privately owned property. The legislation was then appealed in court by the property owner because of the loss it imposed.

Very often the loser of the first trial appealed to a higher court. Through this process of litigation and appeal, the extent and the limitations of the public power to control private land use has been and continues to be defined.

A very early case in this long history was *Mugler* v. *Kansas* in 1887. The U.S. Supreme Court sustained a Kansas prohibition law that forced the closing of a brewery without compensation. The owners of the brewery argued that compensation was due, but the court held that a loss imposed through exercise of the police power to protect the health or safety of the community required no compensation. Note the distinction between "police power" and "eminent domain" here. Had the brewery been taken under eminent domain, compensation would clearly have been required. In 1899 a bill passed by Congress limited the heights of buildings in residential sections of Washington, D.C., to 90 feet, and heights of buildings on some of the widest streets to 130 feet. Light, air, and traffic congestion in the streets were the considerations behind the ordinance. In 1904 the Massachusetts legislature passed somewhat similar legislation for Boston. Structures in the business district were limited to 125 feet, and structures elsewhere to 80 feet. Several years later the Boston ordinance was challenged by a property owner, but the Massachusetts courts sustained the law as a valid exercise of the police power.

In 1909 the city of Los Angeles carried the idea of public control over the private use of land further by dividing the city into a number of commercial districts plus a residential district. In the later, commercial uses were permitted only as exceptions. In what became a landmark case, the city compelled a brickyard in a residential area to case operations. The item of "public welfare" being protected was the interest of residents in having an environment not subject to undue noise, dust, and traffic. The owner sued the city, a series of appeals followed, and the case ultimately went to the U.S. Supreme Court. In *Hadacheck* v. *Sebastian* the Court sustained the city. Though this was, literally, a nuisance abatement rather than a zoning case, the effect of the decision was clearly a strengthening of municipal rights under the police power.[5]

The city that enacted what might be considered the first modern zoning ordinance—though it left much to be desired by present standards—was New York. In the early twentieth century, lower Manhattan was growing rapidly as a commercial center. Steel-frame construction and the elevator were making it practical to build to unprecedented heights of 40, 50, or even 60 stories. The horizontal expansion of the business district was limited by the fact that Manhattan is an island. In fact, at the latitude of Wall Street—then, as now, the center of the financial district—one can walk across the island from the East River to the Hudson River in perhaps 15 minutes. To add to the congestion, the city was in the process of building a subway system, which permitted employers in the business district to reach far out into the other boroughs for their labor forces. Thus the same rapid transit that permitted central residential densities to fall was, paradoxically, permitting increased employment densities downtown.

With downtown space at a premium, builders tended to cover the entire lot and to build without any setbacks. The result was a building shaped like a child's building block set on end. Such buildings darkened the streets below and cast shadows several blocks long. By being allowed to build straight up from the property line, builders could accidentally or otherwise impose major losses on adjacent property owners by casting the facing wall of an adjacent structure in a perpetual shadow.

At the same time that concern over skyscraper development was growing, merchants in the fashionable Fifth Avenue retailing area were concerned that the invasion by manufacturing firms displaced from lower Manhattan would lower the tone of the area and drive away customers. They thus put pressure on the city government for some sort of relief.

Prompted by these concerns, the city in 1916 enacted a comprehensive zoning ordinance covering all five boroughs. The city was divided into

The stepped-back configuration of an old-style office building in the foreground shows the effect of New York's 1916 zoning law. The modern structure at the rear rises without distinct setbacks but has a gradual taper in its lower floors and does not cover the entire lot.

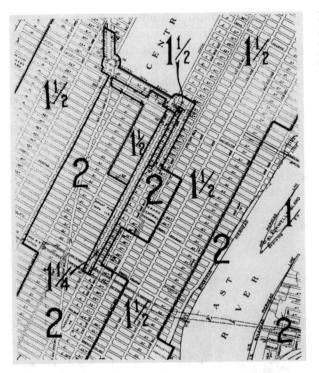

Midtown Manhattan zoning districts as designated in the 1916 plan. The numbers are building height limits expressed as multiples of street width.

three districts on the basis of land use: residential, commercial, and mixed. Overlaid on these use districts were five height districts, where the heights were expressed as multiples of street widths, ratios justified on considerations of congestion and sunlight. Also overlying the entire city were five districts that specified ground coverage requirements such as minimum lot sizes. Beyond that, the ordinance also specified a building "envelope" for skyscrapers, which mandated that there had to be setbacks from the street at higher levels. The stepped-back design that can be seen today in dozens of Manhattan office buildings comes from this ordinance and has been caricatured by some as a modern ziggurat (from a Babylonian temple built as a series of stepped-back terraces). But regardless of the aesthetic merits (or lack thereof) of many of these stepped-back structures, they were a major improvement over structures that rose straight up from the lot lines.[6]

The ordinance was designed by an attorney, Edward M. Bassett, who is generally regarded as the father of zoning in the United States. Bassett designed it in such a way as to ground every facet in some matter of public health, safety, or welfare. Thus he produced an ordinance that proved invulnerable to the inevitable court challenges. Again, the fact that the provisions of the ordinance rested on the police power further established the principle that compensation need not be paid for any loss of property value that the zoning might impose. This point is critical for if compensation had to be paid, public control of land use would be more expensive, far more cumbersome, and far less widespread than is now the case. A theoretical argument can be made that there are some disadvantages to the fact that municipalities can essentially treat the zoning power as a free good, but we reserve this more modern view to Chapter 9.

In 1926 any lingering doubts about the constitutionality of zoning were relieved when a zoning case finally reached the U.S. Supreme Court. In the case of *The Village of Euclid* v. *Ambler Realty Co.*, the court sustained a village zoning ordinance that prevented Ambler Realty from building a commercial structure in a residential zone.[7] The point that a municipality could impose an uncompensated loss upon a property owner through the mechanism of land-use controls was now firmly established. In effect, the court had ruled that such a loss need not constitute a "taking" of property, for a "taking" of property would require compensation as in the "taking" clause of the Fifth Amendment quoted earlier. The term *Euclidean Zoning* named for the town of Euclid is now used to refer to conventional zoning ordinances rather than some of the more modern and flexible types discussed in Chapter 9.

The 42nd Street facade of Grand Central Station, part of what was saved by the Penn Central decision.

In the years after 1926, backed by the *Euclid* decision, state and local courts supported and expanded the power of municipal governments to zone and otherwise regulate the use of privately owned land, and zoning became almost universal in urban and suburban areas. With one minor exception, the Supreme Court did not hear another zoning case for half a century.

In 1978, litigation over New York City's landmark preservation reached the court as *Penn Central Transportation Company* v. *New York City.*[8] The company, which owned Grand Central Station, had sought to build a skyscraper atop the station, but it was blocked because the city Landmarks Preservation Committee had designated the station as a historic site. The company argued that the loss it sustained by being denied permission to build over the station was so severe that it constituted a taking. The company won in the lower court, was reversed in New York State's appellate court, and then appealed to the U.S. Supreme Court. In a split decision the Supreme Court rejected the plaintiff's appeal and sustained the city. Most planners were very pleased with the decision because it seemed to expand the scope of the zoning power. It made it clear that the behavior of a private property owner could be constrained for purely aesthetic reasons. It also made it clear that such control could be applied to a single structure or parcel rather than just to an entire district. In the years since the Penn Central decision, the U.S. Supreme Court has ruled in a number of land-use cases. These cases are summarized in the box beginning on page 82.

Beginning about the end of the 1980s, something of a property rights counterattack began, and this event bears explanation. The question of whether, and if so, how much, government should be able to regulate the use of private property has an ideological dimension. Those on the political right will generally take the view that government's ability to regulate should be sharply limited, for the relative sanctity of the rights of private property is a fundamental part of the right-wing political position. By contrast, those on the political left are far more likely to place less value of the rights of private property and thus to favor greater public regulation. As the United States moved to the right politically toward the end of the twentieth century, what came to be called the *property rights* movement became more powerful.

A number of states have passed laws that required "takings impact analyses" before the implementing of environmental regulations.[9] These laws are too new to tell whether they will have a major effect. To the extent that they do, it will presumably be to reduce the ability of the states to control, without compensation, the uses to which environmentally sensitive land may be put—or, perhaps, to assert that land is environmentally sensitive. Bills to require governments to pay compensation for losses imposed by regulation have been proposed in approximately two dozen state legislatures, but so far, only one bill has passed. That one, in Mississippi, applied only to forest land. Nationally, "takings" bills have been introduced in both House and Senate, but none have become law.

The movement to define as "takings" all reductions in property values caused by regulations has made most progress in Oregon. In November 2000, the voters passed Measure 7. This referendum, backed by a property rights organization called Oregonians in Action, required governments to "compensate landowners for loss of value resulting from government actions that restrict or curtail the use of their property." Opponents argued that converting almost any restriction on land use into a "taking" would impose a huge financial burden on both the state and the local governments.[10] The state estimated the total cost of the measure at $4.5 billion annually, with about two-thirds of that falling upon local governments and the remainder on the state government. They argued that because of this burden, the ability of governments to protect beaches, impose urban growth boundaries, and even enforce zoning laws would be greatly reduced. The opponents took the position that although advocates of the measure couched their arguments in terms of fairness—government should pay for what it takes—the measure was actually a huge blow to government's ability to protect the public interest in land development and represented a type of initiative that Oregon voters had turned back several times before. One opponent of the measure, an attorney for the League of Oregon Cities, stated that "you have stripped the government of a fundamental power to regulate." Opponents of the measure made a procedurally based argument that the measure was impermissibly broad in that it affects, in a single action, a very wide variety of government powers. In 2002, to the relief of many planners and environmentalists, the court accepted the plaintiff's argument and struck down Measure 7. The planners' relief, however, was short-lived. On November 2, 2004, the voters of Oregon approved Measure 37, which essentially repeated the substance of Measure 7 but which was more narrowly drawn so as to be able to resist challenge in court. The key passage in Measure 37 is

> If a public entity enacts or enforces a new land-use regulation or enforces a land-use regulation enacted prior to the effective date of this amendment [to prior state legislation, ORS chapter 197] that restricts the use of private real property or any interest therein and has the effect of reducing the fair market values of the property, or any interest therein, then the owner of the property shall be paid just compensation.[11]

The measure does exclude from compensation regulations pertaining to public health, compliance with building codes, and some other matters. But it potentially makes almost any other kind of regulation that imposes a loss on a property owner a taking and thus subject to compensation. Further, the measure is retroactive back to the time that the property owner acquired the property. Thus for example, if some years ago after you had bought a piece of land it was rezoned from, say, single-family housing at two units to the acre to single-family housing at one unit per acre, you might have a potential claim against the municipality that did the rezoning.

Not surprisingly, Measure 37 was the subject of litigation. On February 21, 2006, in *Mac Pherson* v. *DAS* the Oregon Supreme Court found for the plaintiff and sustained the measure, an obvious setback for the planners. But then, in November 2007 the voters of Oregon passed Proposition 49 which repealed some of what the planners had considered to be the more onerous aspects of Proposition 37. Again, the boundary between the rights of property owners on the one hand and the rights of government to limit the use of private property without compensation had shifted with the changing political scene.

As might be expected, a wide array of environmental organizations are intensely opposed to "takings" bills. The American Planning Association (APA) was also strongly opposed and mounted a serious lobbying effort. Should such requirements become commonplace, they could exert an enormously inhibiting effect upon regulatory agencies at all levels of government. Fears of incurring huge bills for compensation would make agencies extremely cautious and prompt them to err on the side of under-regulation. They might also, as the APA has claimed, enrich attorneys and consultants by producing an explosion of litigation over whether or not a reduction in value sufficient to require compensation had occurred.

THE SUPREME COURT AND THE "TAKING" ISSUE

In the decades after the *Euclid* v. *Ambler* decision of 1926, the U.S. Supreme Court heard only one other zoning case. Then, beginning in 1987, it heard a succession of five cases. In the first four, the court somewhat expanded the definition of what constitutes a "taking," Another way of saying this is that it somewhat reduced the ability of state and local governments to impose uncompensated losses on property owners and thus somewhat reduced the range over which land-use controls, as a practical matter, could be applied. In the last case the court leaned in the other direction, to the relief of the planners.

In California the owner of a beachfront property sought to be allowed to enlarge his house. In return for granting permission, the California Coastal Commission required that he dedicate a portion of his property to provide public access to the beach. The owner then brought suit to have this requirement voided. On appeal the Supreme Court in *Nollan* v. *California Coastal Council* (1987) sustained him, taking the position that there was no "essential nexus" between the granting of the variance and the required dedication of property. Note that the Court did not deny the state the power to regulate or to impose a loss upon a property owner, but it did deny the state the power to impose a loss that was not closely tied to the issue at hand. Clearly, the relationship between house size and public access was not close.

In *Lucas v. South Carolina Coastal Council* (1992), the Court again sustained a property owner against a state agency. David Lucas, the plaintiff, purchased two beachfront lots with the intention of building a house upon each. At the time of the purchase, it was legal to build upon the lots. But subsequently state legislation prohibited any further building on the seaward side of a setback line. This prohibition rendered his two lots unusable, and he brought suit claiming that the passage of the law constituted a "taking." The Court sustained him and required that the state pay him $1.6 million in damages. Subsequently Lucas formed the Council on Property Rights and has been campaigning against what he considers to be excessive government regulation of private property. Lucas's case may have been favored by the fact that the legislature's act did, in fact, render his properties almost entirely worthless. Had they taken only, say, half of the properties' value, the decision might have been different. Perhaps another point in Lucas's favor was that there were houses built before the legislature had prohibited development on the seaward side of the line, on lots adjacent to his.

In *Dolan v. City of Tigard* (1994), the Supreme Court also seemed to broaden the definition of "taking" somewhat. Several years earlier the Dolans had requested permission to build additional parking spaces outside their plumbing supply store. The City of Tigard's Planning Commission approved the request on condition that the Dolans dedicate a fraction of their lot, which bordered a park, for flood-control purposes and the construction of a bike path. The Dolans brought suit to have the dedication requirement voided and, upon appeal, were sustained by the Supreme Court. The Court's verdict again turned on the notion of "nexus." It said, in effect, that for a local government to impose a burden upon a property owner, there must be some reasonably direct connection between the burden imposed and the proposed actions of the property owner.

In *Palazzolo v. Rhode Island,* the plaintiff brought suit because repeated rulings by Rhode Island's Coastal Resources Management Council denied him permission to fill a coastal wetland that he owned and to build a 74-unit housing development on it. He claimed that the prohibition reduced the value of his property so much as to constitute a taking, thus entitling him to compensation from the state. A Rhode Island state court sided with the state on the grounds that when Palazzolo bought the property in 1978, the regulations prohibiting the site's development were already in place. The State Supreme Court then sustained the state court on procedural grounds. However, in July 2001, the U.S. Supreme Court by a 5 to 4 decision reversed the state Supreme Court and ordered the state court to rehear the case to ascertain the facts and determine whether a taking had occurred. The Supreme Court instructed the state court to use the somewhat more permissive standard of whether Palazzolo had reasonable "investment backed" expectations of developing the property when he bought it. State regulations in effect at the time that he bought the property barred it from development, but the Court did not regard this fact in itself as sufficient to deny his claims.

Members of the Property Rights movement saw the Supreme Court's decision as a victory because it took the position that even if the property owner bought the property knowing that current regulations prohibited development, the property owner might still hope either to be permitted to develop or to receive compensation.

Planners and environmentalists were not pleased by the decision, for it suggested that developers might buy properties on which development was barred and then use the threat of a Palazzolo-type lawsuit to compel state or local governments to alter the regulations and permit development. More generally, the *Palazzolo* decision seemed to have an inhibitory effect on environmental regulation by raising the financial risks to state and local governments.

The justices finding for Palazzolo were Rehnquist, O'Connor, Kennedy, Scalia, and Thomas. The Court's more liberal justices—Ginsburg, Breyer, Souter, and Stevens—opposed. The line of votes here was the same conservative-liberal split as in the vote in the *Bush* v. *Gore* decision that settled the disputed year 2000 presidential election, perhaps another reminder that planning questions and ideological questions often overlap.

The issue in *Tahoe-Sierra Preservation Council et al. v. Tahoe Regional Planning Agency et al.* was whether a 32-month moratorium to allow time for the development of a regional plan constituted a taking. The plaintiff held that it did because in this time period, the plaintiffs had been denied any productive use of their land. The court, however, decided in favor of the defendant, the Tahoe Regional Planning Agency, holding that the delay, which served to achieve a useful public purpose, did not constitute a taking. The court noted that, unlike the situation in the *Lucas* case, the denial of all productive use was only temporary, and it argued that when the moratorium ended, the property owners could then recoup the value of their investments.

Planners were very relieved by the decision. If the court had gone the other way and taken the view that "time is money" and that any delay could be a taking, the hand of the planner, particularly at a large-scale level, would have been very much weakened. The moratorium had been imposed in the early 1980s. The case was heard in January 2002 and decided in April 2002. Judicial review can be a very slow process.

THE FIGHT OVER EMINENT DOMAIN

As noted before, it has long been accepted that government can take property, with just compensation, for public purposes. If governments could not do this, a single intransigent property owner could permanently block the building of a road, the assemblage of land for a park, the building of a school, and the like. But within this overall understanding there is much room for what the term "public purpose" means.

The Urban Renewal program (see Chapter 11) which got underway shortly after passage of the Housing Act of 1949 used a particular process that angered many people. Local governments would use eminent domain to assemble blocks of land for projects and then, when site development work had been done, sell or lease the land to developers who then built housing or commercial structures. This meant that eminent domain was used to transfer property from one private party to another private party, rather than from private party to government. The private party to private party transfer occasioned much resentment. In time a property owner went to court to prevent an urban renewal agency from taking his property for this purpose. The case was appealed to the U.S. Supreme Court and in 1954 in *Berman* v. *Parker* the court found against the plaintiff. That is, the process was constitutional.

That decision seemed to settle the matter, but resentment simmered. Half a century latter in *Kelo* v. *New London* [Connecticut] the issue came to the Supreme Court again, and again the court found against the plaintiff. In effect, the court affirmed *Berman* v. *Parker*. But this time the decision unleashed a torrent of anger against the eminent domain process and its real or imagined abuses.

In the year after the *Kelo* decision, all 44 state legislatures that met in that year (not every state legislature meets every year) took up eminent domain bills. Of the 44 legislatures, 28 passed bills restricting the use of eminent domain.[12] There was considerable variation among the bills, but the most common feature was language that restricted the right of state and local governments to take private property if it was to be transferred to another private party. Generally, there were a few exceptions to this so that private property could be transferred to a common carrier which would include, for example, railroads and pipelines, and to utility companies. But the sort of transfers done in urban renewal and community development programs were banned. Many of the states specifically banned private party to private party transfers for "economic development" purposes, effectively saying the same thing in different terms.

To some degree, how you feel about this legislative overruling of *Kelo* will be a matter of your overall political stance. If you basically trust government and if private property rights are not that sacrosanct to you, you are likely to feel that the *Kelo* decision was right and the state legislatures have made a mistake. If you feel the reverse on those two matters, then you are likely to be pleased to see the state legislatures, in effect, reverse *Kelo*. In short, the more to the left you are politically, the more likely you are to be happy with *Kelo* and the more to the right you are, the more likely you are to be happy to see it cancelled out. Beyond the ideological, there was resentment against the whole process of eminent domain because of instances in which government agencies treated property owners in a high-handed manner or in which the private party to private party transfer process was abused.

In addition to the bills passed by state legislatures, there were in 2006 a number of referenda intended to restrict the use of eminent domain. Of these, nine passd, often by large majorities, and two failed. One of those that passed, Arizona 207, also carried language that drastically expanded the definition of a regulatory taking. Basically, the referendum stated that if a restriction on the use to which property could be put reduced the value of a property after the owner had purchased it, the owner was entitled to compensation. There were a few exceptions, such as for matters of public health and safety.

The restrictions on the use of eminent domain and the expansion of the definition of regulatory taking are separate issues and you could argue that if they were to be put up for referendum they ought to be separate, for that would give the voters maximum freedom of choice. But in fact they were bundled together so the voter could vote for them only as a pair. Whether the regulatory taking definition would have passed had it been separate is an open question. As a matter of political strategy, those who favored it were shrewd getting the two items bundled together, for their cause clearly benefited from a groundswell of anger against the perceived abuses of eminent domain.

One might wonder where things stand given that Supreme Court upheld *Kelo* but legislation and referenda blocked that which *Kelo* allowed. The answer is quite straightforward. All the Supreme Court said is that private party to private party transfers via eminent domain cannot be blocked on constitutional grounds. But when a state chooses to ban them, then they cannot be done in that state.

What is the planner's stake in all of this? Regardless of what one feels about the rightness or wrongness of the state bans on private party to private party transfers, it is clear that states and local governments have lost one important tool for a variety of community and economic development purposes. Urban Renewal, as described in Chapter 11, would have been a very different, and probably much smaller, program had such transfers not been possible.

How the part of Arizona 207 that pertains to regulatory taking will play out in practice is not yet clear, for inevitably there will be a court case, the loser will appeal, and that entire process will take awhile.

STATE-ENABLING LEGISLATION

Another change in the legal framework of planning since the days of the Plan of Chicago has been the passage of state legislation that defines in broad terms the local planning function. Legislation varies greatly from state to state. In most cases, legislation merely permits localities to engage in particular planning activities. But in other cases, the legislation requires that communities perform certain planning acts. Note, incidentally, that state-enabling legislation also defines municipal obligations and powers with regard to taxation, borrowing, the judicial system, the provision of police protection, and many other matters.

As an example of state-enabling legislation with regard to planning, consider the state of Virginia.[13] Legislation requires that all cities, towns, and counties establish a planning commission and adopt a master plan. The intent of the state's local planning legislation is given as follows:

> To encourage local governments to improve public health, safety, convenience and welfare of its citizens and to plan for the future development of communities to the end that transportation systems be carefully planned; that new community centers be developed with adequate highway, utility, health, educational and recreational facilities; that the needs of agriculture, industry and business be recognized in future growth; that residential areas be provided with healthy surroundings for family life; and that the growth of the community be consonant with efficient and economical use of public funds.

Having laid out the general reasons for requiring communities to plan, the law then goes on to state,

> The governing body of every county and municipality shall by resolution or ordinance create a local planning commission. . . . In accomplishing the objectives . . . such planning commissions shall serve primarily in an advisory capacity to the governing bodies.

The law requires that each city, county, or town draw up a master plan, and then, in a general way, it suggests the areas the plan is to cover:

> The local commission shall prepare and recommend a comprehensive plan for the physical development of the territory within its jurisdiction. Every governing body in this state shall adopt a comprehensive plan by July one, nineteen hundred eighty.

Note the requirement for adoption as well as for plan preparation. The reason for this wording is that plans themselves are not laws. They become law and acquire force when the legislative body of a community passes a resolution stating that the attached document (the plan) is adopted as the master plan of the municipality.

The legislation stipulates that the plan and accompanying maps, plats,[14] and so on "may include, but need to be limited to" the following:

1. The designation of areas for various types of public and private development and use, such as different kinds of residential, business, industrial, agricultural, conservation, recreation, public service, flood plain and drainage, and other areas
2. The designation of a system of transportation facilities, such as streets, roads, highways, parkways, railways, bridges, viaducts, waterways, airports, ports, terminals, and other like facilities
3. The designation of a system of community service facilities, such as parks, forests, schools, playgrounds, public buildings and institutions, hospitals, community centers, waterworks, sewage disposal or waste disposal areas, and the like
4. The designation of historical areas and areas for urban renewal and other treatment
5. An official map, a capital improvements program, a subdivision ordinance (this term is explained in Chapter 9), and a zoning ordinance and zoning district maps

Where state laws or state constitutions permit municipalities to engage in certain acts of planning, it could be said that they are merely granting permission for municipalities to do that which is implicit under the concept of the police power. There is some truth in this. However, planning-enabling acts and zoning-enabling acts are useful in that they encourage municipalities to plan, define the scope of planning, and furnish legal support for the municipality should its plans be challenged in court. As noted, many planning-enabling acts go beyond simply permitting communities to plan and *require* them to plan. These laws thus establish a minimum planning effort that every community must make.

The Legal Link to State Planning

Many states, as noted in Chapter 4, engage in some statewide planning. Such planning efforts generally impose legal requirements on local governments to ensure that they act in conformity with state plans or planning requirements. For example, if a state engages in planning designed to preserve wetlands, it may require that local governments not grant permits for development in or near wetlands until certain types of studies have been made or hearings conducted. These requirements will prevent local governments from permitting actions that contravene the intent of state plans. Since local governments are "creatures of the state," it is clearly within the power of the state to bind local governments so that they act in conformity to state-established guidelines.

THE FEDERAL ROLE

The 1930s saw the beginnings of a federal presence in local planning. The federal government funded local and state planning agencies, provided funds for public housing, and actually built a few planned communities such as Greenbelt, Maryland. In the years after World War II, the federal presence in local planning expanded enormously. Even in the early 1980s, when the Reagan administration consciously sought to reduce the role of the federal government in local and state affairs, the federal presence was still vastly larger than it had been during the pre-war period.

One way the federal government exerts an influence upon local planning practice is through legal requirements, such as those discussed in connection with air quality in Chapter 16. However, the largest influence is through the giving of grants and the requirements that the federal government attaches to the receipt of those grants. The monies that it takes in through taxes and borrowing substantially exceeds what it spends on goods and services and on transfers to individuals. The excess is used to make grants to state and local governments.

In recent years federal grants to state and local governments have amounted to roughly 30 percent of total state and local government spending, approximately $346 billion in 2002. With this flow of funds necessarily comes considerable oversight and control. This massive flow of funds has not always been a part of the U.S. political picture. In 1960 federal aid to state and local governments was about $7 billion.[15] After adjusting that figure for inflation, there was a tenfold increase in federal aid between 1960 and the present.

Why this pattern of transfers evolved can be explained in various ways. Sometimes it is said that the federal government can raise monies more easily than state and local governments because it has "the best revenue sources." This is largely a reference to the personal income tax, which over the years has proven to be highly income elastic.[16] A more general explanation is simply that state and local governments are restrained in their taxing behavior by fear of losing residents and economic activity to other jurisdictions that tax more lightly. The federal government is not nearly so restrained in this regard.

Another explanation, which places its emphasis on political behavior rather than economic rationality, is offered by the Public Choice theorists. They attribute much of the expansion of the federal government's role in local and state affairs to the vote-seeking competition between politicians to deliver revenues raised elsewhere to their own constituents. An exposition of the Public Choice view would be out of place here, but the interested reader can find an extensive literature on the subject.[17]

Regardless of the reasons for the present pattern of intergovernment transfers, the existence of the pattern gives the federal government enormous influence over localities, both directly and also indirectly through the states. Making certain types of behavior a prerequisite for receiving grants is one way. For example, the federal government has no literal power to compel a community to adopt certain procedures to take citizens into its planning processes. However, if the implementation of the plans, or even the formulating of the plans, will be done partly with federal funds, the federal government can achieve the effect of requirement simply by making citizen participation a requirement for the receipt of federal funds. And in fact, planning at the city, town, and county level is very heavily conditioned by such federal requirements.

Very often the federal government does not even need to monitor the behavior of the recipient government to achieve compliance. The reason is simple. If the local government violates a federal funding requirement, it is likely to face a law-suit from some individual or group seeking to block its use of federal funds on the grounds that it has violated a condition of receiving such funds. For example, failure to take low- and moderate-income citizens into the decision-making process for community development planning is likely to bring such a suit from a low-income or minority advocacy group. Failure to heed guidelines attached to a federal grant for construction of a wastewater treatment plant might bring a suit from an environmental organization. Thus, many of the guidelines attached to grants are self-enforcing.

Another way to influence local behavior is simply by providing funds for the purpose. When Congress wanted to encourage states and localities to do water-quality planning, it provided grants for doing so. Many localities that did water-quality planning in the late 1970s and early 1980s did not want to do it enough to use their own funds. However, they were happy to do it with federal funds from section 208 of the Clean Water Act of 1977.

Mandated Responsibilities

The federal government also influences local and state planning activities by direct requirements, or "mandates." For example, the Clean Air Act amendments of 1970 require the EPA to establish certain air-quality standards. To meet these standards, states are required to produce state implementation plans (SIPs). Although the states have great latitude in the precise manner in which these air-quality standards are to be met, the federal legislation does force them to plan and also establishes minimum targets (levels of air quality) for which to plan. The legislation also specifies in general ways the items that state plans must contain. For example, the state plan must contain provisions for reviewing plans for construction of facilities that might produce sufficient emissions to prevent achievement of federally mandated air-quality standards. Thus plans for a solid waste incinerator that might push levels of air pollutants above federally mandated standards would have to be reviewed. Should a state government fail to make such a review or make the review in an inadequate manner, it might open itself up to legal action by an environmental group or other concerned parties.

The situation just described represents a particular style of regulation that is commonly used by federal and state governments. The regulating body does not tell the regulated party what to do in detail. Rather, the regulated party is told what must be achieved but is left with wide discretion concerning how to do so. Perhaps the best known example of this regulatory style is seen in the rules pertaining to automobile fuel economy. Average mileage standards, Corporate Average Fuel Economy (CAFE), for the total fleet produced by a manufacturer were established, and fines for exceeding this standard were set. But carmakers were told nothing about what technologies to use in achieving these goals.

One advantage of this approach is that overall goals are formulated at a high level, where decision makers have an overview of "the big picture." But technical decisions are made by those who are closer to the problem and thus better informed about details. As a practical matter this style is also likely to be much more acceptable in a political system like that of the United States— one in which power is widely distributed and in which there are strong local governments and a tradition of resistance to excessive central authority.

SUMMARY

Planning occurs within a framework of state legislation, for the municipality as a "creature of the state" has only those powers granted it by the state. It also bears those responsibilities imposed on it by the state. The capacity of a municipality to implement plans is also circumscribed by constitutionally guaranteed individual rights.

Zoning, the best known of land-use control devices, is an exercise of the "police power." The contradictions, real or apparent, between the zoning process and constitutional guarantees relative to property and to due process go far to explain why the process of establishing the rights of municipalities to zone took several decades. Even today, the zoning power is still evolving through a process of legislation, litigation, and judicial decision.

Planning-enabling legislation defines the powers of municipalities with regard to planning and, in many cases, also defines the obligations of the community with regard to planning. For example, it may require that the community have a comprehensive plan and that the plan include certain elements.

The federal government exerts a large influence over the local planning process. In some cases it does so by laws and regulations. More often, it does so through requirements attached to funding or simply through the pattern of federal grants. The predominant flow of funds is downward: from the federal government to state and local governments, and from state governments to local governments.

NOTES

1. John F. Dillon, *Commentaries on the Law of Municipal Corporations*, 5th ed., Little, Brown & Co., Boston, 1911, vol. 1, sec. 237. It can be argued that the "creature of the state" concept is not quite so literally true as it once was. Since World War II there has been a trend for the powers and obligations of local governments to be defined in state constitutions rather than in laws or charters. If one takes the view that the state constitution comes from the people and creates both the state government and the local governments, one could argue that the state and local governments exist in parallel and are thus coequal.

2. Jesse L. Richardson, Jr., Meghan Zimmerman Gough, and Robert Puentes, *Is Home Rule the Answer? Clarifying the Influence of Dillon's Rule on Growth Management*, The Brookings Institution, Washington, DC, 2003.

3. As an example of the antizoning position, both for legal and for other reasons, see Jack C. Harris and William Douglas Moore, "Debunking the Mythology of Zoning," *Real Estate Review*, vol. 13, no. 4, Winter 1984, pp. 94–97.

4. For an account of the legal issues involved in "taking," see Daniel R. Mandelker, *Land Use Law*, The Michie Co., Charlottesville, VA, 1982.

5. For a history of the evolution of zoning, see Mel Scott, *American City Planning Since 1890*, University of California Press, Berkeley, 1971, chaps. 2 and 3.

6. See Charles F. Flory, "Shaping the Skyscrapers of Manhattan," *Real Estate Review*, vol. 13, no. 2, Summer 1983, pp. 48–53.

7. 272 U.S., 365 (1926).

8. Jerome S. Kayden, "Celebrating How the Supreme Court's Preservation of Grand Central Terminal Helped Preserve Planning Nationwide," *Planning*, June 2003, pp. 20–23.

9. John Tibbetts, "Everybody's Taking the Fifth," *Planning*, January 1995, pp. 4–10.

10. R. Gregory Nokes, "Opponents Call Measure 7 Threat to Land, McCall Legacy: Critics Step Up Their Attack on the 'Takings' Proposal, Which a New Poll Indicates Has Solid Support," *The Oregonian*, November 2, 2000, p. A7. See also Charles E. Begs, "Court Hears Argument on Property Compensation Measure," Associated Press Newswire, September 10, 2001.

11. For the complete text of Measure 37, go to www.sos.state.or.us/elections/nov22004/guide/meas/m37_text.html.

12. See the Web site of the National Conference of State Legislatures at www.ncsl.org/programs/natres/emindomainleg06.htm.

13. Code of Virginia, 1950 (as amended), Title 15.1, chap. 11.

14. A plat is a map or diagram showing a parcel of land divided into building lots.

15. By "local governments" are meant all municipal and county governments and also school and other districts.

16. The term *elastic* in this usage means that percentage increases in tax revenues exceeded percentage increases in income.

17. For a very quick, readable summary of the Public Choice view, see "The Public Choice Revolution," James Gwartney and Richard Wagner, *The Intercollegiate Review*, Spring 1988, pp. 17–26. For more extensive treatments, see other works by these two authors as well as works by Gordon Tullock and James Buchanan.

SELECTED BIBLIOGRAPHY

BUCK, PETER L., ED., *Modern Land Use Control*, The Practicing Law Institute, New York, 1978.

BURNS, JAMES M., PELTASON, J. W., and CRONIN, THOMAS E., *Government by the People*, 6th ed., Prentice Hall, Englewood Cliffs, NJ, 1996.

MANDELKER, DANIEL R., *Land Use Law*, The Michie Co., Charlottesville, VA, 1982.

STUART MECK, PAUL WACK, and MICHELLE J. ZIMET, "Zoning and Subdivision Regulations," in *The Practice of Local Government Planning*, 3rd ed., International City Management Association, Washington, DC, 2000, pp. 343–374.

CHAPTER 6

Planning and Politics

WHY IS PLANNING POLITICAL?

For several reasons, planning generally takes place in a highly politicized environment.

1. Planning often involves matters in which people have large emotional stakes—for example, the character of a neighborhood or the quality of a school district. A planning decision that you do not like may intrude itself into your life every day because its fruits are located where you live or work. The often very emotional suburban resistance to subsidized housing is largely a matter of residents' fears about the effect it will have on the local school system. The residents may be right or wrong, but either way it is easy to understand why they become passionate about what they think will affect the happiness and safety of their children. (In Chapter 7, see the box on pages 110–113 about the city of Yonkers.) Vociferous citizens' opposition was the major force that ended Urban Renewal (see Chapter 12). Few actions of government can arouse more emotion than a program that might force the citizen to give up an apartment or relocate his or her business to make way for what one writer called "the federal bulldozer."

2. Planning decisions are visible. They involve buildings, roads, parkland, properties—entities that citizens see and know about. Planning mistakes, like architectural mistakes, are hard to hide.

3. Like all functions of local government, the planning process is close at hand. It is easier for the citizen to affect the actions of a town board or a city council than the actions of a state legislature or of Congress. That feeling of potential effectiveness encourages participation.

4. Citizens correctly assume that they know something about planning without having studied the subject formally. After all, planning involves land use, traffic, the character of the community, and other items with which residents are familiar. Therefore, citizens tend not to defer to planners.

5. Planning involves decisions with large financial consequences. Consider Mr. X, who owns 100 acres of farmland on the urban fringe. Land values in the area are rising, and it is clear that the land will soon pass from agricultural to a more intensive use. If municipal sewer and water lines are extended along the road fronting the property, the land will be suitable for garden apartment development at 12 units per acre, making it worth, say, $100,000 per acre. On the other hand, if the land is not served with utilities, residential development there will be limited to single-family houses on 1-acre lots, and land will be worth $10,000 per acre. Mr. X now has a $9 million interest in whether the municipal master plan shows sewer and water lines down a particular road. Variations on this theme could easily be posed in terms of zoning, street widening, community development, construction of public buildings, flood-control measures, and the like.

Even those who own no property other than the house they live in may feel, quite correctly, that they have a substantial financial stake in planning decisions. For many people, their biggest single source of net worth is not in bank accounts or stock certificates but in home equity (what the home would bring when sold minus what is owed on it). Planning decisions that affect house values may thus assume major importance to homeowners.

6. There can be a strong link between planning questions and property taxes. The property tax is one of the financial mainstays of local government as well as of public education. To the extent that planning decisions affect what is built within a community, they affect the community's tax base. That, in turn, affects the property taxes that community residents must pay. And these taxes are hardly a trivial sum. In 2003 total property tax collections in the United States were $304 billion, or approximately $1,040 per capita. Concern over property tax levels has been very great in recent years. Witness the passage of Proposition 13 in California and comparable property tax limits in a number of other states.

PLANNERS AND POWER

Planners are basically advisors. Alone, the planner does not have the power to do many of the things that cause change within the community: to commit public funds, to enact laws, to enter into contracts, or to exercise the power of eminent domain. Where the planner does have some legal powers, perhaps in connection with land-use controls, as discussed in Chapter 9, they are powers granted by the legislative body and removable by that same body. The planner's influence on events, then, stems from the capacity to articulate viewpoints and develop consensus and coalitions among those who do wield significant power.

A plan is a vision of the future. A planner moves events to the extent that he or she can cause that vision to be shared. In the early years of planning—as noted in connection with the Plan of Chicago—the view was that the plan came solely, or almost solely, from the head of the planner. It was then his or her task to sell that vision to the public and to the political establishment of the community. This is exactly what was done with great success in the Chicago case by Burnham and his associates.

A more modern view is that good plans spring from the community itself. In this view the planner's proper role is to facilitate the planning process and to aid it with his or her own expertise, rather than to deliver the plan full blown. Several points can be made in favor of the modern approach. First, it avoids elitism. The planner has particular skills that the average citizen does not have, but that capacity does not make the planner wiser in general. Second, there is no way that the planner, or any other single individual or group, can have a complete and an accurate view of the interests of the citizenry as a whole. Only the individual can really know his or her own needs and preferences. If that is true, only by taking the citizenry into the planning process at an early stage can their interests be fully represented. Last, it can be argued that a plan formed with substantial community input is more likely to be carried out than a plan of equal quality that has simply been drawn up directly by professionals. The very act of participating in the planning process informs the citizen about the details of the plan. Giving time and energy to the process of planning builds the citizens' commitment to the plan. What was "their plan" now becomes "our plan." But there are also some counter arguments. We will come to these shortly.

Planners now view involvement with politics very differently than they did a few decades ago. In the 1920s and 1930s, it was common to try to isolate the planning process from politics—to keep planning "above" politics. A common political arrangement was to have the planner report solely to a "nonpolitical" planning board. In time it was realized that since the political sphere was where decisions were made, isolating the planner from politics rendered him or her much less effective. Then, too, it came to be realized that the term *nonpolitical* is misleading. If one appoints a group of prominent citizens as a lay board, one has, in fact, made a political decision. A group of nonprominent citizens might give the planners a very different set of instructions. No one is really nonpolitical, for everyone has interests and values, and that is the substance of which politics is made.

The notion of the planning function as one that should be nonpolitical is related to the urban political reform movement of the late nineteenth and early twentieth century.[1] Political power was wrested from the old machines like New York's Tammany Hall and vested in civil servants; so-called reform administrations; and in some cities, professional, nonpartisan managers. The city manager form of government, in which the elected mayor has a largely ceremonial role and the real administrative responsibility and authority are vested in a city manager hired by the legislative body, comes from the reform movement.

In the reform view, politics was a seamy and often corrupt process, and the more that planning could be kept out of it, the better. A more modern view would be that the reform movement was in some measure a victory of the upper-middle class over machines, which often represented, albeit with some of the gravy skimmed off the top, the working class and newly arrived immigrants. In short, reform was not the elimination of politics so much as a transfer of political power.

THE FRAGMENTATION OF POWER

The environment in which the planner operates is characterized by a diffusion of political, economic, and legal power. This condition is probably true for any planner anywhere, but it is particularly true in the United States. Political power in the United States is fragmented in several ways. First, it is distributed among different levels of government. State and local governments are much stronger in relation to the national government than is the case in other democratic states of the Western world such as France or England. In general, also, state and local governments raise much more of their own revenues than do their counterparts in other democracies. Financial responsibility and political autonomy are related. The relatively greater autonomy of state and local governments in the United States goes back to the Constitution, which, as its writers intended, sharply limits the power of the federal government. Resistance to central authority is an old American political tradition.

Political power is also fragmented through the so-called separation of powers among executive, legislative, and judicial branches. That separation goes back to the founding of the country and the intent of the drafters of the Constitution to restrain government by structuring it so that the power of each branch would counterbalance the powers of the other branches. Planning as a government activity is clearly a function of the executive branch. However, implementing virtually any plan requires funding. Both the levying of taxes and the appropriation of funds are legislative functions. The powers of both the executive and the legislative branches are, of course, constrained by the judicial branch. That branch, at the federal level, is nominated by the executive branch and confirmed by the legislative branch.

In addition to being fragmented along the executive-judicial-legislative line, local government may also be fragmented in an administrative sense. A metropolitan area that constitutes a single economic and social entity may be divided into dozens or even hundreds of political jurisdictions. In addition to governments, there may be a variety of districts that have some governmental powers and responsibilities. School districts, for example, generally have the power to tax and sometimes have the power of eminent domain. In many states the school-board members are elected directly by the residents of the district, and those members, in turn, choose the district's superintendent. The administrative structure that runs the schools thus exists in parallel to the structure of local government but is not a part of that government. Yet both structures tax the same population; both may make land-use decisions, and both may make capital investments. Similar comments can be made with regard to water, sewer, transportation, and other authorities.

As noted earlier, the United States has a strong tradition of respect for property rights. Conflict over the exact location of the boundary between the rights of the public and the rights of property owners is virtually inevitable. The determination of the boundary is ultimately made in the courts, that is, by the judicial branch. We also note that the courts are often the guardians of individual rights and in this role may require certain actions of the other branches of government. Court-mandated school integration is perhaps the best known example, but there are many others. For example, how the courts interpret the language of the Americans with Disabilities Act (ADA) of 1992 determines exactly what steps municipalities must take and what expenditures they must make for the handicapped.

Power in the nongovernment sphere is also widely distributed. The citizens in their role as voters are the ultimate power. But groups of individuals also constitute power blocs. The citizen as a homeowner is part of a very powerful bloc, as any planner working in a community with a large percentage of owner-occupied housing units quickly learns. In many communities the citizen as a member of a labor union is part of a powerful bloc. The citizen as a member of an environmental group such as the Sierra Club or a local conservation group is a member of another bloc. Those who own substantial amounts of property, whether vacant land or structures, constitute still another source of power. So, too, are the community's employers. There is a very strong relationship among land-use planning, capital investment, and construction activity. Thus the construction industry—both management and labor—is often a major participant in planning decisions and in planning controversies.

Not only do citizens participate in the planning process both as individuals and as members of groups, but there is also a certain amount of *citizen participation* organized by the planners themselves. This is done partly to involve the public in planning questions, as noted before, but also because it is often a legal requirement. Much federal funding for highways, water and sewer systems, local economic development projects, and the like requires evidence of organized citizen participation before monies can be disbursed. Such requirements are not readily evaded. In fact, they are self-enforcing because the planners and municipal officials know that if the requirements are not met, the project may well be stopped by a procedurally based lawsuit that claims that the federal citizens' participation requirements were not met.

Most planners, on balance, look favorably on citizen participation, but it can have its frustrations. The planner who takes a comprehensive view of the city or town may be very frustrated by citizens who are tremendously concerned with what happens in their immediate vicinity but relatively unconcerned about the "big picture." It is the experience of most planners that citizens participate very readily on issues close to their homes but that it is usually very difficult to get them involved in larger-scale questions like regional planning. In a sense, the citizen's perspective is often like perspective in drawing: Objects that are close to the viewer appear much larger than objects of the same size that are farther away.

It is a basic fact of political life that it is easier to mobilize people in opposition than it is to mobilize them in support. Thus it often the case that there are groups that have the power to stop things from happening, but no group that has the power to make things happen. Citizen opposition has shot down many a planner's brainchild. In the sense that any citizen has the opportunity to make his or her voice heard, citizen participation is democratic. But it is not always as representative as one might at first think. Citizens groups and movements are self-selected and may represent a very small percentage of the population, but local governments often respond to the pressure of vocal and determined minorities. The idealistic young planner who sees his or her ideas about affordable housing stomped to death by prosperous homeowners at a public meeting may come away from the experience wiser, sadder, and harboring mixed feelings about the benefits of "power to the people."

The person who had the most effect upon the physical form of the New York metropolitan area is, without doubt, Robert Moses.[2] Moses, whose career started early in the twentieth century, well before the age of citizen participation, was brilliant, forceful, extremely adept at political manipulation, and sure that he was right. In his early adulthood, at least, he was also idealistic. He was, in large measure, responsible for the building of highways and bridges, the building of parks, the construction of all sorts of community facilities, and the destruction of large amounts of housing and many small businesses to make way for his projects. He had little interest in what the public wanted, but rather in what he thought was needed. He was both widely admired and widely detested. It is hard to evaluate his overall effect on the New York region because it is hard to say what the region would be like if he had not lived. All one can only say with any degree of certainty is that it would be quite different.

Nineteenth-century Paris had its own Robert Moses—named Baron Haussmann. He, too, was possessed of an iron certainty, great ability, and great forcefulness. If you go to the center of Paris, the part that most tourists see, it is likely to strike you as a splendid piece of urban design and a wonderful place to spend some time. Of course, if you had been one of the many thousands of poor nineteenth-century Parisians rendered homeless as Haussmann razed whole neighborhoods to make way for his vision (see the photograph and map on page 172), you might have had a very different view of the man. In any case, he would not have concerned himself with your opinion, and probably not with your welfare either.

But regardless of how the planner may feel about citizen participation, and in the writer's experience most have some ambivalence on the subject, it is here to stay. The days when people used "you can't fight city hall" as an expression about accepting the inevitable are long gone. A population that is better educated, more affluent, less deferential to authority, and possibly more generally suspicious of "the establishment" than it was decades ago, is not going to sit passively on the sidelines. The day of the Moses and Haussmanns is long gone.

The planner usually finds little within the community on which there is unanimous agreement. Majority positions can often be found, and compromises can be reached. But it is rare when all parties can agree on precisely what constitutes the public interest. When propositions are stated as generalities, they often elicit more agreement than when stated as specific proposals. For example, we all favor enhanced environmental quality. But raise the issue of shutting down a particular facility, and you quickly find that one person's environmental protection is another person's unemployment. Planning, like politics, is in large measure the art of compromise.

STYLES OF PLANNING

We have suggested that the planner works in an environment of widely distributed power, conflicting interests, and less than total agreement. How, then, are planners to conduct themselves? Styles of planning vary with individuals and also with places. Few planners will fit exactly into any one of the types that follow but rather will display different amounts of the several pure types in their professional role.

1. *The planner as neutral public servant.* In this role, planners take a politically neutral stance and fall back on their professional expertise, which will be used to tell the community how best to do what it wishes to do. They will not, in general, try to tell the community what it ought to do. The advice and technical work they present to the community will largely be confined to "how to" and "what if" and not to "should" or "should not." When choices are to be made, planners will estimate how the various alternatives will play out. If the community decides it needs some low-rent subsidized housing, planners may advise the community on where to locate it, how to design the site, how to finance it, what effect it may have on the tax base, how many additional children it will send to the schools, and what additional public services its residents might require. If the community is drawing up a comprehensive plan and zoning ordinance, planners will help structure these to reflect the community's intent.

If the community does not want such housing, planners will not urge a change of position, though perhaps they might point out legal or other consequences. Subject to the constraints of personal and professional ethics, the planners might even advise the community on what sort of comprehensive plan and zoning law provisions will withstand court challenge brought by a group seeking to force the community to accept such housing.

2. *The planner as builder of community consensus.* This is essentially a political view of the planner. It became more popular in the postwar period as it grew very clear to most planners that the older view of the planner as nonpolitical public servant was at great variance from the way that planning questions actually were resolved.[3]

In this view, planning cannot be separated from politics. Politics is the art of taking divergent views and divergent interests and bringing them into sufficient harmony to permit action to be taken. The role of the politician, then, is that of broker between various interests.[4] Since no plans can be implemented without political will and political action, the planner, too, must be very close to, or perhaps a part of, the political process. The advocate of this view, for example, would hold that the older notion of having the planner report solely to a supposedly nonpartisan lay planning board is a prescription for impotence: it is better to make the planner an integral part of the bureaucracy or the political structure where the decisions are made. This view is consistent with planners' expressing their own values and trying to move the community in directions that they see fit. How much planners can move the community in their own direction varies. The planner who is visibly at great odds with the main values and desires of the community often becomes an unemployed planner.

3. *The planner as entrepreneur.* This is not a role that planners originally envisaged for themselves but one in which many find themselves. When the planners run an agency that is particularly task-oriented, they very often become entrepreneurs. For example, in Urban Renewal programs, public funds were used to clear and prepare sites, which were then sold or leased for development by private capital. The planner who ran an Urban Renewal agency had to market sites, find developers, and negotiate contracts. Local economic development programs have as their primary goal increasing private investment in the community. Thus the economic development planner is necessarily drawn into an entrepreneurial role involving marketing, negotiation, and financing. In recent years many cities used Urban Development Action Grants (UDAGs) from the Department of Housing and Urban Development to revitalize declining areas. Here, too, the planner had to behave more as an entrepreneur than as a traditional planner.

4. *The planner as advocate.* In this role the planner acts as a representative for certain groups or certain positions and chooses to advance particular interests. The concept of advocacy planning, which developed in the early 1960s, sprang from the view that there are groups in society that lack the political and economic strength to advance their own interests adequately. Thus they need to be specially represented in the planning process. Specifically, advocacy planning cut its teeth on the issue of exclusionary zoning (see Chapters 9 and 19). Advocacy planners, the best known of whom was the late Paul Davidoff, took the position that suburban zoning laws locked out the poor and minority group members and then set about to change such laws by means of persuasion and, more important, litigation.[5] The advocacy planner, like the attorney, does not generally claim to represent the majority but rather the interests of a particular client. Those interests may or may not coincide with interests of the majority of the community or, for that matter, of the nation.

In general, advocacy planners who represent less prosperous subgroups of the population will have at least some element of a radical political perspective. It is the view that society exploits, mistreats, or otherwise abuses some of its citizens that is likely to propel one into an advocacy role. If, on the other hand, one sees society as generally fair and just, one is not likely to see much need for advocacy planning.

The notion of advocacy may also be used in a slightly different sense. Rather than serve as the advocate of a particular group in society, the planner may advocate a particular cause or program, such as parks, mass transit, highways, or environmental preservation. The planner who represents a cause may have a somewhat easier time of making a claim to serving the public interest as a whole than does the planner who represents a particular group. But even here, if one picks almost any goal, it will generally turn out that accomplishing it creates some gainers and some losers.

5. *The planner as agent of radical change.* This is a view held by only a few practicing planners. Planners who hold a full-blown radical perspective are likely to find the day-to-day work of planning in most organizations frustrating and painful because they will have to cooperate on a

daily basis with a system for which they have little respect. Among planning academicians there are a fair number, though definitely a minority, who take a neo-Marxian or critical theory position and see the promotion of radical political and economic change as a proper long-term goal for planning. This subject is discussed further in Chapter 19.

HOW PLANNING AGENCIES ARE ORGANIZED

Planning agencies vary greatly in size and purpose. What follows is typical but far from universal. As noted, the old idea of a planning agency's being outside and "above" politics has been almost universally abandoned. The modern planning agency is a part of the executive branch of the municipal government. Its head, like the commissioners of other departments, reports to the chief elected official or, if there is a manager form of government, to the city or town manager. Very commonly, the planning director or commissioner is a political appointee nominated by the chief elected official and confirmed by the legislative body, just as the head of a federal department is nominated by the president subject to confirmation by the Senate. The commissioner is often required to have specific qualifications such as a master's degree in planning or membership in the American Institute of Certified Planners (a certification based on education, experience, and passing an examination). As an appointed official, the commissioner or director can be dismissed at the will of the chief elected official. In that sense, as in many other ways, the ultimate power to plan is vested in elected officials and, therefore, in the body politic of the community.

Beneath the commissioner is a staff who, generally, have civil service status. A position such as assistant planner, associate planner, planner, and so forth has defined requirements such as degrees and education. The newly hired individual typically goes through a provisional period of six months or a year and then receives a permanent appointment. In some cases staff must be hired from a list of people who have passed the civil service examination for the position. In other cases the agency may be able to hire people who have not taken the examination, but the applicants cannot receive permanent appointments until they have passed the exam. Because of the difference between a political and civil service appointment, the staff often have a good deal more permanency than the commissioner has.

In addition to reporting to the chief elected official, the head of the planning agency may also report to a lay planning board, typically made up of citizens who have been nominated by the chief executive officer and confirmed by the legislative body. Its members serve with no or, at most, token pay. The purpose of the board is to provide some citizen input to and oversight for the planning agency. Such boards vary greatly: Some are merely rubber stamps; others may be very active and forceful. Some boards see their role as essentially supervisory, whereas others may use their own status within the municipality to advance the program of the planning agency. A board whose members are articulate and energetic can make a major contribution to building public interest in and support for the cause of planning.

The planning agency may also report directly to the community's legislative body. Often, the municipality's charter or bylaws will specify subjects on which the agency will report. For example, the charter might specify that the agency will deliver an annual report evaluating the various items proposed in the municipality's capital budget.

If the agency is of moderate or larger size, there are likely to be several sections that handle different aspects of the planning task. For example, there may be a group that handles comprehensive or long-range planning. There may be another group that handles land-use control issues and performs such functions as zoning and subdivision reviews (see Chapter 9). Still another group may review matters related to the capital budget such as investment in water and sewer facilities, roads, municipal facilities, and the like. In some agencies there will be a research section, which makes population forecasts and revenue estimates and, generally, tries to provide a solid quantitative and factual basis for the actions of the rest of the agency. In the 1970s, when community development funds began to flow from the Department of Housing and Urban Development, many planning agencies set up sections to handle the disbursement of these funds. For example, a county agency might have had a community development section that reviewed the plans of and funded the community development activities of subcounty units of government or private groups. From time to time, other planning-related functions of government may be lodged in planning agencies. In many communities, economic development agencies have been located within or attached to planning agencies; agencies that are heavily involved in environmental issues may have an environmental section, and so on.

Combined departments are common. Many planning agencies have been merged with community development departments. Which agency is the dog and which agency is the tail depends upon the priorities of the municipality. Another arrangement is the combined Planning and Public Works Department. The argument for the merger is that both deal with different elements of the same process, namely land development. The head of one such combined agency told the author that such an arrangement enlarges the perspective of all parties. The planners become more aware of the engineering realities and the costs of implementing their plans. The engineers become more aware of the larger picture and begin to think in terms of what to do as well as how to do it.

In small municipalities there may be only one or two planners who function as jacks-of-all-trades without the specialization of labor just described. In fact, in many municipalities there is no full-time planner.

Rather, there is a planning board of lay members, and the technical work of planning is performed either by consultants or sometimes by personnel of a higher-level planning agency. For example, a county or multicounty agency might provide technical support to towns within its area.

Planning Consultants

There are numerous planning consulting firms in the United States, and a substantial minority of all planners are employed by consultants. In general, municipalities with larger planning staffs use consultants primarily for specialized tasks such as environmental studies, traffic studies, planning for specialized facilities such as solid waste disposal sites, or major urban design work. For municipalities with small or no professional planning staffs, consultants are likely to be retained for basic planning tasks such as the drawing up of master plans and zoning ordinances. In fact, a very substantial percentage of all master plans and zoning ordinances in the United States have been done by planning consultants.

Having work done by a consultant rather than in-house has both advantages and disadvantages. One advantage may be the consultant's specialized knowledge and breadth of experience. A disadvantage may be that the consultant does not know the municipality very well and so may miss things that someone familiar with the municipality would see. Consultant-community relationships vary. The consultant may proceed as expeditiously as possible—for time is money—and provide the town with a "cookie-cutter" plan or zoning ordinance that draws heavily on work the consultant has done for other municipalities and that may or may not suit this particular municipality very well. In other cases the relationship is a long-term one. In this case the municipality retains the consulting firm over a period of years; the consultant comes to know the municipality, its political establishment, and its citizens very well, and, in effect, serves as the municipality's planning department.

Reaching Out to the Public

Because planning is a collective activity and because no agency will be very successful without a broad political base, planning agencies generally have a number of links to the community through various advisory or lay groups. These links may be formal or entirely casual. One approach is the advisory panel: A group of citizens interested in a particular issue, say environmental preservation, will maintain liaison with the planning agency. The agency will solicit information and advice from the group on planning decisions that have significant environmental impact. Citizens interested in housing might constitute another group with which the agency has frequent contact. In a college town in which I lived, there are citizens' groups concerned with sidewalks, bicycle paths, and urban design, and the planning agency has frequent contact with all of them. Such groups often furnish support for planning department initiatives, as well as useful data and ideas. But even when the citizens and the planners disagree, it is generally better to communicate on a continuing basis than simply to meet occasionally in an adversarial situation. Differences that can often be negotiated through informal contacts may solidify beyond compromise if they first surface in a public environment and people take stands from which it is later awkward or embarrassing to retreat. As discussed in Chapter 8, planning agencies also make extensive use of public meetings and presentations when developing plans. Meetings are useful in building support, in helping the agency to understand and be responsive to citizens' preferences and concerns, and in meeting legal requirements for citizens' participation.

Beyond all these approaches, most planning agencies reach out to the community through a variety of informal means. The planning director or staff members will speak before the Rotary Club, the League of Women Voters, the Chamber of Commerce, and other groups. Many agencies will send out press releases and otherwise seek media coverage so that people know what the agency is doing and why. Perhaps the most recent trend in communicating with the public is the establishment of planning agency or municipal government Web sites.[6] The site can post the most recent information on planning issues, make the municipal master plan available online, and give citizens the opportunity to express themselves instantaneously and without having to leave home.

But one way or another, outreach is essential. The agency that does not build a base of popular support within the community is not likely to accomplish very much. For reasons noted earlier, this is more true than it was some decades ago.

SUMMARY

Planning takes place in a highly political environment because (1) planning often involves issues in which citizens have a large emotional stake; (2) the results of planning decisions are often highly visible; (3) planning questions are more accessible to citizens than those handled at the state or national level; (4) citizens feel they have insight into planning questions and are not overly deferential to planners' expertise; (5) planning decisions often have large financial effects on property owners; and (6) planning decisions may have significant effects on property tax rates.

Planners exercise little or no power directly but rather affect events to the extent that they affect the political processes of the community. In the last several decades, the idea of planning as a nonpolitical process has given way to a more realistic view of the planner as one of a number of participants in the political process. The older view of the planner as presenting a finished plan to the community has now been supplanted by the view that planning is a community process, which the planner facilitates and supports with technical expertise.

Depending on the community and the personality and ideology of the planner(s), a variety of planning styles can be identified: (1) the planner as neutral public servant, (2) the planner as builder of community consensus, (3) the planner as entrepreneur, (4) the planner as advocate, and (5) the planner as agent of radical change.

NOTES

1. For a discussion of the reform tradition in urban politics, see Blake McKelvey, *The Urbanization of America*, Rutgers University Press, New Brunswick, NJ, 1963, particularly chaps. 6 and 7. See also Edward C. Banfield, *City Politics*, Harvard University Press, Cambridge, MA, 1963. For more recent references to work on the reform movement, see John M. Levy, *Urban America: Processes and Problems*, Prentice Hall, Upper Saddle River, NJ, 2000, chap. 5.

2. Robert A Caro, *The Power Broker*, Random House, New York, 1974.

3. One early work that examined the disparity between a purely rational and technical approach with the way decisions are actually reached is Martin Meyerson and Edward C. Banfield, *Politics, Planning and the Public Interest*, The Free Press, Glencoe, IL, 1955. A shorter presentation of some of the same arguments can be found in Edward C. Banfield, "Ends and Means in Planning," *International Social Science Journal*. vol. 11, no. 3, 1959. The article is reprinted in Andreas Faludi, *A Reader in Planning Theory*, Pergamon Press, New York, 1973. Another article in this connection is Norman Beckman, "The Planner as Bureaucrat," *Journal of the American Institute of Planners*, vol. 30, November 1964; also reprinted in Faludi, *Planning Theory*. See also Alan Altshuler, *The City Planning Process: A Political Analysis*. Cornell University Press, Ithaca, NY, 1965; Herbert J. Gans, *People and Plans*, Basic Books, New York, 1968; and Anthony J. Catanese, *Planners and Local Politics*, Sage Publications, Beverly Hills, CA, 1974.

4. A number of planners have become quite interested in mediation techniques in this regard. See, for example, Lawrence Susskind, "Mediating Public Disputes," *Negotiation Journal*, January 1985, pp. 19–22.

5. Paul Davidoff, "Advocacy and Pluralism in Planning," *Journal of the American Institute of Planners* (now the *APA Journal*), vol. 31, 1965. See also Paul Davidoff and Thomas A. Reiner, "A Choice Theory of Planning." *Journal of the American Institute of Planners*, vol. 28, May 1962. Both are reprinted in Faludi, *Planning Theory*.

6. Jonathan Cohen, "Making the Most of the Internet," *Planning*, July 2000, pp. 20–23.

SELECTED BIBLIOGRAPHY

BANFIELD, EDWARD C., *City Politics*, Harvard University Press, Cambridge, MA, 1963.

BROOKS, MICHAEL P., *Planning Theory for Practitioners*, Planners Press, American Planning Association, Chicago, 2002.

CATANESE, ANTHONY JAMES, *Planners and Local Politics*, Sage Publications, Beverly Hills, CA, 1974.

CATANESE, ANTHONY JAMES, *The Politics of Planning and Development*, Sage Publications, Beverly Hills, CA, 1984.

FALUDI, ANDREAS, ED., *A Reader in Planning Theory*, Pergamon Press, New York, 1973.

FRIEDMANN, JOHN, *Planning in the Public Domain: From Knowledge to Action*. Princeton University Press, Princeton, NJ, 1987.

HARRIGAN, JOHN, J., *Political Change and the Metropolis*, Little, Brown & Co., Boston, 1985.

HEFLAND, GARY, ED., *Metropolitan Areas: Metropolitan Governments*, Kendall Hall Publishing Co., Dubuque, 1A, 1976.

HOCH, CHARLES, *What Planners Do: Power, Politics, Persuasion*. American Planning Association, Chicago, 1994.

JACOBS, ALLAN, *Making City Planning Work*, American Society of Planning Officials, Chicago, 1978.

LUCY, WILLIAM, *Close to Power: Setting Priorities with Elected Officials*, American Planning Association, Chicago, 1988.

MEYERSON, MARTIN, and BANFIELD, EDWARD C., *Politics, Planning and the Public Interest*, The Free Press, Glencoe, IL., 1955.

CHAPTER 7

The Social Issues

The two professions from which modern urban planning sprang are architecture and landscape architecture, both of which are concerned largely with physical design. In earlier years planners often tended to emphasize design and physical issues over social issues, as the discussion of the Plan for Chicago indicated. But planners have long recognized that what at first glance appear to be simply matters of design can have powerful social implications.

In the 1960s and 1970s, dissatisfaction within the profession reached major proportions over what many saw as an underemphasis on social issues. Many planners concluded that they should be focusing on social issues, and some began to define themselves as "social planners" and to speak of a subfield of "social planning." This change within the profession had a number of roots.

The Civil Rights movement of the late 1950s and 1960s focused attention on issues of justice and fairness. Many planners felt that they could not simply be neutral civil servants doing the bidding of "the establishment" if they did not approve of its goals and policies. The wave of riots and arson that hit U.S. cities from Newark to Watts in the mid-1960s revealed a deep well of dissatisfaction and distress among minority populations and added to the perception that we as a society must be doing something wrong. Shortly thereafter, the Vietnam War split a generation of Americans. Those who felt that the war was wrong tended to carry that perception over into a more radical position on many domestic issues. If the establishment was wrong in Vietnam, they felt that it was wrong also at home.

Another reason for the change in focus was that many projects that appeared to be well planned in physical terms did not work out well when considered in a broader view. Urban Renewal, discussed in Chapter 12, was one such case. So, too, was public housing. The Pruitt-Igoe public housing project in St. Louis was a large project built according to what were considered good design practices of the time. In fact, the project won a design award from the American Institute of Architects (AIA). Socially, however, the project was a failure, with high rates of crime, vandalism, illegitimacy, and so on. Ultimately, the city, unable to deal with the multiple social problems of Pruitt-Igoe, demolished the buildings and cleared the site, AIA award notwithstanding.[1] Clearly, physical design does not solve people's psychological, family, economic, legal, drug, alcohol, and other problems. Building a project, however well done from an architectural and site design perspective, that isolated large numbers of people with serious problems in a small area simply set the stage for disaster. In general, high-rise construction has worked out very badly in public housing and a number of other projects have been turn down since the Pruitt-Igoe fiasco. On the other hand many high-rise condominiums and cooperative apartments have worked out very well as indicated by the premium prices that they command.

THE SOCIAL ISSUES IN PLANNING FOR HOUSING

Housing is probably the area in which physical planning decisions have their greatest social effects. Land-use controls and decisions about capital facilities like water and sewer lines affect how much housing and what type of housing will be built. That decision affects rents and house prices, and thus who will live in the community. Through the mechanism of cost, one pattern of housing may favor racial integration whereas another will favor racial segregation. Because where children live determines where they go to school, housing policy can turn out to be educational policy as well (see the box on pages 110–13). Where one lives can determine one's access to recreation, to social services, and, perhaps most important, to employment. Policies and economic forces that separate the housing that low-income workers can afford from the jobs for which they are qualified can produce unemployment. Prolonged unemployment can lead to family breakup, which may have links to welfare dependency, alcoholism, crime, and other social pathologies. It has been persuasively argued that the formation of the "urban underclass" is, in part, due to prolonged, large-scale unemployment in urban areas.[2] Thus it is not too far-fetched to say that decisions about housing policy may have some effect on what many regard as one of America's most pressing social problems.

Even if we forget matters of race and class entirely, decisions about housing can have powerful effects on how people live. Suppose the land-use controls in a suburban town permit the building of only single-family houses on half-acre or larger lots. By limiting what can be built to a single, expensive type of structure, the town has made some very personal decisions for its residents. Many of the children who were raised in the town will not be able to afford to live there as young adults. When a couple is divorced, the partner who does not get the house may have to leave town because there is no housing that he or she can afford. That might not be the case if some rental apartments were available. A couple with a grown retarded child who cannot live alone but could function well in a group home may be very affected by whether or not the town permits large, old, single-family houses to be converted into group homes. Many communities have experienced bitter fights over whether or not to permit group homes.

A middle-aged couple who would like an elderly parent to live with them will be concerned about whether or not the town's zoning law permits accessory, or so-called mother-in-law, apartments to be attached to or constructed adjacent to single-family houses. There are vastly more single-parent families in the United States today than there were a few decades ago. Among two-parent households, there is now a much higher percentage in which both parents work outside the home. A pattern of land-use controls that permitted homes, workplaces, and child-care facilities to be close together would make the lives of many families simpler and happier. In some communities expanding the variety of housing types to accommodate the increasing number of smaller households would be useful.

THE YONKERS HOUSING CASE

Yonkers is an old city of about 190,000 located in Westchester County, New York. On the west the city is bounded by the Hudson River and on the south by the Bronx, one of the five boroughs of New York City. To its north and east the city borders prosperous suburban areas of Westchester County.[3] The city contains 27 public housing projects, 26 of which are built in one area of the city, its southwest corner. In some ways this location makes sense. As the oldest and most densely developed part of the city, the southwest corner contained the largest share of old, substandard multifamily housing. Building the public housing there thus cleared many of these obsolete units.[4] The southwest corner of the city is also the part of the city with the best access to public transportation (bus, commuter rail, and New York City subway system). Thus a family that could not afford a car could live there and still have reasonably good mobility for such purposes as getting to work. The southwest corner was also the part of the city in which the poorer part of the city's population was living at the time the public housing was built.

But these respectable planning considerations were not the only reason public housing was concentrated there. An overriding consideration was *political feasibility*. This bland term meant that the predominantly white population of the rest of the city was adamantly opposed to public housing in their neighborhoods because they disliked or feared the poor black population that would occupy it. The city's politicians, administrators, and planners, as well as the officials of the federal government's Department of Housing and Urban Development (HUD), which funded the housing, bowed to that opposition by ruling out sites that failed the political feasibility test.

In 1980 the Justice Department, subsequently joined by the National Association for the Advancement of Colored People (NAACP), brought suit against the city and against HUD, alleging that the siting of the housing had created a condition of *de facto* school segregation. This violated the principles of school integration established in *Brown* v. *Board of Education,* a landmark case decided by the Supreme Court in 1954.[5] In 1985 Judge Leonard B. Sand of the Southern District Court in New York found both the city and HUD guilty. That decision was sustained on appeal by the U.S. Supreme Court of Appeals for the Second Circuit in 1987. In June 1988 the U.S. Supreme Court refused to hear an appeal by the City of Yonkers. At the end of its legal road and under threats by Judge Sand of massive fines, the city in a consent decree agreed to a plan for the building of public housing in other neighborhoods. But the City Council subsequently refused to carry out the plan.

In spite of the disapproval of the city by Judge Sand and much of the press, many Yonkers residents did not feel guilty about their defiance of the court. Many felt that they knew all they had to know about street crime and school problems simply from living next to New York City. In fact, many Yonkers residents were ex-New Yorkers who had moved to the suburbs to get away from crime and other urban problems and, particularly, to be able to send their children to suburban rather than city schools. Rightly or wrongly they were not about to be educated on the subject by judges, sociologists, planners, or editorial writers.

Defiant city residents were sustained in their view that they were morally right, even if legally wrong, because Yonkers had substantially more than its proportionate share of Westchester County's public housing. By an unfortunate coincidence, Judge Sand had a weekend home in Pound Ridge, an upper-income Westchester town whose population was almost entirely white. Pound Ridge could never be accused of mislocating its public housing because it did not have any at all. To dramatize what they felt was the judge's hypocritical position, Yonkers residents took to driving up to Pound Ridge to picket the judge's house.

There followed more than a decade of political maneuvering, at least one mayoral election that turned almost entirely on the housing question, and one law-suit that went all the way up to the United States Supreme Court. Then the city began to implement the court order. About 200 units of low income housing were built on seven different sites. The low income units, typically built in groups of four, are designed to blend in with the surrounding single family housing. According to the Municipal Housing Authority of Yonkers, which operates the units, the new housing has been well accepted by neighborhood residents.

Yonkers residents protesting the proposed construction of public housing. The figure hanging in effigy is Judge Sand. (Mark Vergari, Gannett Suburban Newspapers)

A limited number of so-called 80/20 units of multifamily housing have also been built. In these, 20 percent of the units are at below-market rents and are, in effect, cross-subsidized by the rents paid by the other 80 percent of the tenants. The number of 80/20 units has been small because, until recently, the housing market in the city was not strong enough to cause many developers to be interested in building such units. Since about the year 2000, the city's housing market has tightened, and, at this writing, there is more developer interest in 80/20 units.

In addition to the 80/20 program, the city's Affordable Housing Office has simply purchased individual units of both rental and owner-occupied housing and, using city funds as subsidy, has made these units available to low-income people. Preference has been given on the basis of low income, present residence in public housing, and minority group membership. The preference for present residence in public housing has caused some problems because few public-housing residents have the income required for the less heavily subsidized individual units. Thus the city has tried to place less reliance on that criterion. That attempt, in turn, has led to some litigation. In brief, then, some progress has been made, but the Yonkers housing story is far from over almost three decades after Judge Sand's decision.

The Special Case of Private Communities

Perhaps the most important recent trend in housing construction in the United States is the remarkably rapid growth of private communities. In 1975 there were 340,000 housing units in private communities. By 1990 that figure had increased by a factor of 17 to more than 5.9 million units. By the end of the 1990s it was estimated that there were more than 40 million Americans living in over 200,000 private communities.[6] Those numbers are considerably higher today.

A *private community* is one in which residence also means becoming a member of a community association, paying fees to that association and agreeing to abide by its rules. Private communities almost always begin as areas within a political subdivision such as a county. Planned as a whole, they are not built in conformance with the existing zoning or land-use controls but rather are developed pursuant to rezoning, the issuance of variances, or an overall site-plan review process. Essentially, the developer's architectural or planning consulting firm becomes the planner and the municipal planning agency, and the legislative body that it advises becomes the judge or arbiter of the plan. Often private communities are said to be "master-planned" in that there is a single plan for the entire community. This is a somewhat different usage of the term *master plan* which ordinarily means the plan for an entire city, county, or other civil division. In the great majority of cases, private communities are built in suburbia or outside metropolitan areas entirely, for that is where large blocks of undeveloped land are to be had. Private communities within established urban areas are much rarer, largely because the land assembly problem is so much more complicated (see Chapter 12 regarding the urban land assembly problem).

In some cases private communities ultimately incorporate as separate political entities. For example, Reston, Virginia, began as just described but is now incorporated as the town of Reston within Fairfax County. Columbia, Maryland, with a population of about 80,000, is currently engaged in an internal debate about whether to become a civil division within Howard County or to retain its present unincorporated status.

Many of the first private communities were retirement communities, often with explicit age restrictions. For example, rules might stipulate that at least one member of a household moving into the community must be at least 55 years old and that no permanent member of the household be younger than 18 years old. More recently, however, large numbers of private communities have developed for working-age populations as well.

Many private communities are open in the sense that anyone can enter them and move about freely within them, though many community facilities such as pools and parks are open only to residents and guests. But an increasing number of private communities are now being built as "gated" communities, with entrance denied to all except residents and guests. In 2001 it was estimated that approximately 4 million U.S. households were in gated communities.[7] That number has undoubtedly grown considerably since then.

For the developer, the private community has a marketing advantage because the buyer is getting not just a house but a complete package. That package may include physical security, often a community of somewhat similar and like-minded people, community recreational facilities, and the benefits of an integrated design. For example, many private communities have extensive systems of bicycle and pedestrian paths. These are easily integrated into a *de nouveau* design but are usually difficult to "retrofit" into an existing urban or suburban pattern.

The planner, architect, or urban designer of a private community has the opportunity to work on a larger-than-usual scale and with much more design freedom than would be the case on smaller projects fitted into gaps in an existing pattern of land use and land-use controls. In that sense, working on a private community may be quite satisfying.

But many believe that the trend toward private communities has some negative connotations. The key word of those who decry the trend is *balkanization*. Critics ask what happens to the sense of a larger community as more and more people opt for separate communities. Edward Blakely, a professor of planning at the University of California, Berkeley, argues,

> It has been over three decades since this nation legally outlawed all forms of public discrimination—in housing, education, public transportation, and public accommodations. Yet, today, we are seeing a new form of discrimination—the gated, walled, private community. I call it the "forting up phenomenon."[8]

He then adds,

> Economic segregation is scarcely new. . . . But the gated communities go farther in several respects. They create physical barriers to access. And they privatize community space, not merely individual space. . . . When offices and retail complexes are placed within the walls, the new developments create a private world. . . . This fragmentation undermines the very concept of *civitas*—organized community life.

If large numbers of the more prosperous withdraw to the enclave of the private community, one might ask what will be the condition of the remainder of the population that does not have the resources to make such a move? What will happen to the quality of public services and civic life in older urban places? Blakely puts it differently when he asks, "Do we really want to give up on the American dream of racial and class integration?" But the underlying argument is the same.

This view that the private community and particularly the gated community are fundamentally balkanizing and destroy a more widespread sense of community is held by many.[9] If fits into a larger view that higher-status and higher-income people are increasingly separating themselves from the larger culture. One proponent of this view, though he did not speak specifically of private communities, was the late social critic Christopher Lasch.[10]

Green Valley, Nevada, is a private community built by the American Nevada Corporation in 1978. By 1992 it had grown to a population of 34,000 on 8,400 acres and was projected to reach more than 60,000 early in the next century. Writing from a critical stance, David Guterson says,

> No class warfare here, no burning city. Green Valley beckons the American middle class like a fabulous and eternal dream. In the wake of our contemporary trembling and discontent, its pilgrims have sought out a corporate castle where in exchange for false security they pay with personal freedoms; where the corporation that does the job of walling others out also walls residents in.[11]

How might the proponent of the private community respond to these charges? One response is simply that private communities clearly are giving many people what they want. Their success in the market leaves no doubt about that. If we believe in maximizing consumer choice in clothing and automobiles, why not in communities as well?[12] What the residents of new communities want is not something reprehensible, but simply what they see as a good life for themselves and their families. He or she could argue that the fact that their tastes may not fit a particular social philosopher's integrationist and egalitarian vision does not necessarily make those tastes bad. If one big motivation for moving to a private community is concern for the well-being and safety of one's family, just what is so terrible about that?

To Blakely's comment on class and race integration, the would-be resident of the private community might note that we now have a large amount of class and race segregation in most metropolitan areas. It is not as though private communities were destroying some Eden of integration. He or she might also note that integration may happen most easily and naturally among people who are somewhat similar in terms of income and class, as is the situation in many private communities.

This writer does not mean to pass judgment on the private community phenomenon but only to note the arguments. Clearly, this pattern of development has social implications that far transcend the matter of physical design.

The Problem of Homelessness

In the 1980s and 1990s, most observers of the urban scene agreed that the number of homeless people was increasing. Planners are certainly not the only professionals to be concerned with this problem. The social workers, mental health professionals, the police, and the attorneys have much more direct contact with the problem than do planners. But the problem of homelessness does have a planning dimension.

The number of homeless people is not known with any degree of accuracy, for they are a hard group to count and to define. Those who have looked at the question attribute the homeless problem to several overlapping causes.[13] A certain number of the homeless are so because of mental illness. The number of mentally ill people on the street has been increased by the deinstitutionalization of mental patients in recent years. That occurred partly because of what is generally referred to as the "patient's rights" movement, which took the position that no patient should be held against his or her will unless that patient constituted a threat to himself or herself or to other people. But note that causality can run both ways. If someone's mental health is already shaky, the stress of being homeless may push that person into clinical mental illness. A certain percentage of the homeless population is so because of involvement with drugs or alcohol. Obviously, there is an overlap with the first category. We also note that the stress of being homeless may push someone in the direction of drugs or alcohol.

In addition, there are those who are homeless for economic reasons— they simply cannot afford the housing that is available. Thus unemployment can contribute to homelessness. So, too, can family breakup. As a generality, writers of a conservative bent have tended to lay more stress on the character and behavior of homeless individuals. Writers on the other side of the political spectrum have tended to place more of the blame on the distribution of income and on housing cost. Thus they place much of the problem at society's door, claiming that we do not provide enough adequately paid employment and that we do not spend enough public money on low-cost housing.

The planner may be able to make some contribution to easing the problem of homelessness via his or her involvement with housing policy. Municipal housing policy affects the entire housing stock, and that includes the low-cost end of the housing whose availability is directly related to the problem of homelessness. William Tucker, among other writers, has argued that municipal housing policy has contributed to homelessness by drying up the supply of cheap housing. That has not usually been the intention but has often been the side effect of policies designed to eliminate low-quality housing and to promote area upgrading.[14]

Urban Renewal (see Chapter 11) demolished a great deal of low-rent, low-quality housing. The goal was to eliminate low-quality housing, but doing that inevitably shrank the supply of low-cost housing at the same time. At the very bottom of the rental market, Single Room Occupancy (SRO) hotels and flophouses have been particular targets of neighborhood and business district improvement programs. The desire of residents and business owners to eliminate such structures is understandable. However, if the most that someone can afford to pay for housing is a few dollars a night, then eliminating the SRO or the flophouse renders that person homeless. Note that the SRO that is torn down in one place cannot generally be replaced with one elsewhere, since most zoning codes will not permit their construction. Then, too, the SRO is likely to be an old structure that has depreciated to a fraction of its replacement cost. Thus a new structure to serve the same purpose would not be feasible financially, even if it were legal. William Tucker, cited earlier, argues that rent controls also produce homelessness. He argues that by driving down vacancy rates, they make low-cost housing unavailable. If you need a cheap apartment, the fact that some people are now living in such, thanks to rent control, does you little good if the vacancy rate hovers near zero.[15]

Assuming that there is some truth in the preceding line of argument, what is the planner to do? Part of the planner's role, as suggested elsewhere in this book, is to take a big-picture view and to make plain the connections, like those previously discussed, to the rest of the body politic. But the planner who sees the situation in the terms just suggested is in a difficult situation. The homeless do not constitute a powerful political constituency, whereas businesspeople and permanent residents do. Then, too, it is easy to be sympathetic both with the homeless and also with those who wish the homeless to be anywhere but here. One can feel sympathy for the homeless person who stations himself or herself in the shopkeeper's doorway and also feel sympathy for the shopkeeper who does not want this individual to drive away his or her customers. The planner can advocate housing policies that do not dry up the supply of housing at the low end. He can push for some expansion of the low-cost housing through more flexible zoning—for example, by permitting accessory apartments or apartments over stores. Such units may or may not house the homeless directly, but they will ease the pressure on the remaining low-cost housing stock. For those of the homeless population who for reasons of mental health cannot function on their own, the planner can advocate flexibility in zoning and housing codes so as to make it easier to build group homes and other forms of congregate housing.

OTHER ISSUES

The Social Side of Economic Development

Economic development is another area in which issues of physical planning quickly reveal a social side. Assume that a community needs jobs and new tax revenues but that it is handicapped by a shortage of sites suitable for commercial development. It could use its power of eminent domain to take some land, carry out the necessary site preparation, and then market the land for commercial use (as noted in Chapter 5 this strategy, once very widely used, is now not legal in a number of states). But the land now contains housing, whose residents will be forced to move. Should it do so? Will a functioning neighborhood be destroyed, and if so, are the new jobs and new tax revenues worth it? If it is to be done, what arrangements will be made to rehouse the displaced population? Or will the population that now lives there simply be given notice, a modest moving allowance, and then left to its own devices?

Often the promotion of the local economy involves giving subsidies or tax breaks to firms to encourage them to locate in the community instead of elsewhere. In that case, public funds are being given, through the firm, to entrepreneurs, investors, and stockholders who may be a good deal wealthier than the average taxpayer in the community. Should we be troubled by this treatment?

Some planners are very comfortable with this approach: That is the way the game is played in this capitalist society, and by and large, the system works better than other alternatives. Others, such as Norman Krumholz, a former planning director of the City of Cleveland, are outraged by it.[16] Regardless of what position one takes on the point, it clearly contains serious questions of social philosophy.

Transportation Planning

Transportation planning has many social implications. As noted in Chapter 11, much of the conflict over Urban Renewal had to do with the taking of land for urban expressways, actions that necessarily displace people and that change or destroy the basic fabric of neighborhoods. How a region's transportation system is structured and how transportation is priced affect people's access to work, to public services, and to a whole range of activities. Thus transportation planning decisions have a major social planning component, whether that fact is explicitly realized or not.

Environmental Policy

Environmental decisions can have major social consequences. If an environmentally fragile area is the last site in town that might accommodate some low- and moderate-income housing, there is a serious question of values to be addressed. As noted elsewhere, one person's environmental protection may be another person's unemployment. Again, what looks like a physical question rapidly reveals a social side.

The Question of Environmental Justice

In recent years there has been considerable interest among planners in *environmental justice* and the related term *environmental racism*. The central question is whether the poor and minorities bear a disproportionate share of the burden of environmental problems and, if so, why? Numerous studies have been done on the subject, and books and articles written about it. Some planning schools offer courses in environmental justice. The Environmental Protection Agency (EPA) has become involved in environmental justice both in administration and also in funding research. The department's statement on the subject begins as follow:

> Environmental Justice is the fair treatment and meaningful involvement of all people regardless of race, color, national origin, or income with respect to the development, implementation, and enforcement of environmental laws, regulations, and policies. Fair treatment means that no group of people, including a racial, ethnic, or a socioeconomic group, should bear a disproportionate share of the negative environmental consequences resulting from industrial, municipal, and commercial operations or the execution of federal, state, local, and tribal programs and policies.[17]

Determining the facts of the matter may be difficult. Assume that the municipal landfill or incinerator is surrounded by low-cost housing occupied largely by minority-group members. Is that the result of intentional discrimination in choosing the site of the facility? Is it because, in the politics of making the location decision, the residents of the area had less political clout and, in effect, lost the game of "hot potato"? Or is the explanation more innocent—that the facility, its location chosen in a fair and reasonable way, reduced property values, and so over the years the area gradually filled with residents whose low incomes limited their choice in the housing market? Answering that question may require considerable digging into the history of the site and its surroundings.

Gender Issues

In the 1990s it was asserted that planning decisions might have a sexual-identity element. In 1997 a group called Gays and Lesbians in Planning (GALIP) was formed as a division of the American Planning Association (APA) to represent the interests of gay and lesbians.[18] One item that GALIP members mentioned was the recognition of and planning for districts that, either commercially or residentially, were oriented to gays and lesbians. Within the planning profession, reaction to the formation of GALIP is mixed. Some within the profession take an "it's-about-time" view. Others take the position that planning is about serving a general public interest and that the formation of GALIP and the assertion of a separate gay and lesbian interest was divisive. How much of a set of gay and lesbian issues can be identified and developed remains to be seen.

Feminism and Planning

A number of planning educators who define themselves as feminists have argued that there is a feminist perspective on planning and a set of feminist issues that should be, and often are not, addressed in planning. For example, a number of feminist planners have suggested that the way many suburbs are planned seemed more to suit the interests of men than of women. The argument first surfaced in a major way in the 1960s with *The Feminine Mystique* which, among many other points, argued that the house in a suburban subdivision where there was nothing but similar houses, even though it might be a nice house equipped with all the best furnishings and appliances, was really something of a prison for the woman who stayed home all day with the children, and this isolation contributed to boredom and depression.[19] In fact the author Betty Friedan referred to the matter as "the problem that has no name." Whether that argument has lost some importance in the intervening years as labor force participation rates for mothers of young children have risen and as the percentage of the adult female population living in households with children has declined is an open question. However, more generally, feminists have suggested that in the past, planning (like almost all other professions) was male dominated, that most of its literature was written by men, and that most of its historic figures were male.[20] This naturally tended to "privilege" male over female interests. They suggest that a city or a metropolitan area laid out by women rather than men might be a very different place. For the reader who is interested in pursuing further the feminist perspective on planning there now exists a substantial literature.[21]

Planning and Aging

A whole set of social issues related to the age structure of the nation will be coming into prominence in the years ahead. Generally, the post–World War II baby boom is dated from about 1947 to 1965. That suggests that the leading edge of the baby boom is now reaching retirement age and that the number of retirees in the United States will rise greatly in the second and third decades of this century.

That so-called graying of the population will push a whole range of social planning questions to the forefront. These questions are not absent from the scene now but will be felt with much greater force. Older people will be much more numerous, they will control a larger share of the nation's personal income and accumulated wealth, and they will constitute a larger percentage of the nation's voters. In short, their political power will climb considerably over the next couple of decades.

The place where the changed demographic structure will probably have its biggest effect on planning practice is in housing and land use.[22] Seniors, who live largely in one- and two-person households, will have very different housing needs and housing preferences than other age groups. They will also have different needs for health, recreation, and public services. Transportation planning (see Chapter 12) will be affected. Public transportation in the United States now, with the exception of commuter rail service and metro service in a very few urban areas, is largely used by the less prosperous—those who do not own automobiles. A large number of affluent seniors who cannot or do not want to drive could put a very different spin on that.

Much of the politics of public expenditures comes down to two very basic questions: Who picks up the bill and who benefits from the expenditures? As the nation's demography changes, the political balance of power will change and that will be reflected in the nation's politics and in the practice of planning.

The social issues noted in this chapter reinforce a basic theme of this book, which is that almost all but very minor planning decisions impose gains and losses. This point is made in subsequent chapters in connection with growth control, environmental planning, and economic development planning, among other issues. Planners who define themselves as social planners often feel that they should attempt to tip society's scales toward the less fortunate (or tip them so they favor the fortunate a bit less). But many other planners take the position that their task is to serve the majority of the community or to serve a general public interest so far as they can identify it. These planners might also argue that a single community cannot do much about broad equity issues such as the distribution of income. Therefore, such matters are necessarily left to higher levels of government, where the means are more commensurate with the size of the problem.

WHO DOES SOCIAL PLANNING? _____

If one asks practicing planners or planning educators whether there is a separate field of "social planning" within the planning profession, one will get answers ranging from "Of course" to "What is it?" If a planner is doing something that is directly devoted to a social end, say administering community development funds for day care or an adult literacy program, clearly that planner is engaged in "social planning." The great majority of planners, however, do not spend most of their time on explicit social planning. But almost any decision that involves how sizable blocks of land will be used or how sizable sums of public money will be spent has social implications. In that sense, any planner who is conscientious and competent is engaged in social planning.

SUMMARY _____

All planning decisions of significant size have social implications. For many planners and planning agencies, social issues present themselves most strongly in the realm of housing. This chapter presents some of the older housing issues such as how much variety of housing type is permitted, as well as the implications of the extremely rapid growth of private communities, both the open and the gated variety. It also notes some social issues in connection with economic development and environmental planning. Whether or not one recognizes a separate field of social planning, it is clear that the social side of what at first might appear to be purely physical or design questions should not be ignored.

NOTES _____

1. A graphic and an entertaining account of the Pruitt-Igoe fiasco can be found in Tom Wolfe, *From Bauhaus to Our House*, Farrar, Strauss, Giroux, New York, 1981.
2. See William J. Wilson, *The Truly Disadvantaged*, University of Chicago Press, Chicago, 1987.
3. The county, population of about 870,000, contains a total of 43 municipalities, of which Yonkers is the largest.
4. Whether clearing substandard units is always desirable is arguable because it may have the effect of tightening the market and thus driving up rents. However, the removal of substandard units was standard Urban Renewal doctrine when Yonkers public housing was built.
5. In this decision the Supreme Court rejected the previous "separate but equal" doctrine and ruled that segregation itself, regardless of whether or not the facilities were otherwise equal, was unacceptable. For the reader interested in the Yonkers case, the best source is the *New York Times Index*, for the *Times* has covered the case regularly since Judge Sand's 1985 decision.
6. Clifford J. Treese, ed., *Community Associations Factbook*, Community Associations Institute, Alexandria, VA, 1993 and 1999. Further information on private communities can be found on the Web site of the Community Associations Institute, www.caionline.org.
7. Bureau of The Census, American Housing Survey, 2001.

8. Edward Blakely, "Viewpoint," *Planning,* January 1994, p. 46.

9. See, for example, David Dillon, "Fortress America," *Planning,* June 1994, pp. 8–12.

10. Christopher Lasch, *The Revolt of the Elites and the Betrayal of Democracy,* W.W. Norton, New York, 1995.

11. David Guterson, "No Place Like Home," *Harpers Magazine,* November 1992, pp. 55–61.

12. The idea that a greater number of communities would maximize consumer choice (the citizen is regarded as a consumer of public services) and move the market for public services toward the economists' model of the perfect market goes by the name of the *Tiebout hypothesis,* after the economist Charles Tiebout. A presentation of the idea can be found in Ronald C. Fisher, *State and Local Public Finance,* 2nd ed., Richard D. Irwin Co., Chicago, 1996, chap. 5. The hypothesis was originally propounded in an article by Tiebout, "A Pure Theory of Local Expenditures," *Journal of Political Economy,* October 1956, p. 422.

13. For a good general account of the problem, see Christopher Jencks, *The Homeless,* Harvard University Press, Cambridge, MA, 1994. For a summary of various estimates of the U.S. homeless population through the late 1980s, see Karin Ringheim, *At Risk of Homelessness,* Praeger, New York, 1990.

14. William Tucker, "How Housing Regulations Cause Homelessness," *The Public Interest,* Winter, 1991, pp. 78–88.

15. For a brief discussion of the economics of rent control and references to the literature, see John M. Levy, *Essential Microeconomics for Public Policy Analysis,* Praeger, New York, 1995, chaps. 3 and 10.

16. Pierre Clavel, *The Progressive City: Planning and Participation,* 1969–1984, Rutgers University Press, New Brunswick, NJ, 1987, chap. 3.

17. EPA press release, June 22, 2004. This release and much other information is available on an EPA Web site, www.epa./gov/compliance/environmental justice/.

18. Karen Finucan, "Gay Today," *Planning,* February 2000, pp. 12–16. GALIP's Web site is www.geocities.com/capitolhill/lobby/7016/galip.htm.

19. Betty Friedan, *The Feminine Mystique,* Norton, New York, 1963.

20. At present, enrollments in U.S. planning schools are about equally divided between men and women so that however much male dominance there is in the field should be reduced as more women rise to senior positions.

21. For a sampling of arguments and references to the feminist planning literature, see *Gender and Planning,* Susan S. Fainstein and Lisa J. Servon, eds., Rutgers University Press, 2004, and Barbara Rahder and Carol Altilia, "Where Is Feminism in Planning Going: Appropriation or Transformation," *Planning Theory,* vol 3., no. 2, 2004, pp. 107–116.

22. Jane Adler, "What's Next, Boomers," *Planning,* December 2006, pp. 34–37.

SELECTED BIBLIOGRAPHY

ANDERSON, WAYNE F., FRIEDEN, BERNARD J., and MURPHY, MICHAEL J., EDS., *Managing Human Services,* International City Managers Association, Washington, DC, 1997.

BOLAN, RICHARD S., "Social Planning and Policy Development," in *The Practice of Local Government Planning,* International City Management Association, Washington, DC, 1979.

CLAVEL, PIERRE, *The Progressive City: Planning and Participation,* 1969–1984, Rutgers University Press, New Brunswick, NJ, 1987.

HOWE, ELIZABETH, "Social Aspects of Physical Planning," in *The Practice of Local Government Planning,* 2nd ed., International City Management Association, Washington, DC., 1988.

CHAPTER 8

The Comprehensive Plan

In the planning literature, one sees the terms *comprehensive plan, general plan,* and *master plan* used synonymously. At present, the term *comprehensive plan* is in most common use and will be used here for all three. It refers to the most basic plan prepared to guide the development of the community. One characteristic of the comprehensive plan is that physically it covers the entire community. Another defining characteristic is that it is long-term. Comprehensive plans typically have time horizons in the range of 20 years. Recall from Chapter 5 that having a plan may be optional or may be required by the state.

THE GOALS OF COMPREHENSIVE PLANNING _____

Since municipalities differ, the following list of goals will not be complete, nor will every item necessarily apply to every community. Because the goals overlap, another writer might list them differently yet cover the same ground. Note that all the following goals, with the possible exception of the last, readily fit within the rubric of the phrase *health, safety, and public welfare,* cited earlier in connection with the police power.

   1. *Health.* Achieving a pattern of land use that protects the public health is a well-established planning goal. One aspect might be prohibiting densities of development that threaten to overload water or sewer facilities. In areas that do not have public water and sewer facilities, it may mean spacing houses far enough apart to prevent leakage from septic tanks from contaminating well water. It may involve separating industrial or commercial activities that produce health hazards from residential areas. It may mean banning certain types of industrial operations from the community entirely.

2. *Public safety.* This goal may manifest itself in numerous ways. It might mean requiring sufficient road width in new subdivisions to ensure that ambulances and fire equipment have adequate access in emergencies. Many communities have flood plain zoning to keep people from building in flood-prone areas. At the neighborhood level it might mean planning for a street geometry that permits children to walk from home to school without crossing a major thoroughfare. In a high-crime area it might mean laying out patterns of buildings and spaces that provide fewer sites where muggings and robberies can be committed unobserved.[1]

3. *Circulation.* Providing the community with adequate circulation is an almost universal goal of comprehensive planning. This means a system of streets and perhaps also parking facilities that make possible an orderly, efficient, and rapid flow of vehicular and pedestrian traffic. In many communities it also means providing for adequate public transportation. Planning for transportation and planning for land use are intimately connected, as is discussed in detail in Chapter 13.

4. *Provision of services and facilities.* An important part of most comprehensive planning efforts is determining the location of facilities such as parks, recreation areas, schools, social services, hospitals, and the like. In addition to planning for facilities, it is also important to plan for a pattern of land use that facilitates the provision of public services like police and fire protection, water, and sewers. For example, the pattern of land use will affect the feasibility and cost of providing public water and sewer facilities. The location of housing relative to the location of schools will determine whether children can walk or must be bused to school.

5. *Fiscal health.* There is a relationship between the pattern of development and the fiscal situation of the community. Any development will impose some costs on the community (fire protection, police protection, traffic, education, etc.). Similarly, virtually any development will generate some revenues for the municipality (property taxes, sales taxes, user charges, and other fees of one sort or another). Some uses will yield surpluses, and others deficits. Generally speaking, it is not very difficult to predict which uses will do which. In fact, a fairly substantial literature exists on this very point.[2] Many communities will plan for a pattern of land use that will hold down property taxes. But there are limits here. Does the community have the right to practice "fiscal zoning"—the use of its land-use controls to keep out types of housing or economic activity that are likely to cost the community more for additional services than they yield in additional revenue? How much can a community limit the building of multifamily and small-lot single-family housing to control costs? The courts have not spoken with total unanimity on this matter, and many an attorney has earned a comfortable living litigating such points.

6. *Economic goals.* In thousands of communities, economic growth or maintenance of the existing level of economic activity is an important goal. There is a link here with the fiscal goal, but there may be other motivations as well, most notably providing employment for community residents. Thus a community may seek to develop a pattern of land use that provides for commercial and industrial sites, provides good access to such sites, and facilitates supplying utilities to such sites. Other steps that a municipality may take to stimulate its own economic development are discussed in Chapter 14.

7. *Environmental protection.* This goal is an old one but, as noted in Chapter 16, has become much more common since the 1960s. It might involve restrictions on building in wetlands, steep slopes, or other ecologically valuable or fragile lands. It might involve preservation of open space, ordinances to control discharges into water bodies, prohibition or limitations on commercial or industrial activities that would degrade air quality, and so on. In a broader sense it may be connected to planning for the entire pattern of land use.

8. *Redistributive goals.* Some planners of the political left would argue that a goal of planning should be to distribute downward both wealth and influence in the political process.[3] In a limited number of communities, planners have been able to bend the planning process in that direction. For an account of a few such instances, see the book by Pierre Clavel cited in Chapter 7.

THE COMPREHENSIVE PLANNING PROCESS _____

We noted in Chapter 6 that the last several decades, the comprehensive planning process has changed from one in which a small group handed down a plan to one in which the making of the plan is a participatory process open to the citizens of the community. This section describes a participatory plan-making process. The process will vary from one community to the next, but we can identify some common elements.

1. *A research phase.* One cannot plan very much if one does not have a sense of the present state of events and their probable future direction. Thus many comprehensive planning efforts began with a data-gathering and forecasting phase.
2. *Clarification of community goals and objectives.* At some point, preferably early in the process, there has to be some agreement about what the plan is intended to achieve. This is not to say that agreement will ever be total.

3. *A period of plan formulation.*
4. *A period of plan implementation.*
5. *A period of review and revision.*

Though presented as a sequence, these items necessarily overlap. Insights gained in the research phase will reveal problems that affect the goals the community will formulate. But selecting goals will affect what things a community should know about itself. Thus the research and the goal-formation processes tend to proceed simultaneously. Research regarding population trends might lead to formulating the goal of acquiring an additional 500 acres of parkland. That, however, suggests another research question: Is a purchase of that magnitude realistic in terms of the community's revenues and other fiscal obligations? Thus steps 1 and 2 inevitably become intertwined.

As one formulates a plan, one needs facts and estimates. The results of research modify the plan, and the needs of plan formulation tend to set the research agenda. Then, too, plan formulation tends to modify goals. Detailed planning tends to make plain the real implications of generalized goals; at that point, goals may become modified. A community might set forth as a goal "an adequate supply of housing at affordable prices." It is hard to be against such a goal: few will come out publicly in favor of an inadequate supply of housing at exorbitant prices. But when the community looks at the matter in detail, it may not like what the goal implies. Getting prices down to affordable levels may mean building smaller housing units at higher densities than present residents want. Perhaps getting prices down will also necessitate a major increase in housing supply, with attendant increases in traffic congestion and overcrowding in the schools. Perhaps an increase in the supply of lower-cost housing will impose costs that push up property tax rates. In short, when the community begins to look at the consequences that flow from its goal statements, it may decide to modify the goals. Implementing the plan may also cause modifications of goals as it becomes apparent what can and cannot actually be accomplished.

In the following sections we discuss the five steps in detail.

Planning Research

Most planning agencies, particularly those large enough to have a research staff, make considerable use of planning-related research. One common type of study is the "population forecast." One cannot plan without knowing for whom one is planning, which means having some notion of how many people there will be in the community. It also means knowing something about the likely age structure of the population. One hundred people over the age of 65 make very different demands on the community than do one hundred elementary school students.

There are various approaches to forecasting population. A common technique is the "cohort survival" method. In this, the present population is mathematically "aged" into the future. In other words, each age and sex group, or "cohort," of the population is advanced through time and its numbers adjusted for expected mortality.[4] Adjustments are made for net migration (moves in minus moves out) and births. The advantage of the technique is that it presents a detailed picture of the structure of the population rather than just an estimate of the total number of people. The mathematics are relatively simple, but getting good results is another matter. At the city, county, or town level, the big differences in growth rates between places are largely due to differences in net migration. Predicting net migration accurately is difficult. At the present it is much more an art than a science.

Then, too, there is an interaction between plans and forecasts that can muddy the waters.[5] For example, in many suburban areas, housing stock is the factor that limits population growth. One might estimate net migration on the basis of past performance, but how does one factor into these estimates the effect on population of land-use control ordinances that will be enacted next year and that may be affected by this year's forecasts? In the ideal planning situation, the making of plans and the making of forecasts should be related. However, such coordination between planning and forecasting is not easy to achieve.

Another basic study is the "land-use inventory."[6] Such a study generally begins with a mapping of existing land uses (residential, industrial, commercial, educational, recreational, etc.). The study also characterizes the undeveloped land in the community in terms of suitability for different uses. The common practice is to prepare a series of maps that show various land characteristics such as topography, flood plains, areas of wells or poorly drained soil, and so on. In many cases the land-use study will also contain some information on land ownership, generally distinguishing between public, private, and institutional holdings at a minimum. The study might make further distinctions such as identifying major private or major institutional holders. The study may also identify some infrastructure characteristics, particularly water and sewer service. It may also identify some legal characteristics such as zoning categories, though these are less permanent characteristics than most of the other items mentioned.

In recent years the traditional paper map for the recording of the results of land-use studies has been supplemented by electronic mapping systems generally referred to as Geographic Information Systems (GIS). In a GIS, data are stored in digital form. For example, to store a contour line in the system, a technician moves a digitizer along the contour line of a topographic map, and the path of the digitizer is converted to digital form and stored in the computer's memory. Information such as assessed values, zoning category, census data, and the like can also be entered as numbers or letters. The electronic database can then quickly be used to produce a variety of maps, calculations, tabulations, and so on. The map that might take a draftsperson days to draw can often be produced by a GIS in a few minutes.

At the regional scale, GISs now make use of data from satellite cameras. Images, from both within and outside the visible light spectrum, come from the satellite camera in digital form and are then "imported" into the GIS database. Among the material that can be mapped from such digital information are vegetation, topography, hydrology, land use, temperature, and some geologic features. The level of precision is not usually sufficient for small parcels, but it may be quite adequate for work at a large scale and costs only a fraction of what it would cost if obtained by conventional methods.

Beyond these two most common studies are a host of others that may or may not be done, depending on needs and resources. If economic development is an issue, an economic base study may be undertaken. The degree of sophistication may vary from a simple listing of present employers to a highly sophisticated econometric model built by a consultant specializing in such work.[7]

Almost all comprehensive plans contain a circulation element. Thus studies of traffic flow characteristics along the existing transportation network are likely to be done early in the master-planning process. Some general estimates of future traffic flows based on projections of future population and employment are also likely to be made at an early stage. There is a strong interaction between transportation planning and land-use planning. The amount of development in an area is a major determinant of the number of trips that will be made to and from the area. On the other hand, the accessibility of the area will in large measure determine how much development takes place there. Thus land-use and transportation planning should go hand in hand.

Studies related to infrastructure are common. Water supply and the provision of sewer service are key elements in shaping the pattern of development in growing areas. Studies may be done to determine potential area for sewers and areas that are amenable to the development of public water supply systems. In areas where public water and sewer supply are not feasible, studies may be devoted to ground water supply and quality.

Soil characteristics may come in for serious study at this point. If an area is not to have sewers, for whatever reason, the amount of development that can occur may be limited by the capacity of the soil to absorb safely household wastes from septic tanks. This capacity will vary greatly with soil types. A sandy, well-drained soil may safely permit building several houses per acre. On the other hand, soil with a great deal of clay or bedrock lying close to the surface may require an acre or two of land per house for safe disposal of household waste. Soil characteristics such as shrinkage and swelling as the water content of the soil changes will affect the types of buildings that can be constructed. The capacity of the soil to absorb water will affect flooding potential, an important consideration in considering the type and intensity of development appropriate for the area.

Many communities will do recreation studies as part of a master plan, looking at population, recreational preferences, existing facilities, and so forth. In general, such studies will inventory the present supply of facilities and services. Future needs will be estimated by applying standards (so many acres of parkland per 1,000 of population, for example) to the municipality's projected population. The gap between the existing situation and the estimated need is used to establish preliminary planning goals. Unmet recreational needs may also be estimated by survey techniques, simply asking residents what facilities they use and what additional facilities they would like to have.

In recent years, planning at the comprehensive stage has taken on an increasingly fiscal cast. Many municipalities have found themselves under strong fiscal pressures, the sources of which are various. In many central cities and some small communities, expenses have risen while the tax base has stagnated. In other cases tax bases have grown substantially, but municipalities have still faced very strong resistance to tax increases, as exemplified by California's Proposition 13 noted in Chapter 5.

Fiscal studies generally involve analyzing trends and making forecasts of expenditures, revenues, and tax rates. Studies may also be done to estimate capital needs and capital costs. The basic purpose of a fiscal study is to permit the community to match the other elements of the plan to the resources that it is likely to have to carry out the plan. In fact, it is very difficult to say whether a community's planning is realistic if one does not have some knowledge of its financial underpinning.

Formulating Community Goals

Ideally, goals should be formulated with a knowledge of the essential facts of the situation, a knowledge of the limitations under which the municipality operates, and a realistic view of the options open to the community. Developing such knowledge is the ultimate purpose of the research component just described. The purpose of the goal-setting process is to formulate a limited number of goals that do not contradict each other and that have enough public and political support behind them to give them a reasonable chance of actually coming to pass.

The planning agency's role in this process might be to provide a forum for discussion (organizing meetings, obtaining media coverage, setting up advisory committees), providing facts and laying out options, and synthesizing and articulating the results of the discussions and deliberations. The process of setting goals should be an open one in that citizens and groups who have a stake in the outcome of the planning process are not excluded. This consideration is not just a matter of fairness or legal requirement, but also of practicality. Those who have had a hand in shaping a plan are more likely to support it than those who have not.

The scope of this phase has been expanded in recent years by the advent of computer modeling. For example, planners working with the California Urban Futures Model were able to offer three very different scenarios—business as usual (continuation of present trends), maximum environmental protection, and compact city—for the same community.[8] Such scenario generation does not absolutely require a computer, but the computer makes it possible to produce a larger number of moderately detailed options or scenarios in a reasonable period of time and thus expands the range of public discussion and consideration. At the design level, computer graphic techniques are coming into use to help people visualize how a proposed design for part of a municipality would appear as one moved through it, rather than judging it from, say, an artist's rendering or a model.

Formulating the Plan

When the baseline studies have been done and agreement has been reached on goals, the work of formulating the plan can begin. In larger communities the plan is generally drawn up by the municipality's planning agency. In smaller communities it is common for the plan to be drawn up by a planning consultant and submitted to the community for approval.

The first step in plan formulation is generally to lay out a variety of options. For example, assume that one goal is to reduce traffic congestion in the central business district. One option might be widening or straightening the main street; another, constructing a bypass; a third, building a parking structure and eliminating on-street parking on the main street; a fourth, converting from a two-way to a one-way street system; a fifth option, some combination of these.

When all the reasonable options have been listed, it is time to begin considering their respective costs and merits. This process is sometimes referred to as "impact analysis." One item to be considered is cost and what the costs would imply for the municipal tax rate and debt structure. That study might look not only at direct costs of the options, but also at indirect considerations such as estimated effects on sales tax receipts and property values. Another item would be the number of households and businesses affected by the taking of property and the disturbance of traffic flow during the construction phase. The planners would also examine the relative degree of improvement in traffic flow that might be expected from each option. Aesthetic and urban design issues would also be examined. When the impact assessments have been made, the preferred option can be selected. Note that it is often a good idea to bring affected parties such as the property owners, residents, and businesspersons into the impact assessment and option-choosing process. First, they are likely to make useful contributions. Equally important, no plan can be implemented without political consent, and politics is "the art of compromise." It is better to resolve differences early around a conference table than later in the courts or the press.

This impact analysis can be done for each main element of the plan. At some point, however, their combined effects must also be examined to know whether the total cost is manageable. If it is not, choices among goals must be made.

Implementing the Plan

As noted earlier, the two most powerful tools for carrying out the physical side of the plan are capital investments as called for in the capital budget and land-use controls. Capital investments in roads, public facilities, and utilities create the basic conditions that permit development, which land-use controls then shape and channel. Ideally, capital investments and land-use controls should be consistent with one another and with the comprehensive plan. If coordination is lacking, the results are likely to be disappointing. For example, if capital investments create powerful pressures for development in areas that the comprehensive plan shows as developing at low density, the stage has been set for litigation and controversy. The end results are likely to be very different from what the community envisioned.

Review and Updating

Almost inevitably, community development will not unfold quite as envisioned in the master plan. Planning is anything but an exact science. Rather it is an art still in the early stages of development. Then, too, the pattern of development is shaped by all sorts of forces that are beyond community control and in many cases beyond prediction. Thus after a short time the community will not be quite where the plan would have it, and so some replanning is necessary. Just as a navigator takes frequent bearings and replots the course accordingly, the community checks its situation periodically and adjusts its plans. But the analogy is not entirely accurate. In the case of the navigator, the destination remains the same. In the case of the municipality, the goals themselves may change as realities both inside and outside the municipality change.

For the plan to be effective over a long term, periodic review is essential. Ideally, the review applies to all the major plan elements. First, it applies to the database. Population, revenues, expenditures, housing stock, employment, and so on inevitably will not evolve exactly as predicted. Large disparities may show up fairly quickly. Consider, for example, cost projections for capital expenditures. A major component of the cost of capital expenditures is the cost of borrowing money, that is, interest rates. Twenty-five years ago the interest rate on long-term bonds was twice what it is at this writing. No one doing capital budgeting for a municipality then could have predicted that drop, nor can anyone doing capital budgeting now predict what interest rates will prevail a few years hence.

Beyond updating the database on which the plan rests, it is also necessary to update goals and strategies. Ideally, the municipal government should have a commitment to updating the plan at regular intervals. If this cannot be done, the plan loses its relationship to reality. If government personnel and citizens perceive the plan as a static and increasingly irrelevant document, it soon loses its political force. The act of updating it keeps it relevant and keeps the body politic committed to it. It also institutionalizes planning as an activity within the community.

Maintaining community interest in the planning process is one of the most important tasks of any planning agency. Thus public relations is a major aspect of successful planning. The planning director's speech to the Rotary Club, the appearance in a high school civics class, and the periodic newspaper article on what the city or town or county is planning for solid waste disposal or parklands or economic development or housing or downtown business district revitalization are all part of that effort. In one southern town, planning agency staff have appeared in first- and second-grade classrooms and run six- and seven-year-old children through a simple experience in laying out a neighborhood. That strategy may not pay off for a quarter of a century, but then planning is a long-term process.

HOW EFFECTIVE ARE COMPREHENSIVE PLANS?

To a great degree the effectiveness of the plan depends upon the degree of commitment by the municipal government and the citizens to the plan. If the municipal government and the citizens are committed to the goals of the plan, then the power of government to raise money, to spend money, and to use the municipality's powers to control land use can be used to move toward the vision embodied in the plan. This is the situation in many municipalities. But in other municipalities, commitment to the plan may be less solid. The plan may exist on paper, but little will be done to make it come to pass. In the extreme the plan may just be a *pro forma* document that exists because the state requires every municipality to have an adopted comprehensive plan or because having a plan is a requirement for state or federal grant programs in which the municipality is interested.

Some municipalities are in a stronger position to stick to a plan than are others. A prosperous municipality that has an adequate tax base will have both the funds to make the public investments that support the plan and also the ability to reject development that clearly contravenes the plan. A poor municipality may find that it simply does not have the fiscal capacity to make the investments required to implement the plan. A combination of weak tax base and high unemployment may put it in the position of being unable to turn away any proposed development, even if that development contravenes the intentions of the plan.

Where there is little growth to be channeled and directed, the plan may be relatively ineffectual. At the other extreme, if economic forces beyond the control of the municipality are making it grow at a very rapid rate, it may be very hard for the planners and the municipal government to stay ahead of the game and stick to the comprehensive plan. The crisis of the day will crowd out everything else.

Unpredictable events may have a big effect on whether or not the vision in the plan comes to pass. For example, the county develops a comprehensive plan and sticks to it for awhile. At this point a major investor(s) acquires a large block of land and draws up a design for a planned community (see Chapter 7). Upon reflection, the plan looks good to the municipality in terms of land use and economic and fiscal impact. But it requires rezoning of a substantial part of the county and thus scrapping major parts of the comprehensive plan. It is something that could not have been predicted, but to a majority of the Board of Supervisors and the Planning Board it seems like an opportunity that is too good to pass up. In short order, the plan is subjected to a major rewrite. Comparable scenarios could readily be suggested for a shopping center, office park, and other commercial development, as well as in some cases large facilities constructed by higher levels of government. Prediction is at the base of any long-term plan and life is often unpredictable.

Some populations are fundamentally more supportive of planning than are others. In the writer's observation, college towns often are quite supportive of planning. Their educated and economically comfortable, albeit not rich, populations seem to be comfortable with it and often take a big interest in it.

The overall political stance of the population is very important. As suggested in Chapter 5, where the boundary between the rights of private property and the rights of the public, considered as a whole, should lie is an ideological question, or to to put it another way, a right/left question. So the overall political complexion of the population will have an effect on how much or how little the body politic thinks it ought to plan.

In brief, then, the plan reflects the community from which it springs. There is as much variation in plans and in their effectiveness as there is among places themselves. In Chapter 19 we discuss some alternative approaches to the comprehensive planning approach and the pros and cons thereof.

SUMMARY

The comprehensive plan covers the entire municipality and has a long time horizon, typically 20 years or so. The goals of a municipality's comprehensive planning process might include issues of health, public safety, circulation, provision of services and facilities, fiscal health, economic development, environmental protection, and, perhaps, some redistributive goals.

Since the 1920s when comprehensive plans (also called master plans and general plans) became common, the process has changed considerably. Early plans were usually prepared by a small "nonpolitical" group, and the role of the body politic was to support the plan with appropriate legislation and funding. In the years since World War II, the process has become much more participatory. The modern planner is likely to facilitate and provide technical expertise for a community-wide planning process rather than simply to prepare the plan for community acceptance.

The comprehensive planning process can be divided into these five major stages:

1. Research
2. Clarification of goals and objectives
3. Plan formulation
4. Plan implementation
5. Review and revision

Though shown as separate steps, there is much overlap between them because what is learned in one step may cause the community to modify what was established in a preceding step. For example, the detailed work of plan formulation, by revealing the true costs of pursuing a particular goal, may cause the community to reconsider its goals. We also noted that periodic review of problems and progress and subsequent updating of the plan are essential if the plan is to continue to affect the development of the community.

NOTES

1. For a discussion of the relationship between design and safety from crime, see Oscar Newman, *Defensible Space*, The MacMillan Company, New York, 1972.
2. See, for example, George Sternlieb et al., *Housing Development and Municipal Costs*, Rutgers University Center for Urban Policy Research, New Brunswick, NJ, 1973; or Robert W. Burchell and David Listokin, *The New Practitioners Fiscal Impact Handbook*, Rutgers University Center for Urban Policy Research, New Brunswick, NJ, 1985.
3. Norman Krumholz, "A Retrospective on Equity Planning: Cleveland, 1969–79," with comments, *APA Journal*, vol. 48, no. 2, Spring 1982, pp. 163–184.
4. For an introductory account of this technique and comparison with other techniques, see F. Stuart Chapin and Edward J. Kaiser, *Urban Land Use Planning*, 3rd ed., University of Illinois Press, Urbana, 1979, chap. 6.
5. The terms *forecast* and *projection* are often used interchangeably, but to demographers there is a distinction. The former implies the analyst's best estimate of what will happen. The latter is simply a mathematical exercise showing what the population will be if certain rates of birth, death, in-migration, and out-migration obtain. A forecast can be proven right or wrong by future events. But a projection, if the mathematics is done correctly, cannot be said to be wrong.
6. See Edward J. Kaiser, David R. Godschalk, and F. Stuart Chapin Jr., *Urban Land Use Planning*, 4th ed., University of Illinois Press, Urbana, 1995.

7. For an account of different types of community economic studies, see John M. Levy, *Urban and Metropolitan Economics*, McGraw-Hill Book Co., New York, 1985, chap. 4. See also Thomas S. Lyons and Roger E. Hamlin, *Creating an Economic Development Action Plan*, Praeger, Westport, CT, 2001.

8. John D. Landis, "Future Tense," *Planning*, February 1994, pp. 22–25.

SELECTED BIBLIOGRAPHY

ANDERSON, LARZ T., *Guidelines for Preparing Urban Plans*, American Planning Association, Chicago, 1995. Anderson, Larz T., *Planning the Built Environment*, American Planning Association, Chicago, 2000.

BRANCH, MELVILLE C., *Continuous City Planning*, John Wiley, New York, 1981.

HOCH, CHARLES J., DALTON, LINDA C., and So, FRANK S., eds., *The Practice of Local Government Planning*, International City Management Association, Washington, DC, 2000.

KAISER, EDWARD J., GODSCHALK, DAVID R., and CHAPIN, F. STUART, *Urban Land Use Planning*, 4th ed., University of Illinois Press, Urbana, 1995.

KENT, T. J., *The Urban General Plan*, Chandler, San Francisco, 1964.

So, FRANK S., HAND, IRVING, and McDOWELL, BRUCE W., *The Practice of State and Regional Planning*, American Planning Association, Chicago, 1986.

CHAPTER 9

The Tools of Land-Use Planning

The comprehensive plan, as described in the preceding chapter, largely pertains to the pattern of land use. In this chapter we discuss the tools available to the municipality to effectuate its land-use plans. Essentially there are two broad categories of direct actions by which a municipality can shape its land-use pattern. These are (1) public capital investments and (2) land-use controls. Some land-use decisions, often very important ones, are determined by higher levels of government and other large players that are not a part of the municipal body politic. These decisions are discussed at the end of this chapter.

PUBLIC CAPITAL INVESTMENT

Though we devote more space in this chapter to land-use controls, in the long term, public capital investment is the more powerful shaper of the pattern of development. Public capital investment creates very powerful economic forces that shape development and, unlike land-use controls, public capital investments such as roads or bridges or water mains are there to stay for many decades.

Accessibility is the most important determinant of land value. Retailers want to locate where they are accessible to the maximum number of potential customers and also where they will be seen by the maximum number of potential customers. The builders of office buildings want to place the buildings where they are most accessible to potential employees and visitors. Manufacturers want easy access for workers and suppliers, and easy access to customers. The most accessible sites will thus command the highest prices.

And builders, seeking to make the most efficient use of an expensive resource (land), will develop most intensely on the most expensive land. Thus public expenditures on roads and highways, as well as other investments that determine accessibility, have a powerful effect on the pattern of land development. In a densely developed urban area, investment in mass transportation is a powerful shaper of land values and hence the pattern of development. In a place such as Washington, D. C., where the metro system is an important part of the total transportation picture, the building of a new stop may create hundreds of millions in land values. In a congested area the building of a parking structure may have a powerful effect on land values and the amount of development by rendering that location more accessible.

Public investment in water and sewer lines is another major shaper of the pattern of development. Without public water and sewer service, residential development is generally limited to single-family houses on fairly large lots. Commercial development is also comparably restrained. Thus the extension of water and sewer lines can produce great changes in the intensity of development.

Public investment in facilities such as schools and universities, airports, and harbor facilities can also be major shapers of the land-use pattern. Public acquisition of parkland can also shape the land-use pattern, because by permanently rendering some land undevelopable, it channels the flow of development.

Financing Capital Expenditures

In contrast to the ordinary operating expenses of government, such as paying the salaries of municipal workers, capital expenditures generally are not financed out of current revenues. Capital expenditures are often quite large, and they are "lumpy," that is, they come along in an irregular manner. Then, too, since a capital expenditure delivers its benefits for many years or decades, paying for it all up front would be asking present taxpayers to pay for an item from which they might not derive more than a small share of the benefits.[1] For these reasons, most capital expenditures are paid for with the proceeds of bonds, and then the bonds are amortized (paid off) over a period of many years.

A bond is basically a promise to make repayments to the buyer on a regular, prearranged basis. Generally, interest payments are made once or twice a year, and the principal is repaid on the bond's maturity date. Between the time that a bond is issued and its maturity date, the bond's market value will vary, but the periodic interest payments (dividends) and the final payment at maturity are fixed from the beginning.[2]

Most local governments maintain a separate capital budget and capital improvements plan (CIP). In fact, in many states, local governments are required to maintain a capital improvements plan, often with a time horizon of five years or so.[3] The CIP lays out the expected sequence of investments and thus gives the municipal government a rough schedule of when and in what amounts it will have to issue bonds and also a rough indicator of how much it will have to spend on debt service (payments of interest and principal) each year. Adopting the capital budget is the prerogative of the municipality's legislative body. Generally, the budget that the legislature passes, with or without modification, is proposed by the municipality's executive branch. Because capital expenditures have such a powerful effect on how the municipality develops, it is very important for the planning agency to have a hand in the preparation of the capital budget and the CIP.

Two main types of bonds are issued to finance public capital invest-ment. For a task such as financing a new municipal building, the most common practice is to issue a general obligation (GO) bond. Such a bond is guaranteed by the "full faith and credit" of the municipal government, meaning that if the municipal government fails to make interest or princi-pal payments on time, a court may require the municipal government to use any resources that it has to repay the bondholders. Because such bonds are a direct obligation on the municipal government, they are issued under strict limits. In many states, a municipality's total outstanding general obligation debt may not exceed a certain percentage of its property tax base.[4] For example, in Virginia, state law limits a municipality's outstand-ing general obligation debt to 10 percent of its real property tax base. A referendum is required in a number of states before local or state govern-ment can issue general obligation bonds. Municipal governments are also prohibited from using bonds to pay for operating expenses because the temptation to shift the burden of present operations to future taxpayers would be a very strong one. Most of these restrictions date from the late nineteenth century when there were numerous defaults on state and local government debt stemming from reckless borrowing. Defaults on general obligation debt are now extremely rare.

If the capital expenditure in question can be expected to deliver a reasonably predictable stream of revenue, then it can be financed with a revenue bond. These bonds are generally not obligations of the municipal or state government. Rather, they are backed by a claim on the revenues that the facility is expected to generate. Thus toll roads, parking structures, water and sewage treatment plants, airports, stadiums, and other such revenue-generating facilities can be financed by these bonds. Facilities that do not generate revenues directly cannot be financed with revenue bonds. Given a choice, municipal governments will usually prefer revenue bonds because such bonds are not an obligation of government and therefore are not subject to debt limits and do not require referenda. What they generally do require is the opinion of a bond-rating agency such as Standard and Poor or Moody's that there will be adequate revenues to pay off the bonds. Otherwise, the bonds will not be marketable.

Bonds may be paid off under many different schedules. The most common repayment system is to issue the bonds as annuity serials; that is, the issue is structured so that each year a certain percentage of the bonds is paid off. For example, assume that a new municipal building is constructed with general obligation bonds that are to be paid off over 30 years. Under the annuity serial arrangement, 3.33 percent of the bonds would mature each year. Thus the principal part of the debt service would be constant from one year to the next. The interest part of the debt service would decline each year, since each year there would be fewer bonds outstanding upon which interest was due. The advantage of the annuity series system is that it is easy to calculate and easy to budget for. The fact that the total debt service for the issue is highest at the beginning and then systematically declines may make it a bit safer and discourage casual or excessive use of the borrowing power.[5]

LAND-USE CONTROLS

Although land-use controls are not quite so powerful a shaper of land use as is public capital investment, they are still extremely important. Their development and implementation constitute a major share of the work effort of most planning agencies. In the minds of many citizens, land-use controls are almost synonymous with planning.

In this section we discuss subdivision controls, zoning, and several miscellaneous types of land-use controls.

Subdivision Regulations

Subdivision regulations are an old form of land-use control going back to the early nineteenth century and before.[6] Their enforcement is an exercise by the municipality of the police power within the framework of the powers granted it by the state.[7] Subdivision regulations control the manner in which blocks of land over a certain size may be converted into building lots. Before building lots can be sold or the owner can make improvements, the municipality must approve a plat (map) of the property. The ordinance will require at a minimum that the map show streets, lot lines, and easements (rights of way) for utilities. It also will stipulate what improvements must be made before building lots can be sold or before building permits may be granted. Thus the community is able to compel the property owner to construct internal streets that link up in a satisfactory manner to the municipality's street system and meet its standards for width, safety, and quality of construction. Similarly, it can compel the developer of the property to provide sewer, water, and drainage facilities that meet the community's standards. Subdivision requirements frequently also stipulate that certain land dedications (or payments in lieu of such dedications) be made to the community by the developer for schools, recreation, or community facilities. Many subdivision regulations require that the design of the subdivision be compatible with the municipal master plan and zoning ordinance, thus reinforcing the implementation of these documents. In general, subdivision regulations apply to residential development, but in some communities they also govern some commercial and industrial subdivisions.

Though less well-known than zoning laws, subdivision regulations give communities substantial power to ensure that new residential development meets community standards and fits in with community development plans. Like zoning laws, subdivision regulations are subject to litigation and various forms of political pressure. Like the power to zone, the power to regulate subdivision can be abused. For example, some communities seeking to screen out less affluent people or less expensive housing that will carry a lower assessment and therefore pay less in property taxes have enacted subdivision regulations that impose unnecessarily high costs on builders, thus blocking the construction of moderately priced housing.

Zoning Ordinances

The best-known form of land-use control is the zoning ordinance.[8] This is generally prepared by the community's planners or planning consultant. The document acquires its legal force when the community's legislative body passes a measure adopting it. Generally speaking, there are two parts to the zoning ordinance. The first part is a map that divides the community into a number of zones. The map is sufficiently detailed so that it is possible to tell in which zone(s) any given parcel of land lies. Most commonly, all of the community is zoned. However, there are some cases, particularly nonurban counties, in which part of a community is zoned and part is not. The second part is the text, which specifies in considerable detail what may be constructed in each zone and to what uses structures may be put. The box on pages 000–000 shows some of the details for one zoning classification in Fairfax County, Virginia.

Among the items generally specified by the ordinance are the following:

1. *Site layout requirements.* These may include, among other things, minimum lot area, frontage and depth, minimum setbacks (minimum distance from structure to front, side, or rear lot line), maximum percentage of site that may be covered by structure, placement of driveways or curb cuts, parking requirements, screening requirements, and limits on the size or placement of signs.

2. *Requirements for structure characteristics.* These may include maximum height of structure, maximum number of stories, and maximum floor area of structure. The last is often cast in terms of floor area ratio (FAR), which indicates a maximum permissible ratio of floor area to site area.

3. *Uses to which structures may be put.* In a residential zone the ordinance might specify that dwellings may be occupied only by single families and then proceed to define what constitutes a family. The ordinance might also enumerate certain nonresidential uses permitted in the zone such as churches, funeral homes, and professional offices. In commercial zones the ordinance will generally specify which uses are permitted and which are not. For example, in a manufacturing zone the ordinance might specify that sheet metal fabrication operations are permitted but that rendering operations are forbidden.

4. *Procedural matters.* The ordinance will specify how it is to be determined whether building plans are in conformity to the zoning ordinance. (A common arrangement is that the building inspector shall make such determination and must deny a building permit application if they are not.) The ordinance will generally also specify an appeals procedure by which an applicant can apply for relief. In many communities the initial appeal authority is vested in a special body generally referred to as the Zoning Board of Appeals. If not, the review process is often assigned to the planning board or to the municipal legislative body.

The Popularity of Zoning. Zoning has been, since shortly after its inception, by far the most common means by which communities have sought to control land use. What accounts for its popularity? The answer is quite simple. It has considerable power to achieve goals that the community favors, and it is almost free. Unless a "taking" has occurred (see Chapter 5), no compensation need be paid to property owners for reductions in property values caused by limitations imposed by the zoning ordinance on the type or intensity of use permitted. The only costs to the municipality are administrative and legal expenses.

In principle, the same effects could be achieved by exercise of the power of eminent domain or by contract between municipality and property owner. But either of those courses would necessitate major expenditures by the municipality.

In fact, contracts between governments and property owners have been used to affect land use. Generally, the contract is referred to as an easement. This is an agreement by the property owner to forgo some right(s), for example, that of subdividing the property or developing it in some way, in return for a payment. For example, Suffolk County, New York, has made widespread use of easement purchases to maintain land on eastern Long Island in agricultural use. Such a device can be highly effective, for the purchase of an easement provides an ironclad guarantee to the community in the form of an enforceable contract that property will not be used in a manner proscribed by the easement. In other

THE INGREDIENTS OF A ZONING ORDINANCE

This material is reproduced from a Fairfax County, Virginia, zoning ordinance. Note that it specifies permitted uses, site geometry, ground coverage, and building height and bulk.

Commercial District Regulations
Part 5 4-500 C-5 Neighborhood Retail Commercial District

4–501 Purpose and Intent The C-5 District is established to provide locations for convenience shopping facilities in which those retail commercial uses shall predominate that have a neighborhood-oriented market of approximately 5000 persons, and which supply necessities that usually require frequent purchasing and with a minimum of consumer travel. Typical uses to be found in the Neighborhood Retail Commercial District include a food supermarket, drugstore, personal service establishments, small specialty shops, and a limited number of small professional offices.

Areas zoned for the C-5 District should be located so that their distributional pattern throughout the County reflects their neighborhood orientation. They should be designed to be an integral, homogeneous component of the neighborhoods they serve, oriented to pedestrian traffic as well as vehicular. The district should not be located in close proximity to other retail commercial uses.

Because of the nature and location of the Neighborhood Retail Commercial District, they should be encouraged to develop in compact centers under a unified design that is architecturally compatible with the neighborhood in which they are located. Further, such districts should not be so large or broad in scope of services as to attract substantial trade from outside the neighborhood. Generally, the ultimate size of a C-5 District in a given location in the County should not exceed an aggregate gross floor area of 100,000 square feet or an aggregate site size of (10) acres.

4–502 Permitted Uses

1. Accessory uses as permitted by Article 10.
2. Business service and supply service establishments.
3. Churches, chapels, temples, synagogues and other such places of worship.
4. Drive-in banks, limited by the provisions of Sect. 505 below.
5. Eating establishments.
6. Fast food restaurants, limited by the provisions of Sect. 505 below.

7. Financial institutions.
8. Offices.
9. Personal service establishments.
10. Private schools of general education, private schools of special education.
11. Public uses.
12. Quick-service food stores, limited by the provisions of Sect. 505 below.
13. Repair service establishments.
14. Retail sales establishments.
15. Telecommunication exchanges.

4–506 Lot Size Requirements

1. Minimum lot area: 40,000 sq. ft.
2. Minimum lot width: 200 feet
3. The minimum lot size requirements may be waived by the Board in accordance with provisions of Sect. 9–610.

4–507 Bulk Regulations

1. Maximum building height: 40 feet
2. Minimum yard requirements
   A. Front yard: Controlled by a 45° angle of bulk plane, but not less than 40 feet
   B. Side yard: No Requirement
   C. Rear yard: 20 feet
3. Maximum floor area ratio: 0.50
4. Refer to Sect. 13–108 for provisions that may qualify the minimum yard requirements set forth above.

4–508 Open Space 20% of the gross area shall be landscaped open space

4–509 Additional Regulations

1. Refer to Article 2, General Regulations, for provisions which may qualify or supplement the regulations presented above.
2. Refer to Article 11 for off-street parking, loading and private street requirements.
3. Refer to Article 12 for regulations on signs.
4. Refer to Article 13 for landscaping and screening requirements.

places a similar effect has been obtained through special tax treatment. Where farmland preservation is a goal, land that is kept in agricultural use is taxed very lightly compared with the tax that must be paid on it when it is placed in some other use.

Easements and special tax treatment are used in most states, but, unlike zoning, their application is quite spotty. The explanation for this difference is cost.

The Effectiveness of Zoning. How effective is zoning in shaping land use? There is tremendous variation among communities, ranging from almost totally ineffectual to highly effective. Zoning may be quite effective in a growing area where the land-use pattern is not yet fully determined. Here zoning can shape the urban pattern by blocking or limiting growth in some areas and thus, in effect, diverting it to other areas. Often in prosperous developed areas in which there is substantial pressure for change in land use, zoning may be effective in preventing or moderating that change. For example, a prosperous inner suburb might successfully resist the transformation of single-family neighborhoods to multifamily neighborhoods even though the economics of the local housing market favor such a change.

On the other hand, zoning may be relatively ineffective in older urban areas where the land-use pattern is essentially established and where growth forces are not very powerful. Zoning, by itself, cannot address the redevelopment problem, for controls cannot compel anyone to invest in an area. Zoning may also be relatively weak if the community is so eager for investment that it readily adjusts its zoning to suit developers' preferences. Zoning may be weak or absent, in semirural or rural areas where the residents do not see much need for it.

One key to effective zoning is synchronization between land-use controls and public capital investment. It is possible for a community's land-use and capital investment policies to be at odds with one another and for each to undermine and frustrate the intent of the other. For example, a capital investment program might generate forces for a type or intensity of development that is proscribed by the zoning. In this case either the capital investment has been partly wasted, or economic pressures will force changes in the zoning. Conversely, if the zoning permits levels of development that are not supported by necessary road and utility investment, nothing is likely to happen. The community will have the pleasure of watching its industrial or office zone grow weeds year after year.

The Limitations of Zoning. Zoning is limited by both economic and legal forces. If the value of land in a use permitted by zoning is very much lower than the value of that land in a use that is forbidden but for which a market exists, property owners have strong motivation to try to change the zoning. They may expend substantial funds on litigation, or they may devote substantial effort to building a coalition of forces to lobby for zoning change. If the community is hungry for jobs and additions to its tax base, potential investors may indicate to the community that if it does not show flexibility, their capital will be invested in some other community, one that can recognize a good thing when it sees it.

To illustrate, consider a prototypical suburban scenario. Mr. X owns 100 acres of vacant land, which has been in his family for generations. He rents the land to a local farmer for enough money to cover his property taxes. The land in its present low-density residential zoning category has a market value of $10,000 per acre. A major real estate developer perceives that were development of condominiums at medium density possible, the land would be worth $50,000 an acre. She approaches Mr. X and offers to buy an option. Specifically, for $10,000 Mr. X gives the developer the right to buy the property for $12,000 an acre at any time during the next two years. If the developer chooses not to exercise her option, Mr. X still keeps the $10,000.

Having purchased the option, the developer now tries to change the zoning. If her attorney tells her that the municipality's zoning of the property is on weak legal ground, she may approach the municipality, indicate to it why its position is weak, and suggest that compromise is in everyone's best interest. The municipality's legal position may be weak for any number of reasons. Comparable parcels in other areas of the municipality may be zoned for more intensive development. Hence a charge of inconsistency (of treating equals unequally) may be leveled against the municipality in court. Perhaps the zoning of the property is not in keeping with the municipality's master plan. If so, the developer can argue that the zoning is capricious and inconsistent. Perhaps the developer can show that on the basis of utilities, access, and other considerations, the property could sustain far more development than the zoning permits. In this case she can argue that the present zoning cannot be justified on the grounds of the police power.

Hearing all this and after due consultation with their planning consultant and attorney, the municipal officials might well decide that compromise is indeed in order. In that case they may recommend to the municipality's legislative body that it amend the zoning ordinance. If the community is adamant and the developer is sure the legal situation favors her, she might bring suit and begin to fight it out in court. The issue might be settled in court or, seeing the tide of legal battle flowing against it, the municipality might decide to compromise.

Alternatively, the developer can take a less confrontational tack. She can engage a local planning consultant to design a condominium development for the site. The consultant comes up with a proposal nicely presented with attractive drawings and a model. Then the consultant performs a set of calculations referred to as a "fiscal impact analysis," which shows that for every additional dollar the project will cost the community for services, its property taxes and other contributions to the municipal treasury will amount to two dollars. (See box on property taxes on page 148–49.) The developer's proposal does not fail to note how many dollars of retail sales within the community will be made to condominium residents, a point that will not be lost on the municipality's business community. The report will also note how many years of on-site construction labor the project will require, a point that should bring in a few more allies, particularly if construction employment has been soft recently.

At this point the report is presented to the town government with appropriate newspaper and other publicity. When public hearings are held, the developer or her spokespeople adopt a posture of reasonableness and conciliation. If there are aspects of the plan to which the citizens object, they will listen attentively and endeavor to find mutually satisfactory compromises. For example, if residents worry that the development will send too many children to the local schools, she may offer to build more studio and one-bedroom units and fewer two- and three-bedroom units, thus bringing in more childless couples and fewer large families. The relationship between unit size, household size, and number of school-age children has been studied often and can be predicted fairly well. Thus this sort of "architectural birth control" can often be practiced quite effectively.[9]

The developer will also structure the proposal to give herself room to be reasonable. If she would have been satisfied with building six units to the acre, the initial plan may call for eight units to the acre. This strategy leaves her something that can be given up after suitable protest but without causing her real pain.

The developer may or may not obtain a zoning change in this manner. Any planner who has spent some time working in the suburbs has seen such situations go both ways. The point, however, is that the party desiring the zoning change has numerous avenues open.

Note that if the developer is successful in obtaining the rezoning, she has, in effect, made a very large sum of money before construction begins. She has obtained land worth $50,000 an acre for a price of $12,000 an acre plus the cost of the option. In fact, were she to forget about the project and simply to sell the rezoned land to another developer, she would have made a very large profit.[10]

Because of the large sums of money at stake in some land-use decisions, the practice of zoning is not immune from bribery and corruption. An FBI sting operation in Fresno, California resulted in eight convictions, with the longest sentence being 30 months, in connection with exchange of bribes and campaign contributions for favorable zoning decisions.[11]

The playing of zoning games is hardly limited to those on the private side of the fence. Municipalities often zone substantial amounts of land in economically unrealistic categories. This practice suits the municipal interest quite well, for it gives the municipality a bargaining position that it would not have were the land zoned realistically in the first instance.

In the late 1970s the town of Harrison, New York, became the home of Texaco's corporate headquarters. The headquarters imposes few costs on the town yet provides a substantial property tax payment, clearly a very desirable situation from the town's perspective. How did this arrangement happen? The site was one hundred acres or so of land zoned for single-family houses on two-acre lots. As it happened, the site was in a developing commercial area and was close to the intersection of two interstate highways. It clearly had potential for much more valuable use than low-density single-family housing. The fact that a zoning change was needed for economically realistic development put the town in a strong negotiating

PROPERTY TAXES AND ZONING

Zoning cannot be fully understood without some understanding of property taxes. Property tax collection by local governments and school districts now exceed $200 billion and account for approximately three-fourths of all local tax collections. Given the size of that number, few significant zoning decisions are made without considering the property tax implications. Here, very briefly, is how property taxes are levied. The municipality maintains a ledger (either on paper or electronically), referred to as the property tax roll. Each property in the municipality appears on this roll. Generally speaking, the roll will have one column for "land" and another column for "improvements," the latter essentially meaning structures. In each column is recorded the assessed value of the land or structure. The value, determined by the municipality's assessor, presents his or her estimate of what the property would bring if sold in an "arm's length" transaction.[12] Some municipalities have "full value assessment." Others use "fractional assessment." Where fractional assessment is used, all properties should be assessed at the same fraction of market value.[13] The municipality and other taxing jurisdictions each have a property tax rate that is applied to the assessed value of the property to determine how much tax is owed. For example, if the tax rate is $2.50 per 100 of assessed value and the property is assessed at $50,000 the tax owed is $50,000 × 2.50/100 = 1,250.

For the municipality as a whole, the equation is tax base × tax rate = tax yield. Tax base in this equation is the sum of all of the assessed values on land and improvements subject to tax.[14]

If a given development will bring in more in taxes than it will cost in additional municipal expenses, either (1) the same level of municipal services can be maintained for a lower tax rate or (2) a higher level of services can be maintained at the same tax rate. If the costs of servicing the new development exceed the tax revenues that it will yield at the current tax rate, those relationships are reversed.

Though this discussion is cast in terms of a municipal tax rate, there may actually be several property taxes within a given community. For example, properties in a town located within a county and having an independent school district may be subject to a town tax, a county tax, and a school tax. In some suburban areas, where the structure and responsibilities of government are not as large as in a city and where a large percentage of all households have school-age children, the school tax constitutes the majority share of the total tax burden.

The property tax has been subject to a barrage of criticisms over the years. However, it remains in universal use. For one thing it is easy to administer and enforce. The assessor assesses, and the Receiver of Taxes sends the bill. If the property owner fails to pay the bill, the municipality can foreclose the property and sell it at auction to recover the back taxes. It is probably the hardest tax to evade. The individual or business may be able to conceal some income, but no one has yet figured out how to hide a house or a factory.

The physical immobility of land and structures is also an important reason why local governments place major reliance on the property tax relative to other taxes. Where jurisdictions are small, the heavy use of income, sales, or business taxes can readily chase economic activity and wealthy residents out of town. Thus the property tax is the safest tax, perhaps the only tax, upon which a local government can place very much weight.

---

position. First, the town was able to turn away any development proposal it did not like. In addition, the need for a rezoning gave the town the power to insist on site features, like below-ground parking and deep setbacks, which the corporation might not otherwise have chosen to provide.

Similar comments might be made with regard to residential development. If a rezoning is necessary to permit the building of multifamily housing, the municipality might say no to a low-income housing proposal but yes to a structurally similar development intended for affluent singles—a form of discrimination that few if any courts would sustain were it written into the zoning ordinance.

Zoning and the Courts. As noted in earlier chapters, zoning and other land-use controls all involve some abridgement of the rights of ownership. Specifically, they limit the intensity or the manner in which real property may be used. Over the years the courts have expanded the amount of abridgement that they will tolerate. But the boundary between what is and is not permissible is somewhat ambiguous and may vary from place to place and court to court, leaving much room for controversy and litigation.

At one time it could have been said that the question was one of adjudicating the rights of the property owner versus the rights of nearby property owners and of the community. That is still a major part of the matter, but in the last three decades or so, another major element has been introduced.

The new element is consideration of the rights and interests of those who are neither members of the community nor owners of property in it. Admitting that outsiders have a valid interest in the community's land-use controls gives them standing to bring suit, a standing that formerly they did not have. The inclusion of these formerly outside parties can be considered a part of the national concern with civil rights that has characterized the last few decades.

Numerous suits have been brought against suburban communities for zoning land in an overly restrictive way, many, for example, by restricting development to single-family houses on large lots. Such controls may make it almost impossible for low-income people to live in the community. Opponents of suburban zoning often claimed that policies that kept out lower-income persons also constituted racial discrimination. The argument was that since blacks have, on average, significantly lower family income than whites, keeping out low- and moderate-income families had the de facto effect of excluding blacks. A number of suits against suburban communities have been brought by minority group organizations for this reason.

The courts have also recognized as a legitimate concern the question of regional housing needs. The argument, very generally, is that if the municipality is part of a metropolitan region, it is part of the regional housing market. If the municipality limits the amount of housing that may be built within its borders, it tightens housing markets and drives up housing costs within the entire region. The courts have thus overturned some suburban zoning ordinances on the grounds of regional housing needs.

For example, in 1965 the Supreme Court of Pennsylvania overturned an ordinance that established a four-acre minimum lot size requirement, stating,

> It is not difficult to envision the tremendous hardship, as well as chaotic conditions, which could result if all the townships in this area decided to deny to a growing population sites for residential development within the means of at least a significant segment of the population.[15]

In 1975 in the best known of the exclusionary cases, *Southern Burlington County NAACP* v. *Township of Mount Laurel* (generally referred to simply as *Mt. Laurel*), the Supreme Court of New Jersey found that the entirety of the township zoning ordinance acted to exclude whole classes of individuals (including the poor and minorities) and was invalid under the New Jersey state constitution. The township was instructed to prepare a new ordinance that remedied these defects.

In 1983 a group of cases, collectively referred to as *Mount Laurel II*, pushed the judicial interpretation of a community's areawide obligations even further.[16] Among the points made in the decision were that all municipalities have an obligation to provide housing opportunities for their low- and moderate-income residents, that any municipality that permits economic growth must create opportunities for provision for some portion of the region's low- and moderate-income housing needs, and that municipalities must take steps to make certain that said housing opportunities are realistic.

The court noted certain concrete steps that municipalities could take to bring themselves into conformance with the court's findings. One of these was the removal of all present legal barriers to the building of low- and moderate-income housing. This could be interpreted to mean that any land-use control regulation that increases costs but cannot be shown to be essential to maintenance of the public health, safety, and welfare would not be sustainable. Thus regulations involving matters of minimum street width in subdivisions, buffering from adjacent land uses, and the like might be struck down. So might exactions, discussed later in this chapter. Tax abatement for low- and moderate-income housing, inclusionary zoning devices, and set-asides might also be required to bring a community into conformance with *Mt. Laurel II.* The term *set-aside* means that the law would require that in housing developments over some specified size, a given percentage of units be set aside for low- and moderate-income renters or purchasers. Conservatives might argue that this provision translates into saying that such purchasers would be subsidized by either the developer or the buyers of the units not set aside. They might argue that such subsidization should be done explicitly by the taxpayers as a whole rather than implicitly by the developer or by other buyers. Nonetheless, that was the position the court took.

Finally, the decision discussed the possibility that large blocks of land might have to be zoned for low-cost housing types such as mobile homes. (Mobile homes are anathema to many affluent communities both because they are considered to represent a lower standard of housing than conventional units and they carry low assessments and thus pay less property tax.)

After the *Mt. Laurel* decisions, it appeared that the exclusionary walls would be breached in many New Jersey suburbs. One hundred and thirty-five suits, most of them by developers, were brought against suburban communities. Many of these suits were close to settlement when a series of events leading to what has been termed *Mt. Laurel III* occurred.

In 1985, responding to pressures from suburban towns that were facing legal challenges based on *Mt. Laurel II,* the New Jersey legislature passed the Fair Housing Act. The act established a Council on Affordable Housing. Towns could submit to the council plans for supplying their fair share of low-cost housing. When the plan was accepted by the council, the town would then be protected from Mt. Laurel–type lawsuits.

In 1986 a builder challenged the constitutionality of the Fair Housing Act, for as noted, the act prevented builders and others from suing a community once the community's plans had been accepted by the council. In *Hills Development Co.* v. *Township of Bernards (Mt. Laurel III),* the Supreme Court of New Jersey rejected the developer's claim and held the law to be constitutional. Under the system low and moderate housing quotas are worked out for communities by the Council. The municipality must then facilitate the building of that number of units. All of the units may be within its own borders, or up to half of the units may be within another community.[17]

To satisfy part of the requirement by units built outside its borders, the community must sign an agreement with another community and pay a Regional Contribution Agreement (RCA) charge of $20,000 per unit to that community. For example, Mt. Laurel was assigned a figure of 839 units. As of mid-1998, 178 low- and moderate-income units had been built in Mt. Laurel. The town was planning to meet the rest of the quota partly through the building of additional units within Mt. Laurel and partly through RCA agreements with another municipality in the same county (Burlington).

What is one to think of the *Mt. Laurel* cases and their ultimate resolution? Low- and moderate-income housing is being built in many municipalities that would not have permitted it without the *Mt. Laurel* litigation. In that sense, from the plaintiff's perspective, the litigation was ultimately a success. But the process has been a slow one. The litigation began in 1975, and it took two decades to bear fruit. The RCA agreements have been the subject of some argument. If you believe that the prime goal of the program should be to achieve economic and social integration, then you may be dissatisfied with the RCA concept, for it voids that goal to some degree. However, if you believe that the prime concern is to get low- and moderate-income housing built somewhere in the state, then the RCA agreements look perfectly acceptable. Municipalities that want funds for low- and moderate-cost housing get those funds, and communities that do not want such housing are able to minimize the amount that they must take.

As the two-decade-long Mt. Laurel story indicates, the limits of the zoning power vary from time to time. The exact line between the rights of property owners, on the one hand, and the right of the public, through government, to regulate the use of private property and to impose uncompensated losses upon property owners, on the other hand, is where the courts say it is. For several of the key cases in the last decade or so, see the box on pages 00–00 in Chapter 5.

Recent Developments in Zoning

Zoning, is a crude instrument. It prescribes what cannot be done, but it cannot make anything happen. Its very rigidity may lead to less than optimal results. For example, assume a zoning district permits a certain amount of development on a given sized lot within a given zone. If some lots are developed to the full amount permitted but other lots remain vacant or are developed to only part of the permitted intensity of use, the district may function quite well. On the other hand, if every lot is developed to full intensity, the congestion, traffic, and noise may be overwhelming. Yet a municipality can hardly tell a property owner not to develop as much as the owner of an adjacent plot simply because the other property owner was first. Such a position would carry little weight in court.

"Zoning saturation" studies have frequently shown that if a municipality were developed to the full extent that the zoning allowed, its population would be several times the present level. The population of New York City, the most densely developed city in the United States, has ranged from 7 to 8 million in recent decades. Some time ago a saturation study showed that if built up to the full extent the law allowed, the city could have a population of some 30 million. A saturation study of Yonkers, New York, with a population of about 200,000 on 20 square miles, showed that the city could, if fully developed as the law permitted, have a population of about 600,000. This would make it the most densely populated city in the United States. In neither case is there any chance of such development occurring.

The disparity between actual and theoretical development does raise questions about the precision of zoning. Clearly, zoning is not determining of the structure of the city in fine detail if there is that much space between the overcoat of zoning and the body of development.

Zoning is vulnerable to the criticism that it severely limits the freedom of the architect and site designer and may thus lower the quality of urban design. Rules promulgated to cover the substantial blocks of land are likely to be suboptimal with regard to particular sites or parcels.

Zoning has also been criticized for producing a sterile environment through an excessive separation of uses. The most influential criticism of this sort was delivered in the 1960s by Jane Jacobs.[18] She argued that by excessive separation of uses—residents here, stores there, and so on—planners produced urban environments that were sterile and sometimes dangerous as well. They were sterile because of lack of diversity, she argued, and dangerous because the single-use street was deserted for some part of the day and thus was an inducement to crime.

One area of which Jacobs spoke very highly is Manhattan's Greenwich Village. The West Village is an old area, characterized by small and frequently irregularly shaped blocks and a great mix of uses. Most buildings are not very high, typically four to six stories. The same block will often contain a fine-grained mix of residential and nonresidential uses. In fact, many buildings have stores, restaurants, coffeehouses, and the like on the ground level with apartments above. The area has a lively street life, which lasts into the late hours of the night, and it is generally considered a desirable neighborhood in which to live. Jacobs argued that the sort of diversity, charm, and activity that characterize the West Village is often blocked by the rigidities of zoning and the planners' excessive concern with separation of uses. She argued that the area owed much of its charm to the fact that it had developed before the advent of zoning (zoning is not retroactive). Though Jacobs is not a planner herself, her's criticism made many planners rethink the intent and effects of zoning on neighborhoods. In fact, Jacobs's criticisms of zoning, which were radical in the 1960s, are now part of the standard wisdom of planning. Her ideas about the desirability of a fine-grained mixture of uses are central to the *new urbanism* discussed in Chapter 10.

In April 1996 the *New York Times* reported a case in which areas of New York thrived only because they were able to escape the rigidities of the city's

The two Greenwich Village streets shown here, though photographed in 2004, are very much as they were at the time that Jane Jacobs wrote. In the top photo, there are an off-Broadway theater on the left and a restaurant on the right with a small apartment house in between and apartments over both commercial uses. Access is overwhelmingly pedestrian, for the street that serves the neighborhood is narrower than would be permitted in even the smallest modern suburban subdivision. In the lower photo, note the mix of structure types and the stores under the apartments.

zoning law, partly because budget problems restricted the number of building inspectors available to enforce the rules. In the 1970s, alarmed at its rapid loss of manufacturing jobs, New York City limited the use of many thousands of acres so as to permit almost nothing but manufacturing. These acres included many blocks, particularly in lower Manhattan, of old manufacturing loft buildings that could no longer compete as locations for manufacturing. However, these buildings had another potential. The *New York Times* noted the following:

> The lofts and warehouses of SoHo and Tribeca, where rents were cheap and huge open [internal] spaces were available, proved to be ideal for the hip hybridization of computer technology, art and residence that the city now crows triumphantly about as Silicon Alley.
>   This transformation was possible only because the zoning regulations were not enforced.[19]

Making Zoning Flexible. In an effort to make zoning a finer instrument, a variety of techniques have evolved in recent years. These, in general, are designed to make land-use controls more flexible and more negotiable. The basic idea is that increasing flexibility allows the parties of land-use negotiations to bargain and thus realize what economists refer to as "the gains of trade."

Let us say that the land developer would like to do something that is prohibited under the letter of the zoning law. On the other hand, the municipality might like the developer to do something that he or she is not legally required to do. Why not have an ordinance so structured that some bargaining is possible? Presumably we need not fear that the municipality will lose out. If, on balance, the trade is not in the municipal interest, the muni" "cipality will not consent. A number of newer techniques follow.

"BONUS" OR "INCENTIVE" ZONING. Many communities will allow increased residential densities if developers will include some units earmarked for low- and moderate-income tenants. For example, the law might stipulate eight units to the acre in a particular zone but permit an increase to ten units if 15 percent of the units are reserved for low- and moderate-income tenants. The developer gets the scale economies of denser development, and the community moves a bit closer to meeting its low- and moderate-income housing goals.

Many cities have made comparable arrangements with regard to office development. The zoning ordinance might stipulate a certain height limitation but permit additional height or stories if the developer will provide certain amenities at ground level—for example, a plaza in front of the entrance to the building, a direct entrance to a subway station, or a "vest-pocket" park or sitting area.

TRANSFER OF DEVELOPMENT RIGHTS. The intent of transfer of development rights (TDR) is to concentrate development in areas where it is wanted and to restrict it in areas where it is not. To do so, a sending and a receiving area are designated. Property owners in the sending areas who do not develop

A glass-roofed arcade connects two parallel streets at AT&T headquarters building in Manhattan. Some willingness to deviate from the rigidities of traditional Euclidean zoning is usually necessary to achieve an interesting and unusual result like this.

their properties to the full extent permitted by the law may sell their unused rights to property owners in receiving areas. The technique might be used to preserve open space, to limit development in an ecologically fragile area, or to achieve historic preservation goals, among others.[20]

One might ask, "Can this not be done with conventional zoning simply by permitting high densities in some areas and low densities in other areas?" In a literal sense, the answer is yes. However, in a practical sense, the answer may be no. Assume that the intent of the community master plan is to keep development very sparse in a particular area. If the community simply zones that way, say a minimum lot size of ten acres for a single-family house, it may have imposed large losses on property owners. Even if it can win in court, the municipality has created a constituency opposed to the plan. On the other hand, if it gives the property owners salable development rights, both their motivation and grounds for suit are eliminated. If the municipality wishes to preserve old buildings in a historic zone, one way to do it is to let the property owners there have salable development rights. When they sell their development rights to property owners in an area where the municipality wants growth (the receiving area), they will no longer want to tear down their old buildings, for having sold their rights, they can no longer redevelop at higher densities.

Won't the property owners in receiving areas object to, in effect, having to buy off owners in sending areas? Not necessarily, for if purchasing development rights is not profitable, receiving area property owners will not purchase them. Presumably a market in development rights will develop, the price moving to a position high enough to motivate owners in the sending area to sell yet low enough to make purchase profitable for property owners in the receiving area.

For the municipality, the technique, like zoning itself, is essentially costless. The payments to some property owners come not from the municipality's taxpayers but from other property owners. Whether the municipality's taxpayers may ultimately pick up some of those costs in the form of higher rents and higher prices is another issue.

The technique is relatively new and a matter of some controversy. One way in which it could be misused would be if development rights were to be assigned to areas where the actual possibility of development is small. If one gives the owner of a property in "bottomless swamp" or "rocky promontory" a development right, it is just a windfall, since he or she could not realistically expect to develop anyway. But a developer in an area of high land values may still be willing to buy that right. The possibilities for abuse seem to be considerable. On the other hand, the technique can be very useful as the box on page 00 indicates.

THE HIGH LINE AND TDR

One unusual and important project in which TDR played a key role is in the construction of New York City's High Line, a 1½-mile-long elevated linear park in Manhattan.[21]

The story begins in the mid-1930s. At that time an elevated railroad line, approximately 30 feet above ground level, running midblock between 10th and 11th Avenues in Manhattan, was completed. The line went between buildings, sometimes over one-story buildings, and in a few cases, through buildings. It replaced a ground-level rail line and separated steam-powered freight trains from pedestrian and automotive traffic at ground level. Thus in its day it was a major traffic improvement. At the time the Chelsea district through which the High Line ran contained considerable manufacturing and warehousing activity. Slightly to the west, the docks along the Hudson River were in active use for the handling of ocean freight. The line thus served an important commercial purpose.

In time, the economics of the area changed. Manufacturing and warehousing activity declined and the docks on the Hudson lost their shipping business to other ports that had the space to handle containerized freight. The High Line carried less and less freight. In 1980 the line carried its last shipment, three carloads of frozen turkeys.

The question then became what to do with the High Line. For about 20 years it was simply a rusting eyesore that served no purpose, depressed the value of nearby properties, and looked like a prime candidate for demolition. In fact, it was spared from demolition only because of uncertainty over who was responsible for its demolition.

In 1999 a citizens' group called Friends of the High Line formed the idea of getting the High Line converted into an above–street level walking path, or urban linear park. In 2002 the newly elected administration of Mayor Michael Bloomberg endorsed the idea and brought the city's planning department into the process. One key problem was land ownership. For the project to proceed, the city had to become the owner of the land under the High Line. Buying the land or condemning it and paying the condemnation award would be a complex and expensive proposition. The problem was solved through the use of transfer of development rights. The property owners in question were given development rights which they could sell to property owners along 10th and 11th Avenues. The city obtained ownership without direct outlay or the necessity for condemnation. At this time the Manhattan market for both residential and commercial real estate market was strong and so the property owners who received the development rights found a ready market for them. Note that in this case the sending and receiving areas are very close, about half a block, or roughly 100 yards, apart.

Work on the High Line started in 2006 and should be completed before the end of the decade. Funding comes from the city, federal grants, and private sources. The transferred development rights have sparked a building boom on 10th and 11th Avenues. According to the city's Deputy Mayor Dan Doctoroff, speaking at a start of a construction ceremony in April 2006,

> Today the city owns the High Line, 27 major property owners are able to transfer their development rights and we have a complex rezoning that saved the High Line and created the opportunity for 20,000 units of new housing, a quarter of it affordable.[22]

Above, the High Line right of way before work began. Below, an artist's rendering of the southern end of the High Line linear park. Note the sidewalk café seating area underneath and the entrance ramp behind it. The park will extend continuously northward, most of it in a midblock location between 10th and 11th Avenues, for about 1½ miles,

INCLUSIONARY ZONING. In inclusionary zoning, developers who build more than a specified number of units must include a certain percentage for low- and moderate-income households.[23] It differs from the incentive or bonus approach in that the inclusion of low- and moderate-income units is not discretionary. It is the same, however, in that it shifts some of the costs of housing such households to the developer. He or she, in turn, is likely to shift at least some of that cost to the other buyers or renters.

PLANNED UNIT DEVELOPMENT. Planned unit development (PUD) has been widely used in the last several decades and its popularity is still growing. PUD techniques vary, but a prototypical ordinance might work like this: The entire community is zoned in a conventional (Euclidean) manner. However, the law provides that a property owner with a minimum number of acres, say 20, has the option of applying to develop his or her holdings as a PUD. In this case the property is subject to a different set of controls. The density permitted may or may not be the same as that stipulated by the conventional ordinance, and the uses permitted may or may not be the same. The entire site plan will be reviewed as a single entity under a review process specified by the PUD ordinance.

Some PUDs are entirely residential, and some are entirely commercial. In many cases, however, PUDs contain a greater mix of uses than would be permitted under conventional ordinance. Many PUDs that are predominantly residential contain some retailing. Numerous PUDs contain a mix of residential and commercial uses. Because the entire site plan is reviewed at one time, the benefits of mixing uses can often be had without risking some of the disadvantages. For the urban designer, PUDs can offer vastly more room for creative and innovative design than can be had working under a conventional ordinance.

One problem with many business areas, both downtown and suburban, is that they become almost deserted in the evening. Mixing residential uses with commercial uses tends to make the area more active in the evenings and on weekends. The mixed-use concept can make both commercial and residential areas more interesting and less sterile. Essentially, PUD technique places some power to control land use in the hands of a review board or other group, which looks at that particular site design. It allows a degree of innovation and flexibility that cannot be obtained under an ordinance that must fit all cases.

But, like all other techniques, PUD has its disadvantages and its critics. Fort Collins, Colorado, stopped using PUDs in the late 1990s for two reasons. One reason was opposition from adjacent property owners. The property owner who bordered a PUD knew in general what would be in the PUD but didn't know specifically what land use would border his or her own property. That uncertainty made property owners uneasy and created an anti-PUD constituency. Municipal officials were also concerned that the development of a large number of PUDs, even if each were well designed, makes it harder to produce a unified plan for the area as a whole.

CLUSTER ZONING. Cluster zoning is another technique intended to free the site designer from the rigidity of conventional Euclidean zoning while still letting the community retain control of the overall effects of the development. Cluster ordinances, which generally apply to residential development, permit the building of houses on smaller lots, provided that the space thus saved is used for community purposes. For example, the zoning ordinance might specify a minimum lot size of one-half acre, but cluster provisions permit building houses on one-quarter-acre lots provided that the completed development shall have no more houses in it than it could contain if developed with one-half-acre lots. The space saved is to constitute an open area accessible to all residents of the clustered area, often maintained by a residents' association.

Cluster zoning is very popular with planners. It permits the preservation of open space and reduces development costs. Placing houses closer together reduces the amount of road surface and utility line required per house. Smaller lots also mean less money spent per house on grading and other site-preparation costs.

Although clusters have been built in many communities, the cluster plan is often greeted with some public suspicion. The community sees the combination of closely spaced houses and open space blocks, and suspects that sooner or later the open blocks will fill in with housing. In point of fact, the permanency of the open blocks is easily protected with appropriate legal documents at the time the cluster development is approved by the community, but it can be difficult to convince a community that this is the case. With the passage of time and the accumulation of favorable experience, community resistance to clustering is diminishing.

PERFORMANCE ZONING. Performance zoning is relatively new and not yet in widespread use, but its use is growing, and it holds much promise. Performance zoning codes stipulate what may or may not be done in terms of end results instead of giving detailed regulations on the exact form of development. It can be regarded as an attempt to achieve the same goals as conventional zoning but in a more flexible manner.

In Largo, Florida, a conventional or Euclidean system of 20 zoning districts has been replaced by a performance zoning system. Five residential categories differ only by the maximum density permitted. Intensity of use is controlled by limits on floor area ratio (FAR) and the percentage of site that can be under impervious cover. There are no limitations on the type of housing, side-yard and rear-yard setback, and building height.

Four separate commercial zones have been created. The zones are distinguished by their FAR and impervious-cover requirements. For the downtown zone, a FAR of 0.90 and an impervious cover of 100 percent are permitted. On the other hand, for the flood-prone zone, the FAR is limited to 0.12 and impervious cover to 40 percent. There are no height limitations and no side- or rear-yard setback limitations. Gail Easley, the community's assistant director of planning, explains the decision to go to performance zoning in this way:

> One particular problem [with conventional zoning] . . . is the proliferation of zoning districts. As the number of districts grows, it becomes harder to distinguish among them; as the distinctions become less clear, the purpose of any given district becomes blurred, and the formal distinctions become less defensible. An increase in the number of districts results in fewer uses being permitted in any single district. This decreases the likelihood that an available site will be properly zoned to meet a developer's needs. This, in turn, increases the probability that a zoning amendment will be sought.[24]

But not every municipality that has tried performance zoning has been equally pleased with it. Tallahassee, Florida, adopted performance zoning in 1992 but went back to a modified conventional system in 1997. In their view, performance zoning was too cumbersome compared with traditional zoning.[25]

DEVELOPMENT AGREEMENTS. The state of California passed enabling legislation that permits municipal governments to enter into "development agreements." These essentially bypass the existing zoning, though they must be in conformity with the comprehensive plan. The contract between the developer and the municipality specifies what the developer may do and also what he or she is required to do within the project area. The developer benefits by being permitted to do things not permitted under the existing zoning. The developer of a multistage project also gets the security of knowing that zoning and other controls will not change during the development process or "build out" period because the municipality is legally bound by the contract. The municipality benefits by being able to require things of the developer as a condition for signing the contract.

In the case of Colorado Place, an office development in Santa Monica, the developer benefited by being allowed to build above the 45-foot height limit specified in the zoning ordinance and also by being able to include in the project some uses not permitted under the existing zoning. The city benefited by requiring that the developer build some off-site low-income housing and provide and maintain a small on-site park and a child-care center.

EXACTIONS. In recent years a variety of charges, often referred to as exactions, have become part of the land development scene. Numerous communities have resorted to exactions, sometimes quite substantial, for permission to develop. In some cases they are required only if there is to be a rezoning or zoning variance. In other cases the exactions are charged for development within the existing zoning law. In general, the exaction is charged to pay the costs that the development is presumed to impose on the community.

In some cases the exaction may be for a closely related cost, for example, nearby road construction needed to carry the additional traffic that new commercial development will generate, or school or park construction that the population of a new residential development will require. In other cases the connection may be more tenuous. For example, San Francisco decided that new office development increases the demand for housing in the city. Since 1981 builders of office structures of over 50,000 square feet of floor space must earn housing credits by either building new units themselves or contributing funds to housing rehabilitation or affordable housing projects. Typically, the exaction runs to about $4 per square foot of office floor space. The number of credits is based on estimates of how many square feet of office floor space are required per worker, what percentage of the San Francisco office workforce lives in the city, and how many workers live in the average housing unit.

These examples do not exhaust the variations on traditional land-use controls. Rather, they are a sample of how municipalities in recent years have added elements of bargaining, negotiation, and flexibility to the land-use control process.

Other Types of Local Land-Use Controls

In addition to subdivision and zoning regulations already described, there are a number of other controls that are not quite so widely used. Several are described here very briefly. In some cases these other types of controls are part of the zoning ordinance. In other cases they are separate.

SITE PLAN REVIEW. Typically, site plan review applies to developments over a certain size. The community vests its planning or zoning agency with the responsibility of reviewing site plans for such considerations as internal circulation, adequacy of parking, and buffering from adjacent uses, and makes site plan approval necessary before building permits may be granted. Site plan review does not supersede zoning but rather is another layer of review. It is applied to commercial and multifamily development.

ARCHITECTURAL REVIEW. In architectural review, building plans are reviewed for aesthetic considerations. A town with a predominantly colonial style of housing might review to ensure that new development would be in keeping with the established style. Architectural boards of review are often found in older, upper-income residential areas where preservation of the past and of property values weighs heavily. They are also frequently found in new planned developments. Often they will become involved in what seem like small issues, for example, whether or not a satellite dish antenna can be placed in a yard or what colors are acceptable for the exterior of houses. Feelings about review boards vary. Some applaud them for maintaining the visual quality of the town or development. Others regard them as a dead hand of conformity that makes the community a less interesting and stodgier place. There is a trade-off. If one wants variety and spontaneity, one must risk some instances of bad taste.

HISTORIC PRESERVATION. Many communities designate historic districts and then exercise control over development within them. Controls may dictate that new structures must be in a style and at a scale consistent with the past. They may dictate that when repairs are done, historic appearance must be maintained. For example, if adjacent buildings have old-fashioned leaded glass windows with small panes, a picture window would not be permitted. In some cases, community development funds may be used to help property owners maintain the character of their buildings. Often responsibility for historic preservation will be vested in the planning agency. In other cases, some responsibility will lie with a separate agency, such as New York City's Landmarks Commission. Although there is historic preservation activity in all parts of the United States, it is probably most prominent in New England, where a great deal of colonial-era development remains to be preserved. Historic preservation is unquestionably motivated by a love of the past, but where tourism is important, there is an economic motivation too.

COMBINING CAPITAL INVESTMENT AND LAND-USE CONTROLS

Since capital expenditures and land-use controls are the two principal methods by which municipalities may affect land use, the enlightened community strives to coordinate them so that they reinforce each other. Capital investment in transportation, public facilities, and infrastructure can shape the land market. Land-use controls can permit what is desired and, within the sorts of limitations described, can prohibit what is not desired.

For example, consider the case of Westchester County, New York's, so-called Platinum Mile. The name was chosen by local promoters with the usual lack of modesty that attends such christenings, but it is reasonably accurate. Along the border between two municipalities, the city of White Plains and the town of Harrison, is a massive collection of corporate headquarters and other office development. All told, these facilities provide many thousands of jobs and constitute hundreds of millions of dollars of tax base. It is the sort of complex that most communities would be delighted to have. How did it come into being?

First, the basic preconditions were there. One fact was a good location within the New York metropolitan area. This made it possible to capture firms that were moving out of New York City but wished to remain within the metropolitan area. It also made the area attractive to firms that were moving into the metropolitan area but did not need a Manhattan location, with its very high costs. Second, the Westchester County–Fairfield County (Connecticut) area was attractive to corporations for "quality of life" reasons, such as parklands, good public schools, and an attractive pattern of development. These considerations are very important for personnel recruitment.

But given the existence of these preconditions, it was still necessary to turn them into reality. At the end of the 1950s, White Plains had been planning to build a bypass along its border with the town of Harrison. The road was to have been called the White Plains Arterial. At this time the interstate highway system was being laid out by the federal government in coordination with the states. City officials were quick to see the opportunity. They dropped the concept of the bypass and pushed to get the pathway of the arterial incorporated into the design for the interstate highway system.

The city was successful, and so interstate highway I–287 now runs between the two municipalities, increasing accessibility and greatly increasing land values and the potential for development. The crucial role of capital investment is clear. However, we note that 90 percent of the cost of building the interstate came from the federal government. Only the remaining 10 percent was paid by state and local governments. State and local funds were used to construct wide service roads on either side of the interstate and a series of overpasses across the interstate linking these roads. Thus a motorist leaving the interstate at one of the several interchanges would have quick access to any point in the entire strip.

Having used capital investment—whether local funds or "foreign aid" from the federal government—to create demand on the site, it now remained to control land uses to produce a desirable result. The strategy used was to permit that which was desired and to prevent other land uses from blocking desirable development. Clearly, zoning to permit office development was one part of the strategy. Requiring large minimum sites for development prevented land from being chopped up by small, scattered development. Where there is good highway access in a relatively populous area, retailing is clearly a possibility. But strip commercial development would foreclose the possibility of office park development, both by eating up road frontage and also by creating an environment that was not attractive to corporate headquarters and other "upscale" office development. That eventuality was blocked by simply prohibiting retail uses. Thus, as a gardener favors the plants he or she wants by weeding out others, land-use controls were used to favor particular types of development by blocking other types.

FORCES BEYOND LOCAL CONTROL

The preceding parts of this chapter were written from a local perspective—what a municipality can do to shape its own pattern of development. But many land-use decisions are outside of municipal control.

For example, decisions made by state highway departments about highways are powerful shapers of the pattern of development. Not only do they involve many acres directly, but also they create powerful economic forces that, in turn, shape land uses. Municipal governments have some hand in these decisions, but they are often not the most powerful players. State highway departments, state legislators, and governors may all have more influence over decisions than do the municipality's officials and residents. In addition, major corporations and institutions may play very powerful roles in shaping state highway decisions. The major corporation that indicates that its decision whether to locate in an area or to close up its operations in an area depends on decisions made about highway construction may carry more weight with the state highway department and state government than the preferences of a town or county government. Institutions may also play a powerful role in highway decisions. In one case that the writer witnessed, a major university became a decisive force in a decision to construct a new highway. With a payroll of several thousand, a big enrollment, and tens of thousands of alumni scattered throughout the state, the university was the "five-hundred-pound gorilla" in the conflict over whether or not to build. The university's president was a much more powerful figure in the decision-making process than was any elected official in the region.

In many cases, the impetus for new road construction wells up largely from individuals and private organizations. At this writing, the state of Virginia Department of Transportation (VDOT) is close to deciding which of several routings will be chosen for what will become Interstate 73. Much of the impetus for the new route came from individuals, businesses, and property owners who saw the route as an economic opportunity and therefore beat the drum for it over a period of years. The governments of the municipalities in the area are only a few of the many parties influencing the decision.

In this age in which state and municipal governments actively pursue economic development and court firms with major financial incentives, decisions made in corporate boardrooms can have major effects on the pattern of development (see Chapter 13). Not only does the building of commercial facilities directly shape the pattern of land use, but also state and municipal governments will make decisions about land use and public capital investment with an eye to their effects upon attracting industrial and commercial investment and, in many cases, in part on the basis of negotiations with those firms.

Other decisions by higher levels of government may have profound effects on the local land-use pattern. The building of state or federal facilities, an action generally not bound by local land-use controls, can have powerful effects on the municipal land-use pattern. So, too, can land acquisition by higher levels of government.

Higher Levels of Land-Use Control

In the last several decades, the state governments and the federal government have asserted some control over land-use decisions that were formerly left up to local governments. This assertion has been termed "the quiet revolution." The phrase comes from the title of a book by Bosselman and Callies. They state,

> The *ancien regime* being overthrown is the feudal system under which the entire pattern of land development has been controlled by thousands of individual local governments, each seeking to maximize its tax base and minimize its social problems, and caring less what happens to all others.
>
> The tools of the revolution are new laws taking a wide variety of forms but each sharing a common theme—the need to provide some degree of state or regional participation in the major decisions that affect the use of our increasingly limited supply of land.[26]

Much of the force for such laws comes from environmental concern, which as noted earlier increased greatly during the 1960s. In general, land-use controls emanating from higher than local levels of government do not supersede local controls. Rather, they add another layer of control. The applicant must satisfy not only the local jurisdiction, but also the higher-level jurisdiction. Higher-level controls are found most often where there is a clear public interest beyond the borders of the single community. Very often, also, higher-level controls are found in environmentally fragile areas, for example, coastal zones.

Why Is Higher-Level Control Necessary? One might ask why higher-level control of things like wetland development is necessary. After all, do not individuals as residents of a locality have the same degree of concern with environmental quality that they have as citizens of the state?

Part of the answer comes down to the issue of *externalities*.[27] If a community grants a rezoning that enables a shopping center development to obliterate a wetland, the fiscal gains of that development accrue to that community. So, too, may many of the employment gains. At least some of the increases in land values are also likely to be captured by community residents. On the other hand, the unfavorable effects may be felt outside the community. For example, increased storm-water runoff may have no significant effect on the community but cause flooding down-stream. Expanding the level of decision making to the state reduces the chance that gains for a few individuals will swing the decision and increases the chance that widespread effects will be given their due weight.

The other big reason for higher-level controls over environmental issues is technical complexity. Most local governments do not have the time and expertise to do the data gathering and analysis required for good decision making. A variety of state-level controls on development are mentioned in Chapters 14 and 15.

SUMMARY

Two major ways in which a municipality may shape its pattern of land use are through (1) public capital investment and (2) legal controls over the use of privately owned property.

Public capital investment creates specific public facilities, which make up part of the total land-use pattern. More importantly, public capital investment shapes the development of privately owned land occurs.

Subdivision regulations essentially control the manner in which raw land is subdivided and placed on the market for development. Though subdivision regulations have been the object of less discussion than zoning, they represent a powerful means of control over the development process. The rigid "Euclidean" zoning, which came into being in the early twentieth century, has now been supplemented with a variety of techniques to make it more flexible, more subject to negotiation, and more adaptable to the planning of large developments as single entities. These devices include "bonus" or "incentive" zoning, transfer of development rights (TDR), planned unit development (PUD), cluster zoning, and a number of others. Although the right to zone has been clearly established since the 1920s, the limits of the zoning power are still subject to some change as a result of the process of litigation and the establishment of legal precedent. In particular, since the 1960s the courts have redefined municipal obligations to nonresidents as a result of suits brought against suburban communities.

For the most effective shaping of the land-use pattern, public capital investment and land-use controls should be coordinated. Public capital investment affects the demand for land and structures, and land-use controls channel and shape the way that demand forces play themselves out.

NOTES

1. Public finance texts sometimes use the term "user benefit equity," meaning that with bonds, the same population that receives the benefits from the project also pays the cost of the project through the debt service on the bonds.
2. The market value of a bond moves inversely with interest rates. In general, the further away is the maturity date of the bond, the more its market price will vary with changes in interest rates.
3. Charles J. Hoch, Linda C. Dalton, and Frank S. So, eds., *The Practice of Local Government Planning*, 3rd ed., International City/County Management Association, Washington, DC, 2000, p. 418.

4. Some municipal governments have gotten around debt limitations by the use of leasebacks. Here, the government wanting a facility encourages a firm to build and to own it but then signs a long-term lease on the facility. In effect, the municipality has taken on a long-term financial obligation just as if it had issued bonds, but the obligation does not count as part of its general obligation debt. Though this device seems like a transparent evasion of the debt limit, it has so far been sustained by the courts.

5. An alternative repayment method is the sinking fund. Here, money is put into the fund each year, and the fund is invested in secure investments such as U.S. government bonds. When the bonds mature, they are paid off from the money accumulated in the sinking fund. Such funds are somewhat risky in that they involve the successful forecasting of future interest rates; also, they may subject the government that is using the technique to underfund it, thus holding down expenses in the short term but leaving a deficit to be made up by the taxpayers at maturity. For these reasons, sinking funds are illegal in some states.

6. For a history of subdivision regulations, see Richard M. Yearwood, *Land Subdivision Regulation: Policy and Legal Considerations for Urban Planning*, Praeger, New York, 1971.

7. For an account of the subdivision process, see Charles eds., C. Hoch, Linda C. Dalton, and Frank S. So, eds., *The Practice of Local Government Planning*, International City/County Management Association, Washington, D.C., 2000, chapter 14.

8. For a general account of the zoning process, see ibid., chap. 14.

9. For an example of a work that relates housing type to household size and pupil load, see George Sternlieb et al., *Housing Development and Municipal Costs*, Rutgers University Center for Urban Policy Research, New Brunswick, NJ, 1973.

10. To pursue the matter of profit and loss from changes in zoning, see Donald G. Hagman, Den J. Misczynski, Madelyn Glickfield, et al., eds., *Windfalls for Wipeouts: Land Value Capture and Taxation*, American Society of Planning Officials, Chicago, 1978.

11. "Operation Rezone Brings Prison Terms, More Trials," *Planning*, October 1996, pp. 20–21.

12. Other criteria may sometimes be used, particularly for commercial property. For example, assessors may use estimated cost of replacement or income-generating potential.

13. When fractional assessment is used, an "equalization rate" is generally computed so that the assessed value can be converted into "full value." This is particularly important when funding such as state aid for public education is conditioned by the property tax base of the receiving community. In recent years there has been a general trend toward full value assessment to avoid such complications.

14. Typically, properties owned by nonprofit institutions, as well as properties owned by government itself, are exempt from property taxation.

15. *National Land and Investment Company* v. *Kohn*, 215, A. 2d 597 (Pa. 1965).

16. For a brief account of the collective effect of these decisions, see Wendy U. Larsen, "The Failure to Legislate: Mt. Laurel II," *Urban Land*, April 1983, pp. 34–35. For *Mt. Laurel III*, see Harold A. McDougal, "From Litigation to Legislation in Exclusionary Zoning Law," *Harvard Civil Rights Civil Liberties Law Review*, vol. 22, 1987, pp. 623–663.

17. More precisely, municipalities take the share allocated to them by the council and subtract from that figure the number of low- and moderate-income housing units that have been gained through rehabilitation. Then they may sign RCA agreements for half of that figure.

18. Jane Jacobs, *The Death and Life of Great American Cities*, Vintage Books, Random House, New York, 1961. See, in particular, the section entitled "The Conditions for City Diversity."

19. Kirk Johnson, "Where a Zoning Law Failed, Seeds of a New York Revival," *New York Times*, April 21, 1996, p. 1.

20. For an example of the use of transfer of development rights in regard to historic preservation, see "Large Tower Would Use Depot's Rights," *New York Times*, September 17, 1986, sec. B, p. 1. See also George M. Raymond, "Structuring the Implementation of Transferable Development Rights," *Urban Land*, July–August 1981, pp. 19–25. For recent uses in a number of jurisdictions, see Rick Pruetz, AICP, *Saved by Development: Preserving Environmental Areas, Farmland, and Historic Landmarks With Transfer of Development Rights*, Planners Press, American Planning Association, Chicago, 1997.

21. Lisa Chamberlin, "Open Space Overhead," *Planning*. March 2006, pp. 10–11.

22. www.thehighline.org/press/articles/041206_villager/.

23. See Seymour I. Schwartz and Robert A. Johnston, "Inclusionary Housing Programs," *Journal of the American Planning Association*, vol. 49, no. 1, Winter 1983, pp. 3–21. See also Barbara Taylor, "Inclusionary Zoning: A Workable Option for Affordable Housing," *Urban Land*, March 1981, pp. 6–12; and Gus Bauman, Anna Reines Kahn, and Serena Williams, "Inclusionary Housing Programs in Practice," *Urban Land*, November 1983, pp. 14–19.

24. Gail Easley, "Performance Controls in an Urban Setting," *Urban Land*, October 1984, pp. 24–27. See also Tam Phalen, "How Has Performance Zoning Performed?," *Urban Land*, October 1983, pp. 16–21.

25. "Tallahassee's Performance Zoning Gives Way to Euclid," *Planning*, December 1997, p. 26.

26. Fred Bosselman and David Callies, *The Quiet Revolution in Land Use Controls*, Council for Environmental Quality, Superintendent of Documents, U.S. Government Printing Office, Washington, DC, 1973, p. 1.

27. An economist's term that refers to effects that are visited on "third parties," that is, parties who are not participants in the transactions and whose interest, therefore, may not be taken into account by the participants in the transaction.

SELECTED BIBLIOGRAPHY

CULLINGWORTH, J. BARRY, *The Political Culture of Planning*, Routledge, Inc., New York, 1993.

HAAR, CHARLES, *Land Use Planning: A Casebook on the Use, Mis-Use and Re-Use of Urban Land*, 3rd ed., Little, Brown & Co., Boston, 1980.

HOCH, CHARLES, J., DALTON, LINDA C., and SO, FRANK S. eds., *The Practice of Local Government Planning*, International City/County Management Association, Washington, DC, 2000.

KAISER, EDWARD J., GODSCHALK, DAVID R., and CHAPIN, F. STUART JR., *Urban Land Use Planning*, 4th ed., University of Illinois Press, Urbana, 1995.

NOTE: For the reader interested in keeping up with trends in land development and land-use control techniques, the magazines *Urban Land*, *Planning* and *Real Estate Review* are good and highly readable sources. For a more technical and formal current source on land-use regulation, see the journal *Zoning Digest*.

CHAPTER 10

Urban Design*

> Mind *takes form* in the city; and in turn, urban forms condition mind. For space, no less than time, is artfully reorganized in cities: in boundary lines and silhouettes, in the fixing of horizontal planes and vertical peaks, in utilizing or denying the natural site, the city records the attitude of a culture and an epoch to the fundamental facts of its existence. The dome and the spire, the open avenue and the closed court, tell the story, not merely of different physical accommodations, but of essentially different conceptions of man's destiny. . . . With language itself, it remains man's greatest work of art.[1]

The design of cities has been the conscious task of many throughout history. However, only in the 1950s with the advent of university degree programs did the term *urban designer* and the profession of urban design emerge with a distinct label.

Cities develop over time because of the conscious and unconscious acts of people. Urban designers assume that in spite of the vast scale and complexity, cities can be designed and their growth shaped and directed. A major example of human ability to shape the urban environment is the work of Baron Haussmann from 1855 to 1868 in Paris during the time of Napoleon III.

During this period, Haussmann was responsible for creating a new pattern of boulevards that reshaped the character of Paris. The facades of buildings along the grand boulevards were required to be uniform, giving a sense of rhythm and order to the streets. The grand tree-lined boulevards

*Parts of this chapter were written by Charles W. Steger. He was formerly Dean of the College of Architecture and Urban Studies at Virginia Polytechnic Institute and State University and is now president of the university.

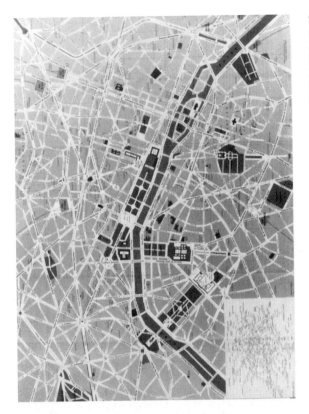

Street map of the central area of Paris (left) shows Haussmann's grand design. Below, a view down the Seine River from the gallery of Notre Dame cathedral shows the reality a century later.

he created became and remain some of the major public spaces of Paris. He addressed the problem of the flow of traffic and the appropriate uses of land. He shaped the skyline and the proportion of space by limits on height and rules governing the space between buildings. The vistas shaped by the boulevards focused on major public buildings and on gardens, giving new character to the nineteenth-century city. This plan for Paris, using grand boulevards as a major orienting force, was copied throughout the world.

WHAT IS URBAN DESIGN?

Urban design falls between the professions of planning and architecture. It deals with the large-scale organization and design of the city, with the massing and organization of buildings and the space between them, but not with the design of the individual buildings.

Several factors distinguish urban design from architectural design. Urban design deals with a large scale, such as entire neighborhoods or cities, and with long time frames, frequently 15 to 20 years. For example, Haussmann's work in Paris required 17 years. This is a sharp contrast to the 1, 2, or 3 years usually required for the construction of a single building. Urban design also deals with a large number of variables, such as transportation, neighborhood identity, pedestrian orientation, and climate. This complexity, combined with the long periods of time involved, results in an environment characterized by high uncertainty. The control over specific development is less direct than with a single building. As a result, many of the techniques employed by urban designers differ from those of the architect.

Although the urban designer and planner have complementary roles, they do have separate and distinct functions. Most commonly, the modern urban designer deals with a part of the city. Very often, the site on which the urban designer works has been allocated as part of a larger planning process. It is after that allocation is made that the urban designer examines the site in terms of massing and spatial organization. The planner, by contrast, must typically consider the entire city. In fact, very often he or she must look beyond the bounds of the city and understand how the city functions as part of a larger region, for example, how the transportation system of the city relates to surrounding suburbs and communities. Thus the planner plays a central role in allocating the uses of land among the competing functions. Planners are more likely than urban designers to be involved in the political process whereby public policy is formulated. Planners and urban designers are each involved with a spectrum of social, cultural, and physical design issues. The difference is a matter of degree.

Numerous urban designers are employed by developers on a variety of residential, commercial, and mixed-use projects. But many urban designers are also employed by public bodies. For example, during the

Market Street in San Francisco remodeled, as visualized by the urban designer. Widened sidewalks and open-air arcades make it an attractive pedestrian area. There is a strong design influence from Baron Haussmann's grand avenues in Paris.

period of Urban Renewal (see Chapter 11), sites were acquired, cleared, and planned by Urban Renewal agencies. Parcels were then sold or leased to developers, who put up buildings or groups of buildings in accordance with the agency's overall plan. In this case the urban design was done by designers on the public payroll, and the architectural design was done by individuals or firms on the developer's payroll.

The Battery Park City development illustrated in this chapter represents a large and highly successful urban design effort done under public

Commercial development at Battery Park City (top) and residential section and riverfront promenade (bottom). The opposite page shows land use allocation and vehicular circulation.

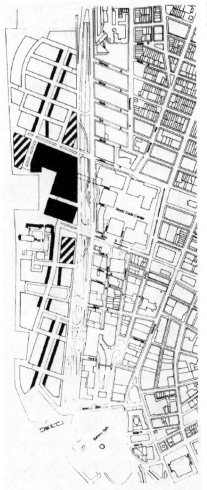

Residential ▭
Permitted Retail Center ▬
Commercial/Retail Center ▬
Potential Commercial or ▨
  Residential Sites

Land Use Allocation

⊕ ||||| | | |
   0 200 400 600

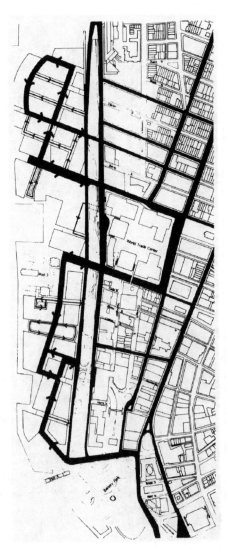

Primary Circulation ▬
Secondary Circulation ━

Vehicular Circulation

⊕ ||||| | | |
   0 200 400 600

REBUILDING THE WORLD TRADE CENTER SITE

The diagrams on page 176–193 were drawn before the 9/11 attack, in 2001. In these diagrams the main north-south route, West Street, divides Battery Park City from the rest of Manhattan. Battery Park City is to the west of the street. Just to the east of West Street, about midlevel in both diagrams you can see the square footprints of the two World Trade Center Towers as well as those of several lower-rise buildings that were so severely damaged that they were torn down after the attack.

At this writing, more than six years after 9/11, the rough outlines of the plan for the rebuilding of the site have emerged, though they may still change, and many of the details remain to be settled. The redesign process has been a complex matter involving many political pressures, questions of symbolism and what sort of message various designs send to the rest of the world, financial issues, important questions about the market for commercial space in lower Manhattan, and legal issues.

Considerable work has been done on the site. The mass transit infrastructure involving the New York City subway system and the Port Authority Trans-Hudson (PATH) tubes has been rebuilt and the foundation of the Freedom Tower, the building that will stand on the site of the Twin Towers has been completed. The present design calls for the Freedom Tower to stand 1,776 feet high. The thick-walled concrete two-hundred-foot-high base will be windowless but will be sheathed with glass to give a reflective effect. The base itself has been the object of some argument, appearing sensible and prudent to some and bespeaking fear and timidity to others.[2] Above the base will rise a chamfered tower, meaning that the corners are cut at 45 degree angles producing an eight-sided shape, containing approximately 2.6 million square feet of floor space. Above the occupied floors in the chamfered section will rise an unoccupied communications tower about 400 feet in height.

Flanking the Freedom Tower will be four other towers, one residential and three commercial. One of these is to be built by the Port Authority of New York and New Jersey, subsequently referred to as the Port Authority, and three by the New York real estate developer Larry Silverstein who had signed a 99-year lease on the World Trade Center towers with the Port Authority a little less than two months before 9/11. Mr. Silverstein will also hold the lease on the Freedom Tower.

To make the Freedom Tower commercially feasible, the Port Authority, after prolonged negotiations with Mr. Silverstein, agreed to lease 600,000 square feet in the Freedom Tower at $59 per square foot per year. New York City agreed to lease another 600,000 square feet, lower down in the building, at $56.50 per square foot. Beyond that, New York state and the federal government have made preliminary arrangements for leasing another 1 million square feet.[3] Without the political decision to relocate thousands of public sector workers into the new tower, it is very doubtful that the tower would be built.

The decision to build so much commercial floor space in lower Manhattan has occasioned considerable criticism. For several decades the market for commercial space in lower Manhattan has been soft. One reason for this is that because of its narrower streets, more irregular street pattern, and smaller blocks, lower Manhattan has tended to lose out in competition with midtown Manhattan. This softness in the lower Manhattan market for commercial floor space is readily apparent on a visit to the area if you simply observe the number of older office buildings that have been converted to rental or condominium apartments. Owners of existing commercial space in lower Manhattan have much at stake if the building of new office space for thousands of workers drives down rental rates and drives up office vacancy rates. Beyond that, those who see the future of lower Manhattan as being largely residential would argue building all of this new commercial space is fundamentally a wrongheaded decision to swim against the tide. Other criticism has flowed from people who thought that the amount and character of the space devoted to those who died in 9/11 were not adequate or suitable. Still other criticism has flowed from people who thought that as a matter of pride and symbolism the two towers that had been destroyed should be rebuilt exactly as they had originally been. Others have criticized the rebuilding design as too cautious and not sufficiently imaginative. In short, everything about the rebuilding of the site has been the subject of intense controversy.

The question of rebuilding also has legal complexities. To take the one with the biggest financial stakes, Mr. Silverstein had insured the towers under a policy which provided up to $3.5 billion per event. He took the position that the destruction of the two towers, which occurred about an hour apart, constituted two separate events. The consortium of insurance companies that had written the policies argued that the two attacks constituted a single event. Thus up to $3.5 billion turned on how the courts interpreted the word "event." Ultimately, the courts decided against Mr. Silverstein and in favor of the insurance companies.

The preceding paragraphs only sketch out a few of the complexities of this major urban design process.

auspices. The developing organization, Battery Park City Authority (BPCA), was set up as a public benefit corporation by the New York State legislature in 1968. Its purpose was to develop 92 acres to be created by landfill on the Hudson shore of Manhattan adjacent to the World Trade Center and the city's financial district.

Streets, blocks, open spaces, utilities, a 1.2-mile-long esplanade along the Hudson River, and the allocation of land uses were all laid out by the project's designers.

The buildings, designed by independent architectural firms, conformed to height, bulk, and other guidelines provided by BPCA.

One characteristic of major urban design efforts is the long time horizon. BPCA came into being in 1968. Funds were obtained through a bond issue in 1972, and the landfill was completed in 1976. Work was suspended for several years because of New York City's financial difficulties, and BPCA was reorganized in 1979. In 1980, construction of the first building began. By 1990, the development contained about 4,000 apartments and roughly 10 million square feet of commercial floor space. Another 8,000 apartments and several million square feet of commercial space still remained to be built. From concept to completion, the project took a quarter of a century.

In years to come, the role of the urban designer is likely to grow because of an important trend in land development in the United States: A growing percentage of all development is taking place within PUDs or other large-scale, unified developments, rather than as lot-by-lot filling-in under traditional Euclidean zoning. One reason for this shift is that better results are often obtained with a unified design approach. Another reason is the emergence of large development organizations that can put together the huge blocks of capital—that such projects require.

But even more important have been changes in the market for residences and commercial space. The emergence of a large and prosperous older population created a market for retirement communities that contain not only houses and apartments but community and outdoor recreation facilities as well—all to be put together in an attractive and a unified design. Comparable comments can be made for the residential demand of affluent "yuppies," who want their squash courts and jogging paths close at hand. (See Chapter 7 for further discussion of planned communities.) Many businesses prefer a business park location because it permits the sharing of common facilities like parking and telecommunications and because a well-designed development gives an "upscale" image that impresses clients and customers. It must also be admitted that a large-scale project may sell partly because its size and physical separation provide a degree of social isolation. Personal safety, security for personal or business property, and even protection from urban unpleasantness like panhandling can be powerful selling points.

THE URBAN DESIGN PROCESS _____

Although each city and its problems are unique, there are some general sets of activities in most urban design studies. Following are four basic phases and some subphases.

1. Analysis
   a. Gathering of basic information
   b. Visual survey
   c. Identification of hard and soft areas
   d. Functional analysis
2. Synthesis
3. Evaluation
4. Implementation

Analysis

Gathering of Basic Information. Basic information is gathered on such items as land use, population, transportation, natural systems, and topography. In addition, the designers make a careful examination of the varied character of the site and the structure of neighborhoods and business areas. Problems and design goals are identified. For a residential development the designer might consider

1. Suitability of the topography, that is, slope or floodplains
2. Land area required for the new units
3. Amount of traffic generated and necessary roadways to accommodate it
4. Adequacy of public utilities
5. Parking space requirements
6. Additional requirements for schools, parks, and playgrounds
7. Relevant zoning and subdivision ordinances

For a commercial development, the designer might also consider the buying income of surrounding residential areas, likely "absorption rates" for commercial space, and the competitive strength of nearby commercial areas.

Visual Survey. In *The Image of the City,* Kevin Lynch describes the concept and key elements of the visual survey.[4] The idea is that as each of us walks around the city, we create a mental map of it. This mental map makes us feel less anxious about finding our way about. Lynch developed a vocabulary of symbols that enables the urban designer to characterize in graphic form the key elements of the urban fabric. The visual survey is now considered a standard part of any urban design study and is used as a tool by designers to communicate their perceptions of the structure and organization of a city or neighborhood to one another. The visual survey examines and identifies components of the city such as the location and views of landmarks and activity nodes. It reveals where the boundaries between neighborhoods are and whether they are clear and distinct or amorphous. The survey also explores the sequence of spaces a pedestrian might encounter in walking from one part of the city to another.

Identification of Hard and Soft Areas. Cities, and the neighborhoods and districts that comprise them, are in a constant state of change. Although this dynamic condition may not be seen easily from one day to the next, over the time span of 5, 10, or 15 years it becomes quite apparent.

The delineation of hard and soft areas helps the designer to know what parts of the city can accommodate growth and change and what parts are essentially fixed because they may be occupied, for example, by a historic landmark or cemetery. A good example of a hard area is a public park near the central business district of a large city. It is extremely unlikely that any development will be allowed to take place in that area. A soft area may be a neighborhood or business district with an increasing number of vacancies. Such information is of considerable value in the latter stages of the urban design process when plans must be evaluated for feasibility.

Functional Analysis. The functional analysis examines the relationship of activities among the various land uses and the way that they relate to circulation systems. This study builds very heavily on the work of the land-use planners. However, the urban designer carries the study into three dimensions.

For example, in virtually every major downtown there is a problem of excessive congestion and traffic on the streets. It is therefore important to consider the real consequences of our plans in three dimensions and the way that they might change over time.

Synthesis

From the synthesis phase emerge design concepts that reflect an understanding of the constraints of the problem and that propose optimum solutions, given the many trade-offs that must be made. The designer is confronted with the resolution of many conflicting demands. For housing units there is an inherent conflict between pedestrian and vehicular traffic. If traffic flow is too fast or too heavy, it will hamper pedestrian crossing unless either traffic lights or pedestrian bridges are installed. Each of these solutions takes additional resources.

It is in the synthesis phase that the data gathered and the analysis of the problem must be translated into proposals for action. Prior to the complete development of the urban design plan, there are several preceding activities. The first component of the synthesis phase is the evolution of concepts that address the problem. In the initial phases, there may be a number of concepts proposed. There is usually more than one way to solve a particular set of problems. Concepts are followed by the development of schematic design proposals. These proposals are more specific in nature. Schematics are followed by preliminary plans.

Evaluation

Evaluation occurs at many levels, ranging from meeting technical demands to the ability to gain public acceptance. It is the time at which the preliminary plans generated in the synthesis phase are compared with the original goals and problem definitions.

After the design proposals are complete, it is essential that they be evaluated in light of the original problem or issue they were intended to address. One of the more complicated tasks associated with evaluation is determining what criteria should be employed. There are two basic questions: (1) How well the solutions fit the problem and (2) how readily the proposals can be implemented.

The task is further complicated by the fact that cities are dynamic and that their problems are constantly changing. Developing solutions for problems that are in a state of flux is like shooting at a moving target.

Implementation

During implementation, the strategy for actual financing and construction is devised. Detailed phasing studies and tools such as zoning ordinances are called into play to realize the project.

Once an urban design plan is developed, the principal tools through which it is implemented are land-use controls and capital expenditures. The land-use controls available to the urban designer include not only the traditional or Euclidean zoning ordinance, but also a variety of modern techniques described in Chapter 9.

Capital expenditures shape the pattern of land development, as noted earlier, by altering land values through the provision of access and utilities. When there is public participation in a project, capital expenditures combined with the power of eminent domain may be used to assemble the land for the project.

WHAT IS GOOD URBAN DESIGN?

In its most general sense, urban designers intend to improve the quality of people's lives through design. They accomplish this through the elimination of barriers as well as the creation of opportunities for people to move about the city in a free, safe, and pleasant way. For example, one should be able to walk through a reasonable portion of an urban area in inclement weather without major difficulty.

Minneapolis, with its long, cold, snowy winters, has accomplished this goal with a system that links the second stories of downtown buildings with climate-controlled skyways. The skyways plus the connecting corridors in commercial and public buildings form a five-mile system. People may travel several blocks from parking structures or apartments to offices or stores without having to go down to street level. Some residents "skywalk" for exercise and recreation.

Clearly, the Minneapolis skyway system has helped the downtown remain competitive with outlying developments, such as the Mall of America located to the south of the city. But skyway systems do have a downside. According to urban designer Wendy Jacobson,

> Both skyways and underground pedestrian systems can drain city streets of the activity that makes them lively, interesting, and safe. With few exceptions, North American cities lack the density of pedestrian activity to fuel both an active street frontage and a competing above- or below-grade system. Something has to suffer and in most cases it is the street.
>
> Privatization is also an important issue. Although they may appear to be public spaces, most skyways and underground walkways link privately owned development. Unlike public streets, access to these systems is normally restricted to certain times and may even be restricted to certain people—those appropriately dressed, for example.[5]

Note that the privatization issue raises questions similar to some of those raised in connection with private communities discussed in Chapter 7. When this writer raised the vitality-of-the-street question with a planner in Minneapolis, he was told that the department believed that the pros of the system substantially outweighed the cons. Thus the city continues to accept applications for new skyways.

Another cold-weather city with an extensive skyway system is Calgary in Alberta, Canada. Its system is named Plus 15 for the required clearance of the skyway over the street. Calgary officials are also aware of the problem of competition between the street and the skyway level. In fact, they note that comparable retail floor space at the skyway level rents for more than it does at the street level. But on balance they are sufficiently pleased with Plus 15 that for every square foot of skyway that a developer builds, the city allows the developer to build 20 more square feet of building floor space than the zoning would normally permit.

People like to see other people and to be seen. Many cities provide incentives for developers who will create public plazas in conjunction with new developments. Such spaces provide an opportunity for people to sit in the sun at lunch and observe the general activity of the street. William Whyte in *The Social Life of Small Urban Spaces* reports a systematic study of

Above, skyways on Minneapolis's Nicollet Mall. The narrowed street is open to buses, taxis, police, and emergency vehicles but closed to passenger cars. Below, the view from Marquette Avenue. The skyways are planned, built, and maintained privately (current cost is about $1 million each), subject to the granting of an encroachment permit. Because they are designed by different architects for different builders, there is considerable variation in their appearance.

the factors contributing to successful urban spaces.[6] He concludes that some form of movable seating and the opportunity to purchase food and drink are key elements.

Another way to evaluate the success of urban space is the way in which it assists in orienting the user. For example, can users find their way from one place to the other without confusion or fear? Are the signs easily understood? Are major pedestrian areas well lighted in the evening so that users can make their way easily and safely? Jane Jacobs made this point forcefully in the early 1960s in *The Death and Life of Great American Cities*.[7]

Other functional criteria such as safety are also important. For example, separation of pedestrian and vehicular traffic reduces accidents. Yet the spaces and circulation areas must be organized so that they can be readily accessible to emergency vehicles and delivery vehicles.

Good design achieves its intentions and often more. For example, the developer's intention in constructing a mixed-use project may simply be to achieve a profitable combination of commercial and residential structures. Yet if the project is well situated and aesthetically attractive, its benefits will spill over onto adjacent areas. The project might increase pedestrian traffic and hence enhance property values in adjacent retailing areas. Its presence might also enhance the value of adjacent neighborhoods by making the area more interesting and varied.

A myriad of factors can affect the success of an urban design project. A list of a number of the more important criteria for judging urban design follows:

1. Unity and coherence
2. Minimum conflict between pedestrians and vehicles
3. Protection from rain, noise, wind, and so on
4. Easy orientation for users
5. Compatibility of land uses
6. Availability of places to rest, observe, and meet
7. Creation of a sense of security and pleasantness

But it must be admitted that urban design is not an exact science, for there is always the element of personal taste. One person's peace and tranquillity will be another person's boredom and sterility. One person's excitement will be another person's soul-destroying cacophony. The area that suits a single person in his or her twenties may seem quite unsuitable ten years later when the same person has a spouse and two children.

The Neighborhood Concept

A very central concept in urban design, and a place where one can see many of the previously noted criteria applied, is the "neighborhood."

Though we now take the idea of neighborhoods and of planning for neighborhoods for granted, it is actually not an old idea. One of the first clear articulations of the neighborhood concept in the United States was that by Clarence Perry done in the 1920s for RPA (see Chapter 3).[8] A neighborhood is a unit that matches the daily scale of most people's lives. Traditionally, the neighborhood planning unit is the area that would contain a population sufficient to supply the pupils for one elementary school. Perry wrote in terms of 1,000 or 1,200 pupils, which in the 1920s implied a total neighborhood population of 5,000 or 6,000.

Typically, the neighborhood plan will provide for residences, a school, shopping facilities for goods that one buys frequently (grocery, drug, and stationery stores but not department stores or automobile dealers), playgrounds, and perhaps small parks. The street pattern will serve the resident population but discourage through traffic. Major thoroughfares will often serve as neighborhood boundaries. In some communities, for example,

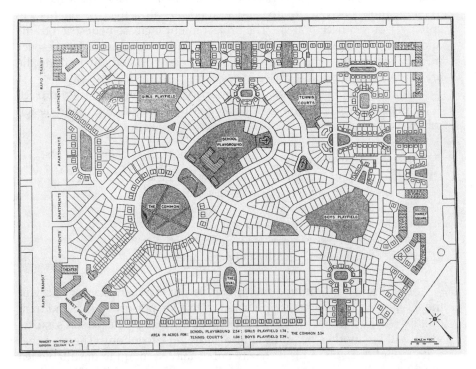

The neighborhood concept circa the 1920s. The separate boys' and girls' playgrounds seem archaic today, but the plan otherwise has many modern features—separation of commercial and residential areas, a curvilinear street pattern to discourage through traffic, the preservation of community open space, concentration of high-density housing near public transportation. Note that the neighborhood is built around a public school.

Above, a pedestrian bridge
connecting the town center
with an adjacent residential
area in the planned community
of Reston, Virginia. Below, a
view of the town center across
Lake Ann (an artificial lake).
Much of the town is designed
to facilitate transportation by
foot and bicycle.

Reston, Virginia, the residents will be further isolated from traffic by separate paths for pedestrians and cyclists. The well-designed neighborhood is likely to be laid out with common areas so that residents encounter each other in ways that promote social relationships. The neighborhood is thus structured to provide conveniently and safely much of what most people need and use in their daily lives.

One complaint about the planning of many suburban areas is that the separation of land uses and, particularly, the large expanses of tract housing eliminate much of what we associate with neighborhoods. One does not meet one's neighbor walking to the corner store because there is no corner store and, given the spreadout nature of many suburbs, one is not likely to walk to many destinations. Similarly, children do not casually encounter each other walking home from the neighborhood school because there is no neighborhood school. Rather, they are bused to and from a consolidated school several miles away.

REPLANNING SUBURBIA: THE NEOTRADITIONALISTS _____

Ask a group of planners to name one urban designer, and the chances are that a considerable number of them will name Andres Duany. The Cuban-born Duany is the most prominent exponent of *neotraditional design*, also sometimes referred to as the *new urbanism.*

Most of the U.S. population growth is going into the suburbs, and Duany and other neotraditionalists insist that, by and large, the suburbs are being planned wrong.[9] They tend to lay the biggest share of the blame on the traffic engineers but still reserve a good deal of blame for the planners. Using Duany's phrase, highway engineers "want cars to be happy" with the result that there is an overemphasis on planning for the automobile. Meeting traffic flow and parking goals takes precedence over designing for people and for walkable environments. New urbanists fault suburban planning for an excessive separation of land uses, particularly residential use from other uses, and for laying out land uses at too coarse a grain. The result is that distances between uses becomes too great for convenient walking and therefore people are forced into excessive dependence on the automobile.

Neotraditionalists argue that excessive dependence on the automobile degrades the quality of life in many ways. Older people lose their independence in the suburbs, not when they are too infirm to walk but when their eyesight no longer permits them to drive. At that point, people who are otherwise able to live independently become dependent. At the other end of the age spectrum, suburban children have much less autonomy than city children have because they have to be chauffeured everywhere.

Neotraditionalists argue that designing for the automobile produces pedestrian-unfriendly patterns that inhibit walking even when the straight-line distances are not great. For example, even if the main road has only two lanes, turning lanes may double the road's width near intersections. The combination of wide streets and absence of sidewalks makes walking unpleasant and sometimes a bit threatening. In traditional urban areas, streets meet at right angles, thereby forcing cars to slow down considerably to turn. By contrast, a rounded corner with a wide radius that permits cars to negotiate the turn without much slowing can make crossing intimidating, particularly for someone who, for reason of age or handicap, cannot move very fast. Yet highway engineers often favor this type of intersection because it speeds the traffic flow.

Neotraditional planning is so named because much of what the neotraditionalists advocate harks back to traditional city and town planning practices that have been rejected in modern suburban planning. Neotraditionalists advocate the mixing of uses at a fine grain. They note that zoning originated to separate incompatible uses but that there is much less need for this technique today than at the turn of the century. For example, much manufacturing today is quiet and clean, and there is no reason why it cannot be located relatively close to housing. It is important that buildings in an area be in scale with each other, but not that they all be for the same type of use or for the same type of inhabitant. Like Jane Jacobs (see Chapter 9), they argue that excessive homogeneity of use and building type leads to sterility and inconvenience. They suggest, for example, that apartments over stores and accessory apartments on single-family lots (for example, the garage that has been converted to a one-bedroom apartment) would go a long way to solving the problems of low- and moderate-income housing. And they note that, regrettably, most suburban zoning codes prevent construction of these types of units.

Neotraditionalists place great importance on pedestrian-friendly streets. The traditional city street with, say, two lanes for traffic, one lane on each side for parked cars, and sidewalks is pedestrian friendly. Because it has only two lanes of traffic that move at a moderate speed, it is easy to cross. The lines of parked cars offer the pedestrian on the sidewalk a sense of security because there is a barrier between him or her and the moving vehicles in the street. Buildings should be brought up close to the street, and parking beyond what can be accommodated on the street should be located behind the building. Neotraditionalists see the typical shopping center or office park design in which the building is set back and isolated from the street by a large parking lot as a design disaster. Even the most unattractive building "gives more to the street," according to Duany, than does a sea of parked cars or, when the cars are not there, a sea of asphalt. Neotraditionalists like alleys, for these permit parking to be placed behind buildings. The alley avoids the need for the typical suburban residential design in which half of the frontage of a house consists of a garage door. And a streetscape that consists largely of garage doors is not a very interesting or inviting public space. The neotraditionalist vision of good design necessarily implies fairly small lots, for widely spaced houses discourage walking.

WHAT IS WRONG WITH THE POD
AND COLLECTOR PLAN

The pod and collector system, with each pod connecting separately to the collector as in the top half of the figure, is a common suburban design approach. It looks good on paper, but, Andres Duany argues, it works badly. First, every trip from a point in one pod to a point in another pod becomes an automobile trip on the collector. This is a prescription for traffic congestion. The problem is not that there is a shortage of total road surface, but that this design forces a large part of the traffic onto a small fraction of the total road surface.

Walking for purposes like shopping is discouraged because there is no direct path from the houses in the pod at the upper right to the mall or the stores fronting on the collector. Walking for purposes of visiting, say between the single-family houses and the apartments, is also discouraged

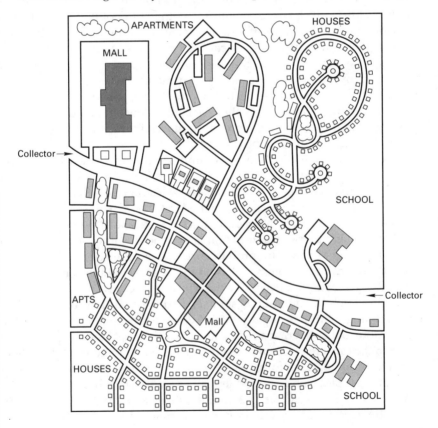

for the same reasons. Even walking from one store to another is discouraged, for the customer at the mall cannot easily walk to the strip shopping because the only link between them is the collector. Thus in addition to concentrating automobile trips as just noted, the pod and collector system also increases the total number of automobile trips.

The half of the drawing below the collector shows a pattern that Duany regards as far superior. The same elements—single-family houses, apartments, stores, and a public school—are contained in each half of the drawing. But circulation is very different. In the bottom half, most trips for shopping and social purposes can be made through secondary streets without having to go out onto the collector. In addition, many trips are easily made on foot. Residents of the single-family houses and apartments can walk to the mall by a reasonably direct path along secondary streets with sidewalks. Similarly, schoolchildren can walk to and from school on secondary streets. The student who stays after school for an activity and misses the school bus can walk home rather than wait to be picked up by a parent. The design promotes a greater degree of social integration because the two different types of housing, apartments and single-family houses, are not isolated from each other in separate pods.

Neotraditionalists rest much of their case on the market. They point out that people will pay very high prices for a fine-grained, pedestrian-friendly pattern. Note, for example, the high price of residential real estate in Georgetown (Washington, D.C.) or Marblehead, Massachusetts, or Greenwich Village and Brooklyn Heights in New York City.

Another prominent neotraditionalist is California-based Peter Calthorpe. His general design philosophy is similar to Duany's although he places somewhat more emphasis on public transportation and the building of a sufficiently large, compact downtown to support public transportation. His name is associated with *transit-oriented development (TOD)*, meaning a high-density area laid out so that every residential unit within it is within ten minutes walk of a transit stop. A series of these "pedestrian pocket" developments strung out along a transit line would give the line sufficient ridership to divert a significant number of trips from automobiles to buses or light rail. (See Chapter 13 regarding the collection and distribution problem in public transportation.) This is particularly important in many parts of California where rapid population growth and heavy dependence upon the automobile have led to serious problems with traffic congestion and air quality. The project for which he is best known in California is Laguna West, south of Sacramento, though *Planning* magazine suggests that he may have had more of an effect on the shape of development in

Two scenes from Kentlands, a Duany-designed new urbanist community near
Gaithersburg, Maryland. The development is characterized by closely spaced
housing, sidewalks on all streets, alleys behind most housing so that garages
and trash cans are out of sight, and, generally, meticulous attention to urban
design details. The town center and adjacent areas contain multifamily rental
units, a senior citizens facility, and a variety of service and retail businesses.

California and elsewhere through his work on a number of town and county transit-oriented master plans.[10]

This writer finds much of the neotraditional design philosophy attractive, but it must be admitted that not everyone does. Much of the large-lot suburban zoning that the neotraditional planners decry is not so much the planners' choice as it is the will of the public.

The planners are often more open to a variety of urban design innovations than were the citizens. The fears of citizens about who their neighbors would be, whom their children would go to school with, and what might happen to their property values if less expensive structures were built nearby, often made these citizens very resistive to smaller lot sizes and mixing of land uses. A substantial segment of the public prefers large-lot development, sharp separation of land uses, and the automobile-dependent way of life that goes with it—just so long as there is plenty of parking and traffic moves quickly. Frank Lloyd Wright's decentralized automobile-based vision embodied in Broad Acre City (see final section) spoke to the taste of a great many people. Seeing the pattern of post–World War II suburban development in the United States, it seems rather prophetic.

Neotraditionalism has received some criticism from the left on the grounds that it is elitist and does not do much for the problems of the central cities. The argument is that houses in neotraditional communities such as Kentlands (see page 192) are expensive and that relatively few neotraditional developments have occurred in central cities. In this writer's view, this criticism is not entirely fair. It is true that housing in most neotraditional communities is expensive, but the fact is that unsubsidized new housing in most of the United States is expensive. By spring 2004 the median new single-family house in the United States cost $221,000. The average figure was still higher, at $270,000.[11] New communities thus will almost inevitably have expensive housing. It is true that most neotraditional development occurs in suburbia or beyond, but it has to be understood that creating a neotraditional community takes a substantial number of acres and, by and large, substantial blocks of undeveloped land in central cities are rare.

As is true with planned communities in general, doing a neotraditional community requires a very large block of capital up front and generally protracted negotiations with the municipality over rezoning and other design questions.

EDGE CITY

At the very opposite end of the design spectrum from neotraditionalism is the *edge city*. Unlike neotraditionalism, which is a very conscious and clearly articulated design philosophy, the edge city embodies no single design philosophy, nor does it have a clear spokesperson such as Andres

Duany. Rather, the edge city is an evolving form of development based on a variety of economic forces and on the understandings that developers and investors have of those forces.

The term *edge city* was coined by the journalist Joel Garreau to describe this new form of development that has been springing up all over America in the last three decades or so. Using Garreau's somewhat arbitrary definition given later, there are more than two hundred edge cities in the United States. Some of those identified by Garreau include Tyson's Corner outside Washington, D.C., Buckhead in Atlanta, the Schaumburg area outside Chicago, Dearborn/Fairfield Village outside Detroit, the Galleria area outside Dallas, Irvine Spectrum outside Los Angeles, the Stamford/Greenwich area in Connecticut, Mitchell Field/Garden City in Nassau County, New York, and the King of Prussia area west of Philadelphia. He defines an edge city as meeting the following five requirements:

1. Has 5 million square feet or more of leasable office space—the workplace of the information age [to convert that figure into jobs, you could use a rule-of-thumb figure of about 250 square feet per worker].
2. Has 600,000 square feet of leasable retail space. That is the equivalent of a fair-sized mall.
3. Has more jobs than bedrooms. When the workday starts, people head toward this place, not away from it. Like all urban places, the population increases at 9 A.M.
4. Is perceived by the population as one place. It is a regional end destination for mixed use—not a starting point—that "has it all," from jobs to shopping to entertainment.
5. Was nothing like a "city" as recently as 30 years ago. Then it was just bedrooms, if not cow pastures. This incarnation is brand new.[12]

What are the market forces that favor the development of edge cities? The peripheral location means that the developer(s) can build a large, unified design at one time and do so without having to absorb the residual value of existing structures (see Chapter 11). The large size may offer substantial economies of scale in planning, construction, and marketing.

Its position on the periphery of the metropolitan area gives employers in the edge city access to a large and suitable labor force. Retailers and providers of personal services prosper in the edge city because they are easily accessible to a large, affluent suburban population. The different activities in the edge city may provide profitable synergy. For example, workers in the office buildings will also be customers for retailers and service businesses in the mall. The edge city is an understandable adaptation to a suburbanized population with a very high rate of automobile ownership and access to high-capacity, high-speed highways. The most basic requirements for the formation of an edge city are good highway access, a large and at least moderately prosperous population within easy driving distance, and a large block of available land.

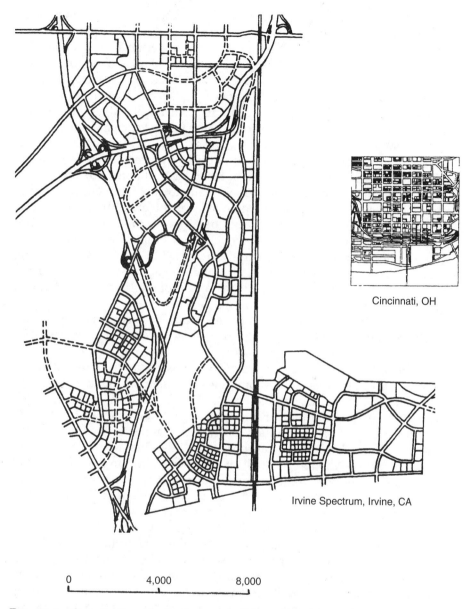

Cincinnati, OH

Irvine Spectrum, Irvine, CA

0   4,000   8,000

Downtown Cinncinati and Irvine Spectrum edge city are shown at the same scale. Note that the longest dimension of Irvine Spectrum is approximately four times that of the longest dimension of the Cinncinati downtown and that the area of Irvine Spectrum is approximately nine times that of the Cinncinati downtown.

Source: Reprinted by permission of the *Journal of the American Planning Association,* 64, no. 3, Summer 1998.

Some edge cities, such as Irvine Spectrum, are planned as a single entity. Others are planned a piece at a time. In either case, the process is very different from traditional urban development under Euclidean zoning. The developer must assemble a sizable piece of land and present the government of the municipality or municipalities with a unified plan. Development is a complex negotiated process, rather than a matter of the developer's acquiring a single parcel and then either building what is allowed by the zoning code or petitioning for a rezoning or variance for that one parcel.

Though the edge city contains many of the same commercial elements as the traditional urban downtown, it differs radically in physical form. The edge city is much more spread out than the traditional downtown. The spread-out form is an adaptation to virtually total reliance on the automobile. Garreau notes that developers regard 600 feet as about the biggest distance that people can realistically be expected to walk without complaint. Thus the typical form of the edge city is a building or perhaps two or three buildings closely grouped and surrounded by some acres of parking space. Larger groupings generally are not done because they would stretch out walking distances beyond what an automobile-owning populace would accept.

Just as the edge city is automobile friendly, it is pedestrian unfriendly. Irvine Spectrum in Southern California, shown on the map on page 195, dwarfs the traditional downtown. Its size alone renders it essentially unwalkable. So, too, does its design. There is no continuous pattern of streets with sidewalks, nor are buildings and their surroundings laid out for walking. Rather, they are laid out for driving, and the visitor is expected to make only the trip from parking space to building on foot. To the extent that there are pedestrian facilities, they will be jogging trails or scenic paths intended for recreation, not transportation. Edge cities do mix a variety of commercial uses, though generally at a coarser grain than the proponent of neotraditional design would prefer. But they separate work from residence very effectively and thus render virtually every trip to work an automobile trip—again, the antithesis of the neotraditional philosophy.

The edge city is only several decades old. Though numerous architects, planners, and others have speculated about the future of urban form, none really foresaw the edge city. In some ways, Frank Lloyd Wright with his vision of Broadacre City anticipated the dispersed pattern of settlement and the overwhelming reliance on the automobile that characterize the larger environment in which the edge city has developed. But neither he nor any other writer anticipated the edge city itself. Joel Garreau notes that because the edge city is a new form, we cannot say what it will ultimately evolve into. Just as the nineteenth-century city that burgeoned as a result of the industrial revolution often evolved into a much cleaner and pleasanter form in the twentieth century, so too may the edge city evolve into a more gracious and subtle form in years to come. But that is only speculation.

VISIONS OF THE CITY OF THE FUTURE _____

Given that the urban designer is concerned with the development of the city not only in the present but also 15 to 20 or more years into the future, it is important to have some concept of what cities in the future might be like. The literature of architecture, planning, and urban design is fortunate to have many such references. Ideas range from Frank Lloyd Wright's Broad Acre City to R. Buckminster Fuller's milewide geodesic dome for Manhattan to Le Corbusier's Ville Radieuse (the Radiant City). Behind each of these concepts was an idea about how city dwellers should respond to social and technological change.

For example, in the Ville Radieuse, Le Corbusier envisioned high-rise residential towers in a parklike setting. Major roadways would link together sectors of the city. Two of his key ideas are reflected in this urban design proposal. The first stemmed from his idea of returning the land for human use. It is for this reason that his buildings are raised off the ground on columns or pilote; in this way, buildings are not barriers to our movement along the ground. The second idea is how the organization of the city should change if we were to accept the automobile. Major roadways connected the high-rise housing with commercial and industrial sectors of the city. Le Corbusier sought to find ways for people to be in closer contact with nature and to use advances in technology to free themselves to reflect on their future and place in the world.[13]

The organization of buildings and patterns of land ownership conceived for Ville Radieuse are in sharp contrast to Frank Lloyd Wright's concepts for Broad Acre City.[14] In Ville Radieuse the land would be owned in common, whereas Wright would have each individual or family own a 1-acre lot. Homes and industry would be connected by major roadways. Wright felt that individual ownership of land by broad segments of the population was important in preserving a democratic society. His political and social philosophies were translated into the design proposals contained in the plans for Broad Acre City.

The differences in the two plans reflect the different political philosophies of the two men. Wright placed great value on the independence and autonomy of the individual, as suggested by each person owning a plot of land. In contrast, Le Corbusier saw a role for collective ownership of property, suggesting that the overall welfare of society is enhanced if individuals see themselves as part of a larger group and fit into a precise grand design.

Other visionaries have suggested more radical approaches to structuring the future city. Drawings and models by Paolo Soleri depict megastructures with heights as great as the tallest skyscrapers but covering as much as several hundred acres of ground. The structures contain both housing and employment for a population of 100,000 or more. Soleri has labeled this general set of studies "arcology." Like ecology,

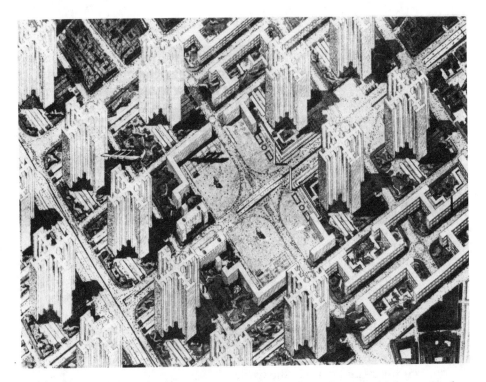

Le Corbusier's "Voisin" plan for Paris 1922–1925 (top). Building very high permitted extreme population density while leaving 95 percent of the land vacant. Though never built, this plan exerted enormous influence on design, both for better and worse, in many countries. At left is the planned community of Roehampton in Great Britain. Note the Corbusier influence in the large amounts of interior open space and the use of columns referred to as *pilote*.

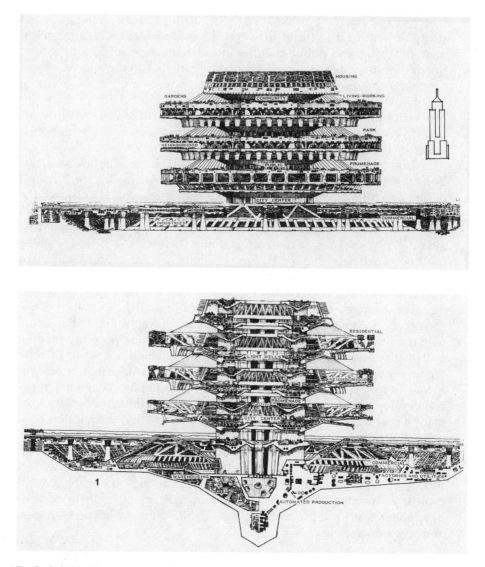

Paolo Soleri's "hyperstructure" in ground-level view, (top) and cross section (bottom). The figure at the upper right is the Empire State Building at the same scale. The structure would be 3,444 feet (1,050 m) high, 10,367 feet (3,160 m) across the base. Population would be 520,000 or about 171,000 per square mile of ground covered, roughly seven times the population density of New York City. Soleri's work is informed by an extremely strong environmental consciousness. The hyperstructure would house and employ a large number of people with a small "footprint" on the earth and with a low per capita energy consumption. Though hyperstructures are not likely to be built in the near future, Soleri's designs have influenced a generation of planners and architects. The influences of his thought can be found in the Houston Galleria and the Atlanta Hyatt-Regency.

which is the study of animals in their natural homes, arcology is the study of how best to build urban structures to accommodate homes, manufacturing, and public facilities in a fashion compatible with nature. In addition to suggesting new ways of organizing living space, Soleri's proposals contain predictions of completely automated manufacturing facilities that might be placed underground. Soleri constructed a small new community called Arcosanti in the desert north of Phoenix, Arizona to test, on a very small scale, some of the concepts embodied in his mega-structure designs.

One task for the urban designer is to combine aesthetic considerations with what we have learned about the relationship of physical design and human behavior to obtain a result that actually improves the quality of people's lives. We have learned through experiences with programs such as Urban Renewal and federally assisted housing that although physical design does affect human behavior, it is not the single most powerful determinant. Rather, it is one aspect of a complex array of physical, social, and economic, cultural, and psychological factors that are present in our everyday lives.

For example, public housing experience has taught us that high-rise construction does not necessarily work out well for all populations. It is hard for a mother living on the twelfth floor to keep an eye on her children as they play outdoors. The relative anonymity of a high-rise seems to make high-rise public housing prone to crime and may also make it more difficult to build a feeling of community and mutual help. On the other hand, high-rise development may work very well for a young, affluent population, as many a successful condominium developer could testify. The negative sociological effects that we now know to be associated with some high-rise, high-density housing were not anticipated by Le Corbusier. Rather than take his proposals literally as ideas to be applied to all urban areas and all urban populations, it is best to consider them as options to be explored and evaluated. The modern city needs a coherent vision of the future to guide its development, yet it must accommodate a wide diversity of values, hopes, and perspectives.

COMING TO TERMS WITH THE AUTOMOBILE

If one wanted to pick a single theme that defined much of urban design in the twentieth century, *coming to terms with the automobile* might be the best choice. Neotraditional planning is clearly planning for an automobile-owning population. It is an attempt to incorporate the automobile into the urban fabric while not letting the automobile destroy that fabric. The edge city and Frank Lloyd Wright's Broadacre City both represent a total accommodation to the automobile, and neither would make any sense without the automobile. One could not live in either city without an automobile, and little remains of the traditional urban fabric in either one. Corbusier's Voisin plan, though it looks radically different from Broadacre City or the edge city, is also an accommodation to the automobile. Travel in it is by automobile. There is no continuous web of small streets and sidewalks, and the distances between the huge structures would discourage walking for purposes other than recreation. Paoli Solieri's megastructure comes to terms with the automobile in a very different way: It banishes the automobile entirely. Vertical travel is by elevator, and horizontal travel is by foot. It is largely meant as an alternative to the sprawling, automobile-begotten metropolitan area of the twentieth century.

If one looks back to the neighborhood drawing on page 190, one sees that it, too, makes a particular accommodation to the automobile. Curvilinear internal streets permit automobile access to all parts of the neighborhood, while the larger streets on its edges carry longer-distance traffic around it rather than through it. In fact, though it antedates the neotraditional movement by at least half a century, it has a certain amount in common with neotraditionalism. Radburn, discussed in Chapter 3, is also an accommodation to the automobile. Like the neotraditionalists, the designers of Radburn acknowledged that automobile ownership and use would be nearly universal, but they sought to keep it in its place and to protect the fabric of the community from it.

The automobile is irresistibly attractive to most people. If there was ever a product that was essentially self-advertising, it is the automobile. It works well in low-density environments but poorly in high-density environments. It is an enormous space hog, both when in motion and when at rest. The automobile takes as much square footage as a studio apartment just to park it. For all these reasons the automobile is not easily reconciled with the urban environment, and it is not surprising that accommodating urban life to it has been and remains a central issue, or perhaps the central issue, in urban design.

SUMMARY

Urban design generally occupies a middle position between architecture and planning. Rather than focusing on the design of the individual structure, the urban designer concentrates on the massing and organization of buildings and on the spaces between them. The physical focus of the urban designer may be somewhat smaller than that of the planner, who is often concerned with the entire city or even the city as part of a larger metropolitan system.

The urban design process is broken into four main phases: (1) analysis, (2) synthesis, (3) evaluation, and (4) implementation. Judging a particular piece of urban design is always a somewhat subjective matter. However, there are some generally accepted criteria, including the following:

1. Unity and coherence
2. Minimum conflict between pedestrians and vehicles
3. Protection from rain, noise, wind, and so on
4. Easy orientation for users
5. Compatibility of land uses
6. Availability of places to rest, observe, and meet
7. Creation of a sense of security and pleasantness

The urban designer, in producing a design that not only looks good but also functions well, must consider many factors beyond the purely physical. These include financial, political, psychological, and sociological considerations.

The chapter summarizes neotraditional design (the New Urbanism) and the edge city as opposing visions of urban design. It then briefly touches on visions of the future of the city by Le Corbusier, Frank Lloyd Wright, and Paolo Soleri. It concludes with the observation that perhaps the greatest challenge to urban design in the twentieth century has been that of reconciling urban places to that most antiurban of technologies, the automobile.

NOTES

1. Lewis Mumford, *The Culture of Cities,* Harcourt Brace Jovanovich, New York, 1970, p. 5, originally printed in 1938.
2. Nicolai Ouroussoff, "A Tower That Sends a Message of Anxiety, Not Ambition," *New York Times,* February 19, 2007, p. B1.
3. Charles V. Bagli, "An agreement is formalized on Rebuilding at Ground Zero," *New York Times,* September 22, 2006, www.nytimes.com/2006/09/22/nyregion/nyregionspecial3/22rebuild.html?ex=11703.
4. Kevin Lynch, *The Image of the City,* MIT Press, Cambridge, MA, 1960.
5. Personal communication.
6. William H. Whyte, *The Social Life of Small Urban Spaces,* The Conservation Foundation, Washington, D.C., 1980.
7. Jane Jacobs, *The Death and Life of Great American Cities,* Vintage Books, Random House, New York, 1961.
8. Clarence A. Perry, "The Neighborhood Unit Formula," reprinted in *Urban Planning Theory,* Melville C. Branch, ed., Dowden, Hutchinson & Ross, Stroudsburg, PA, 1975, pp. 44–58.

9. Andres Duany, Elizabeth Plater-Zyberk, and Jeff Speck, *Suburban Nation,* North Point Press, div. of Straus and Giroux, New York, 2000.
10. Gary Delsohn, "Peter's Pockets," *Planning,* February 1994, pp. 18–21.
11. U.S. Bureau of the Census/U.S. Department of Housing and Urban Development Press Release, May 26, 2004. Data on housing prices can be found on the Web at www.census.gov./newhomesales.
12. Joel Garreau, *Edge City: Life on the New Frontier,* New York, Doubleday, 1991, p. 6.
13. Although Le Corbusier did not build very much himself, his ideas have had a huge influence on both architecture and urban design during much of the twentieth century. Probably the best summary of those ideas is his book *Towards a New Architecture,* Dover Publications, New York, 1986 (first published in 1931).
14. Frank Lloyd Wright, *The Living City,* Horizon Press, New York, 1958.

SELECTED BIBLIOGRAPHY

ALEXANDER, CHRISTOPHER, *A Pattern Language,* Oxford University Press, Oxford, 1977.

BARNETT, JONATHAN, *An Introduction to Urban Design,* Harper and Row, New York, 1982.

BOHL, CHARLES C., *Place Making: Developing Town Centers, Main Streets and Urban Villages,* Urban Land Institute, Washington, DC, 2002.

BRAMBILLA, R., and LONGO, G., *For Pedestrians Only,* Whitney Library of Design, New York, 1977.

CALTHORPE, PETER, *The New American Metropolis: Ecology, Community and the American Dream,* Princeton Architectural Press, New York, 1993.

DUANY, ANDRES, and PLATER-ZYBERK, ELIZABETH, *Towns and Town-Making Principles,* Rizzoli, New York, 1991.

DUANY, ANDRES, PLATER-ZYBERK, ELIZABETH, and SPECK, JEFF, *Suburban Nation,* North Point Press, div. of Straus and Giroux, New York, 2000.

KATZ, PETER, *The New Urbanism: Toward an Architecture of Community,* McGraw-Hill Book Co., New York, 1994.

LARICE, MICHAEL, and MACDONALD, ELIZABETH, eds., *The Urban Design Reader,* Routledge, New York, 2006.

MORRIS, A.E.J., *History of Urban Form,* John Wiley, New York, 1972.

MOUGHTON, CLIFF, CUSETA, RAFAEL, SARRIS, CHRISTINE, and SIGNORETTA, PAOLA, *Urban Design: Method and Technique,* Architectural Press, New York, 2004.

PUSHKAREV, B., and ZUPAN, J., *Urban Space for Pedestrians,* Regional Plan Association of New York, MIT Press, Cambridge, MA, 1975.

REGIONAL PLAN ASSOCIATION, *Urban Design Manhattan,* New York Regional Plan Association, 1969.

TRANCIK, ROGER, *Finding Lost Space: Theories of Urban Design,* Van Nostrand Reinhold, New York, 1986.

Urban Design Associates, *The Urban Design Handbook: Techniques and Working Methods,* W.W. Norton, New York, 2003.

VAN DER RYN, SIM, and CALTHORPE, PETER, *Sustainable Communities: A New Design Synthesis for Cities, Suburbs and Towns,* Sierra Publishing Co., Jackson, CA, 1991.

WALTER, DAVID, and BROWN, LINDA LOUISE, *Design First: Design Based Planning for Communities,* Architectural Press, New York, 2004.

CHAPTER 11

Urban Renewal and Community Development

For several decades, community development has been a major preoccupation of planners. It covers a wide range of goals and activities.

1. *Facilitation of economic growth or, in more desperate cases, measures to retard the loss of economic activity.*
2. *Attempts to increase the quality—and sometimes the quantity—of the municipality's housing stock.*
3. *Attempts to sustain or improve some particular commercial function of the city, most commonly retailing.* (Note the link here with item 1.)
4. *Improvement of some physical aspect of the community such as its parks, recreational facilities, parking facilities, or street pattern.*
5. *Furtherance of urban design goals.* This is often tied to some of the previously listed goals. For example, attempts to beautify—or de-uglify—a downtown street might be tied to attempts to increase downtown retailing activity, which might be part of a larger effort aimed at employment expansion.
6. *Provision of a variety of services.* Examples might be provision of social services such as day care, job training, or drug rehabilitation. Service provision is likely to be directed primarily to less affluent segments of the community's population.

Although the term *community development* is of post–World War II origin, it is not a totally new departure for planning. Planners' concerns with housing go back to the nineteenth century. Then, too, the facilitation of economic growth had been a major motivation behind city planning for decades.

This chapter begins with an account of Urban Renewal, a program that is now history. The reader may wonder why this look backward is necessary. Although the Urban Renewal program is now over, many of its main elements are still central to the urban development process. These elements include, among other things, the use of the power of eminent domain and public funds to assemble large blocks of land for redevelopment, the improvement of this land with public funds, and the transfer of this land to private investors at below cost.

Urban Renewal is instructive in that it illustrates how hard it can be to formulate policy that is free of major side effects and actually does what it is intended to do. For its critics, who grew to be very numerous indeed, Urban Renewal was a classic illustration of the old expression "The road to hell is paved with good intentions."

URBAN RENEWAL

Urban Renewal began with the Housing Act of 1949 and was officially ended in 1973 (though some funding of projects that were started before 1973 continued far into the 1980s). The goals of the program, as expressed in legislation and congressional debate, included

> Eliminating substandard housing
> Revitalizing city economies
> Constructing good housing
> Reducing de facto segregation

The method used was clearance and rebuilding directed by local agencies and supported by large federal subsidies. It was and still stands as the largest federal urban program in U.S. history, and it reshaped parts of hundreds of communities.[1] Statistics published in 1973 when the program was terminated showed that more than 2,000 projects had been undertaken on 1,000 square miles of urban land. Some 600,000 housing units, the dwelling places of perhaps 2 million people, had been demolished and those people forced to move. Roughly 250,000 new housing units had been built on the same sites. Approximately 120 million square feet of public floor space and 224 million square feet of commercial floor space had been built on renewal land.[2] As a measure of economic impact, the floor space figures translate into workplaces for almost one-half million employees. The assessed value of land and structures in renewal areas increased by a factor of 3.6 from what it had been before the program started. Today the figures for new construction would be much larger because the 1973 figures, which actually represented the facts as of about 1971, caught many renewal areas after the demolition phase but well before the construction phase was complete.

By 1973 the Urban Renewal program had spent approximately $13 billion in federal funds, a figure that would be about five times as large if converted into current dollars. To this figure should be added several billion dollars in local funds. Beyond that were the private investments on Urban Renewal sites. These far exceeded the total public investments.

The Origins of Urban Renewal

The rationale for Urban Renewal stems from two very simple economic circumstances. To build on virgin land, the builder need only pay the cost of the land plus the cost of construction. But to build on land containing structures that must be demolished, the builder must also pay the residual value of those structures. A building may be obsolete. Its owner or any objective observer might agree that under present circumstances it would never make sense to build a building like it on the present site. Nonetheless, if the building yields some stream of income to its owner, he or she will not give up the building without compensation.

Consider the following example. Mr. X owns a 90-year-old tenement near the core of the city. The building contains 12 apartments, which rent for an average of $200 per month—a low figure, which represents the fact that these apartments are close to the bottom of the city's housing market. Mr. X is approached by a developer who is interested in the land under the building but must acquire that building to get at the land. A rule of thumb for rental properties is that buildings are valued at 100 times the monthly rent roll, so Mr. X responds with an offer to sell for $240,000 ($12 \times 200 \times 100$). If the building occupies a 50-by-100-foot lot, that works out to about $48 per square foot, or roughly $2 million per acre. Even if the developer thinks Mr. X may come down considerably, that number makes vacant land on a suburban highway at even a million dollars an acre look good.

The second factor that impedes development in built-up areas is the land assemblage problem. Typically, urban land ownership is highly fragmented. A single city block is likely to be owned by many separate individuals or business organizations. In fact, in many cities the basic unit into which land was originally subdivided is the 25-by-100-foot lot (25-foot frontage and 100-foot depth). For the developer setting up a major project, it may be necessary to deal with dozens of different owners. In some instances their titles may have legal problems that cannot be resolved without substantial delays. In other cases the owner of a small parcel may exploit his or her capacity to block a large project by holding out for a price that far exceeds the fair market value of the land. Compared with the urban fringe, where land is generally owned in much larger blocks, the situation can be very discouraging.

These impediments to urban redevelopment were recognized during the latter part of the Great Depression, and the federal government became interested in taking steps to improve the competitive position of the central cities. In December 1941, hardly good timing for proposing a new civilian program, Guy Greer and Alvin Hansen published an article suggesting the creation of City Realty Corporations.[3] These organizations would be able to use eminent domain to assemble land and would have funds from higher levels of government for the acquisition and clearance of sites. The proposed corporations would thus be able to deal effectively with both the residual value and the land assemblage problems.

The idea lay dormant through World War II but was revived shortly thereafter. The Housing Act of 1949 brought the program into being very much as Hansen and Greer had envisioned it. The act provided for the creation of Local Public Agencies (LPAs) analogous to the City Realty Corporation. The LPA would have the power of eminent domain to acquire sites. Two-thirds of the LPA's funding was to come from the federal government, and the remaining third from the municipality. However, some of the local share could be services in kind (services of city personnel, donation of city-owned land, etc.) so that in cash terms, the federal government paid more than the nominal two-thirds. The LPA would use its legal powers and financial resources to acquire, clear, and otherwise prepare sites (grading, provision of utilities, widening and straightening of streets, etc.). These sites would then be sold or leased to private developers at substantially below cost.

By absorbing the residual value as well as many other development costs, the program would greatly accelerate the redevelopment process within the designated renewal areas of cities. By using public powers to acquire and clear large sites, the program would permit far more coordinated and imaginative development than would otherwise be the case.

In order to work as described, Urban Renewal introduced a new practice into law. It previously had been understood that eminent domain could be used to take private property and convey it to a public body for public use, for example, the building of a public school. But under Urban Renewal, government took property from one private party, say, the owner of a dilapidated tenement, and ultimately conveyed it to another private party, the developer building on the Urban Renewal site. This arrangement seemed questionable on constitutional grounds, and a property owner took an Urban Renewal Agency to court. But in 1954 in *Berman* v. *Parker*, the Supreme Court sustained the agency. Had the case gone the other way, the Urban Renewal process as it was then structured would have come to a virtual halt, another indication of the decisive role that the courts often play in planning.

In 2005 the Supreme Court, in effect, reaffirmed *Berman* v. *Parker* in the *Kelo* v. *New London* decision. However, the political uproar that followed the *Kelo* decision caused many states to ban private party to private party transfers so that at present the question of how many redevelopment projects will proceed is not clear. The *Kelo* decision and the states' responses to it are discussed in detail in Chapter 5.

Intention and Reality

Congress intended Urban Renewal as a housing program, as the goals listed earlier indicate. The initial legislation confined renewal activity to sites that either were or would be largely residential. In fact, the initial legislation stipulated that for each new unit of housing built, at least one old unit of housing must be torn down. The intent to eliminate slums by replacing bad, old housing with good, new housing was very clear.

The goals, though praiseworthy, contain some internal contradictions and some not-so-pleasant side effects, which become apparent on reflection. For instance, rebuilding the city's economy is likely to be furthered by a program that demolishes substandard housing and replaces it with a purely commercial development. But where does that leave the goal of adding good, new units to the city's housing stock? Who could be against eliminating substandard housing? Rephrase that view as reducing the supply of low-cost housing, driving down vacancy rates, and thereby tightening the housing market in which the poor must find shelter, and it does not sound so good. Achieving a higher degree of racial integration is a praiseworthy goal. One way to achieve racial integration in a poor, black neighborhood is to knock down dilapidated older housing occupied by low-income blacks and replace it with high-quality—and more expensive—housing to be occupied by middle- or upper-income households, most of whom are not black. Of course, that is a rather stiff price to pay for integration. And, whether real integration will occur or whether the two populations will simply live in the same area but have little to do with each other is a question too.

These points are not made to ridicule the program but to point out that Urban Renewal was major urban surgery, and as such it had many side effects, not all of which were desirable or foreseen. Any major program will have all sorts of secondary effects, some of which are good and some of which are bad. Some will be foreseen, and others will not. Doing good is not simply a matter of having good intentions.

One fact that soon became apparent as the federal funds began to flow was that local intentions and federal intentions were not always the same. With the passage of time, local desires began to change both federal law and federal practice. From the federal point of view, housing was central. But many localities did not care about housing. If rundown housing occupied by lower-income households was demolished and replaced with commercial development, the municipality solved both a housing and a tax base problem. The population that lived in the housing to be demolished would not vanish from the face of the earth. But if that population settled in adjacent communities after being dehoused by "the federal bulldozer," it became someone else's problem. From the local perspective, that solved the problem. Of course, from the federal perspective, that was no solution at all. At best, it was a "zero-sum game" played with federal funds. Clearly, what constitutes a problem and what constitutes a solution vary, depending on whom one considers to be one's constituency.

What happens when federal and local goals differ? The "locals" wanting the federal money do some compromising and accept some conditions that they do not like. On the other hand, the federal official whose job it is to spend the allocated funds wants to see agreements with LPAs signed and projects under way. So he or she does some compromising too. In time the program gets bent from its initial shape into something that both the "locals" and the "feds" can "live with." Gradually both the legislation and the regulations adapt to this reality. In the case of Urban Renewal, that meant relaxing the residential requirements and permitting many projects that had a predominantly commercial emphasis.

But that was hardly the end of the story. With the passage of time, some of the program's side effects became apparent, and both those who suffered from them and their allies began to exert pressure for change.

The most easily identified and numerous victims were those people who lost their housing because of Urban Renewal. In the typical project all the land was acquired at the beginning. Before clearance could begin, all those who resided on the site had to relocate. There then followed a clearance phase during which all the demolition was accomplished. The construction phase might then spread out over a number of years. It might not even begin for several years after clearance was completed. When the construction phase was completed, the number of new units might or might not approximate the number of units demolished. In either case the new units were not likely to do the original residents much good. First, there was the question of where they were to live in the intervening years. Equally important was the cost issue. Good, new housing costs a lot more to rent than bad, old housing. Urban Renewal typically took place in the urban core, where the housing that was demolished was old, relatively inexpensive, and largely occupied by poor people. Most of them could not afford the new housing even if they could wait for it. As Martin Anderson, probably Urban Renewal's most effective critic, noted,

> The people are poor. A great many of them are Negroes and Puerto Ricans. Good quality, conveniently located housing is scarce; good quality, conveniently located housing for $50 or $60 a month is almost impossible to find. It is difficult to picture hundreds of thousands of low-income people, many of them subject to racial discrimination, moving from low quality into higher quality housing at rents they can afford. And then, one might ask, why if all this good housing at low rents is available, didn't they move before urban renewal nudged them along.[4]

Studies of people dispossessed by Urban Renewal often found that they were worse off than before. The process of forced moving tore up individuals' connections to friends, relatives, neighborhood organizations, and the like, and generally left people less happy with their life situation than previously. The only way people seemed better off was that their standard of housing was somewhat better. That effect was almost inevitable since renewal often tore down the most deteriorated units in the municipal housing stock. Of course, with the tightening of the housing stock, they often paid more for their new housing than they had for their old housing.

The effect of Urban Renewal on the city's economy also came under some criticism. There was no question that Urban Renewal did stimulate economic development as described earlier. The question that critics raised was how much damage the process did to the existing economic structure. The first argument was that simply the announcement of impending renewal froze investment both within and nearby the designated area. Within the area no investor would commit funds, for obvious reasons. But even outside the area, investors would be inhibited because they did not know how much competition—subsidized with federal monies—would soon be coming to the renewal site. Whether it be old housing, old retailing space, or old commercial space, spending money on its renovation or modernization would be made more risky if new, competing structures were soon to rise on the nearby site. Another argument was that when businesses were forced to close because their buildings were condemned, they often never reopened. The loss of customers to competitors or the expenses of reopening simply overwhelmed them. It was also said that renewal generally demolished relatively cheap commercial space. This is the space often occupied by struggling new enterprises, which cannot afford newer space. Thus it attacks the "incubator" role of the city and may do long-term damage, which does not show up in short-term statistics.[5]

Ultimately, Urban Renewal accumulated so many enemies that in 1973, Congress terminated the program, although, as noted, funding pursuant to contracts signed previously continued into the 1980s.

Urban Renewal in Retrospect

On the negative side there seems little argument about the human costs of Urban Renewal. The paralyzing effect of impending renewal action seems less important in retrospect, for once the project has been completed, the effect disappears. Somehow, the argument regarding the incubator role of the city also seems less powerful in retrospect. Many cities still retained large amounts of cheap space after Urban Renewal. If there is a substantial vacancy rate on low-cost commercial space, as is the case in many cities, it is hard to argue that much long-term damage has been done by the loss of some low-cost space.

On the positive side what can be said? Probably the biggest gain has been that Urban Renewal projects gave many cities the ability to compete with their suburbs. For example, White Plains, New York (as noted in Chapter 9), has grown as a retailing center in an age when most cities have been losing retail sales and jobs to the suburbs. Clearly, it was the new and efficient street pattern and the availability of large, cleared parcels of land with marketable titles at below cost that made it possible for White Plains to swim against the tide. Without Urban Renewal most of the retailing activity now in downtown White Plains would be out on the highway.

Baltimore's Inner Harbor redevelopment done jointly by the city and the Rouse Corporation. The development includes tourist attractions such as the restored USS *Constellation* (below), restaurants and retailing, large amounts of office space, and hundreds of hotel rooms to accommodate tourists and business travelers. The project works because the mix of uses is mutually reinforcing. Thus such redevelopment can be done only as a unified effort involving many adjacent parcels of land.

The Stamford, Connecticut, Urban Renewal area as it appeared in the 1960s before redevelopment began and as it appeared two decades later at full development. Note the ready access to Interstate 95 and the revised street pattern.

One of Manhattan's big selling points as a commercial and residential location is its preeminence as a cultural center. A part of that preeminence resides in Lincoln Center, a cultural complex built as an Urban Renewal project on several blocks of deteriorated residential structures.

The Boston waterfront, redeveloped as part of the city's urban renewal program, pulls in millions of tourist dollars and also makes the city more attractive as a residence for a young and an affluent population, which might otherwise settle in the suburbs. In that sense it acts as a promoter of "gentrification," a trend that most cities, rightly or wrongly, seem to welcome.[6]

Writing in the 1960s, Charles Abrams stated of Urban Renewal,

> It [Urban Renewal] allows room for more squares and parking spaces and is a useful tool for the long overdue rebuilding of cities enslaved to the 20- to 25-foot lot, and the gridiron pattern. It provides the opportunity for enlarging the street system surrounding the new projects, the closing of streets where necessary, the diversion of traffic, the addition of streets or widening of intersections. It facilitates running the new highways into the city's shopping centers and the creation of off-street parking and enclosed parking space. In short, the renewal project supplies a multipurpose opportunity in place of the piecemeal efforts to correct traffic problems, provide playgrounds and open spaces, provide neighborhood amenities, and new housing public and private.[7]

In referring to the failure of firms that were unable to compete successfully, the economist Joseph Schumpeter applauded the "creative destruction" of capitalism. At its best, Urban Renewal was "creative destruction." It tore away an old and obsolescent urban fabric and replaced it with something newer and brighter and, often, more economically viable. But such destruction is not without pain to individuals and enterprises. Reasonable people may differ over whether the gains justified the pain.

COMMUNITY DEVELOPMENT

A year after the termination of Urban Renewal, Congress passed the Housing and Community Development Act of 1974. This omnibus act replaced Urban Renewal as well as a variety of urban "categorical" programs, that is, programs that provide funds for specific categories of activity, such as sewage treatment, recreation, or housing. The act provided Community Development Block Grants (CDBGs) to permit localities to pursue a wide range of activities including, but not limited to, activities that had been pursued under the Urban Renewal program. The intent of the block grant approach, as opposed to the categorical approach that it superseded, was to reduce the federal role in local affairs by allowing municipalities more discretion. In that sense it was in keeping with the more conservative political philosophy of the Nixon administration in contrast to preceding Democratic administrations. Community Development (CD) funds were distributed on a formula basis, which counted population, age of housing stock, and poverty. Thus virtually every municipality in the nation received some funds. Municipalities were free to expend funds on a wide range of projects, including many types of service provisions as well as capital expenditures. Among the purposes for which CDBG funds could be used were acquisition of real property, public facilities and improvements, parks and playgrounds, centers for the handicapped, neighborhood facilities, solid waste disposal facilities, parking facilities, public utilities, street improvements, water and sewer facilities, pedestrian malls and walkways, flood and drainage facilities, clearance activities, public services, rehabilitation of public residential structures, rehabilitation financing, temporary relocation assistance, and economic development.[8]

The act emphasized services for the poorer segment of the population, but in many communities there was a tendency to spend most of the funds on bricks and mortar. Bricks and mortar last longer and are more visible. Then, too, services are hard to discontinue, so if the source of funding is cut off, the municipality that spent most of its CD funds on services could find itself out on a financial limb.

According to the legislation, municipalities were not to use CD funds for expenditures they would make in the absence of such grants, nor were they simply to use CD funds for tax relief. In the terminology of public finance, CD funds were to be "stimulative," not "substitutive."[9]

The legislation also required the predominant share of CD funds to be used in a manner that primarily benefited low- and moderate-income persons. Essentially, this requirement means either spending CD funds in areas that have substantial proportions of low- and moderate-income residents or spending the funds on facilities or services that will be used by or that will benefit these persons. Presumably day care or land clearance for a factory or warehouse would so qualify; repairing the seawall at the municipal yacht basin would not.

The act required each community to include as part of its grant application a Housing Assistance Plan (HAP), which spelled out community housing needs and laid out plans for dealing with them. The act also imposed significant "citizen participation" requirements on communities. The regulations state

> There shall be involvement of low and moderate income persons, members of minority groups, residents of areas where a significant amount of activity is proposed or ongoing, the elderly, the handicapped, the business community, and civic groups. . . . The applicant shall make reasonable efforts to insure continuity of involvements. Citizens shall be provided adequate and timely information. . . . Citizens, particularly low and moderate income persons and residents of blighted neighborhoods, shall be encouraged to submit their views and proposals.[10]

Clearly, these requirements were motivated in part by criticisms of Urban Renewal, which accused these programs of riding roughshod over the residents of renewal areas. Even if the federal government were to make no effort to enforce these rules directly, they would have considerable force. Any citizen or any group that felt slighted in the community planning process could bring suit against the municipality on the grounds that it had failed to provide an adequate citizen participation process. A successful suit might well enjoin the municipality from spending further federal or perhaps even local funds until this fault was remedied.

In 1977 Congress expanded the scope of community development efforts somewhat by providing additional funds intended specifically for local economic development. These funds were provided under the Urban Development Action Grant (UDAG) program.[11] Communities that met certain criteria for poverty, age of housing stock, unemployment, and slowness of employment growth were eligible to apply for grants. UDAG grants were typically used for site acquisition and clearance to facilitate local economic development. Unlike the CD grants, there was no entitlement. Obtaining a UDAG grant was a completely competitive process. In effect, UDAG monies enabled municipalities to do, on a small scale, a commercial renewal project—site acquisition, site clearance and improvement—and then sell or lease at below cost. In that sense, UDAG was a direct descendant of Urban Renewal. It differed in scale and in the absence of a housing element.

UDAG funds were used in hundreds of cities, and the competition for grants was intense. Although the program was popular with the cities, it was phased out at the end of the Reagan administration, whose hostility stemmed at least in part from ideology. Such grants constitute a public allocation of capital to which the free market conservative is likely to be opposed. But two other factors also contributed to the program's demise: the fact that some instances of corruption and excessive profits were turned up and the general budgetary pressures generated by the federal deficit.

Community Development Versus the Urban Renewal Approach

In general, Community Development has differed from Urban Renewal primarily in its gentler approach and in its emphasis on rehabilitation and preservation, as opposed to Urban Renewal's clear-and-start-from-scratch approach. For example, in the realm of housing, CD programs have expended substantial funds on grants or low-interest loans to homeowners and to the owners of rental properties for rehabilitation and modernization.

One program that has been highly successful in some cities is *urban homesteading*. In declining residential areas, cities often come into ownership of residential properties, primarily through foreclosure for unpaid property taxes. (This is not likely to happen in thriving areas since the higher market values will cause the owner who cannot pay taxes to sell out rather than simply walk away.) In the homesteading program the house is essentially given to a new owner, who promises to "bring it up to code" within a given time period. If the new owner succeeds in doing so, the title then passes to him or her without charge. In effect, the cost of acquiring the property is the expenditure required to bring the building up to the standards set forth in the municipality's building code. That expenditure may be primarily financial, that is, money spent on contractors, or it may largely be labor by the new owner, so-called sweat equity.

In the city of Baltimore, the program has worked quite successfully on old row houses. The lure of home ownership has been strong enough to attract an adequate number of urban homesteaders, but according to city officials, the potential profitability has not been so great as to bring in many speculators. Not only does the program improve housing quality, but also it fills neighborhoods with individuals and families who have a strong commitment to those neighborhoods. It thus contributes greatly to neighborhood stability, a goal that in the long run is probably more important than simply the maintenance of building quality.

In commercial areas many CD programs have taken a less radical approach than Urban Renewal. Low-interest loans have been made to local businesses, sometimes for operating purposes and sometimes for renovation and expansion. Pedestrian malls designed to attract shoppers have been constructed. Of course, some expenditures quite reminiscent of Urban Renewal have been made, for example, the construction of parking structures and street widening and realignment. But in general, the emphasis has been on preservation, rehabilitation, improvement, and gradual change. The intent has been to achieve the same goals as Urban Renewal but with less damage to the existing urban fabric.

In many cases, municipal governments have given up the idea of competing head-to-head with suburban retailers on the grounds that it is impossible to match the automobile access and parking advantages of the suburban shopping center (the case of White Plains, noted earlier, is an exception in this regard). Instead, there has been more of an emphasis on strengthening those assets of the city that are not so readily matched by suburban areas. Such assets might include cultural facilities and areas designed largely for pedestrian traffic, where the denser and more varied pattern of land uses gives the city an advantage over the suburbs. For example, the revitalized downtown in Roanoke, Virginia, includes a museum, a theater, a number of specialty shops, and a small farmers' market, all laid out for pedestrian access. There has been no serious attempt to compete with outlying shopping centers.

In a number of cities, waterfronts that have long since lost their shipping functions have been converted to areas where one strolls, has lunch or dinner, shops, or uses some cultural or entertainment facility. The Boston Waterfront, Manhattan's South Street Seaport, and Baltimore's Inner Harbor are examples. Very often there is an element of historic preservation in such efforts. For example, South Street Seaport includes a number of restored buildings as well as several old, restored sailing vessels tied up at city-owned piers. Again, one might view this as an attempt to capitalize on an asset that the city has and the suburbs generally do not have, namely, the charm of the old.

THE HOUSING QUESTION

Housing, defining the term broadly, is probably the most important issue in urban planning. Housing constitutes the biggest single land use in most cities and towns; in many places it occupies more land than all other uses combined. In many cities housing and the land under it constitute more than half of the entire real property tax base. There are few, if any, planning issues that touch most people more deeply than the condition of their immediate neighborhoods, because that is where they spend most of their time. Moreover, housing is often the single largest item in a family's budget, and the house is the most expensive possession that most people acquire. Equity in a house often constitutes the major share of the estate a person passes on to his or her descendants.

We may all agree that housing problems are important and that they need to be solved, but when asked what the housing problem is, different people will give very different answers. Though we may speak generally of the nation's housing market, it really represents the sum of thousands of separate housing markets. If you live in St. Paul, the state of the housing market in the San Francisco Bay area is likely to be of marginal interest to you at best. If you live in a single-family house in the suburbs, the market for rental housing in the central city of the same metropolitan area is likely to be of little interest to you even though the economist can easily show that those two markets do affect each other to some degree.

For some, the quality, quantity, and cost of housing available to low-income Americans may be the nation's biggest housing problem, though some economists will argue that it is really not a housing problem at all, but rather a problem of income distribution. If you are renting now but want to become a homeowner, you may conclude that the nation's biggest housing problem is that in many housing markets, prices have risen more rapidly than has personal income.

If you are a middle-aged homeowner who wants to build an accessory apartment in your garage for an aging parent, your biggest housing problem may be what you see as the excessive rigidity of the zoning codes that will not let you do this.

If you are a homeowner in a bucolic exurban town that is fast turning into a suburban town, your biggest housing problem may be that too much of it is being built too near you.

If you are a homeowner in a nice suburban house that you have lived in for 25 years, you may not think that there is any housing problem at all. You are comfortably housed now, and when you retire and sell, that big capital gain will make it very easy to buy a nice condo in Florida. You don't get upset about rising house prices because the faster they rise, the better off you are. As an aside, in the writer's experience as a planner in the suburbs, it is very difficult to get homeowners concerned about housing shortages for exactly the reason just suggested.

Where is public policy in all this confusion about what our housing problems really are, you might ask. The answer is *almost everywhere* policies often point in different directions because different elements of public policy are responses to different constituencies.

In 2006 the federal government spent about $38 billion on subsidies for the housing of low-income people. In addition to that, it provided about $8 billion in preferential tax treatment to the builders of low-income housing. (In general, preferential tax treatments are referred to as *tax expenditures* because they achieve a somewhat similar result as do direct expenditures, but they are delivered instead through provisions in the tax code.) Certainly, on balance such expenditure and tax policies can be characterized as pro-poor. However, in the eyes of many, these spending and tax policies are not the largest federal interventions in the nation's housing market. In 2006 the federal government provided about $15 billion in tax expenditures for property taxes paid by homeowners. It also provided a tax expenditure in the $76 billion range for mortgage interest paid by homeowners. On top of that, there was a tax expenditure in the $36 billion range connected with capital gains made on the sale of owner-occupied housing.[12] All together, that adds up to about $127 billion in tax expenditures for homeowners. For reasons explained in Chapter 17, these tax expenditures clearly favor the prosperous. The fact that these two packages of policies point in somewhat different directions is not to say that either is bad. Helping low-income people to obtain better housing certainly seems praiseworthy. Then, too, many would say that encouraging homeownership is also praiseworthy. But if the federal approach had been designed by a single intelligence, say, that of a wise and benevolent despot, it probably would look rather different and would be more internally consistent. But it was not designed by a single mind. It came out of the workings of many minds—out of the democratic political process.

At the local level, policy may not be entirely consistent either. A town may limit the amount of land it zones for multifamily housing and require larger building lots for single-family housing than most planners and urban designers would consider necessary. That treatment tends to raise rents and house prices. At the same time, the town may also have inclusionary zoning requirements that compel builders to set aside a certain number of units for low- and moderate-income renters or buyers. Of course, these policies are somewhat contradictory, but they respond to different constituencies, they may have been enacted at different times, and their inherent contradictoriness may not be readily apparent to the citizen-voter who has many different things besides local housing policy on his or her mind.

Finally, as big as public direct expenditures and tax expenditures connected with housing are, they are dwarfed by private expenditures on housing. In 2006 the nation spent almost $2 trillion on the purchase, ownership, and operation of housing.[13] That was, very roughly, one-fourth of after-tax personal income in the United States. Inevitably, then, government's ability to influence housing is limited.

PLANNING FOR HOUSING

For housing that is to be built purely by the private market, meaning without direct subsidy of any kind, the main step a community can take is to provide the opportunity for the market to work. At the physical level this means providing infrastructure, namely, roads, public water, and sewers. Land cannot be developed for housing without road access, and it cannot be developed at more than very low density without public water and sewers. Beyond these absolutely essential items, other public investment will affect the rate of new housing construction. For example, recreational facilities or an elementary school may make a developing area more desirable.

Land-use controls will limit the quantity of the housing stock by setting an upper limit on the number of units per acre. That affects price. Controls also affect price by the types of units they permit. Garden apartments cost less per unit than do row houses. Row houses, in turn, cost less per unit than do free-standing, single-family houses on small lots. These cost less than houses on large lots. Land-use controls that require particular amenities, for example, recreational facilities, for new developments will raise prices. Subdivision requirements affect the site-preparation costs, which in turn will be reflected in the price of the finished units.

What can the community do to provide low- and moderate-income housing? As stated, it can provide the infrastructure to support and the land-use controls to permit the building of less expensive housing types. It can encourage builders to seek out and use federal and state subsidies for low- and moderate-income housing. It can make it community policy not to use its land-use control and other legal powers to obstruct the building of subsidized housing. Similarly, it can take an accommodating rather than a resisting stance toward group homes. This last item is not an idle point: In many communities, citizens' resistance to group homes can be ferocious. Also, the municipality can use CD funds, or even funds raised through its own tax efforts, to subsidize low- and moderate-income housing. For example, CD funds have been used to make low-interest rehabilitation loans to low- and moderate-income homeowners and to the owners of low-rent apartment houses. This may be done through a revolving loan fund or through the banks, with the municipality picking up a portion of the interest cost and perhaps also guaranteeing the loan. The municipality's zoning laws can provide density bonuses to developers who will include a certain number of units reserved for low- and moderate-income buyers or renters (see Chapter 9).

If particular forces threaten to reduce the supply of affordable housing, municipal governments may sometimes be able to take preventive steps. For example, one trend in many suburban areas where land prices are high and the supply of vacant building lots limited has been that of *tear downs.* Typically these occur in older neighborhoods. A would-be homeowner will purchase a house that may be of good quality and in scale with other houses in the neighborhood simply to obtain the lot. That house is then torn down and replaced with a much larger house, sometimes referred to derisively as a *MacMansion* or *monster home.* Residents often object because such large homes are out of scale with the surrounding development. But another effect is to reduce the supply of so-called starter homes and thus make it more difficult for less affluent people to make the transition into home ownership. Many municipalities have resisted this process with a variety of regulatory tools. In some cases, zoning laws and building codes have been adjusted to limit height, bulk (the cubic footage of the structure), and the maximum floor area ratio, among other building characteristics.[14] Other municipalities have required design review if the new house is to be substantially larger than the one it will replace. However, like so many other matters in planning, such restrictions can be argued both ways. The goals of such restrictions seem quite reasonable, but they do constitute an infringement on the rights of the would-be buyer and may also impose a loss on the homeowner who wants to sell his home. The possibilities for litigation seem to be considerable.

A number of municipalities ranging from New York City to Santa Monica have attempted to render housing more affordable through rent controls. Economists, by and large, are against the practice. They argue that rent controls encourage disinvestment in those units subject to controls and that fear that controls will be extended to new units reduces the rate of new construction. Thus they conclude that controls reduce housing quality and exacerbate housing shortages. However, regardless of the wisdom of controls, no list of policies that address the question of affordability would be complete without mentioning them.

A single community generally cannot do a great deal with regard to low- and moderate-income housing. Federal monies for housing are in relatively short supply. Even if the community makes every effort to see that its land-use controls do not preclude lower-cost housing types, the fact is that any new unsubsidized housing is expensive. The ability of the community to subsidize housing through either CD funds or its own revenues is limited by other demands on the budget and the willingness of the majority of the citizens to be taxed for that purpose. Still, there is a certain amount that can be done if that is what the community wants to do, but as noted elsewhere, not every community wants to do it.

Federal Requirements

The particular federal program that has propelled literally thousands of communities into preparing formal housing plans has been the CDBG program. One requirement for the receipt of funds, whether to be used for housing or other purposes, is the Housing Action Plan (HAP). At present, the rules require the community to certify in its application for CD funds that it is following a HAP approved by HUD. Briefly, HUD requires the plan to contain an inventory of the community housing stock and numerical goals for its improvement. It also requires the plan specifically to provide an analysis of the housing needs of lower-income renters. Finally, the plan must state of how the goals are to be met.

Exactly what aspects of the housing stock and the housing market the study covers may vary substantially from one community to another. If the study is oriented primarily toward matters that are eligible for federal funding, it is likely to focus on the quality and cost of units available for less affluent households.

Good objective measures of housing stock quality are hard to come by. Several decades ago the U.S. Bureau of the Census had its census takers enumerate "deteriorated" and "dilapidated" units but subsequently decided that such judgments were too subjective to provide good data. However, the bureau does provide data on the number of units that do not contain complete kitchen and bathroom facilities. Imperfect as this measure is, it has been used as a "proxy" for housing quality. Another measure of housing quality, though it has nothing to do with the physical quality of the unit, is overcrowding. The U.S. Bureau of the Census defines overcrowding as a situation in which there is more than 1.0 resident per room.

Finally, much attention has been paid to the question of whether low- and moderate-income households can afford housing. For this judgment, planners tend to rely on rent/income ratios, a data item that is also supplied by the U.S. Bureau of the Census. At one time it was thought that a household should not have to spend more than 25 percent of its income on rent. Recently, housing economists have used 35 percent as a rule of thumb. Either figure is somewhat arbitrary.

Thus the community can make some estimates of the number of units that may be substandard and the number of households in need of rental assistance. Vacancy rates may give some indication of whether the community should be seriously concerned with increasing the total number of units.

A More Comprehensive Approach to Planning for Housing

The community, in studying its housing situation, need not be bound by the necessities of federal approval and federal subsidies. One long-term issue to be considered is simply the numerical adequacy of the entire municipal housing stock. Projections of population and employment can be used to approximate future housing needs. A general understanding of market dynamics is also important. Units are added by new construction, sometimes by the subdivision of existing units, and sometimes by the conversion of non-residential to residential units. Units are lost through fire, demolition, abandonment, and the conversion of residential to nonresidential units (e.g., the conversion of a single-family house into an office). Market forces such as personal income, rents and prices in adjacent communities, land costs, the competition between residential and commercial uses for space, and so on, shape the long-term change in the municipal housing stock.

For a long-term analysis, attention should be paid to supply factors, including land, utilities, street capacity, and the like. Thus a really comprehensive study would go well beyond the low- and moderate-income housing questions and attempt to understand the dynamics of the entire housing market. We might also note that housing for low- and moderate-income residents and housing for more prosperous residents are not totally separate matters. If neighborhood conditions deteriorate, we may witness a flight of the prosperous and their replacement by low- and moderate-income households. Conversely, if demand for housing is strong and the supply of housing limited, we may see prosperous households displacing poor households, the "gentrification" process visible in many cities.

SUMMARY

The Urban Renewal program began with the Housing Act of 1949 and was terminated by Congress in 1973. Local public agencies used a mixture of local and federal funds plus the power of eminent domain to acquire and clear redevelopment sites. Sites or portions of sites were then made available to developers at a fraction of their cost. The combination of heavy subsidy and eminent domain was intended to solve two major obstacles to urban redevelopment: problems of residual value and site assembly.

As Urban Renewal progressed, it acquired many enemies, primarily because of its displacement effects. By the time Congress ended the program, it had demolished approximately 600,000 housing units, forcing perhaps 2 million people, most of them having low or moderate income, to relocate. It also forced the closure of thousands of small businesses, many of which never reopened. The destruction of the social and economic fabric of neighborhoods was ultimately considered to be an unacceptably high cost.

The year after Urban Renewal was ended, Congress passed the Housing and Community Development Act of 1974. In place of Urban Renewal's clear-and-rebuild approach, Community Development programs have tended to emphasize preservation and improvement. The urban homesteading program noted in connection with the city of Baltimore typifies the emphasis on preserving the existing urban fabric that characterizes many CD programs. As a reaction to what were regarded to be the excesses of Urban Renewal, CD legislation contains numerous requirements for citizen participation, particularly that of low- and moderate-income citizens.

Housing plans may be narrowly keyed to federal funding programs, or they may take a broader approach. In the latter case, estimates of housing demand based on employment and demographic studies are compared with projections of future supply in order to estimate future needs. In general, housing is one of the more frustrating items with which the planner deals. The sums of money on the public side are very small compared with total expenditures. Thus the capacity of government programs to affect the basic housing picture is limited. In addition, housing issues are often major sources of social and political controversy within the community.

NOTES

1. It can be argued that two other federal programs or policies have actually had more effect on cities than did Urban Renewal. These are (1) the construction of the interstate highway system and (2) the structure of the IRS code and the tax benefits it provides for homeownership. However, as powerfully as these may affect cities, they are not specifically urban programs, nor were their urban effects foremost in the minds of the legislators who enacted them. In fact, it seems likely that their urban consequences, though now well recognized, were largely unanticipated.

2. Congressional Research Service, Library of Congress, "The Central City Problem and Urban Renewal Policy," prepared for the Subcommittee on Housing and Urban Affairs, Committee Banking, Housing and Urban Affairs, United States Senate, Washington, DC, 1973. Note: Subsequent figures on Urban Renewal expenditures or any other federal housing or urban development programs can be found in the *Annual Yearbook*, Department of Housing and Urban Development (HUD), Washington, DC.

3. Guy Greer and Alvin W. Hansen, "Urban Redevelopment and Housing," National Planning Association, 1941.

4. Martin Anderson, *The Federal Bulldozer*, MIT Press, Cambridge, MA, 1964, p. 64.

5. The hypothesis, an old one in urban economics, is that the city incubates small, growing industries. When they reach a certain degree of maturity, they then move out to more peripheral areas, which provide lower costs, albeit in a somewhat less rich and varied business environment. The city survives even though it loses one mature industry after another because it is constantly generating new industries. For an account of this idea, see Wilbur Thompson, *A Preface to Urban Economics*, Johns Hopkins Press, Baltimore, 1965.

6. The term *gentrification* comes from *gentry* and refers to the movement back into older neighborhoods of people of higher economic or social status than the present occupants.

7. Charles Abrams, "Some Blessings of Urban Renewal," in *Urban Renewal: The Record and the Controversy*, James Q. Wilson, ed., MIT Press, Cambridge, MA, 1966, p. 560.

8. This partial listing is drawn from regulations published in the *Federal Register*, March 1, 1978, p. 8441. The *Federal Register* is a daily publication of the federal government, which provides detailed regulations for the implementation of legislation passed

by the Congress. It runs to many thousands of pages per year.

9. Enforcing such a distinction is not always easy. If the community intended to build a playground in any case but allocates part of its CDBG to that purpose, how can we ever say with certainty how the general purpose funds thus freed have been used? Can we say with certainty that the funds freed by the CD grant have not been used for a purpose that is not an approved CD activity? In fact, can we say with certainty that the knowledge that it was to receive a CDBG did not cause a municipality to tax its property owners at a somewhat lower rate than it would otherwise have done?

10. See *Federal Register,* March 1, 1978, p. 8462.

11. The basic ground rules for the UDAG program were spelled out in the *Federal Register,* October 25, 1977, part III, and January 10, 1978, part IV.

12. Table 469, *Statistical Abstract of the United States,* 2006, 126th ed.

13. Table 658, *Statistical Abstract of the United States,* 2006, 126th ed.

14. Terry S. Szold, "Mansionization and Its Discontents," *Journal of the American Planning Association,* vol. 71, no. 2, Spring 2005, pp. 189–200.

SELECTED BIBLIOGRAPHY

Dalton, Linda C., Hoch, Charles J., and So, Frank S., *The Practice of Local Government Planning,* 3rd ed., International City/County Management Association, Washington, DC, 2000, chap. 11.

Wilson, James Q., ed., *Urban Renewal: The Record and the Controversy,* MIT Press, Cambridge, MA, 1966.

Ford, Larry R., *America's New Downtowns,* Johns Hopkins University Press, Baltimore, 2003.

Paumier, Cy, *Creating a Vibrant City Center,* Urban Land Institute, 2004.

CHAPTER 12

Transportation Planning

In this chapter we consider transportation planning as practiced at the municipal and metropolitan level. Before we begin, some background on transportation trends since World War II would be useful.

RECENT TRENDS IN URBAN TRANSPORTATION

In 1945 the US had a population of 133 million people who owned 25 million automobiles. By 2005 the U.S. population had grown to 295 million, There were 136 million passenger cars registered as well 53 million vans and SUVs (which federal statistics count as light trucks) for a total of 189 million vehicles for personal transportation.[1] That is roughly one vehicle for every 1.6 people. Whereas the human population of the United States had increased by a factor of about 2.2, the automobile (and van and SUV) population had increased by a factor of 7.5.

One powerful force behind the increase in automobile ownership was the large increase in average real personal income in the years following World War II. Not only did the general prosperity enable more people to own automobiles, but that same prosperity also facilitated a great wave of suburbanization. The postwar suburbanization and the increase in automobile ownership were complementary phenomena. Widespread automobile ownership facilitates suburbanization. On the other hand, moving from central city to the suburbs increases one's need for an automobile.

The public transportation situation in the postwar period was very different. As the term *public transportation* or *transit* is used here, it refers to buses, subways, light rail (a term for trolleylike vehicles), commuter rail, and the like. It does not include intercity rail or bus, air transportation, or taxicabs. Ridership reached an all-time high in 1945, when wartime employment peaked, gasoline was rationed, and civilian production of automobiles had been suspended for several years. From 19 billion trips by fare-paying passengers in 1945, the total declined to a postwar low of 5.6 billion in 1975. By 2006 that figure had risen to 10.0 billion, in part because of heavy federal investment in public transportation over the last three decades and partly because of increases in the price of gasoline.[2] Despite this increase, transit still constituted a smaller percentages of all trips in 2006 than it did in 1975.

The decline in public transportation is the opposite side of the coin from the forces already discussed. Increased automobile ownership eliminated millions of potential transit customers. Suburbanization meant the movement of millions of households into areas where, because of reduced congestion, the automobile works better than in central cities. Conversely, the dispersed suburban land-use pattern makes the provision of public transportation, which depends on high volumes on fixed routes, more difficult. The spreading out of residences and workplaces with the process of suburbanization complicates both the *collection* and the *distribution* problems. The former refers to getting the rider to the boarding point for the public transportation vehicle. The latter refers to getting the rider from the end of the transit trip to his or her actual destination.

Public transportation is also bedeviled by the trade-off between the spacing of stops and average speed. The more closely spaced the stops are, the lower is the average speed. But increasing the distance between stops makes the collection and distribution problems more severe. Because of the need for frequent stops, public transportation tends to be slow. In 1996, buses averaged 13.1 miles per hour and light rail—what used to be called the trolley car—averaged 14.3. Commuter rail, with its own right-of-way and less frequent stops, did better, averaging 33.1 miles per hour.[3] These figures do not include waiting time.

The ideal environment for public transportation is seen in a number of the large, older, eastern cities—masses of jobs concentrated in the urban core and masses of apartments concentrated near transit stops. This arrangement simplifies the collection and distribution problems and provides a large enough market to sustain frequent service. The high densities also make automobile usage less attractive. But that pattern of development is very much the opposite of the dominant land-use trends since World War II.

Over three-fourths of all public transportation trips to work occur in central cities. Of the subway and elevated trips shown in Table 12–1, the great majority occur in just two cities, New York and Chicago. Transportation to work is emphasized here because it is the mainstay of public transportation demand. When public transportation use declines, it is generally the journey to work that holds up best. Trips for shopping, recreation, and the like decline most rapidly.

TABLE 12–1 Transportation to Work in 1990 and 2000 (figures in millions)

Mode	Persons in 1990	Persons in 2000
All modes	115.1	128.3
Car, truck, or van	99.6	112.7
Drove alone	84.2	97.1
Public Transportation	6.1	6.1
Bus	3.4	3.2
Subway or elevated	1.8	1.9
Railroad	0.6	0.7
Selected Other		
Walk	4.8	3.8
Work at home	3.4	4.2
Ride bicycle	0.5	0.5

Sources: *1990 Census of the Population, Social and Economic Characteristics,* Table 18; and *2000 census,* Summary File 3 (SF 3), Table P30, U.S. Bureau of the Census, Department of Commerce.

Measured in percentage terms, the growth area in transit has been in *paratransit,* also referred to as *demand response systems.* These systems, with names like Dial-a-Ride, send a vehicle in response to a call. They do not operate on fixed routes or have a fixed schedule. Such systems may serve a specialized population such as the handicapped or the elderly, or they may service an area in which it is not economically feasible to provide scheduled, fixed-route public transportation. In that sense, these systems are a kind of publicly supported taxi service to serve those with few other transportation choices.

As Table 12–1 makes clear, the great majority of commuters get to work by automobile, most of them driving alone. From 1990 to 2000, total commutation to work increased by 13.2 million people. Of that increase, 12.9 million was in the *drove alone* category.

PAYING FOR TRANSPORTATION

To understand transportation policy, it is important to understand how private and public transportation are financed. In terms of direct costs, private transportation is largely self-financed. Vehicle purchase, fuel, maintenance, insurance, parking, and other costs are paid directly by vehicle owners and operators. Roads and highways are, by and large, paid for by a variety of taxes and charges levied on automobile users. Such charges include license fees, registration fees, and state and federal gasoline taxes. For example, federal contributions to road construction come from the Highway Trust Fund, which is supplied largely by federal excise taxes on the sale of motor fuel.

It has been argued, however, that the automobile exacts a variety of hidden costs that are not so covered—air pollution; death and injury from accidents; and a more scattered pattern of land use, that results in increased costs of public services. If one dislikes the suburbs, one might argue that suburbanization is a cost the automobile has imposed on America. Conversely, if one prefers the suburbs to the city, as millions of Americans evidently do, one can say that suburbia is a blessing the automobile has conferred on America. But regardless of these arguable matters, the fact is that in a direct sense, automobile transportation is primarily paid for by those who use it.

The economics of public transportation are very different. At present fares pay only one-third of transit expenditures. The remaining two-thirds of transit expenses are paid for by nonfare revenues of transit agencies such as tolls and taxes and by a variety of grants and subsidies from local, state, and federal government. Without heavy subsidization, public transportation would virtually disappear in the United States.

We subsidize public transportation for several reasons. There are people who cannot use private transportation, and society must provide them with some means of personal mobility. Such people include those too young to drive, those too old to drive, those who have some handicap that prevents them from driving, and those who cannot afford automobile ownership. We also subsidize public transportation because we think it improves circulation in urban areas by reducing the number of private vehicles in use. Shifting people from cars to buses or trains may also improve environmental quality by reducing the total amount of emissions. Heavier reliance on public transportation also permits a more compact urban design, which many planners favor. These last several points suggest that subsidizing public transportation confers benefits on nonusers as well as users.

Finally, some suggest that we ought to subsidize public transportation as a matter of income redistribution. The argument is that by providing at below cost a product used by low-income people, we are, in effect, transferring income to them. This is the weakest of the arguments because subsidizing transit is a very inefficient means of transferring income. Not all poor people use public transportation, nor are all users of public transportation poor. In fact, patrons of at least one type of transit, commuter rail lines, have above-average incomes.

TRANSPORTATION PLANNING AND LAND USE

Land use and transportation planning are very much a chicken and an egg situation. In the short term, land use shapes the demand for transportation. Many a highway has been built because population or commercial growth produced congestion and delays, which generated political pressures to deal with the situation. On the other hand, the provision of roads changes land values and thus alters the intensity with which land is used, and, with that outcome, alters the entire pattern of land use. The interstate highway system, to take the largest example, was designed to facilitate movement of vehicles from one existing urban center to another, something it does very successfully. However, it has also done a great deal to reshape urban areas, as discussed earlier, an effect that was not one of the motivations behind its construction. Beyond that, it has reshaped the balance between metropolitan and nonmetropolitan areas in the United States by making formerly isolated rural areas far more accessible than they were a generation ago. In fact, it is believed that much of the movement of manufacturing activity out of metropolitan areas and into rural areas has occurred for just this reason. Thus it can be argued that the system has had a major impact on the economies of both metropolitan and nonmetropolitan areas.

In the ideal case, transportation planning and land-use planning go hand in hand. At the national level, this has clearly not been the case. At the state level, it sometimes is and sometimes is not. In the best case, state highway departments will take into account the fact that their decisions not only affect how the population now in place is served but also shape land use for decades to come. Highway planning and more general land-use planning are coordinated. In the less satisfactory case, the highway engineers tend to think in terms of meeting demand rather than a combination of meeting demand and shaping the future of land use.

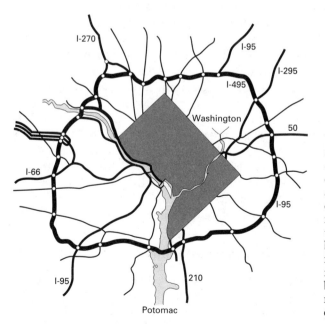

The interstate highway system with its ring road, or "beltway." design creates masses of highly accessible land outside the city, particularly where radial routes coming out of the city intersect the beltway. Though not intended in that way, this feature of the system has been a powerful force for moving people and jobs out of the central city.

It is often at the municipal level that transportation and land-use planning are most closely coordinated. The issues are simpler, and the numbers of people involved are smaller. Thus coordination is easier. The fact that both the planners and the highway department report to the same mayor and the same city council can prevent them from going off in different directions.

THE TRANSPORTATION PLANNING PROCESS

Transportation planning is a basic function of many planning agencies, for adequate circulation is and traditionally has been a major planning goal. As practiced in the last several decades, particularly at the multijurisdictional level, it is perhaps the most elaborate and mathematically well-developed area of planning. The modern multijurisdictional transportation planning process represents a fusion of engineering, economics, and urban planning, all facilitated by modern computing equipment. The field in its present form was brought into being by a coincidence of forces shortly after the end of World War II. The rapid increase in automobile ownership and the suburban housing boom created a massive demand for increased highway capacity. The Highway Act of 1954 provided 50 percent matching subsidies for urban highways and funds for transportation planning. It also required planning as a condition of eligibility for the matching subsidies—still another example of the conditioning of the local planning scene by federal funding requirements. In 1956 Congress passed the National Defense Highway Act, which initiated the building of the interstate highway system. (See Chapter 18.) Federal legislation and funding thus set off a wave of highway building in the decades after the war. The digital computer, which was invented at the end of the war and became a practical planning tool a decade to a decade-and-a-half later, made it possible to "crunch" huge amounts of data and thus make feasible the modern style of highway planning.

The following pages focus on highway planning at the metropolitan level. At smaller geographical levels, the process is necessarily simpler and less mathematical. More than most other planning processes, transportation planning necessitates a multijurisdictional effort, for the flow of travelers is no respecter of municipal boundaries. Thus the same communities that may do their land-use planning in relative isolation will often be part of an areawide metropolitan transportation planning process.

Modeling Metropolitan Area Transportation

The goal of the transportation planning process is to assist governments in providing an adequate transportation system at an acceptable cost. This involves modeling the behavior of the present system, estimating future travel demand, and estimating how changes in the system will affect travel behavior and the operation of the transportation system in the future.

The approach described later was first used in the 1950s in the Chicago Area Transportation Study (CATS).[4] Variations of it were subsequently done in many other major metropolitan areas. The general approach has also been used in many smaller area studies.[5]

Major transportation planning projects usually involve a four-step procedure for estimating travel movements. After such estimates are made, the merits of different possible changes in the transportation system can be evaluated.

Going through the steps requires building a geographic database. In general, the area in question, say a metropolitan area, is divided into zones. In the Chicago study and many studies patterned after it, a rectangular grid is imposed on the region, and data are collected for each square in the grid. A typical grid might cover several thousand square miles. In other cases, particularly in smaller studies, the zones may be irregular, with shapes determined by terrain features, neighborhood boundaries, or other characteristics of the land-use pattern.

The data gathered for each zone include both population and economic information. The former includes such items as the number and type of housing units, number of residents, age structure of the population, household income, number of automobiles owned, and similar items. The economic information will include such items as the number of people employed in the area in various occupations and the number of square feet of floor space and land area devoted to retailing, wholesaling, manufacturing, office operations, and other activities. Each of these broad categories may be broken up into a number of subcategories. Sometimes, just total nonresidential floor space is used. It is often a good predictor of how many trips will be attracted to the zone, and it is much less costly to develop than the more detailed category-by-category data.

The Four-Step Process. Once the database is in place, any given transportation alternative can be evaluated. In general, a four-step process is used.

1. *Estimating trip generation.* Before deciding where people will go from a given point of origin, it is customary to estimate how many trips a given place will generate regardless of where those trips are destined. For estimating trip generation from a residential area, variables such as household income, number of persons in the household, number of vehicles owned by the household, and possibly population density might be used to estimate average trips per household per day. In general the number of vehicular trips would be positively related to the first three items and negatively related to the last. The reason for the last relationship is that trips that may be made on foot or by mass transit in a dense area are likely to be made by auto in a sparsely populated area, where trip distances are longer, and parking and congestion problems are minimal.

2. *Estimating trip distribution.* After trip generation has been resolved, the next issue is to distribute the trips. Suppose a given zone in a region contains one thousand households, whose average size, vehicle ownership, and income are known. The total number of trips that they will make can thus be estimated, but the question is how the trips will be distributed among possible destinations. A variety of estimating methods has been developed over the years. The most commonly used is the gravity model, originally developed in the 1920s to analyze shopping patterns. (The original formulation was known as Reilly's Law of Retail Gravitation, and in the past, gravity models were sometimes known as Reilly models.) The force of gravitation between two objects is proportional to the product of their masses and inversely proportional to the square of their distance. By analogy, the force of trip attraction between, say, a housing complex and an office complex would be proportional to the product of the number of households and the number of square feet of office floor space and inversely proportional to some function (perhaps the square or some value near the square) of the distance between them. In principle, then, one might estimate the relative number of trips made from origin A to destinations B and C by computing the relative force of attraction between A and B and between A and C. This process is illustrated in the box on page 233. For a region with a large number of zones, the database and the number of calculations are huge. Thus such a planning exercise was impossible before the computer.

Such an exercise could be done for an actual distribution of housing and floor space or for a hypothesized one. Distance might be taken as straight-line distance from the center of one zone to the center of another. Or it might be taken as actual road mileage, travel time, or some composite of both.

3. *Estimating modal split.* Where there is more than one mode of transportation available, say, automobile and bus, it is important to apportion by mode the trips distributed in the previous stage. Over the years considerable experience has been accumulated, and a number of mathematical estimating techniques worked out. In general, the two main criteria that determine which mode an individual takes are quality of service and cost. Quality of service is largely a matter of travel time. Quite frequently there is a clear trade-off between speed and cost. For example, in public transportation, commuter rail service is much faster than bus transport and also substantially more expensive. Knowing the income distribution of the population using public transportation would thus help to make estimates of how that population would divide between the two modes.

4. *Trip assignment.* Once the choice of mode has been settled, the last issue is predicting how trips will be distributed between alternate routes

A SIMPLE GRAVITY MODEL ILLUSTRATION

Assume that in the trip-generation step, we have determined that the area shown as the origin will generate 1,000 trips to work per day. This will go to the three destinations shown in the accompanying figure. The force of attraction of each destination is proportional to its square feet of floor space divided by the square of the distance. Then the trips will be distributed as shown in the calculations below the figure. If there are actual data on trips, the model can be made to approximate reality by adjusting the exponent of distance to some value other than 2.0 or by adjusting the values of distance.

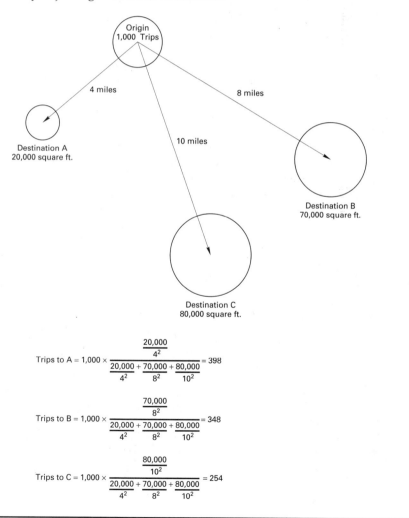

$$\text{Trips to A} = 1{,}000 \times \dfrac{\dfrac{20{,}000}{4^2}}{\dfrac{20{,}000}{4^2} + \dfrac{70{,}000}{8^2} + \dfrac{80{,}000}{10^2}} = 398$$

$$\text{Trips to B} = 1{,}000 \times \dfrac{\dfrac{70{,}000}{8^2}}{\dfrac{20{,}000}{4^2} + \dfrac{70{,}000}{8^2} + \dfrac{80{,}000}{10^2}} = 348$$

$$\text{Trips to C} = 1{,}000 \times \dfrac{\dfrac{80{,}000}{10^2}}{\dfrac{20{,}000}{4^2} + \dfrac{70{,}000}{8^2} + \dfrac{80{,}000}{10^2}} = 254$$

from the same origin to the same destination. Again, the question is resolved by mathematical modeling. Consider that there are two routes, A and B, from zone X to zone Y. Imagine, also, that we begin by assuming that all traffic takes route A. As travelers shift from A to B, travel times on route A fall while those on route B lengthen. Mathematical models are used to predict when equilibrium will be reached.

In general these four modeling steps are used in the following way. First, the existing state of the transportation system is modeled mathematically, using the steps just described. Then the model is calibrated to produce results that correspond to the actual flow of traffic. The data used for calibration will come from measurements of traffic flow, for example, those made by counters that are tripped by the weight of a vehicle passing over a rubber hose. Once the model duplicates the observed travel behavior, alternative situations can be modeled. For example, a planner might assume an increase in the number of households in a given zone.

The model can be run again, and the region will show a slightly different pattern of trips. The transportation planners might then postulate changes in the road pattern to see how these will affect the pattern of trips. Since the speed of travel on a road depends on its volume of traffic, such simulations will give planners insight into how potential changes in the road system will affect travel times. Travel in metropolitan areas has morning and evening peaks, corresponding to commuting hours. Traffic flow is very different in peak and nonpeak hours. The model can be run to stimulate different times of the day.

The real strength of the computer model is that the speed with which it does calculations makes it possible to experiment with numerous different possibilities. In principle, there is no calculation done by the computer that could not be done by hand, but the computer opens up a range of exploratory possibilities that would otherwise be prohibitively time-consuming and expensive.

The Policy Decision

Computer modeling can and does help to examine possible improvements and additions to the transportation system but by itself cannot make any decision. How is the actual decision about policy reached?

One technical aid to decision making is benefit/cost analysis. This is a process of systematically enumerating the benefits and costs of a particular option, say, a new link in the road network or an extension of a transit line, and assigning to them monetary values. The ratio of benefits to costs can then be calculated. Where many projects are competing for limited funds, the benefit/cost ratios may be used as a means of deciding which ones to fund.

On the benefit side of a proposed improvement might be listed time saved by travelers. Doing this means that a monetary value must be assigned to time, and in fact, a large number of studies have been done by transportation analysts to find out how travelers value their time. Other benefits might include lives saved and injuries avoided if the new route is safer than the old one. Savings in vehicle operating costs would be considered if the new route were shorter or reduced stop-and-go traffic. Costs would include land acquisition costs, construction costs, and repair costs, among others. Typically, the three biggest items in highway benefit/cost studies are construction and land costs, time savings, and vehicle operating costs.

Benefit/cost analysis has its subjective side. For example, how does one assign precise values to human life and health? Measures such as estimated lifetime earnings and the award of courts in negligence cases have been used. The favored technique at the present time is a statistical one that combines information on wage rates and fatality rates in different occupations to determine how much more people demand to be paid in order to accept a certain amount of risk of loss of life.[6] For example, if a person would accept a death risk of one chance in 1,000 for a wage difference of $1,000, then one might say that implicitly the person placed a value of $1,000,000 on his or her own life. This method may seem to be cold-blooded or even a bit bizarre, but if we are going to make expenditures to reduce the risk of death or injury, there is no way to get around placing a monetary value on life, even though we all concede that no one really has that kind of godlike wisdom. There are also many other items that cannot readily be converted into dollar terms. For example, urban design and aesthetic issues do not lend themselves well to being "monetized." Nonetheless, benefit/cost analysis is far superior to reliance on pure intuition.

Transportation questions often generate tremendous citizen involvement and can become highly emotional and political. New construction takes people's property and can have great impact on neighborhoods. A freeway through a neighborhood can constitute a formidable barrier between the remaining halves, greatly raise the noise level, lower the air quality, and generally make life there a good deal less attractive. Changes in the flow of traffic may bring windfalls to some businesses and large losses to others. Citizens whose daily travel, particularly the commute to work, is slow and frustrating constitute a powerful force for public investment in new roads and, in more densely developed areas, for public transportation as well.

Some citizens' disillusionment with highway building has come from what planners and engineers refer to as the "induced demand" phenomenon. When the capacity of the road network is increased, for example, by the opening of a new expressway, it is often observed that traffic congestion does not fall very much on the other roads and that in the peak hours, the new road may be operating at close to maximum capacity in a very short period of time. The building of new capacity has induced additional traffic; also, some people who previously traveled during off-peak hours because of congestion now travel in the peak hours. The highway planner may be satisfied with the result in that more people are now getting what they want, namely, the ability to travel where they want when they want. But to the citizen who used to drive to work in the morning rush in one hour and now drives in 59 minutes, it may appear that little has been gained.[7] The next time a highway bond issue comes up for referendum, he or she is likely to vote no.

In recent years citizens' opposition to highway building has become formidable. In San Francisco in the early 1970s, the Embarcadero Freeway was halted in midconstruction by opposition, based largely on concerns that this elevated road would block views of San Francisco Bay. When the portion that had been built and was in use was damaged in the October 1989 earthquake, the city did not move to rebuild it. Rather, the remaining portions were torn down. Since then, the north and south portions have been replaced by an at-grade road. In the 1970s New York City planned Westway, a highway along the west side of Manhattan to divert through traffic from the city's congested street system. The project had the support of the mayor, the governor, organized labor, planners, and probably the majority of the city's population. It was opposed for over a decade by a determined group of citizens who simply did not want any more highways. In 1985 after $200 million had been spent on land acquisition and design costs, the city conceded defeat and filed an application with the federal Department of Transportation (DOT) to have some of the funds that would have been spent on Westway switched to mass transportation projects. The term *freeway revolt* has been used to describe rising resistance to highway building. Not only does resistance come from affected residents, businesspeople, and property owners, but a certain amount also comes from environmentalists, who in general do not favor anything that will increase automobile use.

A variety of business interests may weigh heavily in the decisions about highway construction. Firms wanting the better access that a new highway would bring may lobby for it. Major property owners who do not want their property bisected by a new highway may make every effort to oppose it. In some cases a new roadway may go through whichever neighborhood or municipality is politically weakest and therefore least able to resist it.

The details of how a new highway or highway improvement will be funded may be critical. A local government may know that on a pure calculation of benefits and costs, alternative A is distinctly superior to alternative B. But if alternative B will be paid for primarily by state and federal funds whereas alternative A will require a substantial local contribution, the local government is likely to go for alternative B. All projects look more favorable if funded with OPM (other people's money).

In short, in the final analysis, the ultimate decision is a political one. Modeling, benefit/cost studies, and other types of analysis can and do help to move the decision process in the direction of greater rationality. But ultimately, in a representative democracy, it is the political body that makes the decision and appropriates the funds.

Planning for Public Transportation

The approach to planning public transportation infrastructure is similar in principle to that of highway planning. The same sorts of computer studies done for automotive travel can be done for transit. Then, too, benefit/cost analysis is as applicable to transit as it is to highways and streets.

In recent years the public in large cities and metropolitan areas has generally been more favorably disposed to transit improvements than to the building of new highways. Improving transit tends to decongest the streets by reducing automobile travel. It appeals to environmentalists for reasons of air quality and fuel consumption. Those concerned with urban design often favor transit because it leads to a more compact land-use pattern that is much friendlier to pedestrians than is a city designed for automobile transportation. Distances between destinations are shorter, and less land area is given over to streets. Taking a walk in a transit-oriented city like Chicago or Boston and then taking a walk in an automobile-oriented city like Albuquerque or Los Angeles is likely to convince one that there is some truth in this argument.

A major problem with transit, as noted before, is that financially it is far from self-sustaining. It must be heavily subsidized, and most of that subsidy must come from higher levels of government.

In the mid-1970s the long-term decline in transit ridership halted, and a ridership has slowly increased since then was noted. This reversal was due in large measure to increased federal funding beginning with the Urban Mass Transit Act of 1964. Since then mass transit ridership has grown modestly, largely on the basis of modest federal support. Behind the less than overwhelming political support for subsidizing transit is a basic geographical fact. To function adequately, transit requires population densities of at least two thousand or so persons per square mile. Therefore, a substantial part of the U.S. population, including much of its metropolitan area population, lives in areas that cannot adequately be served with transit at any conceivable level of public expenditure. Thus many members of Congress do not have constituencies that care much about transit.

At this writing the construction of light-rail systems proceeds at a modest pace in a limited number of U.S. cities. *Planning* magazine noted that some light-rail mileage has been constructed in eight U.S. cities since 1981 (San Diego, Buffalo, Portland, Sacramento, San Jose, Los Angeles, Baltimore, and St. Louis). In general, these routes are of modest length and operate with heavy subsidy. They are designed to take advantage of and to promote high density, corridor-type development. Construction costs for light rail are extremely high. The city of Sacramento cites a *per mile* cost of $9.6 million for its 18.3 miles of light-rail routing and claims that this is the lowest per mile cost of any federally funded light-rail system.[8]

In the past both light-rail and heavy-rail (commuter railroad) systems have been built on a radial plan to carry suburban workers to downtown jobs. With the increasing decentralization of employment, there has been discussion of building circumferential light rail to carry workers from suburban residences to jobs in suburban subcenters, but as yet there has been little action in this regard. The high cost of construction and the formidable collection and distribution problems noted earlier would make, this type of system extremely expensive.

In this writer's view, the future of public transportation probably lies much more with buses than with light-rail. The capital costs are generally much lower, and routings can be changed to accommodate changes in the pattern of residential and commercial growth.

A relatively recent compromise between light rail and buses is Bus Rapid Transit (BRT).[9] The bus operates on its own right of way, generally with longer spacing, say, a mile, or so between stops, than does an ordinary bus. The stop resembles a railroad stop more than a conventional bus stop, particularly in that it has boarding from a platform at the same level as the bus floor, rather than the usual step up from street level with an ordinary bus. This considerably shortens loading times. In some cases the system may be set up to automatically shift traffic lights to green as the bus approaches intersections. Capital costs are higher than with conventional bus systems but lower than with light rail. The system has greater flexibility in that the bus can also run on ordinary streets and those routes can readily be adjusted.

CHANGES IN THE FEDERAL ROLE

For planners concerned with transportation, the most important event of recent years was the passage of the Intermodal Surface Transportation Efficiency Act (ISTEA) of 1991. Often pronounced as "ice tea," the act retained the basic structure of very substantial federal transportation aid to the states and localities financed largely by the Highway Trust Fund. But the act also contained some new features that held out the prospect of integrating transportation planning with land-use and environmental planning into one sensible whole.

For several decades it has been widely understood that the building of transportation facilities, especially highways, has had a huge effect on how and where people lived. But, in too many cases, highway planning has been based almost solely on pure transportation issues with little respect for its effect on the overall pattern of settlement and on the natural environment. ISTEA requires states and cities to incorporate nontransportation into their transportation planning. In effect, ISTEA moves the side effects closer to the center of the planning process by forcing states and localities to look ahead and if possible, eliminate the negative consequences of road building.[10]

In areas where current air quality is not up to federal standards, so-called nonattainment areas, the metropolitan planning organization will not be able to receive federal funding unless it produces a plan that deals with automotive emissions. These plans might involve car and van pooling, increased investment in transit, elements of land-use planning designed to place jobs and housing closer to each other, and the like. Foot and bicycle paths might also be part of such a plan.

A total of $24 billion over the life of the act was earmarked for "flexible" funds that could be allocated to a wide range of transportation projects ranging from highways to bike paths. Ten percent of each grant had to be earmarked to safety and another 10 percent to "enhancement." The latter might include scenic, recreational, or other improvements along or near the transportation route in question. Funding for such "enhancements" was continued for another six years by the Transportation Equity Act for the Twenty First Century (TEA-21) of 1998 and again by the ponderously named Safe, Accountable, Flexible, Efficient, Transportation Equity Act: A Legacy for Users (SAFETEA-LU) passed in 2005.

SAFETEA-LU provides $244.1 billion in funding over a six-year period, of which approximately one-fifth will be for transit and "flexible" uses.[11] Most of the funding for SAFETEA-LU will come from the Highway Trust Fund.

FINE-TUNING THE SYSTEM

By the late 1980s the interstate highway system of some 40,000 miles was virtually complete. A future comparable episode of highway building in the United States does not appear to be possible. In recent years the attention of highway engineers and planners has turned to the question of extracting more performance from existing road networks. One set of techniques is referred to as transportation system management (TSM).

One TSM technique is the high-occupancy vehicle (HOV) lane to encourage carpooling. Another is the use of traffic metering techniques. With these, entry from a feeder road onto a main artery is controlled so as to maintain good traffic flow conditions on the main route and thus maximize its carrying capacity. Charging higher transit fares or vehicle tolls during peak hours is another technique. In Los Angeles all businesses with over one hundred employees are required to develop a program to reduce single-occupant automobile trips to work. Promoting telecommuting, offering financial incentives to carpool, subsidizing transit fares, and the like might be elements of such a program. The common element is that programs take a managerial rather than a construction-based approach to increasing system capacity and improving the quality of travel. A number of TSM techniques are listed in Table 12–2.

Travel Demand Management

Within the general category of TSM are a range of travel demand management (TDM) techniques that are intended to improve transportation system performance by reducing travel demand. For example, encouraging telecommuting reduces total travel demand. Encouraging bicycle commuting would reduce total automobile traffic particularly during morning and evening peaks. Note that TSM and TDM are overlapping concepts. The HOV lane listed earlier as a TSM technique could also be considered a TDM technique.

THE GROWING ROLE OF TOLLS AND PRIVATIZATION _____

Economists will tell you that the way to utilize resources efficiently is to get the prices right. If something is free, then it will be used down to the point where the last user gets just the most trivial amount of benefit from it, but the cost that last user imposes may be much more than trivial. If the resource is priced right, then the last user gets just as much benefit as the cost he or she imposes, In the jargon of economics, there is an efficient adjustment at the margin.

One recent trend has been a growing use of tolls. More roads are being tolled and in many cases the toll is adjusted by time of day. That makes sense in terms of efficient use of the road, for the more crowded the road is the more an additional car slows down the other cars and thus the higher cost that last car imposes. It also maximizes toll collections by raising the charge during the morning and evening peak when demand is greatest.

One new wrinkle in the matter of toll roads is that the building and operation of toll roads is attracting private capital. One notable example in the East is the Dulles Toll Road that connects the Washington, D.C., beltway (I-495) with Dulles Airport. People value their time, sometimes quite highly, and investors are realizing that there is money to be made in selling people time savings. From the municipal or state perspective the privately built toll road achieves the public goal of improving traffic flow without the expenditure of public funds and the creation of public debt.

Not only is private capital being attracted to the construction of toll roads, but also to the operation of existing roads on a toll basis. In a case that received widespread notice the city of Chicago sold a 99-year lease for the

TABLE 12–2 Transportation System Management (TSM) Techniques

1. Improved vehicular flow:
   - Improvements in signalized intersections
   - Freeway ramp metering
   - One-way streets
   - Removal of on-street parking
   - Reversible lanes
   - Traffic channelization
   - Off-street loading
   - Transit-stop relocation
2. Preferential treatment of high-occupancy vehicles:
   - Freeway bus and carpool lanes and access ramps
   - Bus and carpool lanes on city streets and urban arterials
   - Bus preemption of traffic signals
   - Toll policies
3. Reduced peak-period travel:
   - Work rescheduling
   - Congestion pricing
   - Peak-period truck restrictions
4. Parking management:
   - Parking regulations
   - Park-and-ride facilities
5. Promotion of nonauto or high-occupancy auto use:
   - Ride-sharing
   - Human-powered travel modes
   - Auto-restricted zones
6. Transit and paratransit service improvements:
   - Transit marketing
   - Security measures
   - Transit shelters
   - Transit terminals
   - Transit-fare policies and fare-collection techniques
   - Extension of transit with paratransit services
   - Integration of transportation services
7. Transit management efficiency measures:
   - Route evaluation
   - Vehicle communication and monitoring techniques
   - Maintenance policies
   - Evaluation of system performance

Source: U.S. Department of Transportation, Urban Mass Transportation Administration, *Transportation System Management: State of the Art,* Washington, DC, 1977.

toll rights on the Chicago Skyway to a group of investors for $1.8 billion. The city took the position that the money would be used for investments that would have a long-term payoff for the city and thus the sale was well advised. The skeptic could argue that politicians, who stand for election on a two-or four-year cycle, have a short time horizon and that in the long term selling that significant revenue source will turn out to be a mistake.

The trend toward the privately built or operated toll road has been given a considerable boost by SAFETEA-LU. The law permits investors to build toll roads using tax exempt revenue bonds. The term "revenue bond" means a bond whose interest and principal are paid out of the revenues earned by the project built with the bond. The term "tax exempt" means that the buyers of the bonds do not have to pay income tax on the interest payments that they receive from the bonds. That, in turn, means that the bonds can be issued at lower interest rates, thus reducing the debt service costs of the investors in the toll road. That constitutes an implicit federal subsidy (a tax expenditure as discussed in Chapter 11) in the building of the road. The amount of the subsidy is not trivial. On a billion dollar road the cumulative interest cost savings from the tax exemption feature might come to several hundred million.

Another feature of the law expands the types of roads that states can subject to tolls. In a number of states, major roads in metropolitan areas have high occupancy vehicle (HOV) lanes, open only to vehicles with at least either two or three occupants during the morning and evening rush. SAFETEA-LU permits states to convert these HOV lanes into high occupancy tax (HOT) lanes.[12] Vehicles with the required number of passengers will still be able to use the lane free of charge, but the lane will also be open to single-occupant vehicles if they pay a toll. The most high-tech HOT lane is one that uses *dynamic tolling*. The charge for using the lane can vary as often as every six minutes and the rate is posted on electronically operated signs along the roadway so that motorists can adjust their choice of HOT lane or untolled lanes accordingly. A transponder in the automobile is tripped electronically when the car is in the HOT lane and the motorist is billed periodically. The system brings in revenue and puts any excess capacity in the HOT lanes to use, thus reducing congestion on the remainder of the roadway. The dynamic tolling feature permits optimizing traffic flow, for as the number of vehicles in the HOT lane rises sufficiently to cause significant congestion, the fares rise to discourage use of the lane. It was feared that these so called Lexus Lanes would be used only by upper-income drivers, but a multiyear experiment on HOT lanes on San Diego's I–15 has not shown this to be the case. HOT lanes are now in use in California, on I–10 in Houston, in Denver, and are now in the planning stage in the Washington, D.C., area. In the case of the D.C. area, HOT lanes planners are now thinking in terms of charges that may top $1 per mile at peak times, a clear indication that they believe that motorists will pay very substantially to ease the pain of their daily commute.

SMART HIGHWAYS, INTELLIGENT VEHICLES, AND NEW MACHINES

Transportation system performance may also be improved in coming years by the application of electronic and other control and decision-making technologies. The *smart highway*, as the term is now used, means equipping the roadway with sensing devices and computing equipment so as to permit instantaneous decision making that optimizes traffic flow. For example, motorists can be diverted to other routes, entrances to main routes can be metered as noted previously, speed limits can be adjusted, and the like.

Toll booths are notorious for slowing the flow of traffic. However, recent electronic technology permits toll collection without slowing down. A transponder in the car registers its entrance onto the toll road and debits the driver's account automatically.[13] Such systems are now in use across the United States from parts of the New York metropolitan area to Los Angeles. Some systems, such as the one in the Los Angeles area, charge higher tolls during the morning and evening peaks with a view toward diverting some traffic to nonpeak hours and also maximizing revenue.

Intelligent vehicle technology, probably combined with smart highway technology, holds much potential, both for improving safety and for increasing the capacity of a given road network. Radar or other distance-sensing devices combined with computing and control technologies would permit building vehicles whose acceleration, braking, and steering are controlled automatically. Much of the technology is here now. For example, collision avoidance devices using either radar or infrared technologies to sense objects in front of the car are now showing up in higher priced automobiles.

A system whose reaction time is measured in microseconds and that never gets bored or sleepy could permit much safer and faster traffic flows. The driver of such a vehicle might guide it on local roads but once on the main route would shift to automatic control and then relax and read the newspaper as the car proceeded on its way.

Just as airliners are guided by air-traffic-control decisions made on the ground and a combination of human and machine decisions made in the cockpit, we can envisage a system in which drivers, computing and control equipment in the vehicle, and the smart highway together guide vehicles on the ground. The gains in safety and faster traffic flow might be considerable.

Onboard electronic computing equipment has also made the gasoline/electric hybrid possible. At this writing the hybrid seems to be making the transition from relative rarity into the mass market. Automobile dealers report waiting lists for hybrids at the same time they have large backlogs of unsold conventional vehicles. A variation on the hybrid that is now in the design stage is the *plug-in hybrid* such as the Chevrolet Volt. This type of vehicle would have batteries sufficient to power it for several dozen miles and would be rechargeable from a 110-volt outlet. It would use gasoline only on longer trips, which constitute a minority of the miles driven by most automobiles. If effect, the plug-in would do most of its mileage on coal, nuclear, natural gas, hydroelectric, or whatever energy source the owner's electric utility company used to generate power. About half of America's electric power is generated by coal which on a BTU basis is considerably less expensive than gasoline. Thus the plug-in will probably have relatively low fuel cost. It will be good for the U.S. trade deficit since only a small fraction of U.S. electric energy is generated by burning petroleum, and to the extent that it reduces U.S. dependence on imported oil it will have some geopolitical advantages as well. Its net environmental effects will depend on what choices we make about electric power generation in the years to come.

It is widely believed that in the longer term, the fuel cell, in which hydrogen and oxygen are combined in the presence of a catalyst, will bring about still higher mileage and lower emissions. The widespread use of the fuel cell is still many years off, for the big question to be solved is where the hydrogen to power the fuel cell will come from. It takes as much energy to pull a molecule of water apart to obtain hydrogen as is gotten back when the hydrogen is burned to form water. Until the question of how to produce the hydrogen needed is solved, mass use of the fuel cell cannot happen. The hydrogen-fuel-powered vehicle itself would emit no pollution, since all that comes out of the tailpipe is water from the oxidation of hydrogen. How much pollution the system as a whole would emit would depend on the energy source used to produce the hydrogen.

Although technologies that improve the speed, safety, and fuel efficiency of the automobile are obviously desirable in their own right, not everyone will be happy about their urban design implications. For whatever improves the performance of the automobile/highway system will be inherently decentralizing and will move us in the opposite direction from the compact, fine-grained pattern advocated by designers like Duany and Calthorpe (see Chapter 10).

Whether there will be major changes in specifically urban vehicles remains to be seen. The very-short-wheelbase Smart Car that is widely seen in European cities is a rarity in the United States, and quite possibly questions of safety will keep it that way. The latest candidate for producing a major change in intraurban transportation is the Segway, a high-tech machine that was first unveiled in 2001, accompanied by a massive publicity campaign. Invented by Dean Kamen, the Segway is roughly the size and shape of a lawn mower. Stabilized by a system of gyroscopes and position sensors, backed by circuits having the computing power of several PCs, the Segway transports its single standing rider at speeds up to 17 miles per hour. Forward and backward motion are controlled by sensing changes in the rider's posture. Thus no accelerator or brake pedals are required. Though the machine is now being primarily marketed to commercial and public users, including police departments, the U.S. Postal Service, and firms wanting to give their employees quicker mobility around factories and warehouses, Kamen sees the ultimate market as the general public. According to *Time* magazine, "He believes the Segway 'will be to the car what the car was to the horse and buggy.'"[14] As Kamen sees it, the Segway will fill the niche between the human foot and the automobile. It will make its mark in areas that are too congested for the automobile but where people want to move faster than the 3 to 4 miles per hour walking speed of the average person.

How well the Segway would mix with pedestrian traffic is a big question. Thus it remains to be seen whether it will produce major changes in how we travel in urban areas—and how we design urban areas—or whether it will just be a very high-tech novelty that fits into the niche now filled by lower-tech forms like the bicycle and the motor scooter.

SUMMARY

Since World War II, per capita ownership of automobiles in the United States has more than doubled, partly because of the increase in real income. Increases in automobile ownership have gone hand in hand with the process of suburbanization, each reinforcing the other. In terms of direct costs, private transportation more or less pays for itself, whereas public transportation requires heavy subsidization. The decline in public transportation since World War II was attributed partly to increased automobile ownership and partly to a more spread-out pattern of land use.

The present pattern of land use shapes the present demand for transportation, and transportation investment decisions shape the future pattern of land use. In the best of circumstances, land-use and transportation planning proceed as coordinated rather than isolated processes.

Large-scale transportation planning is a four-step process:

1. *Estimating trip generation.* Without considering destinations the planners, using such variables as household size, household income, and number of vehicles per household, estimate the total number of trips that will originate from each zone.
2. *Estimating trip distribution.* Using a gravity model or other mathematical model, the planners will then estimate the number of trips from each zone to each zone.
3. *Estimating modal split.* If more than one mode of transportation is available, say automobile and bus, the planners will use mathematical models to estimate the number of travelers using each mode from each origin to each destination. The main variables in such models are cost and travel time.

4. *Trip assignment.* Where there is more than one route from one zone to another zone, the final item to be modeled is the number of trips that will be made via each route.

After the model is built, it is calibrated, that is, adjusted, so that its output duplicates the actual travel behavior of the region. Then the model can be used to examine different transportation alternatives. Benefit/cost analysis is frequently used to evaluate and rank different investment possibilities. Ultimately, though, deciding on major investments is a political matter because transportation system investments can have large consequences for land values, neighborhood quality, and the entire pattern of development.

From the planner's perspective, the most important federal initiative in transportation was the Intermodal Surface Transportation Efficiency Act (ISTEA) of 1991. Its intent is to bring about much better coordination between transportation planning and urban and regional planning in general.

For reasons discussed in the chapter, another period of massive highway building comparable to that which produced the interstate highway system is unlikely in the foreseeable future. Much attention has thus turned to transportation system management (TSM) and transportation demand management (TDM) techniques as a way of obtaining more performance from the existing road network. In the next several decades, we will probably also see substantial change in automobile transportation as a result of a combination of "intelligent vehicles" and "smart highways," sometimes referred to more formally as the intelligent transportation system, from the increasing application of sophisticated pricing systems to roadways, and from new technologies for vehicle propulsion.

NOTES

1. Federal Highway Administration, *Highway Statistics Annual*, 2006, www.Federal HighwayAdministration.
2. *Transit Fact Book*, 2006, American Public Transit Association, Table 44, www. ATPA.com.
3. *Transit Fact Book* 2006, Table 14, www. ATPA.com.
4. *Chicago Area Transportation Study: Final Report* (3 vols.), published jointly by the State of Illinois, County of Cook, City of Chicago, and the U.S. Department of Commerce, Bureau of Public Roads, 1959–1962.
5. John W. Dickey, *Metropolitan Transportation Planning*, 2nd ed., McGraw-Hill Book Co., New York, 1983, chap. 6.
6. For a discussion of this technique, see Michael J. Moore and Kip W. Viscusi, "Doubling the Estimated Value of Life: Results Using New Occupational Fatality Data," *Journal of Policy Analysis and Management*, vol. 7, no. 3, 1988, p. 476.
7. Anthony Downs, "The Law of Peak-Hour Congestion," *Urban Problems and Prospects*, Rand-McNally, Chicago, 1976.
8. Harold Henderson, "Light Rail, Heavy Costs," *Planning*, October 1994, pp. 8–13.
9. Christopher Swope, "L.A. Banks on Buses," *Planning*, May 2006, pp. 33–36.
10. F. K. Plous, Jr., "Refreshing ISTEA," *Planning*, February 1993, pp. 9–12.
11. Federal Highway Administration, Office of Legislation and Inter governmental Affairs,

Program Analysis Team, "A Summary of Highway Provisions in SAFETEA-LU," Washington, DC, 2005, www.fhwa.dot.gov/safetea-lu/summary.htm.

12. Janusz Supernak, "HOT Lanes on Interstate 15 in San Diego: Technology, Impacts and Equity Issues," San Diego State University, 2005. This article, and many others on the subject, is readily available by Googling HOT Lanes.

13. "Drivers Buy into Congestion Pricing," *Planning*, July 1996, p. 24.

14. John Heilemann, "Reinventing the Wheel," *Time*, December 10, 2001, pp. 76–85.

SELECTED BIBLIOGRAPHY

DICKEY, JOHN W., *Metropolitan Transportation Planning*, 2nd ed., McGraw-Hill Book Co., New York, 1983.

MEYER, MICHAEL D., and MILLER, ERIC J., *Urban Transportation Planning*, 2nd ed., McGraw-Hill Book Co., New York, 2001.

CHAPTER 13

Economic Development Planning

Many thousands of municipalities, probably the majority of couties, and all 50 states make serious efforts to promote their own economic development. There are well over 15,000 organizations in the United States devoted to promoting local and state economic development. The exact amount of money spent on local economic development is not known. But when the operating expenses of economic development agencies, direct expenditures on economic development, and a wide variety of indirect expenditures in the form of tax abatements are added together, the figure may be as high as several tens of billions of dollars annually. The present U. S. political scene is characterized by a high level of intermunicipal and interstate economic competition.[1]

Such competition is driven partly by labor market considerations. Citizens expect local and state governments to foster job growth so as to tighten labor markets, thus pushing up wage rates and pushing down unemployment rates. Local and state governments are also driven to economic competition for tax reasons. Caught in the squeeze between the cost of providing services and citizens' resistance to being taxed, broadening the tax base by bringing in new commercial and industrial activity looks like an attractive course of action. Interplace economic competition has a certain amount of "positive feedback" built into it. If one state or municipality offers firms an attractive subsidy for locating there, or launches a massive publicity campaign to promote itself as a good location, other states and municipalities are likely to respond in kind. Thus offer begets counteroffer, and interplace economic competition becomes more intense over time. This interplace competition has promoted economic development planning as a major subspecialty of the planning profession. Planning schools offer courses in economic development planning, and the American Planning

Association has for several years had an economic development planning division. Before we turn to the subject of economic development planning, some historic and national background will be useful.

HISTORIC ROOTS

Planning for economic development is an old American tradition. In many ways it antedates the sort of city planning we have discussed in this book. In the nineteenth century a great many cities took steps to strengthen their competitive position vis-à-vis competing cities. Quite naturally, much of the push came from the city's merchants, for it was they who would profit most from municipal economic success. Most often, such planning efforts were directed toward the transportation infrastructure—to increasing the accessibility of the city. In a day when overland transportation costs per ton/mile were a large multiple of what they are today, a significant reduction in those costs could give the merchants in one city or town an overwhelming advantage over competitors in other cities.[2]

Probably the best-known example in the nineteenth century was the building of the Erie Canal. In the early 1820s a group of New York City merchants perceived that obtaining good access to the Midwest would confer a tremendous economic advantage on the city. The way to do this in the prerailroad era was to build a canal connecting the Hudson River to Lake Erie. Private capital was quickly raised for the task, and within a few years the canal was completed. By the 1830s, a decade or so after its completion, the canal was carrying close to 1 million tons of freight per year, giving New York an enormous commercial advantage over its two main rivals of the time, Boston and Philadelphia. The great age of canal building in the United States, roughly 1800 to 1830, was largely a matter of municipal initiative, each city trying to steal a march on its competitors.

The age of canal building ended abruptly with the coming of railroad technology, but the same story of municipal competition was repeated. Many of the early railroads were built with municipally raised funds, and the competition between cities and towns to be on a rail line was intense. In many cases municipalities purchased railroad bonds to provide the capital to build a line that would put them on the map commercially. In other cases municipalities guaranteed bonds to make them marketable. One writer described this period as an age of "urban mercantilism," so intense was the competition.[3]

When the U.S. rail system was fairly well developed, competition switched to other areas. For example, in the period after the Civil War, a number of southern communities actively promoted the development of the textile industry by offering various forms of financial assistance to firms in New England, which was then the textile manufacturing center of the United States. Again, the impetus came largely from local merchants, whose primary motivation was to promote commerce and development that would boost profits and property values. These motives for local economic development efforts are not unknown today, but some additional and, in some cases, more altruistic motives have been added.

PERSPECTIVES ON LOCAL ECONOMIC DEVELOPMENT _____

To discuss the present situation in local economic development, it is necessary to make clear two different perspectives. For several decades local economic development efforts were heavily shaped by federal funding and federal legislation.

Thus there is a national perspective to be considered. There are also strong local motivations, and what is good for a particular municipality or state may or may not be good for the nation as a whole.

The Federal Presence in Local Economic Development

In the years after World War II, a new term was added to the economic vocabulary of the nation: *structural unemployment.* It refers to a mismatch between the supply of labor and the demand for labor. The mismatch may apply to skills. For example, in the 1960s numerous former farmers and farm workers were unemployed because the postwar mechanization of agriculture had forced them off the land, and they lacked skills for doing other kinds of work. At the same time, the burgeoning computer industry was experiencing shortages of programmers, systems analysts, and technicians. In recent years manufacturing employment in the United States has declined sharply while health care has been a major growth area, so high unemployment rates among industrial workers coexist with severe shortages of nurses. Thus labor shortages may coexist with labor surpluses because of a mismatch between the skills of the labor force and the needs of employers. To a great extent this type of structural unemployment is the result of technological change. The faster the change occurs, the more serious the problem is likely to be.

The other aspect of structural unemployment is geographical. An area may lose jobs because firms have moved out or because changes in technology have reduced their labor needs or because they have gone out of business. If the loss of employment is not matched by corresponding out-migration of population, a sustained condition of high unemployment may result. In general, capital is more mobile than population, so that structural unemployment does in fact occur in just this way. A company's board of directors can in a single, rational, bottom line–based decision decide to close a plant here and transfer its production operations to a site elsewhere in the nation or, for that matter, elsewhere in the world. It is not so easy for a comparable part of the population to decide to pull out of a labor-surplus area and move to a labor-short area.

The structural unemployment problem did not become apparent immediately after World War II. In welcome contrast to the Great Depression, the postwar period was one of great prosperity. Thus for a time it appeared to many that the only important economic function of government was to maintain this desirable state of affairs by competent management of national (macroeconomic) economic policy.

After a few years, however, it became apparent that even though the nation was generally prosperous, not all regions or all subgroups of the population were doing well economically. The first region for which serious concern developed was Appalachia. Lying between the prosperous eastern seaboard and the then-thriving industrial Midwest, the Appalachian region seemed to be in a permanent depression of its own.

Beginning in 1961, Congress began legislation designed to address both the skills and the geographical mismatch sides of the structural unemployment problem. The measures designed to alleviate structural unemployment because of a mismatch in skills do not bear directly on urban and regional planning as the term has been used in this book; therefore, they are not discussed here. Place-related programs, which are of direct interest, are summarized below.

In 1961 Congress created the Area Redevelopment Administration (ARA).[4] This agency was empowered to make grants to localities to support local economic development. Eligibility for ARA funding was based on county-level data on unemployment and poverty. Similar criteria have characterized the federal presence in local economic development ever since. There is obvious logic to this approach. If structural unemployment is the reason for local economic development programs, how better to decide whether an area needs federal aid than by looking for the consequences of structural economic difficulties, namely, poverty and unemployment? The ARA was replaced in 1965 by the Economic Development Administration (EDA), which essentially did the same thing as ARA. Poverty and unemployment statistics developed by the federal government were examined to draw up a list of counties that were to be eligible for EDA assistance. Eligible counties were then encouraged to set up economic planning organizations, which would submit funding applications to EDA.

A typical EDA-funded project was the community industrial park. A combination of EDA and local funds would be used for purposes like site acquisition, grading, and provision of utilities. When the site was ready, it would be sold or leased at below cost to firms, which would then build and operate plants there. From the municipal viewpoint the expenditure of local funds would be justified by two things: the provision of jobs for local residents and the increase in property and other tax revenues from the new facility. The federal contribution was presumably justified by the decrease in structural unemployment.

Substantial federal support for local economic development has also been available from the federal government through Community Development Block Grants (CDBG), mentioned in Chapter 12. Community development funds can be used for a wide variety of economic development purposes. The Urban Development Action Grant (UDAG) program, described in Chapter 12, was another federal initiative that supported local economic development efforts.

The federal role in local economic development efforts peaked during the Carter administration (1977–1981) and then was scaled back during the Reagan (1981–1989) and the first Bush (1989–1993) administrations. As the accompanying box suggests, there is an issue of political philosophy involved. Attempting to reshape the geographical pattern of business investment by means of government programs is a decision to replace the judgment of the market with the judgment of government, and that is a decision with which conservatives are uncomfortable. Thus it is not surprising that under presidents Reagan and the elder Bush, funding for EDA was cut back, and UDAG was ended.

One favorite tool of economic developers that has persisted to the present time is industrial revenue bond (IRB) funding. Municipalities are allowed to issue tax exempt bonds on behalf of firms building or acquiring commercial or industrial facilities within their borders. The firm benefits by the lower interest rates it has to pay because of the tax exemption feature. Economic developers like this kind of financing because it is essentially costless to the municipality. As is the case with the revenue bonds noted in Chapter 12, the subsidy comes from the federal government because the federal government loses the tax revenue that it would have collected if the bond interest had not been tax exempt. At one time Congress considered amending the Internal Revenue Service (IRS) code to disallow IRB funding, but these bonds had been so widely used that Congress has continued them to the present time, albeit in somewhat scaled back form.

When President Clinton (1993–2001) took office, it seemed that given his somewhat more liberal political position, the federal government might take a more active roll in the support of economic development efforts for lagging areas. However, this did not prove to be the case. The one Clinton-era initiative in local economic development was the Empowerment Zone program.[5] The program, enacted in 1994, is similar in concept to programs described on page 251. It made federal funds available to a limited number of distressed areas in an attempt to make those areas more competitive with more prosperous areas in the quest for business investment. Total funding for the program over the next decade was to be $3.8 billion. Compared with the U.S. GNP of approximately $10 trillion at the end of the century, that was a relatively small sum. President George W. Bush (the son of the previous

DOES PUBLIC INTERVENTION MAKE SENSE?

Whether such federal subsidies to local development make sense from the national viewpoint has been the subject of considerable argument. From an economist's viewpoint, subsidies were being used to move economic activity into an area that was not its most efficient location in order to achieve some gains in equity. This so-called equity-efficiency trade-off deserves a short explanation, since it underlies much argument about what is the proper role of government in influencing the location of economic activity.

In brief, the argument is as follows: If the location in question were the most efficient location for the firm, ordinary market forces would cause it to locate there without any government action. If a subsidy (say, in the form of an industrial park site delivered at a fraction of actual cost) is necessary to cause the firm to locate there, by definition, the site is not the most efficient location. Thus following this logic, there is a loss of efficiency for the whole economy stemming from the use of subsidies to influence economic locations. This situation occurs simply because encouraging a firm to locate at other than its most efficient location means that the cost of producing a given bundle of goods or services will be higher. In return for this efficiency loss, there is an equity gain in the sense that economic activity is directed to areas of more than ordinary need. This, then, is the efficiency-equity trade-off. Those who support powerful public intervention in locating economic activity generally, either explicitly or implicitly, place heavy weight on equity. Those who generally oppose such public intervention are apt to place heavy weight, again explicitly or implicitly, on efficiency.

In general, liberals have tended to favor place-related programs. Conservatives have generally opposed such programs, taking the view that it is the proper role of the national government to provide conditions under which private economic activity can flourish but that the marketplace itself should decide how and where capital is invested.

President Bush), inaugurated January 2001, showed no interest in federal assistance for local economic development assistance through most of his term until the 2004 presidential campaign. At that time, perhaps in part to answer charges of weak overall employment growth and losses of manufacturing jobs, he proposed the creation of a number of *opportunity zones*. Few details on the proposal were offered. The main thrust would be to offer tax breaks for investment in places that have experienced job losses.

Opportunity zones were a low priority item for the administration and, as of this writing little more has been heard about them. The second Bush administration exhibited even less interest in local economic development programs than did the Clinton administration.

However, despite the slackening of federal interest in and funding for local economic development, competition between states and localities has increased in intensity. Voters in every state and most municipalities want more jobs for the local labor market and more tax revenues from industrial and commercial development. Then, too, state and municipal economic development activity seems to have the self-generating quality noted earlier. If community X offers subsidies or tax breaks for new firms, then community Y may feel compelled to do the same, not necessarily to gain an advantage, but just not to fall behind.

The Relationship Between Planners and Economic Developers

Planners and economic developers necessarily have considerable interaction, for both are concerned with public investment in infrastructure, land-use controls, environmental regulations, and anything else that affects the what and where of industrial and commercial development. Sometimes the relationship between the community's planners and its economic developers will be a happy one, but sometimes it will not. To the planner, bringing in new firms and encouraging the expansion of firms already in the community will be one of a number of goals. To the economic developer, these may be, in practice, the only goals. Thus the planners' *we want development but it has to fit into the master plan* perspective can conflict with the developers' *do whatever it takes to bring them in* position. When a potential investor wants to do what the economic developers think is the right thing but in what the planners think is the wrong place, the scene is set for disagreement. The issue can go either way depending on the priorities of the municipality's political establishment.

That planners and economic developers have many professional links is hard to deny. At one time the author and a colleague surveyed a large number of directors of economic development agencies. One question was, *If economic development was not your first profession, what was your previous profession?* The most common single answer was *urban planner.*

STATE ECONOMIC DEVELOPMENT EFFORTS _____

For many years the states have supported local economic development efforts. State departments of commerce provide information on the state and try to guide firms to municipalities within the state. States have offered a huge variety of financial incentives, such as investment tax credits, low-interest loans, infrastructure grants, labor force training grants, and the like, to encourage firms to locate or expand within the state's borders. A majority of states have overseas trade offices in Europe, the Far East, or both to help develop overseas markets for their firms and also to encourage investment in their state by overseas firms. Most important, states have become increasingly involved in major industrial and commercial relocations and expansions and are increasingly willing to spend large sums of money to attract economic activity. A few major and well-publicized deals follow.

In 1978, Pennsylvania provided Volkswagen with a $78 million subsidy package to build an assembly plant in the state. For several years thousands of Volkswagens, and the only ones produced in the United States, were made in Pennsylvania. However, demand for the car declined, and the company suspended all production in the United States, leaving the state sadder and perhaps wiser.

In the 1980s when General Motors indicated that it was seeking a site to manufacture its Saturn car, numerous governors and state representatives made pilgrimages to Detroit, and a keen bidding war developed, with states offering sites, promises of major investments in roads, and substantial tax abatements. As events worked out, GM chose a location near Columbia, Tennessee, which seemed to offer advantages in terms of labor force, transportation, and utility rates, but which did not offer as large a subsidy package as did many other places. But the willingness of states and localities to, in effect, make multimillion dollar bids for GM's presence does indicate the eagerness of states for economic development. Illinois was reported to have offered $200 million in infrastructure, tax concessions, and other expenditures for the Saturn facility.

In 1991 Colorado put together a $427 million package of subsidies, direct and indirect, to attract a $1 billion United Airlines maintenance center to Denver. The bid was unsuccessful, and United Airlines went to St. Louis where the subsidy package was smaller but hardly trivial at a figure of $300 million.

In the 1990s Mercedes-Benz opened an automobile assembly plant in Vance, Alabama, and BMW opened one in Spartanburg, South Carolina. The subsidy for Mercedes was estimated to be in the $250 million range, and that for BMW at about $150 million. On a per job basis, the Mercedes subsidy was about $168,000 and the BMW subsidy in the $65,000 range. The subsidies were a mixed bag of direct payments to the companies, public investment on infrastructure for the companies, and a variety of preferential tax treatments.

In the fall of 1995, Governor George Allen of Virginia and officials of the city of Manassas announced a $165.7 million deal that would bring a $1.2 billion IBM-Toshiba chip-manufacturing plant to Manassas. The state's share of the package was about $48 million, of which $38.4 million was a direct cash payment to the two companies if they met certain stated employment and capital investment targets in years five through ten. The city's share was somewhat over $117 million, of which almost $96 million took the form of reduced taxes on machinery in the new plant.[6] The plant is estimated to employ about 1,200 at full development. That would make the subsidy costs (both direct expenditures and tax forgiveness) almost $140,000 per job. Local officials estimated that for every job at IBM-Toshiba, two additional jobs would develop as a result of the "multiplier" effect. This result would reduce the per job subsidy to about $46,000, still a very substantial sum.

In some cases states have offered major packages to firms not to move in but simply not to move out. Perhaps this trend is inevitable. Bids to move will be matched by bids to stay.

> Illinois officialdom breathed a collective sigh of relief last June [1989] when word came that Sears, Roebuck and Company had chosen the Chicago suburb of Hoffman Estates as the new location of its 6,000-worker merchandise group. Sears had announced earlier in the year that it would leave its landmark building, the Sears Tower, in down-town Chicago.
>
> Although keeping Sears cost the state some $178 million and didn't create a single new job, Gov. James R. Thompson hailed the decision as "a great victory" for his state.[7]

The state of Illinois no doubt had numerous other good uses for the $178 million it spent on relocating Sears. But it had little choice about making the expenditure. One reason for its having little choice was that the Sears distribution center with its 6,000 jobs would be quite a prize for any economic development agency and had undoubtedly attracted other substantial offers. Illinois thus had no choice but to make a counteroffer. In a purely political sense, Governor Thompson had no choice either, for if Sears had moved out of the state, he would have been bludgeoned with that fact day and night in his next election campaign.

For the state or locality that provides a big subsidy package in order to attract a new industry, the net payoff may be positive or negative. On the positive side, there are incomes from new jobs and increased tax revenues from the additional economic activity and property development. On the other hand, economic growth generally promotes population growth, and so there will be additional expenses for schools, social services, handling the increased flow of traffic, and the like. Whether, after taking account of the costs of subsidization, the increased revenues will be more than or less than the additional expenses will vary from case to case. Whether or not a new firm will raise average wages in an area may also be problematical. One would normally expect the general tightening of labor markets caused by increased employment to raise the average wage. However, if the wage profile of the new firm is substantially below the average of employers already in place, the new firm may have the unexpected effect of lowering the average wage.

Beyond using their own funds to attract firms, states will often pursue federal investment within their boundaries. That attempt might mean using the influence and power that the state's congressional delegation has to push for having parts of a multibillion-dollar weapons system made in their state. It might mean pushing for the opening of a new federal facility built in their state rather than somewhere else. Or it might mean having the state's congressional delegation do everything it can to resist a decision to close a military base in the state. Pursuit of federal funds for highway construction would be another example, for accessibility is an important consideration when firms make location decisions.

LOCAL ECONOMIC DEVELOPMENT PROGRAMS _____

At the local level there is intense interest in economic development. Of the more than 15,000 organizations in the United States devoted to economic development, the vast majority operate at the local level—city, county, town, or neighborhood.

Communities have several motives for pursuing economic development. One is employment. Increasing the size of the local economy seems like an obvious way to reduce unemployment. Recall that it is unemployment and its concomitant, poverty, that are the usual bases for eligibility for federal assistance.[8]

Another major motivation at the local level is property tax relief. The property tax is by far the largest source of locally raised revenue for substate levels of government. It is also by far the largest locally raised source of revenues for school districts. Most local governments and school districts find themselves under pressure on the subject of property taxes because they are caught between citizens' resistance to tax increases and their demands for services. One obvious way out of the dilemma is to expand the tax base so that a given tax rate produces more revenue. In many localities the property tax motivation is actually more important than the employment motivation. For one thing, essentially all citizens pay property taxes, whereas at any given time only a minority of citizens are unemployed. Then, too, there is no ambiguity about who captures the tax benefits. If a facility is built within the city or county or town or school district lines, that body receives the tax payments. On the other hand, the labor market and business stimulation effects are likely to spread far beyond the municipal boundaries. Small communities within metropolitan areas often sense that they are part of the metropolitan labor market and are too small to affect it very much. However, it is possible for them to calculate quite clearly how much a new project will add to their tax rolls.

There are other motivations as well. Economic growth is likely to be good for various sectors of the business community. Real estate brokers will benefit from an increased number of transactions. Property owners will benefit from increased demand for land and structures. Retailers will benefit from increased sales resulting from increased personal income.

Construction firms—and their workers—will benefit from increased construction activity. In short, there is a good deal of general support from business and labor for local economic development efforts.

Several decades ago the prime focus of many, if not most, economic development agencies was manufacturing, and in fact the field of economic development was sometimes casually referred to as "smokestack chasing." But that is no longer the case. For several decades manufacturing employment in the United States held more or less steady in absolute numbers but declined as a percentage of total employment. Since about the year 2000 manufacturing employment now accounts for only 10 percent of total U.S. employment. Thus today one is more likely to find municipalities and their economic development agencies pursuing retailing, service, office, recreation, and other categories where there is significant employment growth.

A Crucial Difference

Most of the planning discussed in this book does not involve intermunicipal competition. If town A improves its park system, that effort will not make the park system in town B worse. In fact, it may stimulate town B to improve its park system. But if town A through infrastructure improvements, tax abatements, or other inducements causes Universal Valve and Faucet to locate there instead of in town B, its gain is town B's loss. In that sense of intense head-to-head competition between municipalities, local economic development efforts represent a unique area of public policy and planning.

What a Community Can Do to Promote Its Economic Growth

In a very general way, there are four major things a community can do to facilitate its own economic growth. As will become apparent, there is a certain amount of overlap among them.

Sales and Promotion. The community can engage in a variety of public relations, advertising, selling, and marketing efforts. In effect, it can view itself as a product and then make a concerted effort to sell that "product." For a firm seeking a location, there is no feasible way to gather objective information about all the possibilities. The community that makes itself highly visible thus gives itself an advantage.

Subsidization. The community can subsidize development in a variety of ways. One form is tax abatement. Since the main tax used by local government is the property tax, abatement most commonly takes the form of reduced property taxes for new commercial or industrial development. Some communities will set up revolving loan funds or other credit-granting arrangements to facilitate business growth. If the municipality levies sales, inventory, commercial occupancy, or business taxes, it may offer reductions in these.

The enterprise zone is a variation on this theme.[9] The city, town, county, or state designates an area as an enterprise zone. Within this zone a variety of tax breaks are offered for new investment. These may include property tax reductions, sales tax reductions, reduced corporate income tax, and so on. In addition, direct grants may be offered. Another inducement may be the waiving of some land-use regulations to permit higher densities. The technique has most commonly been used in the attempt to restore deteriorated central-city areas.

The use of municipal funds for subsidies, whether through direct expenditure or through the tax expenditure route such as a property tax abatement, has some inherent problems. If the municipality gives assistance to one firm, it has to find the money to do so. If that pushes up its tax rate, it has simultaneously made itself more attractive to one firm but less attractive to every other firm. The question is which effect predominates. That is not always easy to decide.

Subsidizing is bedeviled with the matter of information asymmetry. In the ideal case a subsidy would be given only if it were decisive. If the firm were going to invest in the community in any case, then the subsidy is just a windfall to the firm and serves no community purpose. Assuming that the subsidy is decisive, the subsidy should be exactly the minimum size to get the firm to do what the municipality wants it to do. Any money beyond that minimum amount is a windfall. Determining whether the subsidy is decisive and whether, if so, it is the minimum amount necessary is no easy matter. It is in the interest of the firm to get as big a subsidy as possible and so the firm will take the position that of course it is necessary and it has to be very large. The firm knows its own motivations and, if it has been shopping for a new location, what offers are available from other places. But this information is generally not available to the municipality or its economic development agency. The firm reveals what it chooses to reveal. On the other hand, the municipality and its development agency as public bodies have to operate in a relatively open manner. In effect, it is a poker game in which one player is allowed to hold his cards close to his chest and the other, by the rules of the game, has to play with his cards face up on the table. The chance that the municipality will get the offer just right is small.

Making Sites and Buildings Available. Availability of sites or buildings is a key factor in determining whether a community can attract new commercial activity and retain existing activity. Let us begin by asking what constitutes a usable site. Consider a planning agency in a suburban or metropolitan fringe area setting up preliminary criteria for identifying potential industrial or commercial land. A first cut might be to rule out any land with a slope of more than 5 percent, for steep slopes push up site-preparation and construction costs. Subsoil conditions such as drainage problems, rock outcroppings, and other characteristics that add to construction costs might be a second cut. If the municipality is traversed by a river or stream, land in the flood plain might also be eliminated from consideration. Availability of utilities such as water, sewers, and electric power is also a criterion. For light manufacturing, retailing, wholesaling, and office activities, adequate road access would also be a requirement. For heavy manufacturing, rail access as well is likely to be needed. In addition to having an adequate number of acres available, there is also the matter of site geometry. For heavy industry, a minimum site depth of 800 feet might be a good rule of thumb. For light manufacturing, minimum depths of 400 to 600 feet are desirable.

To ensure that adequate sites will be available in the foreseeable future, there are various steps a municipality can take. The most direct step is the public provision of sites. Numerous cities, towns, and counties have municipal industrial parks. The community uses public funds (and sometimes the power of eminent domain as well) to acquire and develop sites. The prepared sites are then sold or leased long term to firms, which erect and operate manufacturing or other commercial buildings on them. Very often, there is a significant public subsidy in such operations in that the rent or sales price covers only a fraction of the costs incurred in site acquisition, grading, drainage, building of access roads, running water and sewer lines, and so on.

Some communities will go even further in providing a place for economic activity by erecting a building and then seeking a firm or firms to occupy it. Very often the structure put up is a "shell building." The community puts up the outer shell of the building and then waits until it has found a firm to use the building before it completes the interior. Again, there may or may not be an element of subsidy in the process.

Another community might take a somewhat more tentative approach and engage in land banking, that is, acquiring land or perhaps options on land with a view simply to hold it as a potential commercial site. Of course, such a method is expensive. The financial cost to the community is the loss of interest on whatever funds are tied up in the land. If the community sinks $1 million into land banking and the current rate at which the community borrows is 5 percent, the carrying cost is $50,000 for this year, a burden that must be borne by the municipality's tax-payers.

Use of Land-Use Controls and Provision of Infrastructure.

Beyond the direct provision of land, the community can use its land-use control powers to ensure that adequate privately owned land will be available for commercial development. One obvious step is simply zoning an adequate amount of land in the appropriate categories. The zoning should be applied to land that actually has real development potential, land that meets the sorts of topographic and geometric standards previously described. It also means land that either already has been or has the potential for being provided with adequate access and utilities. As noted in Chapter 8, the zoning should be coordinated with the land uses shown on the comprehensive plan.

The infrastructure question is addressed through the community's capital budget. For sites with near-term development potential, capital funds can be spent to provide utilities and access. For sites with longer-term potential, it is hard to justify immediate expenditure. However, providing infrastructure to these sites can be an item on the community's capital improvements program scheduled for some years hence.

None of these measures will guarantee that a given parcel of land will be used for commercial or industrial use or that it will not be put to some other use. However, by declaring its intent through master planning, zoning, and capital budgeting, the community decreases the odds that lands with economic potential will be preempted by other uses. Assume that a block of one hundred acres has good potential for economic development in the long term but that its chances for such development in the next few years are small. The owner has the chance to sell 5 acres out of its center for residential use now. However, dividing the site in that manner will greatly reduce its ultimate commercial or industrial potential. By telegraphing its long-term intentions as described, the community encourages the property owner to take a long-term rather than a short-term view of the situation.

Cooperation and Competition

At one time local economic development was an almost entirely competitive activity, a sort of intermunicipality "war of all against all," to use a phrase of Thomas Hobbes originally said in a very different context. But in recent years that has changed. For many municipalities, especially as regards manufacturing, the most serious competitor is not the next town or the next county, but a producer ten thousand miles away. As a result there are now a very large number of multijurisdictional agencies that seek to promote an area, rather than a single jurisdiction. These agencies may share advertising and public relations expenses and have a policy of seeking to guide prospective investors to whichever jurisdiction in the area best meets the needs of that investor. For such agencies the old habbit of trying to seduce firms away from neighboring jurisdictions is no longer acceptable.

Pursuit of Investment by Higher Levels of Government

As do state governments, local governments also pursue investment by higher levels of government. Occasionally, for a city or a county, the higher level of government is the federal government. More often, it is the state government.

For example, many counties, particularly in rural or semirural areas, have decided that prisons make a good source of jobs. They are labor-intensive activities, and employment in them is not subject to the vagaries of the business cycle. If there is a site that is suitable for a prison and not too close to a center of population, the municipality may well exert itself to get the next state prison built there. Other state facilities, too, may be the subject of considerable competition by local governments. Local governments frequently seek to influence federal and state investment in highways, for good highway access is often a necessary though not sufficient condition for attracting private capital investment.

Larger Considerations

How much can a municipality can do to promote its own growth? As stated, a municipality can do a considerable amount to make itself known to potential investors, it can (with the caveats noted) use subsidies, and it can do a certain amount in terms of sites and infrastructure. But there are also larger matters that are not within municipal control or only partly within municipal control. When firms are questioned about how they make location decisions, two items that come up very frequently are market access and the local labor market. Market access is primarily a matter of location and that is beyond municipal control. Labor market considerations are a mixed bag. The size of the labor market, prevailing wages, and labor force quality all weigh heavily with potential employers. The last item is a mix of skills, education, and some intangibles like "work ethic." For many firms, "quality of life" questions weight heavily in the location choice. This is partly because the executives and owners making the location decision care about where they will live and also partly because of recruitment considerations. If the recruitment of highly skilled personnel who are in high demand is critical to the success of the firm, then being located in an area that will be attractive to these potential employees is very important. What constitutes a good "quality of life" is a subjective matter, but items like climate, an attractive natural environment, recreational opportunities, cultural opportunities, the quality of public education, and personal safety are likely to be important to a very large number of people.

Some of the items listed in this section are entirely beyond the ability of a municipality to affect and some can be affected to some degree. To a large extent, the municipality and its economic development agency have to play the hand that they are dealt.

The importance of these larger questions also suggests that sometimes investments that are not directly aimed at economic development may have a bigger development payoff than investments that are directly targeted to economic development. For example, investment in a museum or concert hall, or in public parks, or in a system of bicycle paths by their contribution to the quality of life as perceived by potential employers might have a bigger payoff than, say, direct subsidies for investment in the municipality. Similarly, investment in public education might pay off in terms of both the perception of and the actuality of labor force quality. Two researchers studying employment in U.S. central cities concluded that the "only consistent correlate with long term economic success is the level of educational achievement of the workforce."[10]

Of course, investing in education will not always have a guaranteed economic development payoff. For one thing, people do migrate. Many a small town has the unhappy experience of seeing many of its graduating high school seniors take their diplomas and head for more promising labor markets very shortly thereafter. Formulating an economic development strategy that makes the most efficient use of limited municipal funds is no easy task.

A Systematic Approach to Economic Development Planning

The following is a brief account of how a municipality might approach economic development planning.[11]

1. *Needs assessment.* In this phase the municipality decides the purpose of the program. The two most common goals are providing additional employment opportunities and strengthening the municipal tax base. If the main goal is jobs, the municipality should consider whether the goal is simply to increase the total number of jobs or whether it is seeking particular types of jobs, perhaps to address high rates of unemployment or underemployment among particular sectors of its labor force. Being clear about the goals of the program is particularly useful if choices have to be made about the expenditure of public funds on competing projects.

2. *Market evaluation.* In order to develop an effective marketing program, the municipality's economic development agency tries to make an objective assessment of its competitive strengths and weaknesses. This means examining wages and the availability of labor, taxes, land and construction costs, utility rates, the composition of its existing commercial and industrial establishment, strengths and weaknesses in its transportation infrastructure, its educational and cultural establishment, and a variety of "quality of life" items. Such an assessment will help the municipality target its sales and marketing efforts toward those types of firms that are most likely to be interested in relocating to or expanding in that municipality.

3. *Assessment of the consequences of an economic development program.* Economic development will involve fiscal effects, both new

revenues and also new expenditures. It may also affect traffic flow, environmental quality, housing markets and many other aspects of community life. Anticipating and planning for those effects is part of a systematic approach to economic development.

    4. *Plan formulation.* The plan might include some or all of the following elements.

    a. An advertising and marketing program.
    b. A plan for the use of subsidies such as property and other tax abatements, low interest loans or loan guarantees, or public absorption of some of the costs of site acquisition and development.
    c. A program of capital investments in water, sewer, road, and other facilities necessary to support industrial and commercial development. If the municipality decides to take an entrepreneurial role, it might include planning for the development of a municipal industrial or commercial park or the construction of a shell building.
    d. A land-use element. This might involve adjusting the municipality's land-use controls to provide adequate industrial and commercial sites and possibly also the purchase or optioning of land for future economic development.

SUMMARY

Planning for economic development dates back many decades. Early efforts tended to focus on transportation and generally were initiated by the commercial elite of the city.

    Beginning in the 1960s the federal government began to subsidize local economic planning and development efforts with a view to combating structural unemployment. This policy continues to the present time though it was weakened considerably during the Reagan and the first Bush presidencies and was not restored under President Clinton or the second Bush presidency.

    Virtually all states strive to foster their own economic growth through a variety of programs involving marketing, subsidization, and the use of capital expenditures. Many thousands of municipalities also promote their own economic development using marketing and subsidization. Very often, the community will use its capital budget and its land-use policies to assure the availability of an adequate number of suitable sites.

    Steps in a simple systematic approach to planning for economic development include the following:

    Needs assessment
    Market evaluation
    Assessment of the consequences of development policy
    Plan formulation
    Plan review and updating

NOTES

1. For an overall description of interplace economic competition and the general workings of local economic development agencies, see the first several chapters of John M. Levy, *Economic Development Programs for Cities, Counties and Towns*, 2nd ed., Praeger Publishers, New York, 1990. For a current picture of the field, see *Economic Development Quarterly*.
2. For a picture of the economics of transportation in the United States at the beginning of the nineteenth century, see Alan Pred, *City Systems in Advanced Economies*, John Wiley, New York, 1977.
3. Alfred Eichner, *State Development Agencies and Employment Expansion*, University of Michigan Press, Ann Arbor, 1970.
4. A brief review of programs through the end of the 1970s can be found in John M. Levy, *Economic Development Programs for Cities, Counties and Towns*, 1st ed., Praeger, New York, 1981, chap. 11.
5. Renee Berger, "People, Power, Politics," *Planning*, February 1997, pp. 4–9.
6. See Peter Baker, "$165 Million in Incentives Promised for Chip Plant," *Washington Post*, August 9, 1995, p. A1.
7. Robert Guskind, "The Giveaway Game Continues," *Planning*, February 1990, pp. 4–8.
8. It should be noted that 100 jobs added to the local economy will not generally reduce unemployment by anything close to that amount. Some of the jobs will be taken by people outside the labor force who have been drawn into it by the new employment opportunities. Additional jobs are likely to be taken by people who migrate into the area because of the availability of jobs. For a summary of experience on this point, see Gene Summers, *The Invasion of Nonmetropolitan America by Industry: A Quarter Century of Experience*, Praeger, New York, 1976.
9. For a summary of experience with enterprise zones, see Rodney A. Erickson, "Enterprise Zones: Lessons from the State Experience," in *Sources of Metropolitan Growth*, Center for Urban and Regional Studies, Rutgers, NJ, 1992, pp. 161–182.
10. Edward W. Hill and John Brennan, "American Central Cities and the Location of Work," *Journal of the American Planning Association*, vol. 71, no. 2, Autumn 2005, pp. 411–432.
11. The reader should not assume that all communities approach economic development in this systematic manner. In many cases, for a variety of political reasons, communities jump into economic development programs without much planning, and the program largely amounts to a matter of shooting at targets of opportunity. See John M. Levy, "What Local Economic Developers Actually Do: Location Quotients vs Press Releases," *Journal of the American Planning Association*, Spring 1990, pp. 153–161.

SELECTED BIBLIOGRAPHY

BLAKELY, EDWARD J., *Planning Local Economic Development: Theory and Practice*, Sage, Newbury Park, CA, 1989.

FITZGERALD, JOAN, and LEIGH, NANCY GREEN, *Economic Revitalization: Cases and Strategies for City and Suburb*, Sage, Thousand Oaks, Ca., 2002.

GLASMEIER, AMY K., *The High Tech Potential: Economic Development in Rural America*, Center for Urban Policy Research, Rutgers, New Jersey, 1991.

MALIZIA, EMIL, *Local Economic Development: A Guide to Practice*, Praeger Publishers, New York, 1985.

VAL, AVRAM BEN-DAVID, *Regional Economic Analysis for Practitioners: An Introduction*, 4th ed., Praeger, New York, 1991.

WHITE, SAMMIS B., BINGHAM, RICHARD D., and HILL, EDWARD, *Financing Economic Development in the 21st Century*, M. E. Sharpe, Inc., Armonk, New York, 2003.

CHAPTER 14

Growth Management, Smart Growth, and Sustainable Development

Growth management is generally defined as the regulation of the *amount, timing, location,* and *character* of development. Since the late 1960s hundreds of cities, counties, and towns in the United States have instituted growth management programs. Many state plans, too, have large elements of growth management.

The goals of these programs vary. Growth management programs are often heavily motivated by environmental considerations. A related consideration may be ensuring a desirable pattern of land development in future years. Preserving an existing lifestyle and community ambiance are common motivations, as is ensuring that community facilities such as schools, roads, utilities, and recreation will be adequate for future needs. In some cases a major goal of growth management will be fiscal, ensuring that the community will not be swamped by development-imposed costs. Finally, like the exclusionary zoning discussed earlier, growth management may have an exclusionary, or "keeping the good things to ourselves," motivation. Rarely will a program be instituted for a single reason. Untangling the various motivations and saying exactly why a community has entered into growth management may be extremely difficult.

In general, growth management plans or systems are made up of elements that have been well known to planners for years. Growth management systems differ from traditional comprehensive planning not in the elements that compose them but in the synthesis of those elements. Specifically, growth management systems are generally characterized by very close and long-term coordination between land-use controls on the one hand and capital investment on the other. They are often also characterized by the use of more modern approaches to land-use control and often by a great sensitivity to environmental issues. In that all of these points are to be found in planning efforts that are not specifically labeled as growth management, it must be admitted that no absolutely hard line separates growth management from more traditional planning.

When growth management appeared in the late 1960s and early 1970s, several different terms with overlapping meanings came into being. A multivolume anthology of articles on the field, published in 1975, carried the title *Management and Control of Growth.*[1] In addition to the terms *growth management* and *growth control,* the term *no growth* also came into use.

Growth management might be taken to mean management without any implication of limiting growth. *Growth control* carries the implication that growth is not only to be managed or guided but also to be limited. The term *no growth* carries the obvious implication of an intent to stop growth entirely. With time, *growth management* became the standard term covering programs that fit all three senses of the term just noted. Growth management has its staunch defenders, who see it as a sensible and principled way to preserve both community and natural values. It also has its detractors, who see it as serving much more selfish purposes, as will be explained subsequently.[2]

Growth management policies are not common in older central cities, for there the problem is more likely to be shrinkage or stagnation rather than rampant growth. Growth *management* policies are common in suburban areas and in those cities where there is still substantial growth potential. They are also common in counties and towns outside metropolitan areas. The potential for rapid growth and a high degree of environmental consciousness predispose communities toward the establishment of growth management policies. So, too, does a high degree of general prosperity. If people or communities are poor, they are more likely to be pro-growth because that implies jobs and revenues. In that case, environmental and quality-of-life issues seem less important.

THE ORIGINS OF GROWTH MANAGEMENT

Several strands came together to bring about the growth management movement. First was the rush to suburbanize after World War II. People moved outward in metropolitan areas partly to obtain relief from central-city conditions: to breathe cleaner air, to be less crowded, to be safer, and to be closer to nature. The person who has made such a move would in many cases want to be the last person who does so—thus the "I'm on board, now pull up the ladder" syndrome. No one who is active in suburban planning is unaware of such motivations.

These motivations were joined by growing environmental consciousness that began, roughly, in the early 1960s. Growth control proponents could gather strength and respectability from a general climate of environmental concern. Proposals to limit growth could now be supported on environmental grounds. At a local level of analysis, it is hard to refute such arguments, for it is undeniable that any development, whether residential or commercial, will have some adverse environmental impact.

Whether environmentally based opposition to growth can be justified when the physical scale of analysis is expanded is another matter. If a town takes some action that keeps a particular area in, let us say, low-density residential use when it might otherwise have gone into high-density residential use, it has unquestionably reduced the environmental impact on that area. Fewer trees will be cut down, less ground will be covered with impervious cover, fewer sources of air and water pollution will be present in the area, and so on.[3] However, it is obvious that much of the growth that was prevented will be displaced elsewhere. In that case one cannot say, a priori, whether the total effect of the growth limitation has been to decrease or increase environmental impact. The environmental impact argument is commonly used by proponents of growth limitations, but the issue of displacement effects is less often discussed.

Regardless of the displacement effects issue, there is no doubt that the growing environmental consciousness of the 1960s and 1970s lent much strength to the growth management movement. Even global concern with overpopulation lent strength to the growth control movement because of the superficial resemblance between planetary population control and local population control.

> Undoubtely this [local efforts to stop population growth] has much to do with the new Malthusian concern with the consequences of unlimited population growth at national and world levels. Some seem to think that the place to start controlling the nation's population growth is at the level of their city, metropolis or state. Others hope that, as the nation moves to zero population growth (ZPG), so will their communities. Both these views are misleading half-truths.[4]

Ernest F. Schumacher's book *Small Is Beautiful* and similar works that railed against the increasing scale and complexity of modern life also lent strength to growth control movements.[5]

One of the first and best known growth management programs in the United States was that enacted by Ramapo, New York, in 1969. The town, located about 28 miles northwest of midtown Manhattan, felt itself on the verge of being overwhelmed by new development. The town was at the very fringe of what was then commuting distance from Manhattan but was in easy reach of masses of new commercial development in the outer portions of the New York metropolitan region located in southern New

York State and in adjacent parts of New Jersey. Ramapo was already zoned so that only single-family development was permitted, but it then added rules which made it possible to turn down development proposals that met the zoning requirements if the development did not have enough points for such infrastructure as sewers, nearby recreational facilities, public roads, and proximity to a firehouse, all items keyed to the town's 18-year capital improvements program. Opponents of the plan saw it simply as exclusionary zoning carried to a new level and took the town to court. On a split decision by the state's appellate (appeals) court, the town was sustained. The ordinance, which seems very primitive by today's standards, and which probably would not be sustained today, has since been rescinded. But it did mark judicial approval of growth management.[6]

WINNERS AND LOSERS IN GROWTH MANAGEMENT

In principle, many municipalities could slow growth with equal effectiveness by limiting either residential or commercial development. Slowing residential growth would slow commercial growth by limiting the size of the labor force and the number of customers. Similarly, limiting commercial growth would slow the growth of the housing stock because the presence of jobs is a major factor in the demand for housing.

In fact, most growth management systems emphasize limiting residential growth because such a policy tends to produce tight labor markets and high housing prices. That result is much more attractive to the population already in place than a commercial limitation policy, which would produce higher unemployment and lower housing prices. And, of course, it is the population resident at the time who establishes the growth management policy.

Assume that a growth management program has the effect of slowing residential growth relative to employment growth. Who wins, and who loses? The homeowner wins simply through the workings of the law of supply and demand. Restrict the supply of any item, and, all other things being equal, its price rises. The owner of rental property benefits in the same manner. A lesser supply of rental units in the long run means higher rents, which is capitalized as a higher value for the building in question. Of course, by the same token, the renter loses. The nonresident of the municipality, if he or she has the desire to become a resident, is also a loser, for it is now more difficult to find housing in the community. In a general sense, those who own developed property in the community benefit, and those who would like to own property lose. Those who would profit from community growth—for example, builders, construction workers, and real estate brokers—also lose. Owners of undeveloped land within the community are losers in the process, for there is a general relationship between the value of land and the intensity with which it can be developed. Restrict that intensity, and the value of land is diminished.[7]

Financial effects will be felt outside the municipality as well. If town X and town Y are in the same metropolitan area, they are to some extent part of the same housing market. If town X reduces its rate of housing construction, it deflects some housing demand to town Y. Thus housing prices in town Y (as well as in X) will rise, benefiting those who already own housing there and penalizing those who seek to buy there. Comparable effects may be seen for rental property.

Fiscal effects can also be demonstrated. If town X restricts residential development but accepts a new corporate headquarters, its tax rate may go down because the tax revenues from the headquarters exceed the new expenses that the headquarters will impose on the town. Town X is capturing the tax surplus from the headquarters while shifting the population-related costs to other towns. Town Y now has to pay the cost of educating the children of people who work in town X and whose place of work contributes handsomely to town X's tax base.

The "Defense of Privilege" Issue

Beyond the purely financial issue of winners and losers is a larger but less demonstrable issue. Much argument over environmental and planning issues is bedeviled with the question of "defense of privilege," with charges of hypocrisy by opponents of growth management and protestations of virtue by its proponents. Without trying to pass a blanket judgment over a complex situation, let us simply present an argument.

There are some goods whose enjoyment by one party does not diminish the enjoyment of comparable goods by another party. If I enjoy a fine steak, that enjoyment does not diminish your enjoyment of another steak. On the other hand, my enjoyment of a day on the ski slope may well diminish your enjoyment of your day on the slope because my presence makes the trails and the lift lines just a bit more crowded for you.

As the U.S. population becomes more prosperous, the possession of goods of the first type becomes less significant as a way of distinguishing between the affluent and the nonaffluent. Instead, the distinction increasingly becomes a matter of being able to enjoy goods and services of the second type—those whose value is lessened the more that others have access to the same or similar items. Increasingly, wealth becomes important not because it buys consumer goods but because it buys quiet, solitude, clean air, or access to relatively unspoiled nature. We can always produce more stereos, but the supply of mountain streams is fixed.

If one accepts this argument, it is only a short step to seeing much environmental and planning conflict in terms of the defense of privilege. The population of a prosperous, attractive community that seeks to limit growth is simply defending its privileges. It is seeking, by means of political action, to protect or enhance the value of those goods of the second type that it now enjoys. One might say that it is using the political process to impose losses on outsiders, that is, denying them temporary or permanent access to the community.

An interesting aspect of this argument is the lineup of combatants in fights over environmental issues. Very often business and labor will be allied in favor of development, and the opposition will be largely upper middle class, perhaps as represented by a coalition of environmental groups like the Sierra Club. The lineup of players is not hard to understand. The same project that means profit to the developer means jobs to the construction worker, and so they make common cause. The upper-middle-class opposition earns its living neither by investing capital nor by doing construction or industrial labor. If one accepts the defense of privilege argument, this class opposes the project for the reasons presented earlier.[8]

A SAMPLING OF LOCAL GROWTH MANAGEMENT PROGRAMS

The city of Boulder, Colorado, which is located in a beautiful physical environment and offers what seems to many to be a superior quality of life, limits growth in a number of ways. Within the city, building permits for residential units are limited to 400 units a year, about 1 percent of the city's total housing stock. If there are applications for more than 400 units, each applicant gets a proportional share of what he or she has requested. Given the long-term decrease in the average number of persons per unit, the 400-unit cap means an end to population growth in Boulder.[9] This limit is becoming moot in that vacant land in the city suitable for residential development is in short supply. In fact, the city planning department estimates that at recent rates of growth, the city will reach "buildout" in another decade or so.

Ordinarily, growth pressure that cannot be accommodated in the city would be accommodated in peripheral development. But that possibility has been blocked in Boulder's case because the city, along with some other jurisdictions, has bought up land outside the city line for permanent open space. The squeeze on Boulder housing prices is further intensified, since Boulder, like many other municipalities, restricts housing development more than it restricts commercial development. Thus the workforce grows faster than the housing stock.

Boulder recognizes that its tight housing market produces very high housing prices and tries to eliminate this side effect of growth management with an affordable housing program. If a new development has five or more units, then 20 percent of those units must be "affordable," meaning a price in the $90,000 to $120,000 range. If there are four or fewer units in the development, the developer can meet the affordable housing requirement with a cash contribution. In 2001 that was $16,156 per single-family unit built or $14,424 for each attached unit built. For the limited number of low- and moderate-income people lucky enough to get an "affordable" unit, the system works. For the person who falls above the income limits for an affordable unit but does not have a big income, the Boulder housing market is a tough nut to crack. In 2001 the average cost of a single-family house in Boulder was well above $300,000.

Bucks County, Pennsylvania, in the Philadelphia metropolitan area, reacted to growth pressures in a somewhat different manner. Here the county has no direct control over local land use since, under Pennsylvania state law, zoning powers reside at the municipal level. The county planning department designates development districts largely on the basis of projected population change. Within those districts it recommends infrastructure (such as sewer lines, water mains, and roads) to facilitate development consistent with the natural environment and expected or planned population change. It suggests that the county outside those districts be considered a "holding zone," with land-use controls that hold population to very low density levels. This purpose is achieved by large, lot zoning requirements and tax policies that encourage farmers to keep their lands in agricultural use.[10]

In the areas designated for development, Bucks County suggests a performance zoning approach with some Euclidean elements (see Chapter 9). Rather than specifying the nature of residential development in great detail, as does the conventional or Euclidean ordinance, the country will simply suggest zoning districts that specify the amount of permissable impervious cover and the number of units per acre. Whether, for example, the units in question are to be single family or multifamily is a matter for community determination. The impervious cover requirements are cast in terms of percentage of the site covered. The intention is to control land use in terms of what is really important (in this case, population housed in an area and volume of storm-water runoff) rather than to specify a large number of details of secondary importance. From a design point of view, performance zoning achieves the overall goals of zoning but gives the designer far more freedom and should encourage much more interesting and varied design. It relies on the marketplace rather than the zoning ordinance to achieve functional, aesthetically sound development.

As in the Boulder case, one side effect of the growth management program is higher house prices. The holding-zone approach prevents some peripheral growth that would relieve pressure on the housing stock. Because residential development is limited more strictly than commercial growth, there is also the labor market pressure noted in the Boulder case.

Although the county's role with regard to zoning is only advisory, the county is not entirely toothless. Under state legislation passed in 2001, if a municipality's land-use plans are not in conformity with the county's recommendations, the chance that the municipality will receive state aid for infrastructure development is reduced. Thus there is a substantial financial motivation for local governments to go along with county plans.

Many jurisdictions have been seen the growth management problem as a largely financial issue—how to provide the infrastructure for growth before growth occurs and how to pay the infrastructure costs that growth imposes. As noted in Chapter 9, an exaction is a payment that a jurisdiction demands in return for permitting development to take place. Fairfax County, Virginia, uses a system of "proffers," a variation on the exaction theme, which requires developers to offer to pay the infrastructure costs of major projects. The county is immediately west of Washington, D.C., and has experienced extremely rapid growth, particularly in office activity. It is very concerned with providing the infrastructure to keep up with this development. Because demand for commercial space is strong, the county has considerable leverage in its dealings with developers.

The county uses the ability to grant or deny rezonings as a means of obtaining proffers. For example, in the Fairfax Center area, which, roughly speaking is a 3,000-acre development node in the county, the master plan recognizes three levels of development. There is a base level, which is essentially single-family large-lot development; an intermediate level; and an overlay level, which permits intensive commercial and multifamily residential development. Under Virginia state law, government cannot literally demand a contribution from a private party. Thus if the developer builds "by right"—that is, under the existing zoning—he or she cannot be compelled to contribute to infrastructure or other costs that the development may impose upon the county. However, if the developer wants a rezoning, the county can choose not to grant the request unless a "proffer" is made. The making of the proffer is thus, in a sense, voluntary. The developer makes it in the hopes of receiving something of value in return, namely, the higher profit obtainable from developing at a greater density. The proffer may take the form of actually doing off-site physical work such as improving an intersection or widening a roadway. In other cases it may take the form of a cash contribution to a housing, parks, road, or recreation fund. In order to provide "affordable housing," the county requires that developers of large residential projects either include a certain number of low- and moderate-income units within the project or make a contribution to the housing trust fund to help build such units elsewhere.

Fort Collins, Colorado, uses a technique designed to direct growth into specified areas and also to require new development to pay its own infrastructure costs first. The city is located within a county, and over the years it has grown by annexation. Under the terms of a joint city-county agreement, a 65-square-mile "urban growth area" has been defined. The understanding is that all land within the growth area is ultimately subject to annexation. Within this area, urban services will be provided, and urban development standards—paved roads, public water, public sewer facilities, and the like—will apply. As urban development takes place, the city annexes the area. In addition to providing necessary infrastructure on-site, developers are required to provide off-site infrastructure such as roads and sewer and water lines. How much they are required to provide is based on traffic and other studies, for which they themselves are required to pay.

In the Fort Collins case, rather than contribute to a development fund, the developer is literally required to provide the specified infrastructure. A subsequent developer may be required to make payments to a prior developer if he or she makes use of the infrastructure the latter has provided. For example, if developer A builds a mile of road to serve his or her project and developer B subsequently builds in such a manner as to make direct use of that road, a compensating payment from B to A may be required.

The Fort Collins approach, as seen by the city's planning agency, is "growth management" as opposed to "growth control" in the sense that the effort is to shape growth rather than limit it. In fact, in the late 1970s a growth limitation initiative analogous to Boulder's was soundly defeated by Fort Collins's voters.

STATE-LEVEL GROWTH MANAGEMENT

Many states exercise considerable control over the process of growth, particularly in environmentally sensitive areas. These controls constitute much of Bosselman's "quiet revolution," noted in Chapter 9.

The first statewide land-use controls were instituted in Hawaii in the early 1960s. The motivation behind them was that the land area of the islands is small, growth pressures were strong, and agriculture was important to the state economy. According to Bosselman, the goal was to keep Honolulu, the main center of population in the state, from sprawling out, Los Angeles–like, into the adjacent Central Valley of Oahu. Under legislation passed in 1961, all land in the state falls into one of four major categories: urban, rural, agricultural, and conservation. Within the urban areas, county zoning regulations prevail. In effect, counties may (but do not have to) permit urban-type development in any area that the state designates as urban. In rural and agricultural areas, land uses are controlled by the State Land Use Commission, a board set up when the system was created. In the conservation district, land use is controlled by the state's Board of Land and Natural Resources.

Perhaps it is no surprise that the first statewide system developed in Hawaii. A small, scenically beautiful state, subject to major growth pressures and having a limited supply of highly productive agricultural land, would appear to be an ideal candidate for such a system. The fact that much of the growth pressure came from outsiders, people from the U.S. mainland, may also have contributed to the passage of the act.

Partly as a result of the limitation on urban growth, Hawaii is characterized by very high housing prices. But is that bad? The person who already owns property in the state is likely to take a very different view than the person who lives on the mainland but thinks it would be nice to buy a condominium in Honolulu for retirement. Again, we see that planning decisions, no matter how well intended, create winners and losers.

The state of Florida faces serious environmental problems in several regards. Its population growth has been extremely rapid in the last several decades and is likely to continue at a brisk pace in the foreseeable future. Its swampy areas are environmentally fragile, as is often the case with tropical soils. Its groundwater supplies are readily threatened by saltwater intrusion because much of the state lies very close to sea level.[11]

In 1972, after considerable lobbying by environmental groups, the state legislature passed the Environmental Land and Water Management Act, as well as several ancillary pieces of legislation. In "areas of critical state concern" and on "developments of regional impact," the state can overrule local land-use decisions if they fail to take into account effects that extend beyond the locality's boundaries.[12] John M. DeGrove quotes the key language of the legislation defining areas of critical state concern as

1. An area containing, or having significant impact upon, environmental, historical, natural, or archeological resources of statewide importance
2. An area significantly affected by, or having significant effect upon, an existing or proposed major public facility or other area of major public investment
3. A proposed area of major development potential, which may include a proposed site of a new community, designated in a state land development plan

The "new community" provision is particularly germane to Florida because much of its population has been accommodated in major new developments, frequently carved out of environmentally sensitive former wilderness. Developments of regional impact are defined as projects that "because of [their] character, magnitude or location, would have a substantial effect on the health, safety or welfare of the citizens of more than one county." Thus, for example, a regional shopping center that would affect the pattern of vehicular traffic in adjacent counties could be classified as being of regional impact. So, too, could a power plant or an industrial facility whose emissions could have measurable effects on the air quality in adjacent counties.

In 1985 the state enacted the Growth Management Act, which added another level of control through "concurrency requirements."[13] These requirements stipulate that before new development can occur, local governments must demonstrate to the state Department of Community Affairs (DCA) that the infrastructure required to support the development is in place. For example, before new housing is built, it must be shown that the water and sewer capacity necessary to support it exists. Similarly, it must be shown that the road capacity exists to handle the additional traffic at an acceptable level of service. If the capacity cannot be shown to exist, then DCA can prevent the project from going forward. Concurrency requirements thus constitute a powerful tool both for imposing some higher-level control and also for avoiding environmental degradation and congestion. But the actual workings of the concurrency requirements are another demonstration that in planning, as perhaps in life in general, all things are more complex than they first appear. One goal of state planning is to avoid excessive sprawl. Suppose a developer would like to do some development on skipped-over parcels in an already developed area (sometimes referred to as "infill"). Traffic congestion in that area, however, is already such that without new road construction, the area cannot meet concurrency requirements. The developer may then choose to invest in a less-developed area where traffic flow is not congested and there is no concurrency problem. In that case, the concurrency requirements promote sprawl. To deal with this problem, the Environmental Lands and Management Act (1993) contains provisions for the creation of Transportation Concurrency Exemption Areas (TCEAs). These can be created if the local government will commit itself to improving public transportation or engaging in various transportation demand management initiatives. (See Chapter 12.) The 1993 act also permits local governments to average traffic conditions over an entire "district" rather than have a project blocked because conditions on one segment or link are below standard.

Oregon has had a state growth management plan since 1973. At this time Oregon was growing at about twice the rate of the United States as a whole, with much concern about the consequences of such rapid growth. The state, considered as a whole, was not and is not densely populated, but growth was highly visible because most of it was occurring in one area, the Willamette Valley south of Portland. The phrase "Don't Californicate Oregon" appeared on bumper stickers at about this time. The state's then governor, Thomas McCall, was a strong environmentalist and a proponent of limiting its population growth. Under the plan all cities and counties are required to make their own land-use plans conform to the goals of the state plan. Though the state plan has 19 separate goals, the core elements in the plan are closely related ones of preservation of natural resources and containment of urban growth. The state Department of Land Conservation and Development is required to certify that local plans are in conformity. An important feature of the plan is the use of Urban Growth Boundaries (UGBs). Land-use controls and public capital investment are designed to encourage growth within the UGBs and to discourage it outside. Local governments are encouraged to promote fairly dense development within the UGBs so as to minimize sprawl. One benefit of this has been to reduce pressure on housing costs, for the policy has resulted in smaller lot sizes for single-family homes and more multifamily development than would otherwise be the case. By increasing the amount of development proximate to central areas, growth boundaries contribute to revitalization of central-city areas.[14]

The 19 goals include, in addition to the items mentioned earlier, a variety of provisions connected with shoreline preservation, estuary preservation, economic development, air quality, energy conservation, and citizen participation, among others. The goals themselves were evolved in a public process involving many thousands of citizens, thus gaining some support for the inevitable political and legal battles over limiting growth. The plan also receives considerable political support from a nonprofit organization, the 1000 Friends of Oregon, an organization that came into being in 1975, partly founded by Governor McCall. More generally, the plan gains support from the strong pro-environmental ethos that characterizes the Pacific Northwest in general.

The state of New Jersey has good reason to pursue a state growth-management program. With approximately 8 million people living on little more than 8 thousand square miles, it is the most densely populated state in the nation. Although the state does not have any very large cities within its borders, it is subject to development pressures from the New York metropolitan area on its northeast and the Philadelphia metropolitan area to the southwest. The resulting suburban sprawl is readily visible, particularly in the parts of the state that fall within the New York City commutershed. The state uses a variety of approaches to pursue the goals of channeling growth into designated development areas. The goals are to help protect the natural environment and also to minimize the cost of servicing population growth. Meeting those goals will also give New Jersey residents convenient access to the natural world.

The state plan is only advisory to municipal governments, but it does provide a financial carrot for local governments in that state agencies are required to use the state plan in making decisions about capital investments. Thus the state's power of the purse with regard to roads, water and sewer mains, the location of public facilities, and the like serves to reinforce the plan.

Coastal areas of the state fall under the authority of the Coastal Area Facility Review Act (CAFRA) passed in 1973. Under this act, development along the state's Atlantic and Delaware Bay Shores and along some of their tributaries requires both local government and state approval. Thus the state has a say over development on much of the most ecologically fragile and desirable land in the state.

Beyond that, there are two areas of the state subject to regional authorities. The 17-square-mile Hackensack Meadowlands area, best known to sports fans as the home of Giants stadium, falls under the province of the Hackensack Meadowlands Development Commission (HMDC). Within this area, local governments have ceded their zoning powers to the commission so that the area can be planned as a single entity. Farther south about 1 million acres (roughly 1,600 square miles and one-fifth of the state's total land area) fall under the jurisdiction of the Pinelands Commission. The area contains 52 municipalities and parts of seven counties. Throughout the area, local plans must conform to the commission's plan. Thus the commission has control over the density of development and types of land uses permitted in this large and environmentally fragile area.

All of the preceding program does not guarantee that New Jersey will be able to control the process of sprawl, for there are very powerful forces behind sprawl—in particular, the economic dynamism of those parts of the state near New York and Philadelphia, and the public demand for housing and for what H. G. Wells a century ago (see 15) called that "private imperium." However, this program does give the state a fighting chance to contain sprawl and to achieve an orderly pattern of development in those parts of the state where there are still substantial blocks of land that remain to be developed.

Numerous other states have growth management plans at the state level. Most plans have some of the elements noted before. Many designate development areas and seek to divert growth into those areas. Many use the state's ability to make capital investments as a carrot to induce municipal governments to make their plans conform to the state's overall plan. State plans generally place emphasis on protecting environmentally fragile areas, whether they be shorelines, wetlands, estuaries, or in the case of Vermont and other mountainous states, land at high elevations. A number of states also seek to protect areas of particular scenic or historic value from excessive development, and they use a mix of regulation and financial incentives for this purpose.

GROWTH MANAGMENT—PRO OR CON?

Growth management, like any other planning technique, is subject to use and misuse. At its best, it can be used to step into the future in a planned manner and emerge with good results—with a sensible and an attractive pattern of development, with the public treasury in good shape, with community services adequate to the tasks demanded of them, and with the natural environment disrupted to a minimal degree. At worst, growth management techniques can be used to block legitimate growth, to defend the privileges of those already privileged, and to displace the inevitable costs of development to other jurisdictions.

Quite probably, the best results will be obtained when the government doing the managing corresponds in size to a natural labor market or housing market. If the primary purpose of the growth management system is environmental, it seems likely that all other things being equal, the best results will be obtained if there is a correspondence between the physical jurisdiction of the managing unit and the realities of the environmental processes. In this case the displacement effects of growth management decisions will be taken account of to a substantial degree. On the other hand, if the jurisdiction is small with regard to the economic, social, or physical effects resulting from its actions, the temptation to consider only parochial interests and to ignore the numerous effects of local decisions on outsiders may be hard to resist.

THE CHALLENGE OF SMART GROWTH

In the mid-1990s the term *smart growth* appeared on the planning scene and rapidly became the buzzword of the day. The term was first used in connection with the Maryland state plan under then governor Parris Glendenning. Whether smart growth is inherently different from growth management as just described or whether it is basically growth management under a more attractive name—who could be in favor of "stupid growth"—is arguable. In either case, smart growth refers to a set of issues that will be with us for years to come.

From 1990 to 2000, U.S. population grew by about 32 million people. That rate of growth, about 3 million per year, continued into the first several years of the twenty-first century and shows, at this writing, no signs of slowing. Most of that growth has gone into those parts of metropolitan areas outside the central city, what we refer to as the suburbs, even though not all of these areas are suburban in character.

Much of the concern with smart growth has been driven by a concern with suburban sprawl, a condition that derives directly from that population growth. There is no standard, unambiguous definition of sprawl, though many of us may take an I-can't-define-it-but-I-know-it-when-I-see-it position. Reid Ewing suggests that indicators of sprawl are the following:

1. Leapfrog or scattered development
2. Commercial strip development
3. Large expanses of low-density or single-use development (as in sprawling bedroom communities)[15]

He then goes on to argue that these readily observable signs do not tell the entire story and that there are some functional indicators as well. The most important of these is "poor accessibility." In an area of sprawl, getting around is inconvenient. One must drive past undeveloped areas to get to one's destination. On roads characterized by strip development, one must pass many commercial uses before getting to one's destination. Because potential destinations are scattered about, it is difficult to combine errands or trips—each destination may be in a different direction.

Ewing also suggests that lack of "functional open space" is an indicator of sprawl. Though the area will have large amounts of undeveloped land, most of it is in private hands, perhaps with access blocked by other development, and thus unavailable for recreational or other public use.

If we use a definition like Ewing's, then sprawl is not a matter of low density, though there may be some correlation between sprawl and low density of development. A 10-square-mile area with a population of, say ten thousand, might be an example of sprawl if it met some or all of the preceding criteria. On the other hand, if the same number of people were grouped in several centers with jobs, shopping, and other destinations generally within short distances of residences and if there were substantial blocks of undeveloped land accessible to and open to the public, then by a definition like Ewing's we would not call it sprawl. We might, in fact, consider it to be an exemplar of desirable low-density development.

The biggest force behind smart growth has been citizen concern over one aspect of sprawl, namely, traffic congestion. The suburban resident who finds that his or her commuting time is increasing because of growing congestion on major roadways and who finds that trips to shopping, to visit friends, and to entertainment and recreation are making him or her feel as if the car is becoming a second home, is likely to feel that something needs to be done. Often that something is planning for smart growth. Other forces behind the push for smart growth have been concern over preservation of the natural environment and concern with what some suburban residents may regard as excessive urbanization of their environs. Because smart growth does not have a precise definition, the term means different things to different people, and it is thus a large political tent that can contain many people with different tastes and agendas.

One element in a smart growth agenda might be using land-use controls, tax policy, and perhaps some public subsidies to encourage compact development. In the same vein, the smart growth program might place an emphasis on in-fill development and reuse, whether of old buildings or of previously used industrial and commercial sites. A smart growth program might also involve buying up or acquiring development rights for some undeveloped land to assure a supply of future open space and to channel development into selected areas. Urban growth boundaries, such as those used around Portland, Oregon, might be part of a smart growth agenda. Those who favor smart growth are likely to be fans of the New Urbanism (see Chapter 10). New-Urbanist design emphasizes relatively close spacing between structures and a fine-grained mixture of land uses. Both of these should facilitate trips by foot or bicycle and also reduce the average length of automobile trips.

Because smart growth is an attractive but not a precisely defined term, there will inevitably be disagreement about just which policies really are smart. For example, a county in the fast-growing fringe of a metropolitan area decides to buy up big blocks of farmland (or the development rights for that farmland) in order to channel growth and preserve open space. Proponents of the move argue that the move is good for the county's present and future residents and also good environmentally because it preserves the habitats of many species. But opponents argue that it simply diverts growth to further out-locations—in effect, it simply promotes leapfrog development at a larger scale. It is not always easy to say who is right. Smart growth, because it is such a nice term, may sometimes be used as a flag of convenience by those whose real game is simply NIMBY (Not in My Back Yard).

Smart growth policies may be pursued at many geographic scales—municipal, county, or state. Because the term originated in Maryland, we take a quick look at Maryland's Smart Growth Program. The background conditions that propelled the state into the program were twofold. First, Mayland is a small state with a higher than average population density—over 500 people per square mile compared with somewhat under 100 people per square mile for the average for the coterminous ("lower") 48 states. In fact, only 4 states—Massachusetts, Rhode Island, Connecticut, and New Jersey—have higher densities. Second, a large percentage of the state's population lives within the greater Washington-Baltimore area and thus is sensitive to all of the sprawl-related considerations previously mentioned.

Maryland defines the goals of smart growth as

1. Save our most valuable remaining natural resources;
2. Support existing communities and neighborhoods; and
3. Save taxpayers millions of dollars in the unnecessary building of the infra-structure required to support sprawl.[16]

The core of the state's effort is the creation of Priority Funding Areas. The state directs its expenditures on physical infrastructure and also on some other categories such as subsidies for industrial development into priority areas in order to channel growth there. Priority areas are defined by the state as

1. Every municipality in the state.
2. All the area of Maryland that lies inside either the Washington, D.C., or the Baltimore beltway. Baltimore is entirely within the state of Maryland; and the District of Columbia, not legally a part of any state, is bordered by both Maryland and Virginia.
3. Enterprise zones, neighborhood revitalization areas, "heritage" areas (see later) and industrial areas.

Though the preceding sounds like a lot, it is only a small share of the state's total land area.

The use of the state's capital budget to concentrate development in these areas is backstopped by a number of other programs. The Rural Heritage program uses state funds to buy conservation easements on rural properties with an emphasis on preserving large contiguous blocks. A Brownfields program (see Chapter 15) seeks to reduce the investment risks on disused urban industrial properties and thus to promote infill development. A "Live Near Your Work" program assists workers in buying homes near their jobs. Its goals are neighborhood stabilization and infill development.

PLANNING FOR SUSTAINABILITY

In recent years there has been much interest among planners in the matter of planning for *sustainable development*. In the United States part of the interest is homegrown, and part comes from Great Britain, the Netherlands, and other nations in Western Europe where much higher population densities give many planning questions a sense of greater urgency. Most discussions of planning for sustainable development hark back to a 1987 report of the World Commission on Environment and Development, also known as the Brundtland Commission, for the name of its chairwoman Gro Harlem Brundtland, who was then prime minister of Norway. In its report the commission defines sustainable growth as follows:

> Sustainable development is development that meets the needs of the present without compromising the ability of future generations to meet their own needs.

That is a very general statement, and much thought and argument have been devoted since then to defining exactly what it means. On the surface it might be taken to have a simple environmental meaning. For example, in regard to forestry, it might mean not cutting more board feet of timber in one year than the forest can grow in one year. However, with the passage of time, sustainability has come to be defined more broadly. Although there is no single, unambiguous definition for sustainable development, a very rough general agreement appears to have emerged in the last decade or so. Most writers define sustainable development planning as planning that addresses three overall goals in a coordinated manner. These goals are *environmental quality*, social *equity*, and *economic* development, easily remembered as the three "Es."[17]

The environmental requirement is readily understood as meaning planning for development that does not degrade the quality of the environment from one time period to the next. However, it should be understood that determining exactly what constitutes degradation is not always so easy. For example, suppose years of farming has thinned the topsoil somewhat in a particular area, but, at the same time, years of fertilizer use has increased the nitrate and phosphate content of the soil. Experts might disagree about whether, on balance, the soil is now better or worse than it was.

Social equity is a more ambiguous matter. Most proponents of sustainable development take it to mean greater equality of wealth and more opportunity for poorer and less-advantaged people. To defend the idea that social equity ought to be included in the concept of sustainable development, one might argue that over the long term, any social or economic system must achieve a satisfactory degree of equity or the internal stresses generated by inequity will render it unstable. Whether this perception is really true can be argued. There is no question that inequity and the perception of inequity has been at the root of many social and political upheavals such as the French or the Russian revolutions. On the other hand, there have been inequitable systems that have shown remarkable stability. The caste system of India strikes most Westerners and many Indians as grossly inequitable. But the social and economic order that the system rested on has shown great stability over many centuries and is only now changing at a moderate pace under many pressures of modernity. One might even argue that some social and economic systems may become unstable as they become more equitable, because that change expands people's perspectives and whets their appetite for more change (sometimes referred to by the phrase "the revolution of rising expectations"). In brief, the point that equity is a prerequisite for long-term stability can be argued either way. The skeptic might contend that equity has been added as a criterion, not because it is intrinsically necessary for sustainability, but rather because those who argue for planning for sustainable systems also, as a group, favor more egalitarian systems, in other words, that equity has been tacked on much as a rider is tacked on to a bill in Congress.

It can be argued that at times, sustainability goals and equity goals may be in conflict, just as environmental and equity goals may be in conflict (see Chapter 15). Therefore, planning for sustainable development should address such conflicts. In this writer's view, that is a valid argument. But note that it is a separate argument from the question of whether equity issues are inherently part of the question of sustainability. However, regardless of argument and counterargument, equity is now firmly ensconced as one of the three main elements of the term *sustainability* as commonly used in the planning profession.

If one accepts equity as a key element in planning for sustainability, then the requirement for economic development makes considerable sense. If equity concerns make it desirable to redistribute a certain amount of wealth, that goal will be easier to achieve if average wealth is growing than if it is stable. In a steady-state situation, any redistribution of wealth would necessarily be a zero-sum game and would meet powerful resistance.[18] This observation is no more profound than saying that it is easier to be generous if you are wealthy than if you are poor.

In principle the idea of planning for sustainable development can be applied at any scale ranging from the municipality, or perhaps even a part of a municipality, up to the planet itself. Actions to promote sustainable development at one geographic scale will inevitably have effects on the environment at other geographic scales. Then, too, what looks sustainable or not sustainable at one scale may look different at another scale. For example, the development of Manhattan (the most densely populated urban place in the United States) might look very bad from a sustainable development perspective, if viewed solely at a municipal scale. Most of the natural environment has been paved or built over; the original land form has been substantially changed; creeks, streams, and marshy areas have been filled in; and biodiversity has been vastly reduced.

On the other hand, when viewed from a larger geographic perspective, Manhattan looks environmentally virtuous. The 1.54 million people living on Manhattan's 22.7 square miles have much less environmental impact than the same number of people would if spread out over, say, 750 square miles (at a typical suburban density of 2,000 people per square mile). Transporting one person to work by subway consumes considerably less energy than transporting one person to work by car. It takes less energy to heat one apartment than it does to heat one single-family house. Fewer trees must be cut down to build one high-rise apartment house than would have to be cut down to build single-family houses for an equivalent number of residents.

The amount of impervious cover is one aspect of environmental impact. Manhattan has 508 miles of streets. Multiply that by 5,280 (the number of feet in a mile). Then divide that figure by the population of Manhattan, roughly 1,540,000. The result is that there is approximately 1.7 feet of street length per Manhattan resident. Then, make a casual estimate of how many feet of street there would be per resident on a suburban street of single family houses built on 100-foot-wide lots. The difference is very substantial. Thus in considering the sustainable development, one may come to very different conclusions depending on whether one thinks in terms of what happens at a particular location on the map or whether one thinks in terms of accommodating a specific number of people or specific amount of economic activity.

With all of the preceding caveats, we turn now to planning for sustainable development in a single municipality.

Implementing a Local Sustainable Development program

What might a city or a county or a town do to pursue the goal of sustainability through its planning process? Very broadly, it might pursue policies that preserve as much of the natural environment as possible from development. Or it might pursue policies designed to minimize energy consumption in transportation and housing. Also, it might require construction practices that minimum adverse environmental effects such as siltation of nearby streams.

A municipality that planned for sustainability might impose strict requirements on building insulation so as to reduce the amount of energy required for space heating. The municipality might also include provisions for solar access in its zoning ordinance so as to encourage a switch from fossil fuel to solar heating. A municipality that took planning for sustainability seriously might adjust its land-use controls and possibly also its property tax policies to favor infill development and thus achieve more compact development.[19] Similarly, it might attempt to encourage redevelopment on *brownfields* rather than development on *greenfields* (see Chapter 15.)

With regard to equity, the municipality might adjust its zoning ordinance and map to provide areas where it is was possible to build relatively lower-cost housing units such as garden apartments or small houses on small lots. It might include provisions that require builders of large developments to set aside some units for low- and moderate-income purchasers or renters. If the municipality were in a strong financial position, it might devote a small part of the municipal budget to subsidizing low- and moderate-income housing. If the municipality pursued an economic development program, as do many thousands of municipalities in the United States, it might tune the program to produce only development that is consistent with its environmental and equity goals, though, as Chapter 13 suggests, that is much easier said than done.

Many advocates of sustainable development are fond of the phrase "think globally, act locally," and, indeed, the sum of thousands of local actions will necessarily have global effects. But it must be admitted that many environmental questions, and many equity questions as well, require national responses. For example, a few years back the United States achieved a massive reduction in the amount of airborne lead because Congress required the phaseout of leaded gasoline. That is the kind of action that can be done only at the national level. Similarly, sulfur dioxide emissions from power plants have been cut back significantly because of an emissions-permit-trading system implemented by the EPA. That action, too can be done only nationally. (Both of these matters are discussed in Chapter 15.)

If in the interest of minimizing the greenhouse effect, we replace some of our fossil-fuel-generating capacity with wind, solar, or nuclear power, that change, too, will be in part conditioned by actions of the federal government with regard to regulations, tax treatment, subsidy policy, and, perhaps, direct public investment as well.

It may also be that for significant change to occur in how we produce energy some compulsion from the national government will be involved. For example, wind-powered electric generators are environmentally benign in that they use no fossil fuel. But residents of many localities have fought them bitterly. Residents of Cape Cod, Massachusetts, have put up a very stiff fight against wind-powered generators that would be put up about 6 miles offshore. Similar opposition occurred in the mountains of West Virginia. Opponents have made environmental arguments including protection of viewsheds, avoiding noise pollution, and the threat that the blades of wind generators poses for migratory birds. Comparable comments can be made about nuclear power. Many people think it is a good idea in principle, but a great many people also think it is a good idea for somewhere else.

Fuel efficiency and emissions standards for motor vehicles are another matter that in principle are best handled by the federal government, because vehicles are manufactured for national or international markets and are not necessarily used in the jurisdiction in which they are purchased.

One reason that local and state governments are limited in how much they can tax or regulate in connection with environmental or equity matters is that they are in competition with each other for affluent residents and for capital investment, as discussed in Chapter 13. A local or state government that gets too far out of line with other local or state governments in terms of personal and business taxes, or in terms of the regulatory burden that it imposes on economic activity, runs the risk of diverting people and investment to other places and thus shrinking its own tax base. Thus the competition between jurisdictions places a very powerful limitation on how much any one place can do in terms of equity. Ultimately, the distribution of wealth and income is a national issue. For this reason a substantial amount of planning for sustainable development, regardless of exactly how the term is used, will necessarily have to be done at the national level. Some sustainable development issues, such as the greenhouse effect, will also be addressed at the global level. (See Chapter 15).

A LIST OF SUSTAINABLE PLANNING TECHNIQUES

In 2001 Edward J. Jepson Jr., surveyed some hundreds of municipal governments to see what steps they were taking to pursue sustainable development.[20] He asked them about 39 categories of actions. These categories are shown in the list that follows to provide a sense of the range of sustainable development. Those whose meaning is not self-evident or are not explained elsewhere in this book are explained in the notes that follow. The measures listed here address all the three E's as well as local self-sufficiency and include both direct actions and steps to gather information to support subsequent actions.[21]

1. Agricultural district provisions
2. Agricultural protection zoning
3. Bicycle-access plan
4. Brownfield reclamation
5. Community indicators program
6. Community gardening

7. Cooperative housing
8. Eco-industrial park
9. Ecological footprint analysis
10. Environmental-site-design regulations
11. Green-building requirements
12. Green procurement
13. Green maps
14. Green-print plans
15. Greenways development
16. Heat-island analysis
17. Import substitution
18. Incentive/inclusionary zoning
19. Infill development
20. Life-cycle public construction
21. Living-wage ordinance
22. Low-emission vehicles
23. Neotraditional (New Urbanist) development
24. Open-space zoning
25. Pedestrian-access plan
26. Purchase of development rights
27. Rehabilitation building codes
28. Right-to-farm legislation
29. Solar-access protection regulations
30. Solid-waste life cycle management
31. Tax base/revenue sharing
32. Transfer of development rights
33. Transit-oriented development
34. Transportation-demand management
35. Urban-growth boundary
36. Urban forestry program
37. Urban-system analysis
38. Wildlife habitat/green corridor planning
39. Wind-energy development

Notes: Explanations are for items not mentioned elsewhere in this text and whose meanings are not readily apparent. 5. Use of community social, economic, or environmental indicators in making plans. 7. Closely spaced housing with many shared facilities. 8. Industrial parks designed to incorporate good ecological practices. 11. Requiring new buildings to use practices that minimize energy use and other environmental impacts. 12. Taking environmental considerations into municipal purchasing decisions. 14. Municipal planning and mapping that show natural areas slated for acquisition and preservation. 20. Costing public construction to include all phases of the project from inception through demolition and disposal. 22. Favoring low-emission types when purchasing municipal vehicles. 27. Writing building codes to favor rehabilitation and reuse 36. Tree planting to reduce CO_2 in the atmosphere and to facilitate heating and cooling of buildings. (The term has also been used in connection with maintaining small amounts of seminatural habital within a municipality.)

Note that items 7, 18, and 21 specifically address equity concerns. Item 17 addresses local self-sufficiency.

Earlier in the chapter we noted that *growth management* relies in large measure for its implementation on planning tools that were in existence for many years before the term came into being. Similarly, many of the techniques that are used in planning for sustainable development have also been around for some time. For example, many localities have been planning for and appropriating monies for open space acquisition for decades. Another example is that many municipalities have had a long-standing commitment to making provisions for affordable housing, and so forth. To the extent that planning for sustainable development is a new idea, it is the overall concept and the long time horizon, not the individual techniques, that will distinguish it from previous planning efforts.

SUMMARY

Growth management is often defined as the regulation of the amount, timing, location, and character of development. Growth management programs generally use techniques that are common to much of planning. Thus such plans are distinguished from more traditional plans by their intent and scope rather than by the implementing techniques they use.

Growth management programs became widespread in the 1960s as a result of reaction to the rapid suburbanization of the postwar period and the growth of environmental consciousness and concern. Growth management also gained strength from concern with national and global population growth even though the logical link with these concerns and local population growth is weak. Such programs raise a variety of equity issues, for controlling the rate and character of growth inevitably produces a variety of winners and losers, a point discussed in some detail in the chapter.

A number of subsequent growth management plans have been instituted in various parts of the country. Some, such as Boulder's, attempt to place a cap on growth, or to hold growth to some predetermined annual percentage rate. Others, such as Fort Collins's, seek to shape the pattern of growth without attempting to limit the rate.

Many states have instituted growth management programs, beginning with Hawaii in the early 1960s. In general, state growth management programs cover only parts of the state, frequently for environmental reasons. State controls on development usually do not supersede local controls. Rather, they constitute an additional level of control intended to see that larger-than-local issues are given adequate weight in the making of development decisions.

The term *smart growth* came into use in the 1990s, first in connection with Maryland's state planning efforts. Interest in smart growth has largely been generated by the perception of growing suburban sprawl and, in particular, by traffic problems associated with sprawl. Whether smart growth is a new idea or whether it is merely growth management under a more attractive name is a matter of some dispute among planners.

The concept of *sustainable development* harks back to the work of the Bruntlandt Commission in 1987. At the local level it shares many techniques with growth management and smart growth. One way it differs is in the very long time horizon, and perhaps another way is that its proponents are concerned with all scales of development from local to global. Still another difference is the very prominent position that it gives to equity issues, though as noted, whether the link between sustainability and equity is entirely logical can be argued either way.

NOTES

1. Randall W. Scott et al., eds., *Management and Control of Growth*, Urban Land Institute, Washington, DC, 1975. Three volumes appeared in 1975; two more have since appeared.
2. For some early recognition of the dark side of growth management, see articles by Wilbur Thompson and Willard R. Johnson in vol. 1, ibid.
3. One might ask what sources of air pollution purely residential development involves. According to EPA estimates, about one-half of U.S. air pollution comes from motor vehicle exhausts. Thus the vehicular traffic associated with residential development is a major source of air pollution. Smaller amounts of air pollution may come from home heating systems. In some areas of the country, for example, Denver, Colorado, emissions from wood-burning stoves have been a major source of air pollution.
4. William Alonso, "Urban Zero Population Growth," *Daedalus*, vol. 102, no. 4, Fall 1973, pp. 191–206. The article is reprinted in Scott, *Management and Control*, vol. 1, chap. 5.
5. Ernest F. Schumacher, *Small Is Beautiful: A Study of Economics As If People Mattered*, Harper & Row, New York, 1975. Previously published in Great Britain.
6. A more detailed description of the Ramapo ordinance and litigation, as well as references to the large planning literature that developed around Ramapo, can be found in any of the first six editions of this book.
7. William Fischel, "The Property Rights Approach to Zoning," *Land Economics*, vol. 54, no. 1, February 1978, pp. 64–81, and subsequent books and articles by Fischel.
8. For a presentation of the view that environmental controls have been used to defend privilege, see Bernard J. Frieden, *The Environmental Protection Hustle*, MIT Press, Cambridge, MA, 1979.
9. The average number of persons per housing unit has been declining ever since the end of World War II. One factor has been the increase in real per capita income in the United States. In the last several decades, a second factor has been the increasing percentage of older adults in the population, a group that typically lives in one- or two-person households.
10. Many counties in or near metropolitan areas use preferential tax treatment to keep land in agricultural use. In general, this means taxing it at a rate appropriate to its value in agricultural use, rather than its market value as sold for nonagricultural use, say, residential or commercial development.
11. In low-lying areas near the sea, a drop in the water table, caused by excessive use of groundwater or a reduction in surface water available for aquifer recharge, will cause saltwater from the ocean to move in. This can cause changes in vegetation and wildlife and also render groundwater unfit for drinking.
12. For details see John M. DeGrove, *Land, Growth and Politics*, Planners Press, American Planning Association, Chicago, 1984, chap. 4.
13. Teresa Austin, "Pay As You Grow," *Civil Engineering*, February 1992, pp. 64–65.
14. Arthur C. Nelson, Raymond J. Burby, Edward Feser, Casey J. Dawkins, Emil E. Malizia, and Robert Quercio, "Urban Containment and Central City Revitalization," *Journal of the American Planning Association*, vol. 70, no. 4, Autumn 2004, pp. 411–425.

15. Reid Ewing, "Is Los Angeles-Style Sprawl Desirable?," *Journal of the American Planning Association*, Winter 1997, Vol. 67, No. 1, pp. 107–119.
16. Details on the Maryland plan can be obtained from the state's department of planning Web site www.mdp.state.md.us/ smartgrowth/smartwhat.htm.
17. For a discussion of the meaning of *sustainable development* and some of its history, see Virginia W. MacLaren, "Urban Sustainability Reporting," *Journal of the American Planning Association*, Spring 1996, Vol. 62, no. 2, pp. 184–202; and Scott Campbell, "Green Cities, Growing Cities, Just Cities," *Journal of the American Planning Association*, Summer 1996, Vol. 62, no. 3, pp. 296–311.
18. The idea that no-growth conditions would tend to lock the poor in their place indefinitely has been present in the planning literature for many years. See, for example, Willard R. Johnson, "Should the Poor Buy No-Growth?" *Management and Control of Growth*, Urban Land Institute, Washington, DC, 1975, Vol. I, pp. 415–425. The term *zero-sum game* means a game, such as cards between friends, in which the sum of the winnings necessarily has to equal the sum of the losings.

    Some writers argue that the terms *economic development* and *economic growth* do not mean exactly the same thing. Economic growth clearly means an increase in total or per capita output. Economic development is taken by some to mean some movement toward a better economic situation without necessarily implying an increase in total output. For example, if the same output were achieved with less environmental impact or with better working conditions, some might argue that economic development had occurred even if there were no increase in total output. However, for purposes of this argument, the terms *economic development and economic growth* can be used synonymously.
19. When vacant land is taxed very lightly, it tends, all other things being equal, to produce a more scattered pattern of development because the low carrying cost encourages the speculative holding of land. When land is taxed more heavily, the higher cost of holding it tends to push it into development.
20. "Edward J. Jepson, Jr., "The Adoption of Sustainable Development Policies and Techniques in US Cities," *The Journal of Planning Education and Research*, Winter 2004, no. 23, pp. 229–241.
21. Some writers on sustainable development have included a degree of local self-sufficiency in addition to the three E's as a goal.

SELECTED BIBLIOGRAPHY

ABBOT, CARL. HOWE, DEBORAH, and ADLER, SY, EDS., *Planning the Oregon Way*, Oregon State University Press, Corvallis, OR, 1994.

BROWER, DAVID J., GODSCHALK, DAVID R., and PORTER, DOUGLAS R., *Understanding Growth Management*, Urban Land Institute, Washington, DC, 1989.

BURROWS, LAWRENCE B., *Growth Management: Issues, Techniques and Policy Implications*, Rutgers University Center for Urban Policy Research, New Brunswick, NJ, 1978.

DEGROVE, JOHN M., *The New Frontier for Land Policy: Planning and Growth Management in the States*, Lincoln Land Institute, Lincoln, Nebraska, 1992.

DEGROVE, JOHN M., *Planning, Policy and Politics*, The Lincoln Institute of Land Policy, Cambridge, MA, 2005.

DOWNS, ANTHONY, ed., *Growth Management and Affordable Housing*, The Brookings Institution, Washington, DC, 2004.

HOLCOMBE, RANDALL, and STALEY, SAMUEL, eds., *Smarter Growth: Market-Based Strategies for Land Use Planning*, Greenwood Press, Westport, CT, 2001.

LAYARD, ANTONIO, DAVOUDI, SIMIN, and BATTY, SUSAN, eds., *Planning for a Sustainable Future*, Spon Press, London, 2001.

CHAPTER 15

Environmental and Energy Planning

Environmental planning covers a wide range of concerns having to do, generally, with minimizing the damage that human activity does to the natural environment. The goals may pertain to any of the following:

Minimizing threats to human health and life, for example, by reducing the concentration of dangerous pollutants in the air or the water supply or by limiting development in hazardous areas like flood plains

Preserving resources for future use, for example, minimizing soil erosion

Achieving aesthetic and recreational goals such as preserving some areas in a pristine condition

Minimizing damage to the environment for its own sake rather than humanity's sake, for example, by preserving the habitat of a rare species that has no known or readily foreseeable use to us

Energy planning has a much simpler goal: the saving of nonrenewable energy resources. An example would be designing a subdivision so that all the houses have unobstructed southern exposures to facilitate solar heating. Often, energy conservation will help achieve environmental goals. For example, solar heating will conserve energy, but it may also reduce the degradation of air quality by reducing the amount of fuel burned for home heating.

THE ENVIRONMENTAL PLANNING PROBLEM

Environmental problems can be difficult to deal with for several reasons:

1. Environmental processes may be complex and not fully understood. For example, both the physical and chemical pathways a pollutant takes through the environment may not be fully understood, nor may be its exact effects as it is dispersed and transformed.

2. Environmental problems are not respecters of political boundaries. Agricultural chemicals sprayed on fields in Kansas may find their way into tributaries of the Mississippi River and end up in the drinking water supplies of a Louisiana community a few months later. Sulphur dioxide from smokestacks in Ohio may come down as acid rain in Vermont. In 1985 the United States and Canada held talks on acid rain because acid rains in eastern Canada result in part from oxides of sulphur and nitrogen released in the American Midwest. The ultimate environmental problem may be the greenhouse effect resulting from increased levels of carbon dioxide in the atmosphere. Fossil fuel burned anywhere on the planet contributes to the problem, so that it can be fully addressed only at an international level.

3. The solution of one environmental problem may become the cause of another. For example, air quality regulations require "scrubbers," which remove a certain percentage of sulphur from the smokestacks of coal-fired electric generating facilities. However, the resulting accumulation of sulphur-containing sludge can prove to be a source of groundwater pollution.

4. Environmental issues can arouse strong emotions and produce formidable political conflict because environmental decisions may deliver both large gains and large losses to particular individuals and groups.

In general the approach to environmental problems has been piecemeal, one pollutant or one source of emissions or one land-use question at a time. This approach is not because of shortsightedness or lack of vision. The problem of achieving higher levels of environmental quality is simply so complicated that a unified approach in which all side effects are considered has yet to be devised.

ENVIRONMENTAL PROGRESS AT THE NATIONAL LEVEL _____

For the reasons suggested, much of the attack on environmental problems must be made at the federal level, and indeed, the federal government has been very active in this area.

The U.S. commitment to environmental quality, as indicated by pollution-control expenditures, has grown substantially since the passage of the National Environmental Policy Act (NEPA). For 1972, pollution control expenditures were estimated at about $44 billion in 2004 dollars. Pollution control expenditures by 2004 were estimated at about 2 percent of gross domestic product (GDP), which for 2004 was about $11.5 trillion. Thus 2004 pollution control expenditures were $200 to $250 billion, roughly five times that in 1972.[1]

The figures include both direct public expenditures and expenditures by firms to comply with environmental regulations. The costs appear in the form of higher taxes and higher prices and, in that sense, represent a reduction in living standards. However, and more important, they also represent a contribution to our living standard by improving the air we breathe, the water we drink, and the environment in which we live. In a populous, industrialized society, environmental quality does not come cheap.

Despite the complexities noted before, considerable environmental progress has been achieved in many areas. Figure 15–1 shows trends in the emissions of six major air pollutants from 1960 to 2000. The figures should be viewed in the light of changes in the United States since 1960. Specifically, from 1960 to 2000 the U.S. population grew by 57 percent, U.S. gross domestic product (GDP) by 288 percent, and motor vehicle registrations by 200 percent. Had we made no effort at environmental regulation, we would see a picture of sharply increased pollution rather than the picture of stabilization and decline shown in Figure 15–1.

In many cases, the imposition of uniform national standards is absolutely necessary. If different standards prevailed, polluting activities would simply be shifted from places with tight standards to places with loose standards.

Progress is often most rapid when there are a few sources that can be clearly identified and a substitute product or technology can be introduced. Note that the most striking reduction shown in Figure 15–1 is that for airborne lead, a pollutant that can contribute to, among other maladies, mental retardation and developmental problems in young children. The primary source was leaded gasoline. When automobile manufacturers were required to market only cars that ran on unleaded gasoline, the problem was on the way to an almost total solution.

When the pollutant has multiple sources, when substitute technology is not available, or when the problem is global rather than local, solutions are much more difficult.

THE QUESTION OF GLOBAL CLIMATE CHANGE

The idea that humans could change the earth's climate is an old one. In 1895 the Swedish chemist Svante Arrhenius suggested that mankind's emissions of carbon dioxide might cause the earth's temperature to rise by several degrees. He calculated that at the rate of emissions that prevailed in 1895 the process would take several thousand years. His work, in turn, was based on even earlier work. In 1859 the Irish scientist John Tyndall had identified two gases, carbon dioxide and water vapor, as trapping heat in the atmosphere and causing the earth to be warmer than it would otherwise be. Since Arrenhius's day the combination of population and industrial growth has caused carbon

Sulfur Dioxide Emissions

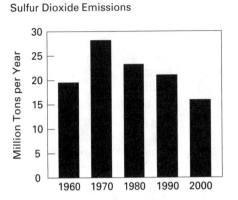

PM–10

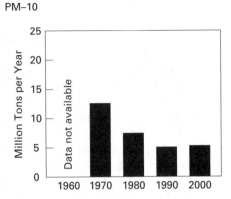

Nitrogen Oxide Emissions

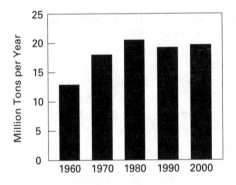

Volatile Organic Compounds

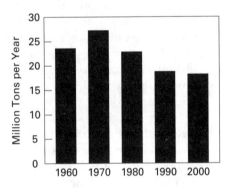

Carbon Monoxide Emissions

Lead Emissions

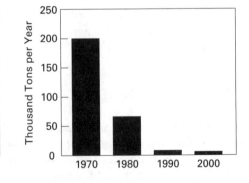

FIGURE 15–1 U.S. Air Pollution Trends

Note: PM-10 signifies particulate matter less than 10 microns in size.

Sources: Data through 1990 is from Environmental Quality; 22nd Annual Report of the Council on Environmental Quality, U.S. Government Printing Office, Washington, DC, 1992, p. 11. Subsequent data are from the *Statistical Abstract of the United States,* 122nd edition, 2002, Table 348.

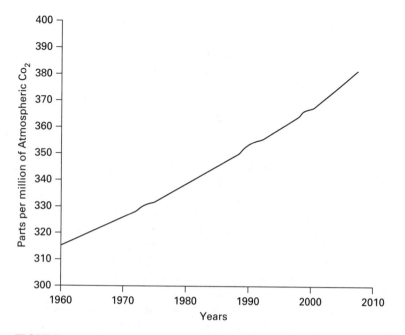

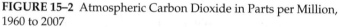

FIGURE 15–2 Atmospheric Carbon Dioxide in Parts per Million, 1960 to 2007

Note: Pre-Industrial Revolution CO_2 levels are estimated from ice core samples to be in the 260–280 parts per million (ppm) range.

Source: Measured at Mauna Loa Observatory, Hawaii.

dioxide emissions to increase enormously, shrinking Arrenhius's timeline from millennia to decades (see Figure 15–2).

Serious concern with human-caused (anthropogenic) climate change did not begin until approximately a couple of decades after World War II. During the last three decades or so climatologists have increasingly focused on the subject and large sums of money have been spent on data gathering and climate modeling.

Acceptance of the seriousness of anthropogenic climate change, until very recently, has come sooner in Europe and some other parts of the world than it has in the United States. At the International Earth Summit Conference held in Rio de Janeiro in June 1992, many nations wanted an agreement that set forth goals and timetables for stabilizing the levels of greenhouse gas (primarily carbon dioxide) emissions. President George H.W. Bush (father of President George W. Bush) resisted this on the grounds that the high costs of changing so many production processes could not be justified given the uncertainty and disagreement about the predictive power of global climate models. Ultimately, other nations gave way, and the conference adopted a statement in principle that contained no numbers or dates.[2]

The general consensus about the Rio Summit five years later was that its effects on the production of greenhouse gases had been minimal.[3] Under United Nations auspices a second attempt to reach global agreement on greenhouse gases was made in Kyoto, Japan, in December 1997. After 11 days of discussion, the delegates signed a treaty referred to as the Kyoto Protocol. It committed the industrialized nations of the world together to reduce emissions of carbon dioxide and other "greenhouse gases" such as methane to 5.2 percent below the 1990 level. Then it specified targets for the United States and a number of the other industrialized nations. The United States target was 7 percent. The treaty did not specify targets for developing nations such as India and China.[4] That omission, so far as ratification by the U.S. Senate was concerned, was the treaty's Achilles heel.

One argument raised against the treaty was that it would impose huge costs on U.S. industry without placing any burden on producers in the developing world. That requirement would put the United States at a competitive disadvantage and would promote job losses in the United States, especially in manufacturing. It was also argued that prospective increases in greenhouse gases in large developing nations such as India and China were so great that nothing that the United States and other industrialized nations could do would prevent an increase in global emissions. Almost immediately, it became evident that chances of ratification by the Senate were close to zero.

The hand of the treaty's opponents was strengthened by the scientific uncertainties about the greenhouse effect, as was also the case with the Rio Summit in 1992. There was then widespread, though not universal, agreement among climatologists that the effect was real. But there was uncertainty about how big the increase in average world temperatures will be or about what specific climatic effects will occur. Thus treaty opponents could argue that it was premature to incur major economic costs before the scientific picture became more clear. Opponents of the treaty also argued that because some nations would be subjected to limits whereas others would not, one effect of the treaty would be to cause industries that discharged large amounts of CO_2 and other greenhouse gases to relocate to parts of the globe not covered by the treaty. Therefore the United States would incur major economic losses without effecting a significant worldwide reduction in greenhouse gases.[5]

The U.S. Government's "we're concerned, but let's not be hasty" attitude matched the attitude of the U.S. public fairly well. Although many Americans were environmentally conscious and supported environmental efforts like recycling, they showed little willingness to make major adjustments for environmental reasons. For example, by far the fastest-growing segment of the automobile market was for sport utility vehicles (SUVs). These are essentially light trucks (the federal Department of Transportation classifies them that way), which generally weigh from half a ton to a ton more than standard automobiles and which get substantially poorer gas mileage. Rather than having to meet Corporate Average Fuel Efficiency (CAFE) standards of 27.5 miles per gallon, they are required to meet the 25 percent lower light-truck standard of 20.5 miles per gallon. The shift to vehicles with substantially higher fuel consumption suggested that there was little public will to make major adjustments for the greenhouse effect. Nor was there much political will either. In March 2002 the U.S. Senate by a substantial majority voted down a bill that would have mandated a moderate increase in CAFE standards over the next several years.

But in the last few years the national mood has changed considerably. Several states, most notably California, passed legislation aimed at restraining carbon dioxide emissions from automobiles and powerplants. Then in early 2007 several different events occurred which together suggested that perhaps the United States was coming to a turning point on the subject of Greenhouse gases.

The fourth report of the International Panel on Climate Change (IPCC) asserted strongly that the gradually warming observed in recent years was almost certainly caused by human activity and that significant further change was virtually inevitable.[6] The report also outlined many consequences, some of which were quite dire. The report left little doubt that the overwhelming majority of climatologists were in agreement and that, for all practical purposes, the controversy about the greenhouse effect was over.

Earlier in the year President Bush had finally stated that global warming was problem. Environmentalists were not happy with his view that dealing with it should largely be a matter of voluntary cooperation, nor were they impressed that his main program for dealing with automotive emissions was increased use of ethanol, a strategy they thought to be inadequate to the problem, and also partly crafted with a view to its political appeal in big corn-growing states. But, at least he had finally agreed that global warming was a problem.

On April 2, 2007, the U.S. Supreme Court in *Massachusetts* v. *The Environmental Protection Agency (EPA)* found for the plaintiff and against the EPA. Environmentalists and others concerned with the greenhouse effect had pushed for the EPA to regulate the carbon dioxide emissions of new vehicles under section 202 of the Clean Air Act, but the EPA, following the generally antiregulatory line of the Bush administration, had maintained that it did not have the authority to do this. The Supreme Court stated that the EPA could only avoid regulating such emissions if it found that greenhouse gases "do not contribute to climate change or if it provides some reasonable explanation as to why it cannot or will not exercise its discretion to determine whether they do."[7] Given the overwhelming consensus of scientists, there appeared no way that the EPA could meet the first part of that requirement. Nor is it easy to see what argument the EPA could advance as to why it cannot make the determination. The decision delighted environmentalists and was a sharp setback to the environmental position of the Bush administration. In effect, the high court had ruled that greenhouse gases, of which the most important one is carbon dioxide, met the meaning of the word pollutant and it was incumbent upon the EPA, as well as other federal agencies, to deal with it.

Other straws in the wind were also visible. In the same month a group of retired three- and four-star admirals and generals connected with CNA Corp., a think tank in Alexandria, Virginia, issued a statement that global warming was a threat to U.S. national security.[8] Beyond making suggestions related to defense policy as such, they also took the position that the United States should take steps to counteract global warming. The report may not have been particularly consequential in itself, but it did show that concern with the greenhouse effect was going mainstream and showing up in some very establishment and conservative places.

In the same month TXU, the largest electricity producer in Texas, agreed to be taken private in a leveraged buyout of $44 billion. The deal required approval by the federal government. In order to, in effect, buy off potential critics and opponents the group buying TXU agreed to drop plans for building 8 out of 11 coal-fired plants that TXU had planned to build. The agreement reached was after consultation with the Environmental Defense Fund. The fact that the group buying out TXU even felt it was important to cover their flanks on the environmental side was an indicator of the growing political power of those concerned about global warming.

In the latter part of 2007 Congressional interest in dealing with global warming increased as exemplified by the Lieberman-Warner bill (not enacted as of this writing) that would have created a national "cap and trade" system for carbon dioxide emissions. Global warming also showed up as a subject for discussion in the 2008 presidential primary campaigns.

Greenhouse Winners and Losers

Recently there has been an increasing awareness that climate change will not affect all nations and populations equally but rather in the coming decades is likely to create both winners and losers.[9] In a very general way, it is not hard to guess who the presumptive winners and losers are likely to be because the gross effects of global warming are coming into view, even though many details will remain uncertain for years to come. In general, warming will be greater in high latitudes than in low latitudes, but most parts of the globe will warm to some degree. Overall, rainfull is likely to increase in higher latitudes and decrease in lower latitudes.

In the Western Hemisphere the obvious big winner will be Canada. Warming will not only make its climate generally more agreeable, but it will also lengthen the growing season and possibly open up hundreds of thousands of square miles for agriculture. For the United States the situation will be a mixed bag. Alaska and states in the northern tier along the U.S.-Canadian border may come out winners. On the other hand, states in the southern tier are likely to be hit with a range of warming problems including unpleasantly warm summer temperatures and decreased rainfall. The latter is likely to be a big problem in the Southwest where rainfall is already low and where aquifers are now being pumped much faster than they can recharge. Along the Gulf Coast rising sea levels and increasing storm intensity are likely to increase the risk of flooding and result in some loss of coastline.

By the same general logic, global warming is not likely to be good news for Mexico, the rest of Central America, and much of South American. In Brazil parts of the rainforest may turn into savannah as rainfall diminishes.

One can apply the same sort of thinking to the Eastern Hemisphere. Parts of Scandinavia and Russia and perhaps parts of China and Mongolia may benefit from global warming, but the results may be very bad in India, Bangladesh, much of Africa, and other places at lower latitudes.

When the retired generals and admirals spoke of global warming as a "threat multiplier," it was the effects of this winner/loser dichotomy to which they were referring—political and military instability caused by conflicts over scarce resources like water or by mass migrations that result as long-established agricultural patterns change.

This writer does not claim to know what the results of climate change will be in the United States itself, but one can readily imagine some possibilities. Climate change might moderate or even reverse the Frostbelt to Sunbelt population shift as the Frostbelt warms and the Sunbelt gets hotter and drier. Changes in rainfall patterns may change the distribution of agricultural production in the United States and that would change the pattern of economic activity and population distribution. At present over half of U.S. population growth comes from immigration. How much immigration we receive will partly depend on conditions in other nations and those conditions will partly depend on climate change. How big our population is and how fast it grows ultimately affects every aspect of planning.

How we try to reduce our contribution to global warming by cutting back on our emissions of carbon dioxide, and to a lesser extent on emissions of other greenhouse gases, will affect what we produce, how we produce it and how we transport it, and ourselves, too. Climate change and our reaction to climate change are likely to ramify through our entire society and life in ways that we can only perceive dimly at present. Virtually all our smaller-scale environmental problems, for example particular habitats, will have to be viewed and dealt with against the larger background of planetary-wide climate change.

As concern with climate change increases, choices will have to be made about environmental priorities. For example, the damming of rivers has destroyed many habitats, disrupted the migration of fish, and from the perspective of many, ruined some natural areas. As a result, there has been much pressure from environmentalists, fishermen, Indian tribes, and others in parts of the United States to tear down dams so as to restore the original environment as much as possible. And, in fact, a number of dams have been torn down and others are scheduled for tear down. However, dams do have the virtue of producing hydroelectric power without releasing greenhouse gases. Tear down a dam to restore the habitat of a threatened species and you shift some power generation to fossil fuel and thus contribute to global warming. There is a serious trade-off to be considered.[10]

Environmental Policy During the Second Bush Administration

George W. Bush assumed the presidency in January 2001. He succeeded William J. Clinton, who had served two terms as president after defeating Bush's father, George H. W. Bush, in November 1992.

In general, environmentalists were less pleased with George Bush than they had been with his predecessor, Bill Clinton. In keeping with his more right-wing political stance, Bush was more inclined to give economic and market considerations relatively more weight and environmental considerations less weight than had President Clinton. In March 2001, he declared the Kyoto accords "fatally flawed" and, so far as the United States was concerned, officially dead. Environmentalists in both the United States and Europe were distressed with his position. His defenders argued that he was only making explicit what people who were informed about the situation already knew—that there was no chance that the U.S. Senate would ever ratify the treaty. They also argued, for some of the reasons noted in the previous section, that his characterization of the treaty was an accurate one.

In the spring of 2001 the state of California experienced a crisis in electric power characterized by blackouts, brownouts (drops in voltage without complete interruption of power), and big swings in the price of electric energy for some utilities and other bulk buyers of power. That put the Bush administration under some pressure to formulate a national energy policy.

The basic choices facing anyone formulating such a policy are (1) conservation, (2) development of alternatives to fossil fuels (currently our main source), and (3) increasing the supply of fossil fuels through drilling and mining, and building additional power plants in which these fuels would be burned. To the distress of environmentalists, the Bush administration placed heavy emphasis on the last of the three alternatives. In a widely quoted speech on the subject, Vice President Dick Cheney stated the following:

> Now, conservation is an important part of the total effort. But to speak exclusively of conservation is to duck the tough issues. *Conservation may be a sign of personal virtue, but it is not a sufficient basis all by itself for sound, comprehensive energy policy.* [author's italics] We also have to produce more.[11]

Though the Bush administration did propose some funding to explore new energy technologies, the main thrust of policy was clearly to produce more fossil fuels (coal, oil, and natural gas). The words in italics were widely quoted and taken by environmentalist as a very bad omen regarding the basic attitude of the Bush administration with regard to the climate change issue.

In other areas environmentalists were also very unhappy with President Bush. Environmentalists accused the administration of weakening the Clean Air Act by having the EPA change the regulations for New Source Review (NSR) for electric power plants. In essence, the new rules stated that if investment in a power plant amounted to less than 20 percent of the cost of replacement of the plant, the company did not have to install new pollution-control equipment as required by NSR provisions of the Clean Air Act. Environmentalists argued that several less-than 20 percent investments, with some time between each, could could provide a very wide path around the intent of the law.

Under the Clinton administration road building had been forbidden on 60 million acres of federally owned forest. The Bush administration ended that policy and declared that subsequently each request for permission to build roads would be decided separately.[12] In a similar vein, the administration proposed to revamp the relicensing procedures for some thousands of privately owned dams that produce hydropower.[13] Under the proposed rules, only dam owners would be permitted to appeal Interior Department rulings on the licensing and operation of dams. In effect, only those who took the position that rulings were excessively stringent would have a voice in the process. Those like local and state governments, citizen and environmentalist groups, sport fishermen, Indian tribes, and others who might take the position that the regulation was not stringent enough would be effectively out of the loop. To many environmentalists, it was more evidence of their view that the Bush administration favored the needs of business over the needs of the environment. Soon angry environmentalists added the sobriquet "Toxic Texan" to the United States' already rich collection of political epithets. As noted in the previous section what many people saw as the Bush antienvironmental position softened somewhat in 2007.

THE INTERGOVERNMENT CONTEXT OF ENVIRONMENTAL PLANNING

For reasons noted at the beginning of this chapter, much of the impetus for environmental improvement and planning must necessarily come from the federal government. Since 1970, federal legislation has been the major shaper of environmental planning and the nation's efforts to deal with environmental problems. In fact, to a large extent the environmental planning professions have been brought into being by legislation passed by Congress.

As discussed in Chapter 4, environmental consciousness in the United States grew substantially during the 1960s. At the end of 1969, Congress passed the National Environmental Policy Act (NEPA).

> The Congress, recognizing the profound impact of man's activity on the inter-relations of all components of the natural environment . . . declares that it is the continuing policy of the federal government, in cooperation with State and Local governments, and other concerned public and private organizations, to use all practicable means and measures, including financial and technical assistance, in a manner calculated to foster and promote the general welfare, to create and maintain conditions under which man and nature can exist in productive harmony.[14]

NEPA was signed in 1970 as President Nixon's first official act that year. Subsequently, the Environmental Protection Agency (EPA) was created by executive action. During the 1970s many states enacted their own versions of NEPA, generally known as "little NEPA" acts. Within the next few years, a variety of other major environmental acts became law. These included the Clean Air Act of 1970; the Clean Water Act of 1972; the Marine Protection, Control, and Sanctuaries Act of 1972; the Coastal Zone Management Act of 1972; the Safe Drinking Water Act of 1974; the Resource Conservation and Recovery Act of 1976; the Toxic Substances Control Act of 1976; and the Comprehensive Environmental Response, Compensation, and Liability Act (CERCLA) of 1980, more commonly known as "Superfund."

In 1990, amendments to the Clean Air Act placed stricter limits on emissions of sulphur dioxide, a primary component of acid rain. Most of the 22 million tons of sulphur dioxide discharged in the United States in 1990 came from the burning of coal in electric generating plants. The act permitted an innovation that most economists see as a more efficient way of reducing pollution than the usual flat regulatory standards. It permitted the creation of a market in pollution rights to be run by the Chicago Board of Trade.[15] So far, the program appears to have been an outstanding success, with goals reached well ahead of schedule and at much less than estimated costs.

From 1990 to 1995, U.S. emissions of sulfur dioxide dropped from about 10 million tons to under 6 million tons. Given this record, it may well serve as the model for many other pollution abatement programs. The act also required the phasing out of chlorofluorocarbons (CFCs), widely used as a refrigerant, and carbon tetrachloride and methyl chloride, believed to be the main causes of ozone depletion. The deadline was originally set for the year 2000, but the first Bush administration subsequently moved the deadline up to 1995. As of the end of 1995, the United States was on the verge of a complete phaseout of CFCs, far sooner than had been anticipated only a few years earlier.

Under the Clean Air Act and its amendments, states are required to create State Implementation Plans (SIPs) for metropolitan areas not meeting federal National Ambient Air Quality Standards (NAAQS) and to implement programs to reach the NAAQSs. This requirement includes measures to reduce both point source (a nonmoving source such as an industrial operation) and mobile (automotive) sources. The EPA identified 84 areas not meeting the standards.

Considerable progress has been made in many areas such as Los Angeles. The South Coast Air Quality Management District (AQMD) includes Los Angeles and Orange County, as well as parts of San Bernadino and Riverside counties. It contains about 14 million people and over 9 million motor vehicles in a 12,000-square-mile area. The area's air pollution problem, considered the worst in the nation, is compounded by its topography, for mountains ringing the area create a bowl that restricts air circulation. Although the area's air quality problem is still far from solved, officials of the agency note that ozone levels are half what they were in 1950 despite a tripling of the area's human population and a quadrupling of its automobile population. They also note the following:

> In the past decade, we have reduced by half the number of Stage 1 Smog Alerts, the level at which schools are advised to keep children from playing outside. And, we almost never reach Stage II levels, which used to occur 15 times a year a decade ago.[16]

Among the measures taken have been regulation of many types of industrial and commercial processes, as well as some personal activities such as barbecuing, and stringent emissions standards for automobiles. The AQMD is responsible for point source pollution, and other California agencies for mobile sources. The regulations are backed by fines and, in the extreme, criminal prosecution.

In October 1992, Congress passed a wide-ranging energy bill. The legislation contained provisions to reduce both the use of nonrenewable energy sources (fossil fuels) and pollution from energy use. The bill requires that small energy producers be allowed to make use of the transmission lines of electric utility companies. In effect, this use permits the small producer to sell power to the utility company that will, it is hoped, create a market for small-scale wind, solar, and hydrogenerated power.

The buyback provisions of the bill appear to be successful in that they are creating a market for small-scale generators. Few wind generators would be in existence if their builders were not able to make use of the existing electric grid. In the 2004 election, voters in Colorado passed Amendment 37, which stipulated that by 2015 at least 10 percent of the electricity used in the state must have been generated by renewable means, of which the majority share is expected to be from wind-driven generators. This was the first such requirement adopted by a direct vote, but other states have adopted such requirements by legislative act.

The bill mandates efficiency standards for lightbulbs and home heating systems. The latter is not a trivial item. About one-third of all U.S. energy use is for space heating, and a large part of that is residential.

The bill authorized the Department of Energy (DOE) to enter into agreements with companies to develop electric vehicles. Note that this step may not reduce dependence on fossil fuels or total energy consumption if the vehicle's batteries are charged by electricity generated by burning coal or oil. However, air quality in the area where the vehicle is driven will be improved. The bill also contains provisions to encourage the use of cleaner burning alternative fuels such as alcohol and natural gas. Again, there may be no net energy saving, but air quality, particularly in large metropolitan areas, will benefit. Some environmentalists were skeptical about the push for electric vehicles (and for subsequent efforts toward fuel-cell-powered vehicles) because they saw both as distractions, perhaps intentional, from the immediately doable step of simply raising CAFE standards.

The bill provides for the "environmentally sound use of our nation's abundant coal resources through research and development of advanced coal technologies. . . . " The situation with regard to "advanced coal technologies" is not entirely clear at this time. A clean coal technology might simply meaning burning coal in such a way that the production of pollutants like sulfur dioxide is minimized. But from a greenhouse gas perspective, the main villain is carbon dioxide, which is not reduced by scrubbers and other conventional pollution control technologies. It is the converting of carbon to carbon dioxide that is the energy source in coal.

Recently there has been much discussion of *sequestration* of carbon dioxide, which has been done on a small scale in Norway. The idea is to pump under extremely high pressure the carbon dioxide generated by the burning of coal into places in the earth, such as spaces that once held oil or natural gas or, perhaps, disused coal mines, where it would remain for the indefinite future. In this way coal could be burned without contributing to the greenhouse effect. Large-scale sequestration appears to be complex, and the technology is not fully developed. Whether it will be feasible on a mass scale is not known at this writing.

The NEPA Process

For planners and environmental professionals, the most significant aspect of NEPA has been its requirement for environmental impact statements (EISs) as a precondition for large projects making use of federal funds. In brief, the NEPA process works like this.[17] The agency considering an action that might have significant environmental effects must prepare an environmental assessment (EA). This is a relatively brief document that describes the project in general and includes a "discussion of the need for proposed action, the environmental impacts of the proposed action, and alternative actions, and a listing of the persons and agencies consulted." The EA either concludes that an environmental impact statement is necessary or that there is "no significant impact," in which case an EIS is not required. The EA is a public document, and it can be expected that if there is serious public concern with the issue, it will be subject to considerable scrutiny. The process is designed for visibility and accountability. Thus an agency could not readily rule that an EIS was not necessary if, in fact, serious environmental effects could be demonstrated.

If an EIS is called for, a complex process begins. Notice of the agency's intent to prepare an EIS must be published in the *Federal Register*. This is a daily newsletter published by the federal government detailing regulations and a variety of other federal actions. The first step is a "scoping" process involving other federal agencies, lower levels of government, and the public. At this time, too, a lead agency, or agency having overall responsibility, is designated. Once the scope (hence the term *scoping*) of the work to be done has been determined, a draft EIS is prepared, either by the federal agency or an agency of a lower level of government or a party under contract to a body of government. The latter might be a consultant. The draft EIS includes

> a discussion of the purpose of and need for the proposed action, alternatives to the proposed action (for example, a highway EIS might include discussion of the merits of expanding mass transit instead), including a no action alternative, analysis of the affected environment and of the environmental consequences of the proposed action and alternatives, a list of persons who prepared the document, a list of agencies, organizations and persons to whom the document is being mailed.[18]

At this point the draft document is circulated for both official and public comment. The lead agency, after considering the comments, then produces the final EIS. There again ensues a comment period, and following this, the lead agency prepares a "record of decision." This is a summary of the agency's decision and indicates the basis for the decision, alternatives that were considered, and so on.

The process is an open one. The turn-of-the-century "muckrakers," who were fond of the expression "sunlight is the best disinfectant," would be quite pleased with the process. It prevents government from acting in secrecy, makes the process open to any concerned citizen, and makes it as practical as possible for interested parties to comment.

The EIS may be a long document, or in the case of a large project, a shelf of documents, often supported by large amounts of data. EIS requirements have brought a fair-sized consulting industry into being. EIS requirements have also provided an enormous amount of employment for attorneys. For the individual or group opposed to a particular project, the most effective action often is to sue. A common basis for suing is to claim procedural flaw in the environmental review process. The litigant does not necessarily have to show that the project is a bad plan. If it can be shown that there has been some fault in the process itself, that is, a violation of a law or regulation, the project can be stopped until that flaw has been remedied.

To take a well-known example, New York City's Westway project, noted in Chapter 13, was killed by such litigation. In the last chapter of a decade-long saga, a federal judge found that state and federal officials had "colluded" in concealing information about the effect of the project on the Hudson River and, particularly, on striped bass in the river.

Whether the litigants actually cared about the striped bass is a moot point. The complexity of the review process presents numerous opportunities for delaying actions, in this case sufficient delays to kill the project. Critics of the environmental review process have complained that it provides too many legal weapons for naysayers and that it permits small, determined groups to thwart the will of the majority. Defenders of the process argue that the law is meant to be obeyed and that if it has not been, the project should be delayed until it is.

The field of air quality planning was essentially brought into being by the Clean Air Act of 1970 and its subsequent amendments. The preparation of SIPs and the evaluation of proposed projects for their effects on NAAQSs (see page 302) created the demand for air quality planners. For the biggest moving source, the automobile, Congress itself set the emissions standards rather than delegating that task to the EPA. The emission control equipment on all new cars sold in the United States is there because of requirements that, although periodically modified, date from this time.

The Federal Water Pollution Control Act (FWPCA) brought into being state and local water quality planning efforts on a massive scale. Specifically, section 208 of the act required states to produce water quality plans, either directly or by delegating responsibility to substate governments. Accompanying the planning requirements were substantial sums of grant money to fund the work. The Coastal Zone Management Act imposed coastal zone planning requirements on the states. We note that about half of the U.S. population lives in counties that border on a coast, that coastal areas are often ecologically fragile, and that for many reasons, coastal areas can be extremely attractive for commercial and residential development.

ECONOMIC AND POLITICAL ISSUES IN ENVIRONMENTAL PLANNING

Environmental protection and environmental planning are inevitably contentious for a number of reasons. Envrionmental legislation and regulation often impose large losses on some parties and deliver large gains to others. Consider shoreline protection. Suppose that protecting a certain stretch of beachfront requires that further residential development be stopped or sharply curtailed. People who already have beachfront properties are winners. Their privacy will be protected and the market value of their houses will rise because no more can be built. Conversely, people who own beachfront property that they can no longer develop are losers (see the case of *Lucas* v. *South Carolina Coastal Council* in Chapter 5). People who would like to buy beachfront houses but cannot do so because no more can be built are also losers.

In many places it is now difficult to get a permit to open a marina. This difficulty is understandable because the dredging necessary to keep channels open, spilled fuel, and boat exhausts all damage the marine environment. This situation makes winners out of those who already own a marina because it protects them from the emergence of new competition. People who might like to open marinas are losers. So, too, are boat owners because with less competition, prices for space at marinas will be higher.

Environmental regulations that mandate additional pollution-control expenditures for a firm will increase that firm's costs and thus decrease its profitability, clearly a loss to its stockholders. In the extreme, the costs of complying with environmental regulations may put the firm out of business, a loss to the stockholders and an even larger loss to the employees.[19] But those same regulations will deliver benefits to firms in the business of making pollution-control equipment. Any pattern of laws and regulations that delivers gains and losses on a large scale will inevitably produce controversy and provide much employment for attorneys.

The Special Case of "Superfund"

Environmental regulation can produce unpredicted side effects. Superfund (more formally CERCLA, the Comprehensive Environmental Response, Compensation, and Liability Act of 1980) noted earlier is a case in point. The act provided authority to the Environmental Protection Agency to designate contaminated sites. Owners of these sites are required to bring them up to EPA standards. The law requires this "remediation" even if the actions that polluted the site were legal at the time they were taken. For example, a site might have been contaminated by dumping of paint solvents when such dumping was not prohibited. Beyond that, present owners of the site may be held responsible for contamination caused by previous owners of the site. Thus by buying a site that subsequently turns out to have been contaminated by a previous owner, a firm or individual may be inadvertently "buying" a liability that is much greater than the value of the site. That possibility will make potential buyers of used industrial or commercial sites very hesitant. But it goes still further than that. Suppose XYZ Corp. goes bankrupt while still owing $1 million to the bank that holds its mortgage. Normally, the bank would foreclose the property, sell it, and thus recover some of its loss. But if the site has been in industrial use for, say, the last century, Superfund's liability provisions will make the bank hesitate. If the site subsequently turns out to be contaminated, the bank may now become the unhappy owner of a site that takes $10 million to bring up to standards. Maybe it would be wiser just to accept the loss and not foreclose. But the next time the bank is asked to make a loan to a firm on an old, possibly contaminated site, it will remember what happened when the XYZ Corp. went under, and it will say no.

The liability provisions of Superfund have brought into being the terms *greenfields* and *brownfields*. A greenfield is a site, usually suburban or rural, that has never been used for industrial or commercial purposes. A brownfield is a site, usually urban, that has been or is in commercial or industrial use. Greenfields pose no threat of unforeseen liability under Superfund, but brownfields do pose a threat. This will bias the market for industrial and commercial sites against urban areas in favor of suburban and rural sites.[20] For cities struggling with problems of structural unemployment (see Chapter 13) and inadequate tax bases, that bias is very unfortunate. It was also completely unintended.

After perhaps a decade, these antiurban side effects became widely recognized, and some steps have been taken to nullify them. For example, some state environmental agencies have devised arrangements that, in effect, immunize firms against Superfund liability for contamination that comes to light in the future if firms will agree to appropriate remediation of presently known contamination. Banks sometimes can protect themselves against the sort of risk described earlier by making mortgage arrangements such that in the event of default, they can foreclose on property other than the potentially risky brownfield property. In the previous example that would mean that the bank could foreclose on some nonbrownfield property owned by the XYZ Corp. Of course, doing that presumes that XYZ Corp. has such a property and that said property is not encumbered by other liens. Insurance arrangements against Superfund liability risk are also emerging. Thus the side effects of the law are being dealt with, at least to some extent. The point of the digression, though, is that environmental legislation and regulation can create powerful and unintended side effects.

Friendly Criticism

Current environmental policy has been subject to what we might term *friendly criticism* from economists, policy analysts, risk analysts, and others who take a rationalistic, quantitative approach to environmental issues. The economist, the benefit/cost analyst, and the policy analyst would, if they could, have us balance the costs and the benefits of environmental regulation at the margin—the last dollar spent on conforming to environmental regulations would yield exactly one dollar of benefit. In a rational system, they would argue, proposed environmental regulations (or at least major ones) would be subject to benefit/cost analysis. Unless it could be shown that the proposed regulation would yield benefits at least equal to the costs that it imposed, it would not be accepted. But environmental policy is not made that way. Laws and regulations may use language such as "best available technology" or "adequate margin of safety." In some cases, laws and regulations may direct that the regulated industry strive for a zero-risk standard without any adjustment for the relationship between costs and benefits. Nor, generally speaking, is there any balancing between the benefit that could be obtained by expenditures on one environmental problem or hazard as against another problem or hazard. William Reilly, a former head of the Environmental Protection Agency, notes,

> No law has ever directed that [the EPA] seek out the best opportunities to reduce environmental risks in toto; nor that we employ the most efficient, cost effective means of addressing them.[21]

But, of course, that global, rationalistic approach is exactly what the academic critic of present policy would favor. Present environmetal policy offers the critic some fine targets.

> Although relatively low in total costs, EPA's rule regulating wood preservatives costs at least $5 trillion [not a misprint] per life saved and is estimated to avert only one case of cancer every 2.9 million years.[22]

If one thinks about environmental quality purely from the perspective of human health and well-being, it turns out that environmental expenditures that have a very high ratio of costs to benefits can actually increase human mortality and morbidity (illness). Statistically, more prosperous people live longer and are healthier than poor people. This is true if we compare the populations of rich and poor countries and also if we compare rich and poor people within the same country. Suppose that we require more effective but also more expensive emission controls on automobiles. We will then breathe cleaner air, which will contribute to our health. But the increased price of automobiles will leave us less to spend on medical care, more healthful food, bicycle helmets, and other things that contribute to health and safety. Which effect will predominate? One cannot answer that question a priori. Answering it takes careful study as well as the economist's balancing of benefits and costs at the margin. From the economist's perspective then, one can both favor substantial or even increased environmental regulation and expenditures, and be highly critical of current environmental policy.

Unfriendly Criticism

After the 1994 congressional elections that gave the Republicans control of both houses of Congress for the first time since 1948, national environmental policy came under sharp attack. Based largely in the House of Representatives and presaged in the "Contract with America," the attack came from a general animus to regulation, a feeling that the federal government was simply too large and powerful, and a strong preference for the rights of private property. Much of the force behind the attack came from congresspersons from western states. They were often influenced by, and spokespersons for, a loose coalition of antiregulatory forces referred to as the "Sagebrush Rebellion." As discussed in Chapter 17, a large part of all land west of the Mississippi is owned by the federal government and managed by federal agencies such as the Bureau of Land Management. As a result, logging interests, grazing interests, mining interests, and others whose incomes derive from the use of public lands constitute a powerful antiregulatory force. This force gains support from a general ethos of "rugged individualism" that figures heavily in the political culture of many western states.

Many groups and individuals interested in scaling back federal environmental regulation in the West organized as the "Wise Use" movement. The movement, well named from a public relations standpoint, takes positions on a variety of regulatory and control issues, claiming "wise use" to be a combination of commercial use and environmental conservation. Clearly the movement is not beloved by environemntalists. In controversies such as the one in the Northwest over the needs of the timber industry versus the preservation of the habitat of the spotted owl, the movement could be counted on to take a relatively pro-industry position. The Wise Use movement has been another weight on the antiregulatory side of the balance.

The wave of referenda and legisation on takings (See Chapter 5) that came in the wake of the *Kelo* decision is part of the same antiregulatory mindset.

LOCAL ENVIRONMENTAL PLANNING

Planning at the local level can make a contribution to the quest for environmental quality in several ways, including the following. (They are discussed in detail in subsequent sections of this chapter.)

1. Control of the intensity of development
2. Control of the type of development
3. Control of the location of development
4. Public capital investment
5. Control of the operation once development is complete

Analyzing the Physical Environment

The physical environment can be analyzed in several different ways. The least comprehensive approach is simply to deal with each land-use issue as it arises. If major development is proposed, if citizens are complaining because the city water has acquired a slight odor, or if the fish are becoming less plentiful in a particular stream, the issue can be dealt with as a problem on its own. This approach may be likened to the physician "treating the disease and not the patient" and may be criticized on the grounds that it may give less than optimal results because it ignores the larger picture. For example, displacement effects, as we noted in Chapter 14 on growth management, may be ignored. Yet the case-by-case approach may still produce useful results. Many a patient has been cured by a physician who did, indeed, treat the disease and not the patient. The case-by-case approach is very common. Local governments tend to act most vigorously when their citizens put pressure on them. And that pressure is often strongest over a specific issue.

A more comprehensive approach is *land capability analysis*. Here the planner looks at all the land in a planning area, or at least all the land not now committed to a particular use, in terms of development cost. The technique makes use of geologic, hydrologic, soil, and other physical data to estimate the costs that these physical conditions will impose on various types of development: residential, commercial, industrial, and agricultural. The physical conditions that enter into the calculation are items such as slope, drainage conditions, settlement potential, shrink-swell potential, flood hazard, and earthquake hazard.[23] For discrete risks (an event that either will or will not occur, such as a flood), the amount of damage likely to be done if the event occurs is multiplied by the possibility that the event will occur, to get what statisticians refer to as "the value of the expectation." For example, if it is estimated that there is one chance in 20 that a flood will occur in the time period under consideration and that such a flood would cause $15 million in damage, the value of the expectation is $750,000 ($15 million × 0.05). That value is the figure entered into the cost calculation. Essentially, the area is mapped in terms of development cost for each type of land use. Thus for a given development type, say, residential, any point on the map would fall in some cost zone, expressed in dollars per acre.

The technique is obviously limited in that it does not take into account social, aesthetic, and other considerations. Thus there may be occasions when it should be used in combination with other techniques. But even if land capability analysis is used alone, it will probably still help avoid some environmental mistakes simply because steep slopes, wetlands, flood hazard areas, and the like, which should be treated with care for other reasons, will show up as high-cost areas.

A still more comprehensive approach was developed by landscape architect Ian McHarg. He took the view that to design well, the designer must design with nature rather than impose his or her will on nature. McHarg has been a crusader for this particular viewpoint and, among landscape architects, became something of a cult figure. Behind his work there is a strong feeling about nature and our proper relationship to it—about, in his words, turning from an attitude that is "exploitive and destructive" to one that is "deferential and creative."[24] The technique he advocates involves detailed study of the natural features of an area, followed by a graphic analysis that shows least and most desirable areas for the particular land use in question.

In connection with the Richmond Parkway (in the borough of Richmond, a part of New York City also called Staten Island) location study, McHarg considered the following: slope, surface drainage, soil drainage, bedrock foundation, soil foundation, susceptibility to erosion, land values, tidal inundation, historic values, water values (lakes, ponds, streams, etc.), scenic values, forest values, recreation values, wildlife values, residential values, and institutional values. Each of these characteristics was mapped on a transparent sheet with three different tones, the darkest for the greatest value or cost.

> Let us map physiographic factors so that the darker the tone, the greater the cost. Let us similarly map social values so that the darker the tone, the higher the value. Let us make the maps transparent. When these are superimposed, the least-cost areas are revealed by the lightest tone.[25]

The optimal location is then revealed when all the transparencies are overlaid in a single stack. McHarg does not try to rank some values more highly than others. In fact, he asserts that it is impossible to do so meaningfully. Rather, he states that his technique shows us the "maximum concurrence of either high or low social values." Note the difference between McHarg's approach and benefit/cost analysis discussed in Chapter 12.

> By abandoning absolute economic values . . . and employing a relative system of most to least, it is possible to include all of the important factors that defy pricing by economists. While this denies an illusory precision of cost-benefit economics, it does show the relative concurrence of positive factors and their relative absence. Although we are unable to fix precise money values on these, it is safe to assume that, in the absence of any supervening value, the concurrence of the majority of positive factors in any one location does indicate its intrinsic suitability for the land use in question.[26]

In the case of the Richmond Parkway, there was already a great deal of development in place. Thus a large number of social values were considered. In doing a comparable study for an undeveloped area, some of the social values would be absent. For example, the "residential values" item, an overlay that simply reflects the market value of housing, would be absent. So, too, might be the "historic values."

McHarg's approach is considerably more comprehensive than land capability analysis. Yet it, too, leaves much unaccounted for. For example, it largely ignores fiscal considerations. "What a crass and philistine matter to raise," a McHargian purist might object. Yet municipal funds might be used for environmentally virtuous purposes such as open space acquisition, sewage treatment, or planting grass and trees to stem erosion on publicly owned beaches. More generally, a purely McHargian approach neglects many social and economic issues. To some extent, it also neglects some large-scale planning questions. For example, suppose an overlay analysis suggests a land-use pattern that does not make sense in terms of, say, the regional transportation network or minimizing the amount of energy used in transportation. What is the comprehensive planner to do? A fully comprehensive land-use planning approach has yet to be devised.

AN EXAMPLE OF ENVIRONMENTAL PLANNING

The issue of what to do about solid waste has bedeviled many communities. Typically, solid waste just from households averages several pounds per person per day. To this is added solid waste from manufacturing, commerce, and the like. Basically, it can be disposed of in landfills, burned, or dumped (though ocean dumping is being phased out under pressure of federal legislation). In general, landfills are not popular with people who have to live near them. Such sites involve truck traffic and may be unsightly or odiferous. Beyond these essentially aesthetic issues, they can often engender real fear in nearby populations. If solid waste is buried in landfills, there is fear of groundwater contamination because acids in surface water or rainwater dissolve pollutants in the waste and carry them into the groundwater. Fears, quite obviously, are even greater if the landfill is to contain toxic wastes. Siting landfills is often more difficult as a political problem than as a technical problem.

Incineration causes fears regarding air quality. Reassurances from experts often do not carry much weight with nearby residents. For one thing, it takes a certain amount of technical background to interpret figures cast in terms like "parts per million" or "micrograms per liter." Then, too, there is often some fundamental distrust of the expert. If the town government hires a consultant who tells the citizenry that the planned incinerator poses no threat to their health, there is always the suspicion that he or she is singing the song of those who pay the consulting fee.

Having admitted that the decision on how to dispose of solid waste is politically sensitive, let us look at how the more technical side of the process might be carried out. Very often, a community is propelled into solid waste planning when the present system begins to look as though its days are numbered. If the community is now using landfill disposal, it may be that the landfill area is now nearly filled to capacity. It may be that the community is shipping its solid waste to a landfill in another municipality, which has indicated that when this waste disposal contract expires, it will not be renewed. Or, perhaps, the cost of upgrading the municipal incinerator to meet air quality standards appears to be more than the community can manage.

A planning approach might be as follows:

1. *The dimensions of the problem are established.* Population and employment projections are used to estimate the probable load of solid waste that must be handled. The present disposal system is examined to see how long it can be expected to function adequately. For example, pounds of solid waste would be converted into cubic yards, and that figure laid off against the remaining capacity of the community's landfill.

2. *A preliminary reconnaissance of alternative disposal methods might be undertaken.* These are likely to include landfill, incineration, and rail haul. The latter essentially means shipment out of the area to someone else's landfill or incinerator. This alternative is becoming less available as the cry of "NIMBY," an acronym for "not in my back yard," becomes more common. Within the incineration alternative there are several possibilities. Incineration may be combined with power generation. The heat might be used for generation of electric power or simply to produce steam for heating. In both cases a big question is whether there is a good market for the energy. In the case of steam, the market has to be close by because generally it is not practical to pipe steam for more than one thousand yards or so. After incineration, various material recovery schemes might be considered. For example, magnetic separation might be used to extract ferrous residues. Other systems might be used for glass and nonferrous metals. Some schemes for disposal of the residue after separation need to be considered. The residue might be buried in landfills. It might be disposed of at sea, though, as noted, this alternative is becoming less widely available. It may be possible to process the unburned residue into a useful product such as construction aggregate if a user who will enter into a long-term contract can be found.

At this stage a final selection cannot usually be made because the costs and risks of each alternative may not be fully known. However, it may be possible to eliminate some possibilities and find some other possibilities that look promising. Consider, for example, the landfill alternative. A common way to approach it would be to make a list of criteria and then find all the sites in the jurisdiction that qualify. Such a list might include minimum site size; minimum distance from residential population; minimum distance from schools, hospitals, or other institutions; minimum distance from streams and aquifer recharge areas; minimum distance from wetlands; area outside of one hundred year flood plain; maximum distance from main road; acceptable site geology; and soil characteristics.[27]

3. *Cost estimates are developed.* For example, site acquisition costs might be estimated by examination of assessed values of land and consultations with assessors, appraisers, or real estate brokers. Operating costs on the site itself might be estimated by obtaining figures from presently operating sites.

Transportation of solid waste to landfills can be a major cost, so this too might be estimated. Recent experience from the municipality itself or nearby communities could be used to obtain an average ton/mile figure. The community can be divided into a number of "wastesheds," and the distance from the center of each wasteshed to a given site measured. The population and commercial activity are then estimated and hence the ton/miles estimated.

4. *Site selection is made.* A common way to approach this final step is with some sort of scoring system. A system might assign so many points for cost, so many points for environmental impact, so many points for traffic impact, and so on. Thus potential sites identified in step 3 could be ranked from most to least acceptable. Such scoring systems are not entirely objective, for the matter of what weight one assigns to each consideration is necessarily judgmental. Nonetheless, a point system is a step in the direction of rationality. Then, too, the person who chooses to call its results into question has to state what attributes he or she thinks have been weighted incorrectly. That act in itself forces the participants in the process to be explicit and thus helps clarify discussion of the issue.

These steps are a fairly straightforward technical process. The next step—actually designating a site—is often the most difficult. Even if one site is clearly superior, the process of site selection is far from over, and the choice of site not necessarily determined. In general, opposition from nearby residents can be expected. The opposition may take the form of political and public relations activity—neighborhood organization, protest meetings, letters to newspapers and legislators, and the like. It may also take the form of litigation. The state has an environmental permit system, and groups opposed to the plan may mount legal challenges either on procedural or substantive grounds.

In practice, the location of such sites is often determined by a political process that bears some resemblance to a game of hot potato. In a multijurisdictional body—for example, a county made up of a number of municipalities—such a site may end up in that municipality that is least able to resist it.

Public participation in such a decision is likely to be substantial. State legislation pertaining to the granting of permits for such facilities is likely to require that plans be made public, that hearings or public meetings be held, and that the public be given an opportunity to comment. But even in the absence of any such legal requirements, public participation is likely to be high simply because of a high degree of interest and concern. In recent years many states have passed so-called sunshine laws, which make many government meetings and internal documents open to the public. Thus as a practical matter, most local governments could not go very far in siting such a facility without the process becoming public knowledge. In many cases, the best policy for a local government seeking to choose a site may be to conduct the entire procedure in a very open way. Doing that will not prevent conflict or even feelings of victimization on the part of the "losers," but it will at least protect the government against charges of secrecy and impropriety. A basic rule of politics is that no one likes surprises.

The reader might well ask, Why go through the procedure outlined if politics is likely to figure so heavily in the outcome? One answer is that the process, though not entirely rational, is not totally irrational either. One role for the planner—and not just in this situation—is to lay out options clearly and accurately in order to move the decision-making process in the direction of rationality as much as possible. In a democratic society the planner is only advisory to the elected political body, and it is unrealistic of the planner to expect that his or her advice will necessarily be followed as given. At a practical level, if the actions of local government are challenged in court, there is no better defense than a well-documented, well-researched, systematically arrived at position.

ENERGY PLANNING

The field of energy planning emerged quite abruptly at the end of 1973. It resulted from the energy price increases and shortages that followed the Arab oil embargo at the time of the Arab-Israeli War in October of that year. Interest in energy planning was further increased by the second round of oil price increases in 1979–1980 occasioned by the Iranian revolution. Subsequently oil prices declined considerably, reducing national concern with energy conservation. At this writing, energy prices are high, and world energy demand is growing strongly, particularly because of the rapid growth of the Chinese economy. The chance that we will soon be returning to a period of low energy costs appears slim. Beyond the matter of price, interest in energy planning may be augmented by an interest in energy independence for reasons of national security. It is also now intimately connected to the question of the greenhouse effect, an item that was not on the public agenda in 1973.

Many facets of energy conservation are best handled nationally, for example, mileage requirements imposed on automobile manufacturers. Funding research on new energy sources like hydrogen fusion also makes most sense if done nationally—or, perhaps, internationally. How energy is priced will affect how it is used. Thus energy pricing could be considered a form of energy planning. Clearly, steps like increased taxes on gasoline are best considered at a national level. However, a number of steps can be and have been taken at the local level.

Steps that a municipality can take to conserve energy can be divided into four general categories.

1. Land-use planning
2. Changes in building characteristics

3. Changes in transportation
4. Community energy sources

Land-use planning can be used to reduce energy consumption in a variety of ways; the most obvious is by minimizing transportation requirements. One way to do this is by favoring development that reduces the average distance between the origin of a trip and the destination. However, the long-term trend in the United States, as noted in Chapter 2, has been to lower urban densities. An alternate, and probably more feasible, approach is to encourage mixed-use development. For example, mixing commercial and retailing uses with residential uses may permit shorter average commuting and shopping trips than would be the case if the three uses were strictly separated.

Another way that land-use planning can encourage energy efficiency is by making nonautomotive modes convenient. This might mean providing separate bus lanes along major thoroughfares.[28] In a major metropolitan area, it might mean designing major highways with a median that would be suitable for future installation of rail lines. For example, Route 1-66, which extends westward from Washington, D.C., was laid out in this way. In the mid-1980s the Washington Metro was extended into adjacent parts of northern Virginia along that routing. In a smaller community, planning for energy efficiency might mean providing bikeways to separate bicycle from automotive traffic, thus eliminating a major discouragement to bicycle use. The community in the United States best known for this plan is Davis, California. There, approximately 25 percent of all passenger miles, as opposed to about 2 percent statewide, are made by bicycle. In general, land-use planning can facilitate the development of public transportation by arranging residential and non-residential uses to reduce the "collection" and "distribution" problems noted in Chapter 12. A community might also decrease the use of private automobiles by greater expenditures for public transportation, setting up new initiatives in public transportation such as van pooling and dial-a-ride systems, and encouraging carpooling.

Building characteristics can be altered to produce very sizable reductions in energy expenditures. In some cases these changes are closely linked to land-use planning decisions; in other cases they can be effectuated independently. A land-use plan might encourage row housing as opposed to free-standing single-family units. This choice need not mean higher density in the development but might, for example, mean clustering, with the provision of common open space. Row or attached housing, in general, reduces energy used in heating because it reduces the amount of building surface exposed to the elements. To see this, just imagine two free-standing units moved into a side-by-side position. The two side walls which have been brought together become interior walls and can no longer conduct heat to the outside.

Siting buildings with regard to the sun will affect the ease with which sunlight can be used to supply part of the energy used for heating. Streets that run east-west facilitate placing houses so that they face south for maximum solar exposure. A number of communities have adopted solar access zoning, which prevents structures or trees from being placed in such a position that they block the direct access of other buildings to the sun.

There are also building-related steps that are unrelated to overall land-use planning. A number of communities impose minimum insulation requirements on new houses. Some municipalities have implemented programs designed to encourage property owners to retrofit old buildings. These may be limited to giving technical advice or may also include low-interest loans and other financial incentives. A few communities require that before a house can be resold, it must be brought up to some minimum standard of insulation, a technique that gradually forces a retro-fitting of the existing housing stock.

The number of municipalities that have "green building codes"—codes that mandate a variety of energy saving and other environmentally friendly features in new buildings—is increasing rapidly. Many municipalities now build or retrofit their own structures with energy conserving features such as solar heating or photovoltaic panels.

A number of communities have begun community energy production systems. In a sense these do not represent energy conservation, but by their nature they tend to, and are intended to, conserve traditional energy sources. Many communities have developed or are developing so-called low head hydroelectric systems, for example, using a source that was used for power but subsequently abandoned when relatively low-cost power from central sources became available. One factor that makes such development practical is state laws that require utilities to buy power from small-scale generators and thus create a market for the output of such facilities. New England, with a large number of dams dating from the period when many mills and factories ran on waterpower, is the national center for such activity.

In many communities, solid waste, which was once disposed of in landfills or burned in incinerators, is now used as the fuel for power generation. The power is either used locally or sold back to the area utility and distributed through the utility's transmission grid. A number of municipalities have looked at the possibility of *cogeneration,* a system in which waste heat from one process is put to a second use rather than simply discharged into the atmosphere. For example, waste heat from a municipal power generating facility might be converted to steam and used to supply heat for municipal or other buildings.

SUMMARY

Much environmental planning and regulation must be done at the national level because of the scale of the problems and the great distances pollutants can travel through the environment. Local environmental planning often takes place within a framework of federal grants and regulations. Concern with environmental problems grew rapidly in the United States during the 1960s, culminating in the passage of the National Environmental Policy Act (NEPA) in 1969, the creation of the Environmental Protection Agency (EPA) in 1970, and the passage of a number of other major pieces of national environmental legislation in the 1970s. The passage of NEPA produced a massive increase in the number of planners and firms specializing in environmental planning because of its requirements for environmental impact statements (EIS) as a prerequisite for the federal funding of large projects.

At the national level, environmental planning involves the establishment of standards and the funding of such activities as the construction of waste-water treatment facilities. At the local level, much activity is related to federal legislation and funding, for example, EISs, or to planning for projects that involve joint local and federal funding, such as waste-water treatment. However, much to enhance environmental quality can also be done at the purely local level, including controls on the intensity of development, and the type of development, the matching of development to the physiographic character of the area, the pattern of public capital investment, and regulation of the character of development and operation. There are various ways of thinking about environmental issues, from a purely case-by-case approach to the fairly comprehensive techniques advocated by Ian McHarg. The water quality planning process and a solid-waste disposal site location process discussed in the chapter are examples of how environmental planning questions might be approached by a municipality.

Energy planning arose with the oil price increases that followed the 1973 Arab-Israeli War. The original concern of the energy planner was the conservation of nonrenewable energy sources, that is, fossil fuels such as petroleum. At the local level, reductions in consumption of nonrenewable energy may be achieved by urban design, which reduces trip lengths and facilitates public transportation or the use of nonautomotive modes (foot or bicycle). Energy savings can also be affected by site design and land-use control ordinances, which facilitate the use of solar energy, and by regulations that mandate minimum insulation standards. With the decline in energy costs during the 1980s and much of the 1990s, national concern with energy planning also declined. In the last several years a combination of rising oil prices, apprehension over global warming, and concern with the geopolitical issue of energy independence have put energy planning back into an important place on the planners' agenda.

NOTES

1. D. Morgenstern, R., A. Pizer and J. S. Shih, *Review of Economics and Statistics*, "The Cost of Environmental Protection," November 1, 2001, vol 83, no. 4, pp 732–737.

2. Adam Rogers, *The Earth Summit: A Planetary Reckoning*, Global View Press, Los Angeles, 1993, p. 188.

3. "5 Years After Environmental Summit in Rio, Little Progress," William K. Stevens, *New York Times*, June 17, 1997, p. C8.

4. William K. Stevens, "Meeting Reaches Accord to Reduce Greenhouse Gases," and James Bennet, "Warm Globe, Hot Politics," both in the *New York Times*, December 11, 1997, p. A1.

5. Jon E. Hilsenrath, "Eco-Economists Back Bush on Kyoto Pact," *The Wall Street Journal*, August 7, 2001, p. A2.

6. Neil Agder et al., Working Group II Contribution to the Intergovernmental Panel on Climate Change, *Climate Change 2007: Climate Change Impacts, Adaptation and Volnevability*, available on the Web at www.IPCC.org.

7. Edward Strohbenn et al., "Supreme Court Decision Forces EPA to Reconsider Greenhouse Gas Emission," available on Web, www.mondaof.com/article.asp?articleid=47684.

8. Stephen Nodvin, "Ex-generals: Global Warming Threatens U.S Security, blog.nodvin.net/?p=204.

9. Gregg Easterbrook, "Global Warming: Who Loses and Who Wins," *The Atlantic Monthly*, April 2007, pp 52–64.

10. William Yardley, "Climate Change Adds New Twist to Debate Over Dams," *New York Times, April 23, 2007*, p. A12.

11. Marjorie Williams, "Energy Amnesia," *The Washington Post*, May 2, 2001, p. A21. The entire speech can be found at www.whitehouse.gov/vicepresident/news-speeches/speeches/vp20010430.html.

12. Elizabeth Shogren, "White House Reignites Battle on Forest Roads," *Los Angeles Times*, May 5, 2001, p. a-1.

13. Blaine Harden, "US Seeks to Restrict Appeals on Dams," *Washington Post*, October 28, 2004, p. A1.

14. From Title I of the National Environmental Protection Act (NEPA) of 1969, PL 90–190.

15. For a detailed discussion of this process and an explanation of the economic rationale for pollution rights, see John M. Levy, *Essential Microeconomics for Public Policy Analysis*, Praeger, New York, 1995, chap. 12.

16. See the Air Quality Management District's Web site: www.AQMD.gov.

17. For an account of this process, see *Environmental Quality*, 1983, pp. 253ff.

18. Ibid.

19. Some writers have referred to "the export of pollution." The phrase refers to a process in which more prosperous nations enact such stringent controls that certain polluting operations are no longer economically feasible. The operations will then move to poorer nations, which are willing to tolerate a higher level of pollution for the jobs and income that the polluting activity will bring. This point was raised during the 1992 presidential campaign in connection with the North American Free Trade Agreement (NAFTA) that had been negotiated by the Bush administration but not yet approved by the Congress. Those opposed to the agreement and those who wanted it modified argued that one reason that U.S. manufacturers were locating plants in Mexico just south of the Rio Grande was that Mexican environmental standards were much lower than those of the United States and that, therefore, the cost of complying with them was much lower.

20. A large literature has developed on the greenfields-brownfields issue, with a heavy emphasis on the how-to-do-it aspects of brownfields redevelopment. See, for example, David Yaussy, "Brown-fields Initiatives Sweep Across the Country," *Environmental Compliance and Litigation Strategy*, vol. 10, no. 11, April 1995, p. 1; "Redeveloping Contaminated Sites: Economic Realities," *Urban Land*, June 1995; and James A. Chalmers and Scott A. Roehr, "Issue in the Valuation of Contaminated Property," *Appraisal Journal*, vol. 61, no. 1, January 1993, pp. 28–41.

21. Bradley K. Townsend, "The Economics of Health Risk Analysis," in Levy, *Essential Microeconomics*, p. 217.

22. Ibid., p. 219.

23. For an account of some of the conditions considered and some types of simple calculations that can be done regarding land suitability, see John H. Baldwin, *Environmental Planning and Management*, Westview Press, Boulder, CO, 1985, chap. 3.

24. For a presentation of McHarg's design philosophy, see Ian McHarg, *Design with Nature*, Natural History Press, Doubleday & Co., Inc., New York, 1969.

25. Ibid., p. 34.
26. Ibid., p. 115.
27. An aquifer recharge area occurs where surface water such as a stream, lake, or wetland overlies an underground layer of gravel or porous rock, permitting recharge of the underground from the surface source.
28. In general, bus transportation is more energy efficient than automobile transportation. "Big Wheels: How Dreams of Clean Air Get Stuck in Traffic," *New York Times,* March 11, 1990, sect. 4, p. 4, gave the following average energy use for moving a person one mile. All are expressed in calories: bicycle, 35; walking, 100; rail transit, 885; bus transit, 920; single-occupant automobile, 1,860. The reader may wonder why the difference between bus transit and single-occupant auto is not greater. Part of the answer is that the full bus that one might picture describes the situation only part of the time, most typically at rush hour.

SELECTED BIBLIOGRAPHY

BALDWIN, JOHN H., *Environmental Planning and Management,* Westview Press, Boulder, CO, 1985.

COUNCIL ON ENVIRONMENTAL QUALITY, *Annual Report,* Washington, DC. (This series begins in 1970.)

DANIELS, TOM, and DANIELS, KATHERINE, *The Environmental Planning Handbook,* APA Press, Chicago, 2003.

MABEY, NICK, HALL, STEPHEN, SMITH, CLARE, and GUPTA, SUJATA, *Argument in the Greenhouse,* Routledge, New York and London, 1997.

MANGUN, WILLIAM R., and HENNING, DANIEL H., *Managing the Environmental Crisis,* 2nd ed., Duke University Press, Durham, NC, 1999.

MASER, CHRIS, *Sustainable Community Development: Principles and Concepts,* St. Lucie Press, Delray Beach, FL, 1997.

MCHARG, IAN, *Design with Nature,* Natural History Press, Doubleday & Co., Inc., New York, 1969. Second edition, 1992.

MOFFAT, IAN, HANLEY, NICK, WILSON, MIKE D., *Measuring and Modeling Sustainable Development,* The Parthenon Publishing Group, New York and London, 2001.

NATIONAL RESEARCH COUNCIL, *Our Common Journey: A Transition Toward Sustainability,* National Academy Press, Washington, DC, 1999.

RANDOLPH, JOHN, *Environmental Land Use Planning and Management,* Island Press, Washington, DC, 2004.

VIG, NORMAN, J., and KRAFT, MICHAEL E., *Environmental Policy in the 1990s,* CQ Press (Division of Congressional Quarterly, Inc.), Washington, DC, 1997.

CHAPTER 16

Planning
for Metropolitan
Regions

Most of the planning discussed in this book is that done by the individual municipality. But there are many planning issues that transcend municipal boundaries and are much better addressed at a larger-than-municipal scale. In this chapter we discuss planning at the metropolitan area level.

THE POLITICAL PROBLEM

The key problem in planning for a metropolitan area is the political one. By themselves, city governments are generally too small to address adequately metropolitan area problems. Yet it is at the municipal level that much of the power and responsibility lies. The problem, then, is to set up a metropolitan areawide mechanism that has the capacity to do effective planning. That means an organization that can obtain sufficient support and cooperation from the established institutions of government, municipal and state. This is not an easy task. Politicians, like most other people, do not readily cede power and authority to others. They need to be convinced that they and their constituents have a community of interest with the regional organization. Metropolitan planning organizations succeed only to the extent that the local and state political establishments—elected officials and their constituents—see the regional organization as useful in meeting their needs. This is necessarily so, for metropolitan-area planning takes place within the U.S. federal system in which large amounts of authority and responsibility,

The portions of this chapter pertaining to Minneapolis–St. Paul were written by the late C. David Loeks, who was Professor Emeritus in Urban Affairs and Planning at Virginia Polytechnic Institute and State University, and a former Planning Director of the city of St. Paul.

such as the power to control land use, reside with local governments. This situation is very different from that in a number of European nations such as the Netherlands, where a powerful central government can require that local plans conform to higher-level plans (see Chapter 18).

What, specifically, are the planning issues that demand a regional rather than a local approach? The listing that follows is not complete, but it includes the main items that make most lists.

1. *Transportation.* Because large numbers of people cross municipal lines to work, to shop, or to take part in social and recreational events, a regional approach to transportation is necessary. Then, too, many transportation facilities, such as airports, by their very scale must be regional facilities.

2. *Water supply, sewers, and sewage treatment and solid-waste disposal.* Water supply systems must be designed with regard to topography and hydrology, not to political boundaries. Where municipal populations are small, economies of scale in water and sewer treatment facilities may make multijurisdictional plants more efficient. Locating a solid-waste disposal facility means taking account of soil characteristics, ground-water flows, road access, and population distribution. In most cases these design requirements will not correspond to municipal boundaries. Similar comments can be made about flood control, though in some cases that problem transcends the metropolitan scale as well.

3. *Air quality.* A single municipality within a large metropolitan area cannot by itself solve its own air quality problems. There must be cooperative action within the metropolitan area or within the "airshed." (See the discussion of the Los Angeles Air Quality Management District in Chapter 16.)

4. *Parks, outdoor recreation, and open space.* Because population densities and land values in the core of the region are vastly greater than on the periphery, it makes sense for outlying areas to provide more of their share of open space and parkland. This arrangement does not obviate the need for such efforts at the municipal level, but it does make a case for multijurisdictional efforts as well.

5. *Economic development.* If the region unites for this purpose, it can sell itself as a single entity to the rest of the world rather than expend funds on competition between municipalities that are all part of the same regional labor market. Thus some zero-sum game activity can be avoided. A regional rather than a municipal approach may also achieve marketing economies of scale, for example, in having a single development office represent the entire region in London or Frankfurt or Tokyo.

6. *Housing.* Housing and land-use policies in one municipality affect housing prices, rents, and vacancy rates in the entire metropolitan area. Employment growth in one municipality affects housing demand in many other municipalities. Thus one can argue that housing is a regional as well as a local issue. It must be admitted, however, for a variety of reasons noted in the last section of Chapter 12 that regional housing planning is still more of a gleam in the planner's eye than a major force in urban and metropolitan housing markets. Although there is no problem constructing arguments for a regional approach, the political force behind a regional approach is often weak.

Beyond these planning issues there is also a range of services in which a regional approach makes better sense than a municipal approach, often because it permits greater economies of scale. Thus we also see regionwide efforts in manpower training and the provision of various social services. But these services take us beyond the realm of planning as the term is used in this book.

A BRIEF HISTORY OF METROPOLITAN AREA PLANNING _____

In this section we discuss three institutional approaches to planning at the metropolitan level: the regional planning agency, the authority, and the council of governments. Though they are separate forms, they have many points in common.

The need for metropolitan area planning has been recognized at least as far back as the turn of the last century. Recall that the 1909 Plan for the City of Chicago contained regional elements for both transportation and open space. However, the first big surge of interest in regional planning came in the 1920s. The primary cause was the great increase in automobile ownership that occurred during the 1920s and the related growth of the suburbs. As the compact city of the nineteenth century gave way to the metropolitan area of the twentieth century, the need for metropolitan area planning became evident, particularly in regard to transportation and utilities.

One response to this need was the regional planning agency. One of the first, and probably the best known, of these organizations was the Regional Plan Association in New York. The plan, described in Chapter 3, covered more than five thousand square miles in three states, New York, New Jersey, and Connecticut. By the end of the 1920s, there were about 15 regional plans in the United States. Many of them, like the plan for the New York region, were done entirely under private auspices. In such cases the plans done by the organization had absolutely no official sanction or any force of law. The plan had an effect upon the region only to the extent that it influenced the opinions of public officials and their constituents. Because some regional planning agencies of the period were governmentally chartered and funded, they had a certain statutory relationship to the political establishment. But even then, the power of such a group was essentially only the power of persuasion. For it is only the legislative and executive branches that can make laws and appropriate monies.

The Public Authority

Another path to regional planning, also of 1920s origin, was the creation of authorities. An authority is an organization that is generally created by state government or in some cases by the joint action of two or more state governments. Rather than being a general-purpose government like that of a town or city, it is a quasi-governmental organization with some of the usual powers of government. For example, an authority often has the power to raise money through the issuance of tax-exempt bonds. It may also have the power to take property through condemnation or to override local land-use controls. In general, it has a single task or set of tasks assigned to it. In modern administrative jargon, it is set up to be very "task oriented." Authorities were not and are not created to do general-purpose planning in the sense that a regional planning agency is. However, the decisions of an authority may well shape a region and constitute planning decisions under another name.

The authority exists "at the pleasure" of the state legislature(s) that created it, and it can always, at least in principle, be abolished by the same legislative body or bodies. Its board of directors is appointed by the same legislature(s). That feature, too, constitutes a powerful element of legislative control. Yet authorities do sometimes become a force of their own and achieve a substantial degree of autonomy. Though they are ultimately under legislative control, on a day-to-day basis authorities are much further from political control than, say, a city agency such as a public works department. They operate separately from municipal and state government, and they are further from the reach of the voter because he or she does not vote for the board members directly. Rather, the voter votes for the legislators, who then choose the authority's board.

The first authority in the United States was the Port of New York Authority, subsequently renamed the Port Authority of New York and New Jersey. It was created jointly by the legislatures of New York and New Jersey in 1921. As discussed in the next section of this chapter, it has been a powerful force in shaping the New York region.

The fact that both regional organizations mentioned so far, Regional Plan Association and then Port Authority, are of the New York region is not entirely coincidental. Regional planning and development efforts come into being where the disproportion between the size of the real city—the economic and social city—and the political city is great. The New York region was by far the nation's largest metropolitan area in the 1920s, and the problems of achieving coordinated action were compounded further by its being a multi-state region. Thus it is not surprising that much of the apparatus of regional cooperation should evolve where the need for it was greatest.

Regional Planning After World War II

Regional planning in the United States after its promising start in the 1920s developed only slowly over the next several decades. But the pace of development accelerated sharply in the 1960s. One reason for the acceleration was the long period of rapid suburban growth that began after the end of World War II and that continues to the present time. This was a resumption of the same force that had started the trend toward regional planning in the 1920s. A second factor was that we began to give environmental issues more weight, and environmental problems by their very nature tend to be multi-jurisdictional. But perhaps most important was that the federal government began to offer state and local governments irresistible inducements to regional planning.[1] In the 1960s the flow of federal money for highways, urban redevelopment, and environmental projects increased greatly. But to get federal grants, local governments had to meet federal requirements for regional planning. For example, the 1962 Federal Highway Act provided matching funds for highway construction, but to get those funds, the applicants had to show that their application was consistent with a regional plan. The Urban Mass Transit Act of 1964 authorized billions for mass transit systems, but again, the applicant had to show that the funds being applied for would be used consistently with a regional plan. Not only did these and other acts make regional planning a requirement for funding, but many of them also provided funds for the making of regional plans. The carrot of federal funding was a major factor in bringing into being the Councils of Governments (COGs), which today are the main instrument for intermunicipal cooperation in the United States, and which often incorporate regional planning and former regional planning agencies within themselves.

Councils of Government. The name Council of Government is used generically in this section, but numerous other names for the same type of organization are in use, such as regional councils, associations of governments, planning districts, and area development district associations.

According to the National Association of Regional Councils, there are about 450 councils of government, by one name or another, in the United States today. They range in size from three employees to over three thousand employees. In the south and the southwest, virtually all local governments are members of COGs, and in the rest of the nation, the great majority of local governments are members. Some municipal and county governments may belong to more than one COG. For example, every county in the state of Virginia belongs to one of Virginia's 17 Planning District Commissions. But Virginia counties in the northeast portion of the state are also physically part of the Washington, D.C., metropolitan area. Those Virginia counties such as Fairfax and Prince William, which are part of the metropolitan area, also belong to the Metropolitan Washington Council of Governments (MWCOG).

To meet the National Association of Regional Council's definition of a COG, at least 51 percent of the organization's board of directors must be elected officials of its constituent municipalities. In practice, local elected officials usually make up much more than 51 percent of board membership. Those members of boards who are not elected officials are often persons who have some appointed relationship to one of the constituent municipalities, such as being a member of a planning board. The board of the COG sets policy and hires the full-time director, much as a city council hires a city manager. The director is the day-to-day director of the COG, but he or she serves under the direction of the board. Thus the COG is very much the creature of its constituent municipalities. What responsibilities it has and how far it can go in any direction are thus determined by the municipalities that it represents. For a COG to do effective work, it must have the support of its member municipalities, that is, they perceive it as serving their purposes—as being a help and not as being a rival.

As noted, the growth of COGs has been greatly accelerated by the carrot of federal funding. One of the more recent carrots was the Intermodal Surface Transportation Efficiency Act of 1991 (ISTEA) as discussed in Chapter 12. It greatly strengthened the planning role of COGs by designating the COG or COGs in each region as the Metropolitan Planning Organization (MPO) that would coordinate transportation planning and prepare the applications for funding. Since the act involved the appropriation of $150 billion or so in federal highway funds over the subsequent five years, it was a very powerful inducement to metropolitan area planning in the realm of highway and related investments. The 1998 highway bill, which authorized $203 billion in federal expenditures over the next six years, continued the Councils of Governments as the lead agency in metropolitan area planning. That is, it continues to designate the Council of Governments as the Metropolitan Planning Organization. These arrangements were extended further by SAFETEA-LU (see Chapter 12), passed by Congress in 2005.

The Council of Governments serves as a venue for communication and negotiation between municipal governments. For example, imagine that the Council of Governments in its role as Metropolitan Planning Organization is putting together a grant application for highway funds. The approximate total that the region will receive is known, but the cost of every project that each municipality would do if it could is vastly greater. The collective "wish list" must be pared down to approximate the total of funds available. Thus there must be bargaining and compromise among the municipalities making up the COG. The COG serves as a venue for such activity and in that way helps to bring about some meeting of minds among the governments of the metropolitan area or region.

Councils of government are not always well understood by the citizens of their member municipalities. The city or town or country government is much more visible to the citizen. Its actions tend to be much better reported in the local press or covered on the six o' clock news. Then, too, the citizen votes for municipal officials. The COG, as a creation of the various municipal governments, is much less visible. Politicians want visibility because they have to stand for election, and to do that successfully, they must be known. The director of a COG may take a different view. He or she may prefer to be relatively unknown and simply get on with the work of the COG outside the light of publicity and beyond the inquiries of reporters. Thus many councils of government function in relative obscurity.

In the following sections we present three case histories to illustrate the previous general discussion: the case of Minneapolis–St. Paul, for regional planning agencies; the case of the Port Authority of New York and New Jersey for authorities; and the Atlanta Regional Commission for Councils of Governments.

MINNEAPOLIS–ST. PAUL: A TALE OF TWO CITIES _____

At the turn of the century, Minneapolis and St. Paul were two separate cities with a combined population of about 460,000. At that time the need for any sort of collective action was limited. By the 1950s their combined population had risen to about 1.2 million, and the two once-separate cities had coalesced into a single urban area bisected by the Mississippi River. Both cities, like many others of the period, were rapidly suburbanizing.[2]

The problems of suburban expansion as well as those of rebuilding the two cities' downtowns focused the attention of civic and government leadership on the question of how to guide the continuing growth of the Minneapolis–St. Paul region. The issue was brought to a head by problems connected with the expansion of the metropolitan sewer system and by the advent of the Interstate Highway System (see Chapter 18). The sewer problem required a regional approach if duplication of facilities was to be avoided and if the efforts of one municipality were not to complicate the efforts of other municipalities. Since in that region all sewer systems ultimately empty into the Mississippi River, it would not be helpful to have one municipality's discharge pipes located immediately upstream of another municipality's intake pipes. Similarly, it was understood that the highway system, which would serve the entire region, would be best designed if the region were viewed as a whole.

In 1957, after two tries and much bargaining and compromise, the Minnesota legislature passed a bill creating the Metropolitan Planning Commission (MPC). The law that created the MPC provided for a 28-member governing board, of which 21 members represented local governments. The other 7 members were appointed by the governor to represent civic, business, and community interests. The law also specified that the commission's authority was limited to planning and recommending. It had no powers to implement. The MPC had been structured so as to be nonthreatening to the existing political establishment at both the local and the state level. This fact takes us back to the point made earlier, that politicians and the existing political establishment will resist any loss of their own powers and prerogatives. A council that threatened to impose such losses would have been politically dead on arrival.

For the next decade the MPC worked on developing a regional plan. A good part of the time was spent on developing information and promoting public consciousness of the issues and of the need for planning. This effort to reach out to the public comes back to a point made in Chapter 6. No matter how good the plan is on its technical merits, if it does not have public support, there will not be sufficient political force behind it, and it will not come to pass.

The plan that emerged was a development policy designed to minimize sprawl and to concentrate urban development in the two central cities and in a number of large-scale, self-contained satellite communities. These would be separated by open space and farmland but would be linked by the metropolitan transportation system.

One obstacle to achieving intermunicipal cooperation about land-use planning is the matter of property taxes (see Chapter 9). All municipalities want land uses that return more in property taxes than they cost the municipality to service. Thus there will be intermunicipal competition over attractive "ratables" such as shopping centers, office parks, and some types of industrial development. Therefore, the plan called for a tax-sharing arrangement. A portion of the property tax revenues from new nonresidential development would go into a common pool to be shared by all the municipalities in the region. This arrangement would mean that there would be less motivation for municipalities to compete for fiscally desirable developments and more chance of achieving a land-use pattern that made sense in regional terms.[3] By 1966 the planning phase was just about complete, and it was time to begin implementation. In 1967 the Minnesota state legislature created the Metropolitan Council to move from plan to reality.

Within several years the Metropolitan Council was responsible for policy in a number of areas including sewers and sewage treatment, solid waste disposal, open space, sports facilities, public transportation, and highways. The tax-sharing arrangement noted before was set up in 1971. In 1975 a "Metropolitan Framework" law was passed, which stipulated that the Metropolitan Commission would establish the following:

1. Urban service areas in which housing subdivisions would be concentrated
2. Commercial/agriculture areas in which free-standing subdivisions would not be allowed
3. Rural development zones that would not provide urban services (such as public water and sewer) except around preexisting development

Note that this approach is similar to that of many growth management systems, some of which are described in Chapter 15.

In addition to this planning work, the Metropolitan Commission also functioned as a management and service delivery agency for various federally mandated programs in criminal justice, health care, the arts, and services for the aging. In this regard it functioned in the same way as many other Councils of Government.

What Has Been Accomplished?

The council by itself does not literally put bricks on mortar, but it has created the framework in which regional planning takes place. The resident of the region benefits from a better transportation system and better public utilities, a well-planned system of open space, and a higher level of environmental quality.

There are also economic benefits. The region has benefited greatly from investment by such organizations as the 3M (Minnesota Mining and Manufacturing) Corp. The corporation's willingness to commit itself to the region stems in part from its recognition that problems that affect it and its employees will be effectively addressed. The revitalization of the downtowns of Minneapolis and St. Paul has been facilitated because investors had confidence that transportation and other problems of the downtowns would be addressed.

More generally, the Twin Cities area is widely regarded as having a high quality of life as measured by things like public services, employment, education, and recreational and cultural amenities. There is a widespread "pride of place." Some of that emanates from a raised regional consciousness and a sense of national leadership in urban planning, development, and governance.

THE PORT AUTHORITY OF NEW YORK AND NEW JERSEY _____

The first authority formed in the United States was the Port of New York Authority, which was created in 1921 by the legislatures of New York and New Jersey and was subsequently renamed the Port Authority of New York and New Jersey. In the following discussion it is simply referred to as the Port Authority.

The authority's original mission was to improve the transportation of rail freight in the region. The port area is divided by the New York–New Jersey boundary, which lies in the middle of the Hudson River. The interstate problem was compounded by commercial rivalry between the business establishments on the New Jersey and the New York sides of the port. On the New Jersey side, the problem of political coordination was further complicated because the area is divided into a large number of municipalities. To the governors of New York and New Jersey, as well as to other public officials, an authority looked like a way to cut through the problems of multiple competing political jurisdictions. The authority also offered a way to get the public's work done without tax increases. In the words of Al (Alfred E.) Smith, then governor of New York, such an authority would be

> the one method we have discovered of getting work done expeditiously and without overtaxing our people to get it done.[4]

At first the Port of New York Authority concentrated on rail freight improvements, but it quickly became apparent that the future belonged much more to the automobile and the truck than it did to the train. The authority's basic mission—both from its own perspective and also from that of the political establishments in the two states that had created it—soon expanded to that of building in a coordinated way the river crossings that would meld the New York and New Jersey sides of the New York region into a single metropolitan area.

The decisions about what to build and where emerged from a mix of engineering, planning, and political considerations. The decision to let the entire problem of river crossings be handled by a single public agency was a political one, driven in part by the conviction of Governor Smith that such an important public task should not be left to separate groups of investors formed for each project but should be handled publicly as a single undertaking. Once that decision was made, the what and the where questions were decided on the basis of a mix of practical and political considerations.

The first major project was the George Washington bridge, which spanned the Hudson River from the Palisades in New Jersey to 179th

Street in northern Manhattan. The decision to build there rather than to build either a bridge or a tunnel to midtown Manhattan was made for a variety of reasons. The governor of New Jersey and a variety of interests in northern New Jersey wanted the crossing in that location to open up the northeastern part of the state. As is often the case with such decisions, part of the decision-making process turned on a particular personality. Once of the great civil engineers of the twentieth century, Othmar H. Ammann, a Swiss immigrant to the United States, was taken up with the idea of such a crossing to northern Manhattan. The bridge that he conceived would be the longest single span in the world. In the late 1920s a suspended center span of over three thousand feet was an engineering challenge that would push the bridge-builder's art to the limit. Ammann was convinced that it could be done, and he wanted to be the one to do it. A persuasive and an energetic man, he was a major force behind the scenes in bringing about a consensus that the bridge could be built within a reasonable budget, that it would quickly pay for itself, and that it could be completed in a relatively short period of time. He proved right on all counts, and the bridge was finished in 1931 in less than two years and underbudget.[5] Ammann, who had some of the artist in his makeup, as well as being a talented engineer, was very concerned with bridges as works of art. Commenting on the bridge in 1936, Le Corbusier said,

> The George Washington Bridge over the Hudson is the most beautiful bridge in the world. Made of cables and steel, it gleams in the sky like an arch upturned, blest. It is the only seat of grace in a disheveled city.[6]

The bridge was a major planning decision for the region. The direct, continuous, high-capacity link for motor vehicles provided by the George Washington Bridge provided a tremendous impetus to the growth of northern New Jersey. The effect might not be so great today, for suburbs are much more economically self-sufficient than they once were. But in the 1930s the economic role of the metropolitan core, Manhattan in the case of the New York region, was proportionally much greater than it is today. If one says that regional planning to a large extent consists of intervening at a few strategic points that change the overall dynamics of the region, the building of the bridge was clearly one such decision. In subsequent years the Port Authority of New York and New Jersey continued to build, producing many of the links that bind the New York area, cut up as it is by bodies of water, into a unified region.

In addition to building bridges, the Port Authority has also played a role in mass transit. It operates bus lines, and much of the bus traffic between New York City and the New Jersey part of the region uses the Port

Authority's bus terminals. It also operates commuter rail service from New Jersey to lower Manhattan. Though it did not build them, the Port Authority operates the region's three major airports, La Guardia, Kennedy, and Newark.

The Port Authority also has played a major part in shaping the role of New York City as a port. In the period after World War II, the Manhattan docks lost essentially all their ocean freight business. The city's congested streets drove up the cost of moving freight, and lack of available land made it impossible to expand docking facilities to handle containerized freight, which made its appearance during that period. The Port Authority responded by developing the Port Newark–Elizabeth Marine Terminal (often referred to simply as Port Newark) on the New Jersey side of the region. Covering over three square miles, the terminal is set up to handle containerized freight and provides very quick access to the interstate highway system as well as to railroads and Newark Airport. Though its construction did nothing to keep freight handling at its traditional Manhattan location, it does enable the region to retain considerable ocean freight business that would otherwise have gone out of the region entirely.

When economic development became a hot issue with municipal governments, the Port Authority got into that activity, too. With its large and predictable stream of revenues from bridges, tunnels, airports, and ocean freight facilities, the authority had ample resources to do so. One unusual development is its Staten Island "Teleport," which is a one-hundred-acre business park centered around an "11 acre radio-frequency shielded area which provides communications with all domestic and Atlantic Intelsat Satellites."[7] The park is a niche marketing effort clearly designed for the firm with particular communications needs. The venture, built and operated by the Port Authority, was done in cooperation with New York City, which paid some of the infrastructure costs and offers preferential tax treatment to firms using the facility.

The Port Authority was not the only authority that shaped the New York region. On the New York side of the Hudson River, a number of bridges and tunnels have been built by the Triborough Bridge and Tunnel Authority (TBTA) under the direction of Robert Moses.[8] For example, in the 1960s the TBTA built the Verrazano Bridge between Brooklyn and Staten Island. Previously the only links between Staten Island (the borough of Richmond) and the rest of New York City were either a ferry trip to Brooklyn or Manhattan or a very circuitous drive to make use of the Holland or the Lincoln Tunnel. Staten Island in, say, 1960 was a rather quiet place, semirural in many parts, because of its relative isolation. The building of the bridge produced much suburbanization, a major increase in population, and much more commuting between Staten Island and the rest of the city. The Verrazano Bridge is without

Above, the George Washington Bridge, shown looking west from the New York side of the Hudson River, which was the first major project built by the Port Authority. To accommodate rising traffic volumes, a lower deck was added to the bridge after World War II. Below, Port Newark, built by the Port Authority on the New Jersey side of New York Harbor near the confluence of the Hackensack and Passaic Rivers. Note the strategic location. Immediately to the west of the port is the New Jersey Turnpike, a part of the Interstate Highway System, and beyond that is Newark Airport.

doubt the most important planning decision ever made in connection with Staten Island. That the decision was made by an authority that does not have regional planning as a formal mandate makes it no less of a planning decision.

Up to now we have said nothing about the financing of authorities. In the case of an authority such as the Port Authority, the main instrument is the tax-exempt bond (see Chapter 9). The monies received from the sales of bonds are used to build facilities, and charges like tolls are used to pay off the bonds. For the government, whether city or state, that created the authority, this is an attractive arrangement. The bonds are not an obligation of the government, nor do they count in determining whether that government has reached its debt limit. The agency can accomplish the purposes of the government that created it without obligating or burdening that government. If the agency has sufficient revenue-generating assets within the total mix of services that it provides, it can be entirely self-financing, as is the Port Authority. Not every activity must be self-supporting, since the more profitable ones can "cross-subsidize" the money-losing ones. For example, surpluses on bridge tolls might subsidize losses on bus operations.

Is There a Downside?

The picture presented so far is that of the authority cutting the Gordian knot of multiple jurisdictions and doing its work in a condition of relative isolation from the city or state finances. Is there a downside to this otherwise attractive picture?

Although authorities are created with a specific mission, they tend to survive for very long periods of time, and over time their missions may change considerably—experience "mission creep" in Pentagon jargon. The first goal of most organizations, whether they be governments, foundations, businesses, academic departments, or authorities, is to survive and to grow. For example, the Port Authority, born in 1921, has outlived all of its creators. Unless something very remarkable occurs, it will someday have outlived everyone alive in year of its birth. As the prior description indicates, it plays many roles that its founders never imagined. Any authority is more distant from the voters than is municipal government because its officials do not stand for election but are appointed by the municipality's elected officials. Voters tend not to know very much about most authorities. The percentage of New Yorkers who could name one of the 12 directors of the Port Authority of New York and New Jersey is probably very small. In fact, the number of New Yorkers who can say the organization's full name correctly may be relatively small. In ordinary New Yorkese, it is often rendered as "Port of Authority." Thus in some senses an authority is almost another, and a somewhat autonomous, branch of government.

The Port Authority has done many things that had to be done, and it has done many of them very competently. The preceding observations are not a criticism of this particular organization. Rather, they are simply an observation that the existence of a major authority creates another center of political power, and one that is substantially less accessible to the average citizen than are the elected officials in City Hall. That degree of political isolation may allow the authority to be more decisive and efficient at times.

Because the authority is isolated from direct involvement in electoral politics, it may be able to operate with a somewhat longer time frame than the two-or four-year cycle that necessarily looms so large in the minds of those who have to stand for reelection. Thus its relative political isolation may be advantageous. But it may also hold out some possibility of abuse of power. Even without anything that we would call abuse of power, the authority might spend its revenues differently than would a municipal government if it were collecting the tolls and fees—perhaps more wisely, perhaps less wisely, but differently. For example, it has been suggested that if a large share of public spending is in the hands of authorities, it may tend to push the mix of spending toward infrastructure rather than services both because most authorities are originally created to address infrastructure issues[9] and because infrastructure like bridges and tunnels generates revenues.

Though the authority can, in principle, always be abolished by the legislature that created it, a large authority may become a considerable political force in its own right. The Port Authority, for example, has close to eight thousand employees. Its operating revenues in the mid-1990s were over $2 billion a year, and its outstanding debt over $6 billion.[10] Those are the statistics of a fairly large city government.

THE ATLANTA REGIONAL COMMISSION

Councils of Government are now the predominant mechanism for metropolitan area planning, as well as for multicounty and other multijurisdiction efforts outside metropolitan areas. The Atlanta Regional Commission, which bills itself as the "oldest and largest publicly supported, multi-county planning agency in the United States" is also one of the most respected. A brief account of its origins and activities follows.

The history of metropolitan area planning in the Atlanta region began in 1938. Recognizing that growth beyond municipal borders was producing problems, the City of Atlanta, Fulton County, which contains most of the city, and the city's Chamber of Commerce, commissioned a consultant to study and make recommendations regarding intermunicipal cooperation in the Atlanta region. The consultant, Dr. Thomas Reed of the National Municipal League, came out strongly in favor of a regional planning agency:

> We feel that the institution of a metropolitan planning commission would be the beginning of a new day in the growth of the Atlanta region. Planned development is the only sure development. No man today trusts himself to build a structure much bigger than a chicken coop without a set of blueprints. How can such a vast and complicated affair as a great metropolitan community have orderly growth without a plan?[11]

This quote from Thomas Reed perhaps shows a bit more faith in our ability to shape the future through planning than the modern planner, with the benefit of hind-sight into the unplanned effects of major programs like Urban Renewal and the interstate highway system, might have. In that sense it is very representative of the 1930s outlook (see Chapter 3).

The region's move toward regional planning was delayed by World War II. However, in 1947 a Metropolitan Planning Commission (MPC) was created by act of the Georgia state legislature. The membership of the commission was small, only the city of Atlanta and two counties, Fulton and DeKalb. The commission focused primarily on transportation and open space, which appeared to be the critical issues in a growing region. As the region gained population, the initial organization grew. In 1960, Clayton, Cobb, and Gwinnett counties joined, roughly doubling the land area in the planning region, and a new organization was formed, the Atlanta Region Metropolitan Planning Commission (ARMPC). During the 1960s, regional planning for a variety of purposes grew, largely as a result of the flow of federal funding noted earlier. The result was that there were several regional planning agencies operating within the Atlanta region. Beyond the ARMPC there were separate regional agencies for health, crime, and highways. To bring order out of the situation, the Georgia legislature in a bill entitled Act 5 combined these various agencies into a unified agency, the Atlanta Regional Commission, which began operations in 1971. At this point, these separate regional efforts had been transformed into a full-blown Council of Governments.[12]

At present the Atlanta Regional Commission represents ten counties and a population of over 3 million. The City of Atlanta, with a population estimated at 426,000, represents only about 14 percent of the metropolitan population and, of course, a much smaller percentage of the land area under the purview of the Atlanta Regional Commission. As is true of all other COGs, control of the board of directors is firmly vested in the municipalities that constitute the COG. Twenty-three members of the board of directors are elected officials, mayors, and county commissioners. In addition, there are 15 members at large who cannot be elected or appointed officials nor employees of the political subdivisions of the COG.

However, they are not elected by the public but are chosen by the 23 elected officials on the board.[13]

What does the Atlanta Regional Commission do? Its organization chart shows its staff divided among five main areas: Communications, Community Services, Comprehensive Planning, Development Services, and Support Services. From the perspective of this book, the two of major interest are Comprehensive Planning and Development Services.

As is the case with many other COGs, the Atlanta Regional Council provides a database for the region's planning efforts. Thus population, water use, traffic, and other projections made by the council provide a common denominator for planning throughout the region. Having such a shared picture of the future is fundamental to being able to cooperate. It does not guarantee agreement, but it does enable people to talk on the basis of a set of shared assumptions. Much of the council's planning efforts over the years have been devoted to transportation issues. The City of Atlanta was founded as a rail terminal in the 1830s, and its function as a transportation hub has been a key element in its economy ever since. Over the years its efforts in transportation have included planning for the I-285 beltway around Atlanta; Hartsfield Atlanta International Airport; and the region's commuter rail system, the Metropolitan Atlanta Rail Transit Authority (MARTA). After Congress passed the Intermodal Surface Transportation Efficiency Act (ISTEA) in 1991, which included money for so-called "enhancements," the council has participated in planning for bicycle and pedestrian pathways as well.

The council has also been active in water planning. This has included planning for reservoir development and for the protection of watersheds in the Atlanta region. A 1972 study by the council of the Chattahooche River corridor formed the basis for intermunicipal efforts to protect the river and for the designation of river and environs as a National Recreation Area by the Carter administration in 1978. The council has also engaged in collaborative efforts with the states of Alabama and Florida, which share watersheds with Georgia.

The Development Services section of the Atlanta Regional Council has taken a modest role in economic development. The agency produces and supplies data and, most recently, a Geographic Information System (GIS) for firms interested in an Atlanta region location. It also seeks to assist the efforts of municipal economic development agencies and chambers of commerce. It does not, by itself, spend monies on economic development projects such as industrial parks.

As is the case in Minneapolis–St. Paul and other metropolitan areas, the chief contribution of a regional planning agency is not to be found in specific bricks and mortar, but in a spirit and process of intermunicipal cooperation that such an agency engenders. In the case of the Atlanta region, the Atlanta Regional Council has played a significant role in a variety of regional initiatives, particularly in transportation, open space and environmental quality, and water supply.

SUMMARY

The first major wave of planning for metropolitan areas occurred in the 1920s. The primary force behind it was the great increase in automobile ownership and the related increase in suburbanization. As the area of urbanization spilled out of municipal boundaries, the need for planning at an intermunicipal level became apparent.

In the 1920s two types of organizations appeared in response to this need. One was the regional planning agency, of which the best known was the Regional Plan Association (RPA) in the New York Metropolitan area. Some agencies, like RPA, were entirely private organizations with no official aegis at all. Others were created by legislative act. But in either case, regional planning agencies had no power to implement. Instead, they existed purely to advise, with implementation left entirely to the governments of the region. The second type of organization that appeared in the 1920s was the authority. These were organizations created by state legislatures with a definite mission (in transportation, utilities, and the like), and with some, but not all, of the powers of government. Though authorities were not specifically "tasked" with overall metropolitan area planning, decisions that they made about public infrastructure often turned out to be major planning decisions. In the post–World War II period, a third instrument for intermuncipal cooperation at the intermuncipal level appeared. This was the Council of Governments (COG). Today there are about 450 COGs in the United States, and most municipalities in the United States belong to one. Some belong to more than one. The growth of COGs was promoted in large measure by the federal government's regional planning requirements for funding bills in transportation, urban redevelopment, environmental improvement, and social services.

The chapter concludes with three case studies: the evolution of regional planning in the Minneapolis–St. Paul region, the origins and growth of the Port Authority of New York and New Jersey, and the history of the Atlanta Regional Commission.

NOTES

1. Frank S. So, Irving Hand, and Bruce D. McDowell, eds., *The Practice of State and Regional Planning,* American Planning Association, Chicago, 1986, pp. 144–147.
2. Twin Cities Metropolitan Planning Commission, "The Challenge of Metropolitan Growth," Report No. 1, St. Paul, 1952.
3. This arrangement is widely admired by planners and experts in public finance, the former for its land-use effects and the latter on the ground that it will help to equalize the per capita fiscal capacity of different municipalities in the same region. Unfortunately, such systems are rare for a very simple reason. Most municipalites are able to predict whether they will be net gainers or net losers under such a system. There is no way to compel the potential net losers to agree to join the system.

4. David C. Perry, ed., *Building the Public City*, Urban Affairs Annual Review 43, Sage Publications, Thousand Oaks, CA, 1995, p. 221.
5. For a detailed account of the politics of the bridge and Ammann's role, see Jameson W. Doig, "Politics and the Engineering Mind: O. H. Ammann and the Hidden Story of the George Washington Bridge" in *Building the Public City*, op. cit.
6. Ibid., p. 22.
7. Fact Sheet *The Teleport*, Port Authority of New York and New Jersey. Other listings of Port Authority projects are from Corporate Communications, Port Authority of New York and New Jersey, New York, NY. General information can also be obtained from the organization's Web site: www.panynj.gov.
8. For an account of Robert Moses's career and effects upon the city and the New York region, see Robert Caro, *The Power Broker*, Alfred A. Knopf, New York, 1974. The TBTA was merged with the Metropolitan Transit Authority (MTA) in 1965 and essentially survives as that part of the Authority with responsibility for bridges and tunnels. The other part of the Authority is responsible for the New York City subway system, city buses, and the metropolitan area's commuter rail service.
9. Katherine Foster, *The Political Economy of Special Purpose Government*, Georgetown University Press, Washington, DC, 1997.
10. Statistics from the *Annual Report of the Port Authority of New York and New Jersey*, 1996.
11. From the 1938 Reed Report as quoted in *Atlanta Regional Commission: 50 Year Commemorative Report*, Atlanta Regional Commission, Atlanta, GA, 1997.
12. This chronology is adapted from *Atlanta Regional Commission: 50 Year Commemorative Report*, Atlanta, GA, 1997.
13. *Bylaws of the Atlanta Regional Commission*, adopted September 10, 1971, amended through August 28, 1996.

SELECTED BIBLIOGRAPHY

PERRY, DAVID C., ED., *Building the Public City: The Politics, Governance and Finance of Public Infrastructure*, Urban Affairs Annual Review, no. 43, Sage Publications, Thousand Oaks, CA, 1995.

SO, FRANK, HAND, IRVING, and MCDOWELL, BRUCE D., EDS., *The Practice of State and Regional Planning*, American Planning Association, Chicago, 1986.

CHAPTER 17

National Planning in the United States

IS THERE NATIONAL PLANNING IN THE UNITED STATES? ____

Is there national planning in the United States? In one sense the answer is no, for there is no person or organization charged with drawing up a physical plan for the nation. There is no national master plan corresponding to the master plan that a city or town or county might have. In fact, when Congress terminated the National Resources Planning Board (NRPB) in 1943, it expressly prohibited any other agency in the federal government from assuming the board's national planning functions (see Chapter 4). No national planning agency comparable to NRPB has ever been set up since then.

One reason that we do not have a national plan is simply ideological. A national master plan sounds like socialism, and for most of our history, that has not been a welcome sound. Another reason may be the formidableness of the task. A national land-use plan for a small country is feasible. The Dutch engage in national land-use planning and, in the view of this writer, do it very well. But the Netherlands has a land area of a little more than 13,000 square miles, not much bigger than the state of Maryland. That is quite different from the 3 million square miles of the "lower 48."

Finally, and perhaps most important, we have a federal system of government in which a great deal of power resides with the states' congressional delegations. That dispersion of power makes the formation of a unified national plan extremely difficult. The sort of top-down planning that the Dutch do is simply not possible in the U.S. political environment. Note that this is not a matter of democracy versus autocracy, for the Netherlands is just as much a democracy as is the United States. Rather, it is a matter of the degree of centralization of political power within a framework of representative government.

Although there is not now nor has there ever been a master plan for the settlement pattern of the United States, there is no question that the federal government has engaged in a number of acts that have had a major effect upon the pattern of development in the United States. This chapter briefly describes some of these acts that, to an extent, constitute de facto national planning.

All these acts do not fit together neatly as parts of a single grand design. But although there is no grand design, there are some commonalities. The federal style, in most cases, has not been to command but to permit and to encourage. In most cases there has been more carrot than stick, the carrot being federal money or federal land. The general direction is set by a system of federal guidelines and incentives, but the details are decided at the state or substate level. Where the federal government is the actor that actually does the work, as in an Army Corps of Engineers' project, much of the initiative is local.

In general, the federal hand in shaping the pattern of development in the United States looms larger as one moves west. Federal ownership of land necessarily made the federal government a major player in determining the pattern of land development. And it was in the West that the federal government became the major landowner. In the immediate postrevolutionary period, most of the land east of the Mississippi was claimed by the thirteen colonies, though much of that land came into the union as other states. However, west of the Mississippi the Louisiana Purchase, lands obtained from Mexico after the Mexican War, lands ceded by Great Britain in the Oregon Compromise, the Gadsden Purchase, and the Alaska Purchase made the federal government a landowner on a huge scale. Climate has also favored a larger federal role in the West. In most of the United States west of the 100th meridian (a line that runs roughly from North Dakota Southward through the Texas Panhandle) rainfall is generally under 20 inches a year and is not sufficiently reliable to support agriculture other than grazing.[1] Thus agriculture in most of the western half of the country is dependent on irrigation. That dependency makes federal water policy a key shaper of the development of the region.

THE PATTERN OF LAND SETTLEMENT

The Ordinance of 1785, passed by the Continental Congress under the Articles of Confederation, laid out the basic pattern of landownership in what was then the Northwest Territory, a tract extending from the western border of Pennsylvania westward to the Mississippi, bounded on the south by the Ohio River and on the north by the Great Lakes. The act established the six-mile-by-six-mile-square township and the one-square-mile section as the basic units for land division. In the original plan, land was to be auctioned off in blocks of one square mile (640 acres) at a minimum price of $1-per-acre. The money was to provide the Congress with revenue, and the process of auctioning land in relatively small pieces would people this vast area with small, independent farmers. When the $1-per-acre price proved to be too high, Congress backed away from the plan to some extent by selling off large blocks of land to investors and speculators at a much lower price. The area then developed in a manner largely determined by the rate at which these buyers could create new settlements and resell land to individual holders. The effect of the act was to permit the rapid peopling of the area and to lay down a basic grid pattern that is still readily seen on the map of Ohio, Indiana, and other parts of the upper Midwest. The decision to sell farm-sized plots of land to individuals reinforced the rural American pattern of scattered farmsteads as opposed to a pattern commonly seen in Europe in which a rural population lives in hamlets or villages surrounded by the fields farmed by its residents.

In the latter half of the nineteenth century, the settlement of the West was very much influenced by a few other decisions of the federal government. The Homestead Act of 1862 permitted settlers to claim 160-acre blocks of public land at essentially no cost if they would reside on the land for five continuous years.[2] Ultimately, about 80 million acres, roughly 125,000 square miles, were homesteaded. Most homesteading occurred west of the Mississippi and much of it in areas that did not have adequate and predictable rainfall sufficient to support agriculture. This situation, some decades later, helped to propel the federal government into taking a major role in water development throughout the West.

In the same year Congress passed the Morrill Land Grant Act, which granted each state 30,000 acres of federally owned land for each member of the state's congressional delegation. The states were to use the monies from the sale of these lands to establish at least one college that would have as its primary role the teaching of "agriculture and the mechanic arts." A great many of the state universities in the United States today are land grant colleges. The suffix A&M in a university's name dates from the act. In the case of many other schools, the A&M has subsequently been lost. A major intention of the act was to ensure the teaching of practical arts to support agriculture. And in this regard it was extremely successful. Again, the federal government's actions were all carrot and no stick. No state was required to create an A&M college nor told where such a college should be located. The states were simply offered an attractive option, and most of them made use of it. The scattering of major state universities in small towns across the United States is, in part, a legacy of the Morrill Act.

ESTABLISHING THE RAIL NETWORK

The railroad network that facilitated and shaped the rapid development of the United States during the nineteenth century was, itself, shaped, and its construction greatly accelerated, by the actions of Congress. In 1850 there was no national network of railroads. There were under 10,000 miles of track in the eastern United States, mostly connected to large cities but not forming a unified system. For example, the furthest west one could continuously travel by train from New York City was to Buffalo. Other than along the East Coast, there were no major north-south links. Yet by 1860, national rail mileage had tripled, and most of the major cities east of the Mississippi were tied together in a network so that people or goods could travel between any two major cities entirely by rail.

A major factor in this expansion was federal land grants to railroad companies. The grants provided the right of way plus large amounts of land adjoining the right of way that the company could sell or use as collateral against which to issue bonds to pay for construction. The first such grant, totaling 3,736,000 acres (5,837 square miles), was to build a continuous link from Chicago to Mobile, Alabama. By 1860 Congress had granted a total of 18 million acres for railroad construction.[3] That area, about 28,000 square miles, is roughly the area of Vermont, New Hampshire, and Massachusetts combined.

With the rail system of the East relatively complete, the next obvious task was to span the continent with railroads. The First Pacific Railway Act of 1862 provided both the authorization and the financial incentives for a transcontinental railway.[4] The act authorized the Union Pacific Railroad to build westward from St. Joseph, Missouri, and the Central Pacific Railroad to build eastward from Sacramento, California. The act granted the railroads a 400-foot right of way and five square miles of land for each mile of track built (a figure that was doubled by Congress two years later). In addition, the federal government issued bonds to provide construction funds. Thus investors in the project bore relatively little of the total risk. The building of the lines was accomplished with considerable corruption and malfeasance. Exactly how much corruption there was will probably never be known.

> Their bookkeeping was, to say the least, primitive, and such records as existed, were destroyed, possibly by design, in a fire in 1873. But there can be little doubt that the profits were enormous.[5]

Construction proceeded rapidly over formidable obstacles, and the two lines met at Promontory Point near Ogden, Utah, in 1869, making coast-to-coast rail travel possible.

Within a decade or so, other lines crossed the continent, both north and south of the Union Pacific route. Here, too, congressional aid played a major role. In 1863 Congress granted the Atchison, Topeka, and Santa Fe ten square miles of land for every mile of route constructed, and in 1864 the Northern Pacific railroad was given lands that totaled more than the entire area of New England.[6]

Grants of public lands to railroads continued until 1873, by which time approximately 160 million acres (250 thousand square miles) of land had been given to railroads either directly by the federal government or indirectly by the federal government through the states.[7] It is hard to imagine a more powerful stimulus to railroad building. The grants provided a clear and an uncontested title to the route, and the potential sale of land to settlers and speculators made the financial prospects very attractive. U.S. rail mileage grew from about 30,000 miles in 1860 to about 200,000 in 1900, by which time the rail network as we now know it was essentially complete.[8]

WATER AND THE WEST

The combination of the Homestead Act and the spanning of the continent by railroads greatly accelerated the peopling of the western states, and this brings us to the question of water. In the eastern United States, where rainfall is generally adequate to support farming, water policy is rarely the most important public issue. In much of the West, water policy is an absolutely vital issue. In the years immediately after the Civil War, the populations of the plains states grew very rapidly for reasons noted. These years were wetter than usual, and if many western farmers did not thrive, they at least survived. The favorable weather, in fact, caused some to believe that the very act of cultivating large areas of land would cause rainfall, a notion then expressed in the phrase "rain follows the plow."

In the 1880s the weather turned drier, and it became apparent that rain did not follow the plow. In a number of plains states, both the farm population and the total population fell sharply as farmers abandoned their barren lands. By the end of the nineteenth century, of somewhat over 1 million families that had tried home-steading, only about 400,000 had made a go of it.[9]

The failure of rain-fed agriculture in the western half of the nation did not cause the United States to give up on western agriculture but rather promoted a great interest in irrigation to "reclaim" the desert lands for agriculture. But private irrigation efforts, by and large, were not very successful. Inadequate technical knowledge, undercapitalization, and, in many cases, fraud and chicanery doomed a majority of private irrigation projects. Pressure mounted for federal action.

The Reclamation Act of 1902 established the Reclamation Service (which became the Bureau of Reclamation in 1923). Under the act, funds from the sale of public lands were to be used to pay for irrigation projects and the investment repaid (without interest) by the parties using the water. At first the repayment period was to be 10 years, then 20 years with a 5-year grace period, and subsequently was extended even further.[10] The principle of federal subsidization of water development thus became firmly established. From the act's passage to well into the 1920s, the federal role in providing water in the West was modest. But in the late 1920s, a combination of events propelled the nation into almost a half-century of dam building and water projects that shaped much of the modern West.

In the period around World War I, people in the rapidly growing Los Angeles region recognized that growth would be brought to a halt by water shortages if a new source were not found. The nearest major source was the Colorado River, which begins in central Colorado more than two miles above sea level and follows a tumultuous southwesterly course ending in the Gulf of California between Baja California and the main land mass of Mexico. But the river does not flow through California itself, and thus California could not make a direct claim on it. The Californians took the initiative, and after much negotiation the Colorado River Compact to divide the waters of the Colorado was signed by the seven states of California, Arizona, New Mexico, Colorado, Nevada, Utah, and Wyoming. In 1928 Congress authorized the construction of Boulder Dam (subsequently renamed Hoover Dam), smaller dams downstream, and the All-American Canal. The latter was to run westward from a lower point on the river, Lake Havasu, to be formed by Parker Dam, to Los Angeles. The centerpiece of the project was Boulder Dam on which construction began in 1931 under the auspices of the Bureau of Reclamation. Completed in 1936, the dam was a massive testimony to the civil engineer's art. It was 726 feet high, almost a quarter of a mile across the crest, contained 66 million tons of concrete, and was altogether an impressive, if not amazing, accomplishment. A system of canals and aqueducts was then constructed to carry the waters of the Colorado across the width of California to serve the city of Los Angeles. Further south, the All-American Canal carried the Colorado's waters westward just north of the California-Mexico border and turned the desert of California's Imperial Valley into one of the nation's most productive agricultural areas.

The dam was a spectacular demonstration of what could be done both to supply huge quantities of water and to produce enormous amounts of cheap hydro-electric power. At the same time, the Great Depression had left a quarter of the nation's labor force unemployed, and federal job creation looked like the best way to deal with the problem. Dam building and associated reclamation projects were one way to soak up unemployed labor and produce a useful product. The dust bowl of the early 1930s (a result of dry weather and overcultivation) was driving hundreds of thousands of farmers off their land in states like Oklahoma (hence the term *Okies*) and sending them westward toward California. Another use, then, for funding reclamation work would be to open lands for farmers displaced by the storms of the dust bowl. A great era of dam building was soon under way. The prime agency for this work was the Bureau of Reclamation, though some dams were also built by the Army Corps of Engineers.

In connection with the dam building and associated construction done on the Colorado, one writer states,

> If the Colorado River suddenly stopped flowing, you would have two years of carry-over capacity in the reservoirs before you had to evacuate most of Southern California and Arizona and a good portion of Colorado, New Mexico, Utah and Wyoming. The river system provides over half the water of greater Los Angeles, San Diego and Phoenix; it grows much of America's domestic production of fresh winter vegetables; it illumines the neon city of Las Vegas . . . whose annual income is one-fourth the gross national product of Egypt—the only other place on earth where so many people are so helplessly dependent on one river's flow.[11]

What was done on the Colorado was not unique but only a harbinger of what was soon to be done elsewhere. By the start of World War II, Grand Coulee and Bonneville Dams (built by the Army Corps of Engineers) on the Columbia River and Shasta Dam on the Sacramento River in northern California had been completed. The process of damming and controlling the rivers of the West continued with great speed after World War II. By 1971, according to a Bureau of Reclamation tabulation, Hoover Dam ranked only forty-seventh in size among dams built or under construction by the bureau.[12] The largest of these, the earth-filled San Luis Dam in California, had an interior volume of over 77 million cubic yards, more than 30 times that of Hoover Dam.

Construction of water projects peaked in the 1960s with the addition of about 29 million acre feet of storage per year and then slowed in the 1970s. It has since come to an almost complete stop. What happened? First, most of the best dam sites had been developed.

> In the 1920s, a cubic yard of dam produced 10.4 acre feet in reservoir capacity. The average declined in each decade, and by the 1960s only .29 acre feet of storage was produced per cubic yard of dam.[13]

Thus newer projects showed lower benefit/cost ratios than older ones, and it became increasingly difficult to justify large federal expenditures for them.

Then, too, our notions of conservation have changed. To Theodore Roosevelt, the greatest turn-of-the-century conservationist, the idea of reclaiming the desert and making it bloom made perfect sense. The conservationist of today might ask just what prior claim were we "reclaiming." We have come to question how much sense it makes to deliver water to the farmer at 10 cents on the dollar in a nation that uses billions of federal dollars to pay farmers elsewhere to take land out of cultivation. Does it really make sense to grow rice, as is actually done, in the California desert? Then, too, it has become apparent that the great Bureau of Reclamation and Corps of

Engineers' projects of the past make both friends and enemies. Farmers and the industrial users of hydropower love them. But environmentalists become concerned about converting wetlands into reservoirs, for wetlands serve as breeding areas, as sources of biodiversity, and as stopping areas for migrating birds. They are concerned that changing the flow of a river by damming it changes the life within it and may drive some species to extinction. Fly fishermen, canoeists, and kayakers want rivers left in their natural state. Archaeologists do not want to see historic sites submerged forever. In short, the growing strength of the environmental movement helped to bring the era of great water projects to an end.

In 1986 Congress passed the Water Resources Development Act (WRDA). The law mandated much higher local contributions to federal water projects and higher user fees for federal water projects. By shifting a substantial part of the cost downward, it ended the era when state and local governments would lobby for inefficient projects simply because the project would bring them some benefits while imposing almost no costs on them.[14] The law applied to the Corps of Engineers and not to the Bureau of Reclamation, but it affected the bureau nonetheless. At present both the bureau and the corps are much more attuned to issues of conservation and efficient use of resources rather than massive new projects. In the West the key issue in regard to water will not be that of making more available but of making the best use of the amount that is now available. The big conflicts are likely to be over questions of water rights and water pricing and of balancing the needs of growing urban and suburban populations with the prior claims of agriculture.

In the West, water rights have generally been determined on the basis of "prior appropriation," meaning on the basis of who first claimed the right and used the source.[15] Agriculture, which employs a very small part of the total population of the region, uses a very large share of its total water supply. It has a grip on this supply because of the doctrine of "prior appropriation." If water is to be allocated on a more economic basis, whether it be competitive bidding or simply pricing water at its true cost of delivery, that change will favor urban and industrial users over agricultural users.[16] Decisions on this apparently technical issue of how to price water will have a major effect on the future development of the West.

Western Water Policy in Retrospect

Looking back on the era of reclamation, what is one to make of it? Some, like Marc Reisner, the author of *Cadillac Desert* cited earlier, regard much of the damming and reclamation work in the West as a giant combination of hubris, delusion, and scandal. But millions of westerners who like their region and the life they lead in it take a very different view. They will tell you that even if mistakes were made along the way, they are, by and large, pleased with what was done and what it has made possible. Some of them might also tell you that it is not right to judge actions in the past by the sensibilities of today. One should not condemn those who dammed the Colorado and the Columbia in the 1930s because they lacked the particular sensibilities of the Sierra Club members of today.

Projects, some by the Bureau of Reclamation, some by the Army Corps of Engineers, and some by state or municipal public authorities, made the modern U.S. West vastly different than it otherwise would have been. Dams, aqueducts, and canals provided the water for vast metropolitan areas like Los Angeles. Hydroelectric power at a fraction of the cost of fossil fuel–generated power in the East provided a basis for western industry. Western agriculture is largely a product of public water policy. California is first among the 50 states in value of farm output.[17] In California's Imperial Valley, one of the most productive agricultural areas in the United States, rainfall averages two to three inches a year. Without the waters of the Colorado, it would be as dry as the Sahara.

Were it not for the great water projects, the population of the American West would be much smaller than it is, and it would be strung out along the region's rivers. Los Angeles could not exist at anything close to its present scale. Reno and Las Vegas would, at best, be small towns depending on whatever water could be brought up from the wells. The West would be a food-importing rather than a food-exporting region and its industrial base far smaller than it currently is. People would not be able to water-ski on artificial lakes in the desert.

The rest of the nation would be different too. The population of the eastern United States would be substantially larger than it is today, and the centroid of U.S. population would be further east than it now is, for there would have been much less east-to-west migration.[18] The eastern United States would have considerably less forest than it now has, for without so much food production in the West, there would have to be much more land cultivated in the East.

SYSTEMATIC REGIONAL PLANNING

The sort of systematic planning for an entire region that one might call national planning has been done only once. That project was the work of the Tennessee Valley Authority (TVA). The Tennessee River originates in the Cumberland Mountains of the eastern part of Tennessee, flows westward, turns southward into northern Alabama, and then swings north emptying into the Ohio at Paducah, Kentucky, a few miles upstream from the confluence of the Ohio and the Mississippi. Over half of its drainage basin is in Tennessee, but the basin also includes parts of Virginia, North Carolina, Georgia, Alabama, Mississippi, and Kentucky.

> The natural regime TVA of the Tennessee River is characterized by large spring flows that produce destructive floods and low summer flows that inhibit navigation. The intensity and frequency of these events discouraged development and contributed to persistent poverty in the valley.[19]

The idea for integrated development of the valley originated shortly after World War I and was persistently and skillfully backed by Sen. George Norris of Nebraska. One selling point for a project on the Tennessee, aside from the poverty of the region, was that there already was some federal investment in the valley. Toward the end of World War I, the federal government had started to build a dam at Mussel Shoals on the Tennessee River to generate hydroelectric power and an industrial facility to use that power to make nitrates for explosives. The nitrate plant was tested and then "mothballed" in 1919. The dam was completed in 1925. The presence of that wartime investment provided a rationale for more development to properly utilize the original public investment. The nitrates that would have been used for explosives in war would be used for fertilizer in peacetime. In 1928 Congress passed legislation that would have created an organization similar to TVA, but it was vetoed by President Calvin Coolidge.

The Great Depression changed the political equation. In April 1933 President Franklin D. Roosevelt requested passage of legislation creating an authority, and Congress quickly complied.[20] Both job creation and alleviating the persistent poverty in the region were motivations. The act created a single authority to deal with all aspects of water development and policy within the region.

The river was dammed at a number of points to control flooding, and the same dams were used to produce hydroelectric power. The hydropower made possible electrification and furnished power for industry. In time the economic growth of the region raised the demand for electricity beyond what could be produced from the river, and in the years after World War II, TVA branched out into fossil fuel and nuclear-generated power as well. The building of locks rendered the river navigable from Knoxville, Tennessee, to the Missouri and thence to the Mississippi, thus contributing to the commercial growth of the region. Lakes created by the water projects provided recreation for the residents and also contributed to the economic development of the region by bringing in income from tourism.

As a project and as an experiment, the TVA has both its critics and its admirers. From the political right it has been criticized as socialistic and as permitting government to compete unfairly with private power companies. In fact, early in its history, electric power companies brought suit to enjoin it from selling electric power. The appeal went to the Supreme Court, which upheld the right of the governmental body to produce and sell electric power. TVA has been criticized from the left for being too cautious and sticking to an excessively narrow agenda. The agency has concentrated on a few areas—flood control, navigation, and power—and has eschewed a more comprehensive planning and social engineering role. Its admirers will argue that the agency performed yeoman service for the region by ending flooding, rendering the Tennessee River navigable (over a 652-mile stretch from Paducah to Knoxville), and providing the region with low-cost power. It let the region compete rather than languish in a state of underdevelopment.

Congress has never duplicated the TVA, though many "little TVAs" have been proposed. One reason clearly is ideological. A writer who worked for TVA for some years suggests that another reason is bureaucratic rivalry.[21] In the TVA, various functions are all the responsibility of a single commission. Thus, she asserts, "little TVA" proposals have been opposed by the Corps of Engineers, the Bureau of Reclamation, and other agencies because they would take functions out of the hands of those agencies. Although the TVA experiment has never been duplicated in the United States, the project has been the object of study for planners, economists, and administrators from developing nations all over the world as an example of how to do regional development.

As suggested earlier in this book, the effects of Hurricane Katrina on New Orleans and some tens of thousands of square miles of the Gulf Coast suggest that a major regional planning effort for that region might make some sense, for wind and high water are no respectors of municipal or state lines. Certainly, the planning technology today is vastly more advanced than what was available when the TVA was created. Then, high technology for data crunching was the hand-cranked calculator and the sliderule. GIS systems were unheard of and our knowledge of the underlying sciences like hydrology was only a fraction of what it is today. The question is not one of technical capacity but of the alignment of political forces.

THE INTERSTATE HIGHWAY SYSTEM

The design and construction of the interstate highway system represent a major act of national planning. In cubic yards of earth moved or cubic yards of concrete poured, the system, taken as a whole, may well be the largest construction project in human history. The construction of a coordinated system of highways all built to the same standards and linking every major city and more than 90 percent of all cities down to a population of 50,000 or more residents, across a land of about 3 million square miles, was a major act of planning. It was done as a cooperative venture between the federal government and 49 states.[22]

The federal presence in highway construction began with the Federal Aid Road Act of 1916. This act provided federal funds to assist states in the construction of intercity highways. It established a basic pattern of shared funding responsibility and local consent to and participation in highway planning that persists to the present time.

In the 1920s and 1930s, the increase in the number of automobiles and the dispersal of population, largely because of widespread automobile ownership, tended to outpace the rate at which the states and municipalities built roads. Traffic congestion and inadequate highway connections between cities were a continuing fact of American life. In 1934 federal aid legislation authorized funds for state highway planning in addition to supplementing the states' construction expenditures. This set in motion a variety of traffic studies and placed the idea of a national highway grid on the national political agenda.

In 1938 Congress requested the Bureau of Public Roads (BPR, a federal agency that subsequently became the Federal Highway Administration) to study a proposal for a system of six superhighway toll roads, three to cross the country from east to west and three from north to south. Toll roads were suggested because the federal government and the states were starved for revenues during the Great Depression, and tolls appeared to be a way to make the highways self-financing. BPR studied the matter and decided that this proposed 14,000-mile system would not be able to generate enough toll revenues to be self-financing. Instead, in 1939 BPR came back with a proposal that recommended a national highway system of 26,700 miles. A succession of planning studies over the next decade-and-a-half produced a vision of a national highway system of roughly 40,000 miles.[23] The system would be jointly planned by the federal government and the states, would be built to the same design standards across the nation, and would be a system of limited-access roadways. Limited access was necessary to maintain a smooth, high-speed flow. The concept had been proved on a very small number of parkways beginning with the Bronx River Parkway in the late 1920s (see Chapter 2).

Although the vision of a single, integrated, limited-access system was compelling, the passage of legislation that would bring it into being was stalled by the problem of how to finance it. Studies indicated that tolls, despite their financial success on a few roads such as the Pennsylvania Turnpike, could not generate the revenue required to build and maintain a national system. It took a decade after the end of World War II before that problem could be resolved.

In 1956, at the urging of the Eisenhower administration, Congress passed the Federal Aid Highway Act of 1956. Title I of the act called for uniform design standards across the nation, established methods for apportioning highway funding among the states, and dealt with questions of procedure and administration. But the crucial part of the act was title II, which provided for a mechanism that would deliver massive funding for highway construction. The act set up the Highway Trust Fund, which would receive money from excise taxes on new vehicles and sales taxes on motor fuel. These funds would be dedicated, meaning that they could be used only for highway construction. Since the passage of the act, motor vehicle ownership, miles driven, and fuel consumed have risen rapidly, providing a growing tax base to sustain highway construction.

The design of the system was a joint effort between the Federal Highway Administration and state officials. The overall plan of the system was worked out by the federal people, but the exact routing within the states was largely determined by state officials. Design standards were uniform. There were four 12-foot lanes to be separated by a median and provided with shoulders at least 10 feet wide. The highways were designed for maximum speeds of 50, 60, or 70 miles per hour depending upon topography. Early on, it was decided not to permit any services on the highways themselves, in contrast to the practice on toll roads. The argument given for this was to preserve competition and avoid the granting of "monopoly positions." But one might speculate that this decision had the fortuitous effect of increasing support from local businesspeople who would see the highway as a source of additional customers, rather than as a source of additional competition.[24]

The system, at this writing, covers about 42,500 miles and is virtually complete. The total cost of the system is estimated at about $129 billion. In the sense that the entire system is a single entity built to a single set of standards providing high-quality connections between virtually all of the major urban centers in the United States, it is a huge act of planning. And there is no question that it has shaped the development of the nation to an enormous degree. But it must be said that many of the system's effects were unanticipated and that in at least one way, the building of the system has had an effect opposite to that intended.

From the beginning it was recognized that there would be a choice between whether the interstates would go through cities or would bypass them with a circumferential road. It was understood that this choice would have important urban design consequences, and the 1956 legislation provided that where such a decision was to be made, a public hearing would be required. Within a few years enormous public opposition to cutting interstates through cities developed, and the decision was almost always to bypass.

The decision to bypass brought into being the familiar beltway pattern that we see about most major cities. And that is a profoundly deurbanizing design. The beltway (not shown in Figure 17–1) creates a major locus for economic activity around the city. People who work for businesses on the beltway no longer need to live within commuting range of downtown. The beltway, in effect, becomes the new downtown. The "edge city" of which Joel Garreau writes is made possible by the beltway design.

Proponents of the interstate highway system believed that it would strengthen the economy of the city by providing better access to the city's central business districts both from other cities and from the city's hinterland. But it was not foreseen that this effect would be swamped by the larger effect of creating huge masses of highly accessible commercial space outside the central business district and outside the city itself.

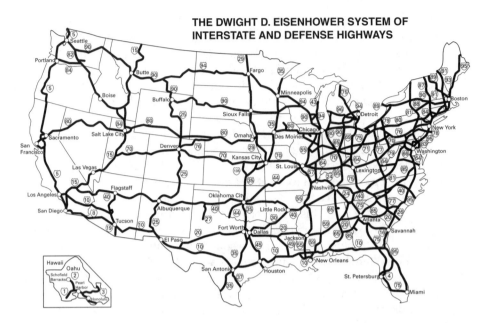

FIGURE 17–1 The interstate highway system as completed. Note that the figure does not show the beltways discussed in the text.

In the cases of the largest metropolitan areas, congestion on the beltway and the areas around it, in time, creates demand for a second beltway. The New York metropolitan area has, in effect, a double beltway system though it has breaks in it because of topographic considerations and bodies of water (Long Island Sound and the lower reaches of New York Harbor). In the Washington, D.C., metropolitan area there is now much discussion of a second beltway 10 or 15 miles farther out. This would spread the region farther and bring many hundreds of square miles of exurbia into the metropolitan area.

The building of the interstate highway system accelerated the shift of U.S. manufacturing from rail-borne to truck-borne freight by providing a road network that greatly increased the efficiency of trucking. That, of course, was also a decentralizing force. It probably also accelerated the growth of the Sunbelt relative to the rest of the country by tying formerly remote rural southern areas into a single, highly efficient national highway system.

One might wonder how different America would look if instead of taking the path we did, we had attempted to keep cities compact and spent much of the money devoted to interstates on a high-quality, heavily subsidized rail system. But although one may wonder about this, there was no real possibility for such a choice. The American love affair with the automobile and the process of suburbanization were well under way by the time the interstate system was begun. The rail served, compact city configuration has its appeal, and it certainly can make a claim for environmental virtue. But it never had the mass support that might have made it a real possibility.

The system accomplishes what it was intended to do. It provides rapid, safe, high-quality automotive transportation between cities, and between cities and their hinterlands. It has also accomplished much that was not intended.

FINANCING THE SUBURBS

Few acts of the federal government have had more effect upon the physical form of metropolitan areas than legislation concerning the financing and taxation of housing. Prior to 1935, mortgage lending was very different from what it is today. To protect themselves from losses when the borrower defaulted on a mortgage loan, banks required very large down payments. That, by itself, prevented many people from becoming homeowners. There were other barriers as well.

> Lenders considered a ten year mortgage to be long term. Many mortgages ran only one, two or three years, with most of the loan amount due in one large payment at the end of the short term. At the end of this short period, the home purchaser faced great uncertainties. Could he persuade the lender to renew his mortgage? At what interest rate? If he failed to get a renewal, he often lost his home. The standard plots in melodramas of the time [the villain about to foreclose on the hapless widow] were not entirely fiction.[25]

This situation was radically changed by a single act of the federal government. In 1935 the Federal Housing Administration (FHA), which had been created the previous year, began to offer mortgage insurance. The insurance fund consisted of a small fee paid by each borrower (the buyer of the house). The fund reimbursed banks should the borrower default on the mortgage. Federal mortgage insurance effectively eliminated the risk of default and thus made banks willing to lend for 25 or 30 years and with little down payment. Shortly thereafter the federal government created the Federal National Mortgage Association (FNMA, often referred to as Fannie Mae) to buy mortgages from banks. The bank could sell the mortgage to FNMA, thus converting the mortgage into cash. The home buyer would continue to make mortgage payments, but they would go to FNMA with the bank acting as intermediary. By creating a secondary market for mortgages, the federal government further increased the willingness of banks to issue mortgages because the bank could now get out of the commitment if and when it saw a more profitable use for its funds. In other words, the operations of FNMA removed much of the "opportunity cost" risks of mortgage lending.[26] After World

War II the Veterans Administration further encouraged home buying by insuring veterans' mortgages that carried little or no down payment.

Congressional intent in passing the required legislation was primarily to increase homeownership, something that is generally considered to be a central element of "the American dream." Another goal during the Great Depression was to reduce unemployment by stimulating residential construction. The stimulating effect during the Great Depression was not very large. But the effect on both construction and homeownership in the prosperous years that followed World War II was enormous. So far as is known there was no spatial intent behind Congress's actions. In fact, there is no evidence that members of Congress were aware early on that these actions would have any spatial effect But the effect of making home-ownership more accessible was to promote rapid and extensive suburbanization, for the suburbs rather than the cities were where the mass of land available for building single-family houses was located.

Suburbanization and Tax Policy

The federal government has also contributed to suburbanization through tax policy. If you own a house, you can deduct from your taxable income both interest on the mortgage and property taxes on the house and the lot. If one rents a house or an apartment, one implicity pays mortgage interest and property taxes because the landlord must cover these taxes through the rent. However, you cannot deduct these expenses from your taxable income. This favorable treatment of the owner vis-à-vis the renter creates a powerful push toward homeownership.[27] A few years ago when marginal tax brackets extended up 70 percent, the push was almost irresistible for the very wealthy, for it meant that at that margin the federal government was reimbursing the homeowner for 70 cents of every dollar that he or she paid in mortgage interest and property taxes.

There is no explicit spatial dimension to this favorable tax treatment, nor was any spatial effect ever intended. One can take advantage of the tax treatment just as well by buying an apartment in a high-rise condominium or cooperative in midtown Manhattan as one can in the suburbs or in rural America. But because in most metropolitan areas most of the land available for new construction is in the suburbs and exurbs, the net effect is deurbanizing.

One should not underestimate the force of this favorable tax treatment acting year after year. For 2006 the Office of Management and the Budget (OMB) estimates the federal revenue loss (tax expenditure) for the deductibility of interest paid on home mortgages at $76 billion. They estimate the deduction for the deductibility of property taxes on owner-occupied housing as being worth an additional $14.8 billion. Even that is not the end of the story. Since the Taxpayer Relief Act of 1997 a couple selling their house can exempt up to $500,000 of capital gain (basically, what they sell the house for minus what they paid for it) from federal taxation. For 2006 that tax expenditure was estimated at $36.3 billion.[28] The three tax expenditures, adding to a total of $121 billion, have a huge effect on people's decisions about whether to buy or rent and how much housing to buy. To the extent that the tax deductions increase the demand for owner-occupied housing they also have a substantial effect on the price of housing.

But Is It Planning?

The question is whether one should refer to the federal government's actions just described as "planning." In the matter of restructuring mortgage lending, there was, in a loose sense, a plan. The goal of the plan was to promote home-ownership. In this regard the federal government was highly successful.

The issue is less clear with regard to tax treatment. Provisions exempting interest and local taxes have been part of the IRS code since its inception. The Tax Reform Act of 1986 took away the exemption on most other local taxes and most other types of interest payments (for example, interest on credit card debt or on a car loan is not tax exempt). But Congress left the homeowner treatment untouched. One reason was that trying to eliminate it or scale it back would have provoked a political firestorm, for about two-thirds of all occupied housing units in the United States are owner occupied. Whether or not there was also widespread feeling in Congress that homeownership was an important national goal to be pursued through continued favorable tax treatment is harder to discern.

LAND MANAGEMENT

The federal government is involved in land management on a grand scale. As of 1989 the federal government owned 662,158,000 acres, about 1.035 million square miles of the United States, most of it west of the Mississippi.[29] The Bureau of Land Management (BLM) manages hundreds of millions of acres. Much of the land that it manages is low-value land for reasons of low rainfall, poor access, or the like. Its role is, therefore, more one of stewardship than of planning for development.

In the United States, 231 million acres (about 361,000 square miles) are designated as National Forest, of which almost 83 percent is actually owned by the federal government. Again, the role of the federal government is largely one of stewardship. Shaping the pattern of settlement in the nation is not a primary intent. Nonetheless, decisions about how much development to permit in national forests and about where to permit the cutting of timber have economic consequences that exert some influence on the pattern of settlement. And, of course, in the long term, decisions by the

Bureau of Land Management and the Forest Service about how hundreds of millions of acres are to be used cannot help but have an effect on the environmental quality of vast areas. The National Park system, often considered to have begun with the setting aside of Yellowstone National Park in 1872 now covers, an area of about 119,000 square miles.

For many years this system of land management has seemed a fixed feature of the American scene. In recent years, however, particularly since the Republican party took control of both houses of Congress in the 1994 elections, there has been pressure on the federal government to divest itself of some of its landholdings and turn these back to the states. This can be regarded as another part of the "sagebrush rebellion" noted in Chapter 15. So far the pressure has been greatest to change the ownership of lands managed by the Bureau of Land Management. There has been somewhat less pressure regarding lands managed by the National Forest Service and much less regarding lands managed by the National Parks Service. The pressure comes largely from grazing, mining, and lumber interests, and takes a variety of forms.

In the Senate, Craig Thomas of Wyoming introduced legislation that would turn back approximately one-half of the federal government's million or so square miles to the states. Litigation brought by a number of western counties has sought to force the turnover of some federal lands to the states on the grounds that federal lands acquired in the nineteenth century were meant for only temporary federal holding, not permanent ownership. One precedent cited is the acquisition of land under the Northwest Ordinance of 1785, noted earlier in this chapter, and its subsequent release to private parties.

The federal position is that the legality of federal ownership has been upheld before by the courts and is beyond doubt. Federal land management agencies and many environmentalists argue that land is being held in stewardship for future generations and it is important that this stewardship continue. Many environmentalists fear that if land is turned over to the states, transfers from state hands to private hands will follow, partly as a result of local political pressures and partly because sales of land will ease pressures on state budgets. Commercial considerations will then, they fear, take precedence over the interests of future generations. But arguments can be made on both sides of the issue. Against the federal stewardship position, it can be argued that the states, being closer to the situation, may do a better job of land management. It can also be argued that if some land, for example grazing or timberland, comes into private ownership, the owners will have a powerful financial interest in its long-term management and thus will do a better job than, say, the Bureau of Land Management. On purely legal grounds the consensus is that the federal government's position is not likely to be shaken. If change occurs, it will happen because sufficient political force has developed to cause the Congress to change the laws.

SUMMARY

The United States has never had a national plan nor, since the termination of the National Resources Planning Board in 1943, a national planning agency. However, the federal government has, through a variety of programs and policies over the last two centuries, played a major role in shaping the pattern of settlement in the United States. In general, the federal style has been to provide guidelines and funding and to let the states, localities, and private parties fill in the details. The federal actions and legislation discussed in this chapter included the Northwest Ordinance of 1785, the Homestead Act, the Morrill Land Grant Act, land grants to railroads, the work of the Bureau of Reclamation, the Tennessee Valley Authority, the building of the interstate highway system, and federal mortgage insurance and the tax treatment of owner-occupied housing. It was also noted briefly that today the federal government owns and manages somewhat over 1 million square miles of the United States, primarily west of the Mississippi River.

NOTES

1. The 100th meridian passes through North Dakota about one-third of the way west from the eastern border of the state, passes through South Dakota, Nebraska, Kansas, Oklahoma, and then forms the eastern edge of the Texas panhandle. The exceptions to this generalization about rainfall are the northwest coastal region about as far south as San Francisco and a few scattered areas in the northwest quarter of the region.
2. In some western states where the dry climate made it impossible for 160 acres to support a farm family, larger homesteads were permitted.
3. Richard Hofstadter, William Miller, and Daniel Aaron, *The American Republic*, 2nd ed., vol. 1, Prentice Hall, Inc., Englewood Cliffs, NJ, 1970, p. 545.
4. The fact that several of the pieces of legislation mentioned in the chapter were passed in 1862 is not a coincidence. Both the opening up of western lands for settlement and the choice of transcontinental rail routes had important implications for the balance of power between free and slave states. Thus prior to the Civil War, congressional agreement had not been possible. But with southern representatives out of the Congress in 1862, agreement was easily reached.
5. Dexter Perkins and Glyndon G. Van Deusen, *The United States of America: A History*,

2nd ed., The Macmillan Co., New York, 1968, p. 73. The interested reader can look up further details under the heading "Credit Mobilier" in numerous U.S. history texts.
6. Ibid., p. 73.
7. Hofstadter, Miller, and Aaron, *American Republic*, p. 683.
8. Perkins and Van Deusen, *History*, p. 69.
9. Marc Reisner, *Cadillac Desert: The American West and Its Disappearing Water*, Viking, New York, 1986, p. 111.
10. On a long-term loan the sum of the interest payments can be significantly greater than the principal. Thus interest forgiveness of these loans represented a very substantial subsidy. In point of fact the actual subsidy was even greater than that would suggest because the bureau would not (or politically could not) force the farmer who became delinquent off his or her land. For a brief account of the early years of the Bureau of Reclamation, see Kenneth D. Frederick, "Water Resources: Increasing Demand and Scarce Supply," in Kenneth D. Frederick and Roger A. Sedjo, eds., *America's Renewable Resources: Historical Trends and Current Challenges*, Resources for the Future, Washington, DC, 1991. For a more detailed presentation, see Richard W. Wahi, *Markets for Federal Water*, Resources for the Future, Washington, DC, 1989.

11. Reisner, *Cadillac Desert*, p. 127.
12. *Major Dams, Reservoirs, and Hydroelectric Plants, Worldwide and Bureau of Reclamation*, release by U.S. Department of the Interior, Bureau of Reclamation, Denver, CO, undated.
13. Frederick, "Water Resources," p. 49.
14. For a detailed account of the events leading to the passage of the act, see Martin Reuss, *Reshaping National Water Politics: The Emergence of the Water Resources Development Act*, IWR Policy Study 91-PS-1, U.S. Army Corps of Engineers, 1991.
15. In the East the law has generally relied on riparian rights, a concept derived from English Common Law, that assigns right on the basis of immediate proximity to the water source. This worked reasonably well in the East but was not practical in the water-short West.
16. Robert Reinhold, "New Age for Western Water Policy: Less for the Farm, More for the City," *New York Times*, October 11, 1992, sect. 1, p. 18.
17. *Statistical Abstract of the United States*, 112th edition, U.S. Department of Commerce, Economics and Statistics Administration, Bureau of the Census, Washington, DC, 1992, Table 1096. Texas ranked second, also largely on the strength of irrigated land. In the case of Texas, however, irrigation waters largely come from wells in the great Ogallala aquifer. Unlike surface waters that are renewable, "mining" the Ogallala is a one-time event, for the aquifer's recharge rate is only-time event, for the aquifer's recharge rate is only a minuscule fraction of the rate of current withdrawals.
18. The centroid is a calculated point "at which an imaginary flat, weightless and rigid map of the United States would balance if weights of identical value were placed on it so that each weight represented the location

of one person on the date of the census." In 1990 the centroid was located a few miles southwest of St. Louis. See Ibid., Table 3.
19. Frederick, "Water Resources," p. 37.
20. For an account of the legislative history, see Marguerite Owen, *The Tennessee Valley Authority*, Praeger, New York, 1973.
21. Ibid., p. 235.
22. There is no interstate mileage in Alaska.
23. This account is drawn from *America's Highways 1776/1976: A History of the Federal Aid Program*, U.S. Department of Transportation, Federal Highway Administration, Washington, DC, undated.
24. For a detailed account of the politics of the interstate highway system, see Mark H. Rose, *Interstate Express Highway Politics*, revised edition, University of Tennessee Press, Knoxville, 1990.
25. Carter M. McFarland, *The Federal Government and Urban Problems*, Westview, Boulder, CO, 1978, p. 117.
26. For further details see an urban economics text such as James Heilbrun, *Urban Economics and Public Policy*, 3rd ed., St. Martin's Press, New York, 1987; Mc-Farland, *Federal Government*: Henry Aaron, *Shelter and Subsidies*, The Brookings Institution, Washington, DC, 1972; or a text on real estate finance such as William Brueggeman and Leo D. Stone, *Real Estate Investment*, 8th ed., Richard D. Irwin, Homewood, IL, 1989.
27. It has been suggested many times that balance could be achieved by extending the same favorable tax treatment to renters, but Congress has never shown much interest in the idea, nor has the idea ever gathered much grassroots support.
28. *Statistical Abstract of the United States*, 2006 Table 469.
29. *Statistical Abstract of the United States*, 1996, Table 343.

SELECTED BIBLIOGRAPHY

FREDERICK, KENNETH D., and SEDJO, ROGER A., EDS., *America's Renewable Resources*, Resources for the Future, Washington, DC, 1991.

OWEN, MARGUERITE, *The Tennessee Valley Authority*, Praeger, New York, 1973.

ROSE, MARK H., *Interstate Express Highway Politics*, revised edition, University of Tennessee Press, Knoxville, 1990.

WAHL, RICHARD W., *Markets for Federal Water: Subsidies, Property Rights, and the Bureau of Reclamation*, Resources for the Future, Washington, DC, 1989.

NOTE: Detailed information about the work of federal agencies such as the Bureau of Reclamation, the Department of Transportation, or the Army Corps of Engineers can be obtained by writing or calling them directly. A number of federal agencies employ a department historian, an especially good source for the student or scholar.

CHAPTER 18

Planning in Other Nations

With coauthors Sonia Hirt and Johann Jessen[*]

In this chapter we look briefly at planning in other nations. Much of the chapter will focus on Europe, not because of a desire to be "eurocentric" but because planning practice in the United States and Europe have many common elements and have exerted considerable influence on each other. Thus European experience can be an enlightening reflection on planning in the United States. We look first at several Western European cases and then briefly at the present situation in Eastern Europe. The chapter concludes with a section on planning in the Third World. It is clearly not possible to present a systematic review of planning practice around the world in a single chapter. This chapter is just a sampling.

PLANNING IN WESTERN EUROPE

Before we look at particulars, let us note a few background differences between the United States and the Western European planning scenes. These differences are generalizations, and not all apply to every country.

1. To understand the history of European planning in the second half of the twentieth century, one must take into account the effects of World War II. In many nations there was enormous destruction of urban areas. Thus in the early postwar period, there was a big emphasis on

---

[*]The section on Eastern Europe was written by Professor Sonia Hirt of Virginia Polytechnic Institute and State University and the section on Germany by Professor Johann Jessen of the University of Stuttgart.

reconstruction and on rebuilding the housing stock destroyed in the war, particularly in inner-city areas.

2. In the last two decades or so of the twentieth century, the planning scene in Europe was affected by another continent-wide force, this time a peaceful one. This was the coming of European unification. The European Community (EC) is increasingly becoming a single nation economically, a process that was completed with the acceptance of a common European currency, the Euro, on January 1, 2002. (Item 1 and 2 are related, for it was the experience of two world wars beginning only a quarter-century apart that provided much of the push for European union.)

3. Socialism was a major political force in many European nations at various times in the second half of the twentieth century, whereas the United States has never had a powerful socialist movement. That ideological difference carries with it a different set of ideas about what are the proper prerogatives and obligations of government. Another way to make this point is to note differences in the share of gross national product (GNP) spent by the public sector.[1] In the United States that percentage is in the low- to mid-30s. For most of the states of Western Europe, it is up in the 40s or 50s, and for at least one country, Sweden, it is in the low 60s. That larger role for the government in the general life of the nation usually also includes a larger role for planning in particular.

4. Most European nations have higher population densities than has the United States. The "lower 48" states have an average population density of about 100 persons per square mile. Great Britain and Germany have over 600 people per square mile, the Netherlands almost 1,200, France about 280, and Switzerland about 470. Thus in many European nations, there is more of an emphasis on concentrating development and on using land more efficiently simply because there is less land per capita.

5. Most, if not all, European nations take a less expansive view of the rights of property owners than do we in America. Thus a degree of control over the use of private property that would not be tolerated politically or legally in the United States is tolerated in Europe. Recall the safeguards for property rights imbedded in the U.S. Constitution (see Chapter 5). The greater degree of control that government can exercise over the use of private property in Europe clearly strengthens the hand of the planner.

6. In the United States only a very small part of the housing stock is publicly built and owned (see Chapter 3). By contrast, in many of the nations of Western Europe, a very substantial share of all housing is publicly built and owned. (Generally it is referred to as "social housing.") This ownership gives government a powerful role in shaping the man-made environment.

7. In a number of Western European nations, particularly in Scandinavia, large amounts of urban land are publicly owned, thereby giving the municipality absolute control over when and how that land is developed.

8. In many Western European nations large numbers of middle- and upper-class individuals seem content to live in apartments rather than experiencing the American dream of the single-family house on a large lot. In general, the middle and upper classes also seem to show a much stronger preference for urban and central city residence than do people in the United States. Then, too, European tax systems are not structured so as to favor homeownership as is the case in the United States (see Chapter 17).

9. In Europe there is generally more reliance on administrative decision and less reliance on the courts to adjudicate planning disputes than is the case in the United States. Thus municipal governments in Europe are less inhibited by fears that their actions in regard to regulating the use of privately owned land will be reversed by the courts.

10. In most European nations, with the exception of Germany, Austria, and Switzerland, political power is much more centralized than in the U.S. federal system. Recall that the U.S. Constitution reserves a great deal of power to the states (some of which the states delegate to substate units of government). Then, too, the U.S. Constitution establishes the system of checks and balances so that one of the three branches of government can block the actions of another branch (see Chapter 5). The higher degree of political centralization in Europe allows national governments to require that local plans be in conformance with the national plan.

11. Finally, there is the matter of physical size. The greater land area of the United States makes the development of a national plan more difficult than would be the case in a smaller country.

Planning in Great Britain

One might think that given many similarities in culture and in law (much of American law is derived from English common law), planning in the United States and Great Britain might be done in a similar manner. But this is not the case. Much of the difference stems from differences between the two nations' political structures and political cultures. In Britain the national government is much more powerful relative to subnational governments than is the case in the United States. For one point, Britain does not have a written constitution. Parliament thus can act with much more freedom than can the U.S. Congress. During the prime ministership of Margaret Thatcher, Parliament simply abolished a number of municipal governments, including that of Greater London, and placed oversight of the affairs of these municipalities directly in its own hands.

Two other features of the British system should also be noted. In general, citizen participation and media coverage of the actions of local government are much more limited than in the United States.

> The British elect their politicians and then expect them to get on with the job: that is what they have been elected to do.[2]

That is a very different approach from the American tendency to elect the politicians, suspect that they are rascals, and watch them like a hawk.

Another feature of the British system is that questions that in the United States would be settled in court are settled administratively. A property owner who is displeased with a decision of a council (a unit of local government) may appeal it to the national level, but he or she does not take it to court. Since the passage of the Town and Country Planning Act in 1947, there has been no zoning in Great Britain. Even a project that conforms in every detail to the land-use plan of the council must have specific council approval before construction can begin. A builder cannot "build by right" as in the United States (see Chapter 9).

Planning in Great Britain Since World War II. In the 1930s, Great Britain, like much of the western world, suffered from the high unemployment rates of the Great Depression. The problem had a strong geographic dimension. The London metropolitan area suffered moderately, but many of the more peripheral parts of the nation experienced real economic disaster. This was particularly so where the economic base was heavily dependent on manufacturing, ship building, or mining. Thus British officials and planners in the late 1930s saw much of the national planning problem as limiting the growth of the London metropolitan area and diverting economic growth to other parts of the nation.

Little could be done to effectuate this vision during World War II (1939–1945), but even in the early stages of the war, when it was far from certain who would win, planning continued. The strategy that emerged was embodied in a series of laws passed by Parliament in the decade after the end of the war. The main thrust of the plan that emerged in the early postwar period was to

1. Limit the growth of London and a few other major cities.
2. Preserve as much as possible of Britain's remaining farmland and countryside from development.
3. Strengthen the economy and prevent population decline in lagging outlying areas.

To effectuate these goals, the national plan had three main elements:

1. A system of greenbelts surrounding London and other major cities.[3]
2. The creation of new towns
3. The use of subsidies and regulations to divert economic growth from London to lagging areas of the nation[4]

The last element, the use of subsidies and regulations to divert growth, was never very successful. For many years the policy was applied just to manufacturing, but in the postwar period, manufacturing was shrinking as a share of total employment. Even when the policy was extended beyond manufacturing, many businesses that wished to locate or expand in the London area found ways around the regulations. But elements 1 and 2 were carried out vigorously and have changed the face of Britain.

The concept of the greenbelt was enunciated in the Town and Country Planning Act of 1947 and remains policy up to this time. The greenbelts are the most striking manifestation of British planning. The American planner making an automobile trip from, say, the City of Oxford to the City of London, located about 40 miles to the east, encounters a very "un-American" sort of landscape. Oxford (population about 100,000) is densely developed by American standards, yet the instant a traveler leaves the city, he or she is in the countryside. There is no transitional suburban or exurban zone. The motorway into London passes through countryside. There are fields, woods, and an occasional house or hamlet in the distance. At the London end of the trip, the transition back from countryside to city is equally abrupt. One moment the traveler is passing through fields and pastures, and the next moment the traveler is in a dense urban environment.

Clearly, the spreading and scattered development that would have been produced by the natural working of market forces has been blocked. How was this done? The Town and Country Planning Act simply froze development in the green-belt areas. The development that already existed was permitted to remain, but new development was simply forbidden. A limited amount of compensation was paid to some landowners for losing the development potential of their land. Basically, though, the government had "nationalized development rights." Parliament had, in effect, ruled that the property owner does not have the automatic right to profit from increases in land value nor the right to be compensated should the government prevent him or her from developing the land in the most profitable use. Though the political pendulum has swung back and forth from left to right in the intervening six decades, the basic greenbelt plan has held.

One might ask what happened to all the population and housing growth that would otherwise have gone into the areas designated as green-belts. Part was absorbed in existing urban centers. In fact, in recent years British planners have spoken of "town cramming." As demand for housing and business locations in already urbanized places increases and property values rise, there is an understandable tendency for denser development to occur in town and for every available parcel of land to be used. The trade-off is inevitable. The more congested town and the unspoiled expanse of the greenbelt are the flip sides of the same coin.

Another portion of the population growth deflected by the greenbelts was housed in new towns. Between the end of the war and 1980, over 30 new towns were begun in Great Britain. The first wave, started in the 1946 to 1951 period, included both towns located around London and towns located in lagging areas of the nation. In the period after 1960, additional ones were begun in order to relieve population pressures around other urban areas. By 1990, according to Peter Hall, new towns that were begun since the end of World War II contained about 700,000 housing units and a population of about 2 million.[5] Though new towns absorbed some of the population growth that might have gone into the greenbelt and led to an increase in long-distance commuting, a result that was not part of the plan.

The British system of strong central government and relatively weak local governments facilitated the building of new towns. The process was set in motion by Parliament in 1946 by the passage of the New Towns Act. The building of a new town was the responsibility of a group of directors appointed by a national official, the Minister of Town and Country Planning. The committee, in turn, hired staff to do the planning and administrative work. The commission had broad powers to acquire land either by purchase or by condemnation, and to construct housing, commercial and public build-ings, and the infrastructure such as roads and sanitary facilities necessary to support the town.[6] The law called for consultation with local councils (governments), but the real power was in the hands of the directors appointed by the national government, and the wishes of local governments could be overruled. The money to support these expenditures came from long-term bonds issued by the national government, subsidized in part by some deferred payment arrangements. The reader might compare this process with the building of planned communities in the United States as described in Chapter 7. In the United States, the planned community, whether it is small or covers thousands of acres as in the cases of Reston, Virginia (see Chapter 10), or Columbia, Maryland, occurs on land owned by the developer and is done as a profit-making venture. The capital involved is entirely or almost entirely private. The community is built pursuant to the permission of local government. If the necessary rezonings and other adjust-ments in land controls are not granted, then the project cannot be done. The land involved is acquired through voluntary sale by private landowners. In some cases, like that of Columbia, Maryland, built by the Rouse Corporation, land was purchased very discreetly through a variety of dummy organiza-tions, for if Rouse's intentions had been known, land prices would have risen sharply, making the project impossible.

The building of the new towns was influenced in many ways by the ideas of the turn-of-the-century planner Ebenezer Howard (see Chapter 3). Howard argued that land values were created by public investment and should be captured by the public, not by individual property owners.[7] In the new towns much of the land and many of the structures were owned by the commission that built the town, and so as land and property values increased, the commission could capture that increase either as rents or, from time to time, sales of property. The monies realized from increases in property value were, in turn, used to pay off the bonds that underwrote the development of the new town.

The physical planning of the town also reflected Howard's thinking. The original town plans generally aimed for populations in the 30,000 to 60,000 range, which was similar in size to what Howard had suggested. (Some new towns, like Milton Keynes, which is about an hour's train ride north of London, have been much larger.) He favored a population size large enough to sustain a significant amount of economic activity so that the town would be more than just a bedroom community. On the other hand, he favored a small enough size so that places of business could be reasonably close to people's homes and so that an ample amount of the natural world would survive within the town. He also favored a ring road (a rail line in the original conception) that took traffic out of the town and also connected the town to the central city and the rest of the metropolitan region. Finally, the original Howard vision called for the location of some industrial activity outside the ring road to keep it from impinging on residential areas. All these design elements showed up in many new town plans.

Though greenbelts and new towns are the most distinctive features of post–World War II British planning, there were other important elements as well. Like all other nations with advanced economies, the British had to confront the postwar explosion in automobile ownership. Thus an important part of British planning in the last several decades has been a system of high-speed limited access motorways similar in overall design to the U.S. interstate system. One of the persistent British planning problems is traffic congestion. The high rate of automobile ownership coupled with high population density make that problem inevitable.

In the years immediately following the end of World War II, much subsidized housing was built in central areas, and as part of that process, there was also a great deal of slum clearance. New housing was needed both to replace housing destroyed by bombing during the war and to make up for the slow rate of construction during the Great Depression and war years. Clearance was needed to replace much very-low-quality housing that had survived the war. Urban housing conditions in Britain had been worse than on much of the continent for a simple historic reason. The Industrial Revolution began in Great Britain, and so the process of rapid urban growth got started there much sooner than in other nations.

Milton Keynes, located about 60 miles north of London, is one of the new towns built in Great Britain after World War II. The commercial center is located proximate to the train station. Most housing is in small hamlets separated by open space. The town has a dual circulation system with roads for automobiles and an extensive parallel system of bicycle and footpaths. Above, a view of the commercial area seen from across a roundabout (rotary) at the intersection of two bicycle paths. Note the underpass for these paths under the automobile road at upper left. Below, a view of one of the hamlets from the path. Automobile access is from the other side of the hamlet.

For example, the coming of rapid industrialization in Germany trailed that of Great Britain by more than half a century, and in Scandinavia the process lagged by approximately a century.[8] Thus Great Britain had masses of densely developed, low-standard urban housing dating from early in the nineteenth century. As measured by physical indexes like overcrowding and poor plumbing facilities, considerable improvement in housing quality was achieved by this combination of building and clearance.

British Planning Since the 1970s. A great deal had been accomplished by the 1970s. But new needs were becoming apparent, and some dissatisfactions with the results of the early post–World War II planning were being voiced. Then, too, Great Britain was changing politically. There was considerable dissatisfaction with the British welfare state, what some have termed the "nanny state," and there was also a feeling that the British economy would perform better if more were left to the market and less to the state. In short, Britain was moving to the right politically. And, as noted previously, planning and political ideology can never be entirely separated. In 1979 the Conservatives, led by Margaret Thatcher, assumed power. Thatcher herself enjoyed the longest period in office of any British prime minister in a century and was then succeeded by the less colorful but quite conservative John Major. The Conservatives did not relinquish power until 1997 with the election of a Labor prime minister, Tony Blair, 1997–2007. By that time the British political center of gravity had moved far enough to the right that on most domestic policy issues, the Blair government looked remarkably like the Conservative government of a few years earlier.

But even before Thatcher took office, the planning agenda began to shift. It had become apparent that none of the accomplishments previously noted did much for the problems of depressed inner-city areas. In fact, it could easily be argued that the building of new towns and new housing developments (called "housing estates" in Great Britain) in peripheral areas actually increased blight in inner cities. This situation is analagous to that in the United States in which post–World War II suburbanization in the United States sucked income and jobs out of the inner cities, leaving behind a stranded underclass that was not capable of participating in the general prosperity of the nation. Then, too, there was the issue of national economic competitiveness. Britain was growing economically at a slower rate than a number of nations on the continent and elsewhere, a fact that many attributed to the effects of regulation and heavy taxation.[9]

The Thatcher government essentially stopped making grand national plans. To use the terminology that will be introduced in Chapter 19, there was a shift from a *comprehensive* to an *incremental* planning philosophy. The British government began to focus on deteriorated urban areas and to try to involve private capital as much as possible. One Thatcher initiative was the Enterprise Zone, a concept developed by the British planner Peter Hall, cited earlier in this chapter. A depressed part of a city would be designated as an Enterprise Zone, and within that part, builders and firms would be eligible for a variety of tax breaks and would be free from many ordinary planning restrictions. Note that this idea then crossed the Atlantic and appeared in the United States in the form of Enterprise Zones in a number of states and at the federal level in the Clinton administration's Empowerment Zones (see Chapter 13).

Another closely related Thatcher administration initiative was the Urban Development Corporation (UDC). These organizations were designated and funded by the national government. In their designated areas they had the power to take property and to override the plans of local government. Their boards of directors were heavily weighted toward business people to give them a probusiness focus. The goal of the UDC was to make the area attractive to private investment by establishing the preconditions for development, such as providing cleared sites and infrastructure improvements. The parallel with the U.S. urban policy, and particularly with Urban Renewal, is very strong.

The most visible single result of the Enterprise Zone and UDC approach is the Canary Wharf development on the Isle of Dogs, a part of the London Dock-lands area. Within the Isle of Dogs Enterprise Zone, an enormous amount of capital, most of it private, has been invested to produce a massive office and retail development. The path was not a smooth one. In fact, the Canadian development firm, Olympia and York, which did a great deal of the actual construction, went bankrupt during the building.[10] Nonetheless, Canary Wharf is a very impressive development. At least for a time, it was the largest office development in Europe, with work spaces for about 45,000 people.[11]

In brief, planning in Great Britain moved in the direction of what is often termed "property led" development, meaning that the pattern of development was largely shaped by the competition for private capital investment in property. When government seeks private capital investment and development depends on private investment, compromise becomes necessary, and some of the decision-making power necessarily shifts from public to private hands. As discussed subsequently, the trend toward "property led" development made itself felt at about the same time in a number of nations on the continent. The cause was basically the same—strain on the public purse and the desire to be economically competitive. In its emphasis on private investment and in the competition between places for private investment, the British planning scene became more similar to the American scene.

The Thatcher government also introduced a variety of American-style programs designed to foster competition and to integrate construction programs with programs designed to attack underlying social and economic problems. Among these were some grants for which cities had to compete and some investment in manpower training programs to increase the employability of the residents of poorer areas. Again, the parallel with U.S. policy is very strong.[12]

Planning policy in Great Britain did not change substantially under the subsequent Labor government of Tony Blair succeeded by Gordon Brown, also Labor, in June 2007). Though it is a Labor government, we note that the

Labor party of the present is a far more conservative organization than it was, say, three decades earlier.

Planning in France

A number of European nations have seen planning as a way to address regional imbalances. One such nation is France. Since the nineteenth century, the Paris region has grown more vigorously than the rest of the nation and it contains disproportionate amounts of the nation's higher educational establishments, cultural resources, and administrative activities. It even contained a disproportionate share of the nation's total manufacturing employment. In many periods the Paris region accounted for a large share of the nation's total population growth. Shortly after World War II, a French geographer, Jean Français Gravier, wrote the very influential *Paris et le désert Français* (Paris and the French Desert). His main point was that the disproportionate growth of the Paris region left the rest of the nation impoverished and that something ought to be done about it.[13]

In response to this problem of Parisian dominance, the French government identified eight growth poles.[14] The actual term is *métropole d'équilibre*, denoting the idea that these regions will balance the economic and demographic mass of the Paris region, the *Ile de France*. Each of these poles consisted of a city or of two or three closely located cities.

These cities form a ring several hundreds of miles in diameter. The eastern part of the ring lies close to the French-German border, and the western part extends to France's Atlantic coast. The northern part extends to the English Channel, and the southern part to the Mediterranean, France's *Côte d' Azur*. For the last five decades it has been national policy to strengthen these poles relative to the Paris region.

> Since the late 1960s, successive French governments have systematically sought to divert public investment into these poles, thus strengthening their economic potential and acting in turn as a device to attract private capital.[15]

Specifically, Peter Hall notes that investment in higher education facilities, in the nation's limited access highway system, and in its high-speed passenger rail system has all been used to favor the growth of these regional centers.[16]

In addition to strengthening other regions relative to the Paris region, French planners also sought to divert growth from the city itself into other parts of the Paris region. Thus public funds were invested in building satellite towns and peripheral development areas. The plan was supported by the building of a regional rail system, the RER, and a circumferential highway.

The sort of national approach to planning just described, in which the planning authorities consciously make national economic and demographic (in the sense of where people will live) policy is feasible only in a

The new new town of Créteil. Built at the end of one line of the Paris Metro, it is within easy commuting range of the center of the city. Above, the town center. Below, mixed residential and commercial development along the shore of an artificial lake.

very centralized state. Historically the French central government was very strong, and local governments, though very numerous, were very weak. In fact, many local administrators, called *préfets*, were appointed by the central government. Planning was a top-down process with the national government laying out the big picture and the local governments filling in the details, pursuant to approval by the national government. In the early 1980s there was major political reorganization in France, and some political power was decentralized.[17] For example, appointed *préfets* were replaced by elected officials. But compared with that of the United States, the French system is still highly centralized. The United States has had no national planning body since the abolition of the NRPB in 1943 (see Chapter 4).

Not only is planning much more centralized and the power of government to control land use much greater than in the United States, but also the government exercises power over development in another way. A great deal of urban development is done by development organizations of mixed private and public ownership, the *Société d'Économie Mixte* (SEM). Thus there is not the separation between development interests on the one hand and government on the other hand.

> Normally the public partner has a majority shareholding in the company. Thus political control is retained [by government] while the company structure allows for greater operational flexibility, free from the bureaucratic rules of town hall. The SEM may be set up by the commune [local government] or by a private party.[18]

The arrangement is very consistent with the French vision of the proper relationship between state and private sector—a mixed system in which the relationship between government and capital is a cooperative one. In the decades after World War II, the French national planning style was termed "indicative planning" in which government and industry jointly set goals and policies.

At the local level, urban planning in France, as in many other nations of Western Europe, often has a somewhat different emphasis than in the United States. There is often more emphasis on the fine texture of the urban fabric—on historic preservation, on the details of urban design, and on pedestrian-friendly environments. There is often more emphasis on spaces that promote interaction between people. Where the design choice must favor either the pedestrian or the automobile, there is more of a tendency to favor the former than is usually the case in the United States.

In recent years observers of the French, like those of the British, have seen an increase in "property led development." In France several factors have contributed to this increase. The decentralization of political power in the early 1980s made local governments become more important decision makers in the development game. At the same time, there were cutbacks in the flow of revenues from the national to the local governments. The response

Two views of La Defense, a major public/private office development about 4 kilometer from the center of Paris. La Grande Arche (top), built to commemorate the two-hundredth anniversary of the French Revolution (1789) is intended to be a twentieth-century version of the Arc de Triomphe. It is a cube 106 meters (347 feet) on edge. The sides contain offices whose windows face the interior of the cube.

The historic district of Annecy, France. Above, the canal, once used for transportation of freight, is preserved as a scenic attraction. Below, preservation of old buildings and protection from vehicular traffic help to keep street life lively in this commercial area.

of local governments was to begin competing for commercial investment. The analogy with the American situation (see Chapter 13 on economic development planning) is quite strong.

Planning in the Netherlands

Another European nation with a strongly centralized planning system and a commitment to national-level planning is the Netherlands. The Netherlands' population density is about 13 times that of the "lower 48." The nation's land form has been substantially changed by a long-time policy of reclaiming land from the North Sea. Thus some of the nation's population lives on land that lies a few feet below sea level and is protected from the sea by dikes. It is no surprise that the Dutch take a different attitude toward planning than do Americans. When it comes to the use of land, the Dutch have learned to cooperate with each other. They have no alternative. Then, too, with a land area only a little larger than that of Connecticut and no major physical barrier that divides the nation, planning the entire nation on the basis of a unified vision is much easier. Peter Newman and Andy Thornley note that the Netherlands has been called the "most planned" nation in Europe. The American planner traveling in the Netherlands is very likely to feel that this description is true.

As in many other parts of Europe, there is a very sharp separation between town and country. Urban development and farmers' fields meet abruptly with no intervening suburban development. The first impression one gets of the Dutch landscape is of great order, of a landscape in which very little space has been wasted, and in which every acre is earmarked for some purpose. The nation's largest city, Amsterdam, is densely developed but also orderly and charming. It is very modern and very functional, yet a great deal of the old survives. The core of the city is not big; there is essentially no vacant land left, and the city is a major magnet for businesses and for tourism, as well as for permanent residential use. It is clear that if the land and property market were allowed to work without interference, the effects of extremely high land values would quickly transform the core of the city. Buildings of five or six stories, the typical height, would quickly be torn down and replaced with much taller structures. The street system would soon be overwhelmed, for it has an essentially preautomobile-era layout. In very little time the charm and the delightful pedestrian character of the city would be gone. Part of the city's charm comes from a well-preserved system of concentric canals that once performed a central transportation function but are now primarily scenic and recreational. The canals, too, would not survive if land uses were determined purely by the market. Planning controls are obviously very strict and effective.

A section of a canal about a mile from downtown Amsterdam.

The Dutch planning system is a top-down one. The national government produces both the laws that govern planning and, periodically, a national plan. Provincial governments, the middle layer in a three-tier system, interpret the national plan and prepare directives and the like for local governments. Local government plans must be in conformity with the national plan. At the local level there is a *struktuurplan* that lays out the overall picture. The U.S. counterpart would be the master plan. To implement that, there is a detailed plan *(bestentminsplan)* that specifies the expected and acceptable use of every parcel. The U.S. counterpart would be the zoning ordinance and map.[19] The system as described here may sound a bit more rigid and autocratic than it is. In actuality there is a great deal of communication up and down, and there is opportunity for the public to comment on plans. But when the period for comments and adjustments is over, the plans are binding. Some years ago the writer attended a presentation by a Dutch planner to a group of American planning professors. When the planner had finished explaining the system described here, one of the Americans asked, in effect, "but does it really happen that way?" The Dutch planner answered that indeed it did, and he seemed puzzled by the question. The Americans understood the question perfectly, for they all knew about the role of politics, the process of litigation and appeal, and our love affair with private property. But they had difficulty in believing the answer.

The most conspicuous example of Dutch planning at the national level is Randstad Holland, the urban heart of Holland. As shown in Figure 18–1, this urbanized area consists of a grouping of six cities around an open core. This arrangement will not happen naturally, for if events are left purely to the market, the central core will fill in because locations inside the core will offer good access to all the cities and thus become very valuable. Rather, the arrangement is made to happen by a large-scale planning and strict controls on land use. The arrangement has several advantages. First, it gives the residents of the Randstad much better access to the natural world than they would have if the same 4.5 or so million people were all contained in a single city. The arrangement also reduces commuting times, for the average trip in a small city will be shorter than the average trip in a large city.[20] There are environmental advantages; for example, the ring of cities will, all other things being equal, have better air quality than would a single city containing the equivalent number of people and economic activity. Peter Hall notes that there is a considerable degree of specialization among the three larger cities of the Randstad. Rotterdam, at the mouth of the Rhine, is a port city, in fact, the largest port in Europe. The Hague is the seat of the Dutch government and also contains some international organizations including the World Court. Amsterdam is a commercial, financial, and cultural center. Much of that specialization is historical accident or is decreed by geography. But some is planned and makes the cities more efficient economically than they would otherwise be. In an economic sense, the group of cities, because they are physically close and linked by a very effective transportation system, constitutes a single economic entity and achieves some of the advantages of large scale that a single metropolis would have.[21] But the group also achieves some environmental and quality-of-life advantages that we normally associate with smaller places.

Planning in Scandinavia

Unlike the case of the Netherlands, planning in Scandinavia has been less a national matter and more a matter for the municipality and the region. One reason for this tendency is that local governments have been stronger relative to the national government than is the case in many European nations.

In Sweden a very high level of municipal and regional control over the pattern of development has been achieved in two ways that render Swedish planning practice very different from American practice. First, municipal governments often own a sizable percentage of the land within their own borders. In fact, the central government encouraged municipal governments to own (land-bank) a ten-year-reserve of developable land.

FIGURE 18–1 The cities in the ring form the Randstad Holland described in the text. The diameter of the Randstad, about 50 miles, is similar to that of the London or New York metropolitan area. The Afsluidijk shown about 70 miles north of the Randstad is a huge dike that forms an enclosed inland sea behind it. To the east of the sea lie polders, flat low-lying agricultural land reclaimed from the sea.

Vallingsby, a new town located in the Stockholm metropolitan area. The town is laid out around a stop on the city's metro, providing its residents easy access to employment in the city's central business district. Above is a pedestrian-oriented shopping area proximate to the metro station. Below, a short walk from the station, is a residential area fronting on a combined pedestrian and bicycle path. Automobile access is on the other side of the buildings.

Skarpnack, another new town in the Stockholm metropolitan area, located about 20 minutes from downtown Stockholm via the metro. Essentially an in-town bedroom community, it is oriented to families with children. A system of interior paths connects groups of apartments located around courtyards. Parking is located in a multilevel structure several blocks away from where the pictures were taken. Most housing is low-rise multifamily. As in Vallingsby, there are no single-family houses.

Legislation permitted municipal governments to take privately owned land for purposes of land-banking.[22] Doing this would be the equivalent of a U.S. municipal government condemning private property not for a specific public use but simply for holding it for unspecified purposes at an unspecified time. It is doubtful that any U.S. court would sustain this action or that many municipal legislatures would appropriate funds for it.

Public ownership of land gives government a very strong grip on the process of development. It controls the timing of development through the release of land for sale or lease. It also provides total control over the way that the land is developed because the developer of the land is bound by whatever contracts are part of the sale or lease agreement.

The second way in which Swedish municipal governments achieved tight control over the pattern of development was through a very extensive role in the production of housing. For many years of the post–World War II period, housing was essentially a nationalized industry in Sweden. The national government provided the financing, and local governments directed the what and the where of residential construction. Though most construction was done by private firms, the firms were, in effect, acting as contractors to local governments.

> The government adopted a strong social housing policy for the whole population and believed that people had the right to a good home regardless of income. In contrast to most other developed countries the Swedish government sought to control the whole housing stock and not just that for low income earners. A massive programme of suburban high rise took place called the Million Homes Programme and large numbers of existing town centers were also redeveloped. An organisational structure was set up to deal with the huge programme. This resulted in wide-ranging controls on residential development which extended far beyond the traditional planning system. The production of housing was steered by the public sector with the aim of removing speculation from land and housing. Central government was responsible for regulation and the supply of resources while municipalities ensured that the building took place.[23]

This approach was very much in accordance with Swedish political ideology in the postwar period. Sometimes this has been referred to as the "social democratic" model and sometimes as a "third way," one that is more socialistic than the capitalist model and more capitalistic than the socialist model.

As noted elsewhere in this book, housing is the largest single land use in most cities. In some cities it is a larger use than all other uses combined. Thus government's tight control over almost the entire housing market easily translates into great influence on the entire pattern of development.

In and around the capital city of Stockholm, the basic plan, which has been carried through and is widely admired, was to deal with growth pressures and the spreading of the city by concentrating further growth in planned communities centered around stops on an underground railroad system. Development was to be concentrated and new towns separated by green areas to be used for recreation and summer housing. In recent years the scheme has been extended somewhat with smaller developments linked by road rather than by rail. But the basic scheme of tight development surrounded by greenbelt has held. The resemblance to Ebenezer Howard's vision is strong. Since the 1980s the Swedish planning system has become a little more free-form for many of the same reasons noted in connection with Great Britain and France. Dissatisfaction with some aspects of the welfare state has caused some rightward movement along the political spectrum. Slowing economic growth has caused fiscal pressures. In short, there has been some turn toward "property led" development. As noted before, where government courts private investment, there must necessarily be negotiation and compromise.

Many elements of the approach just described can be found elsewhere in Scandinavia. For example, in Helsinki, the capital city and by far the largest city in Finland, planners have exercised a fairly tight control over the pattern of development through the mechanism of public land ownership. As of the mid-1990s, about half the land in the city was owned by the city.[24]

Perhaps the best-known Finnish planning accomplishment is the satellite new town of Tapiola, located a few miles outside Helsinki and linked to the city by frequent, high-speed bus service. The town has a linear commercial core with housing and open space on each side. There is some single-family housing but a predominance of multifamily. This arrangement permits a moderately high population density to coexist with a considerable amount of open space within the town. The entire town is automobile accessible, but it is also very pedestrian and bicycle friendly. Distances from residences to the commercial core are short, and there are numerous pedestrian and bicycle paths. The resident of Tapiola can reach downtown Helsinki in half an hour or so by bus, and then at the end of the business day, can return to an environment that offers real closeness to the natural world.

Planning in Germany

Modern urban planning in Germany dates back to the last decades of the nineteenth century, when the first planning laws were enacted and planning agencies were established. The first planning textbook was published in 1879. Regional planning emerged during the early 1920s when the Ruhr Coalfield Settlement Association (Siedlungsverband Ruhrkohlenbezirk, or SVR) was formed to protect the landscape in the Ruhr area, which was almost completely devastated by the rapidly expanding mining and steel industry. The SVR is said to be the world's first regional planning agency, predating the Tennessee Valley Authority (TVA) in the United States by about a decade.

General Features. Germany is a federal state with three levels of government: the federal government (Bund), the states (Länder), and the municipalities (Gemeinden). The constitution, written after World War II, clearly defines the division of power among the three levels. The planning system in Germany is characterized by a "strong legal framework and a decentralized decision making structure."[25] On the central state level, there are only general legal guidelines. The legal framework consists of the Federal Regional Planning Code (Bundesrau-mordnungsgesetz) and the Federal Building Code (Baugesetzbuch), which provide the legal instruments for regional planning on the state level and for urban planning on the local level. This framework is to ensure a certain degree of consistency of planning on the lower levels (Länder and Gemeinden). However, each Land has its own regional planning system. Municipal governments enjoy a high degree of autonomy in planning and have fervently defended this against all demands for centralization of power.

The general aim of planning in Germany is to achieve living conditions of "equal value" all over the country by equalizing the distribution of economic resources. There are both economically strong and weak urban regions. Munich and the Stuttgart region in the south with their modern industries such as automobiles and electronics are very prosperous. By contrast, the Ruhr area with its declining mining and steel industry and the harbor cities like Bremen with their declining shipyard industries suffer from high unemployment and little, if any, economic growth. Since the reunification of Germany in 1990, these south-north differences between regions in the former West Germany have been overshadowed by the much greater differences between the poorer former East Germany and the rest of the nation. There are also very large differences between nonmetropolitan areas, of which some are prosperous and booming, attracting modern industries like Oberbayern (Upper Bavaria) and Oberschwaben (Upper Swabia) near Lake Constance; and some are remote and rural, with poor agriculture and no prospects for new industries and/or tourism, like the Emsland in the west or Vorpommern in the far northeast of the country.

Planning in Germany Since the End of World War II.

Planning in Germany Since the End of World War II. The main challenge to urban policy and planning all over Europe after the end of World War II was the reconstruction of cities. In Germany every city with more than 100,000 inhabitants (with the exception of the city of Regensburg) had been bombed. As a result of the war, there was a tremendous housing shortage of 5.5 million units. The shortage was intensified by the presence of more than 6 million refugees from the former East Germany. Thus extensive housing programs were quickly put into operation. In most of the cities, the reconstruction followed the old street network, for the infrastructure (sewer, power, and water supply systems) was damaged only in places. This phase of restoration and rebuilding in the established urban areas lasted deep into the 1950s.

The 1960s was the period of rapid economic growth, low unemployment, rising personal income, and rapidly increasing automobile ownership. This long economic boom fired urban growth. People from the rural areas continued to move into the urban agglomerations where the labor markets were booming. In addition, thousands of foreign workers from southern European countries such as Italy, Spain, Greece, and the former Yugoslavia, as well as from Turkey, immigrated to Germany. Today more than 5 million people from other countries live in Germany. In Frankfurt every third resident carries a foreign passport. Kreuzberg, the inner-city district of Berlin, is said to be the fourth-largest Turkish city in the world. Construction of social housing remained on the agenda. Big housing developments were built in the suburban zones. At the same time, the accessibility of the inner city was increased by new inner-city motorways, new parking facilities, and the modernization of the public transport system. In many cities, pedestrian zones were established in the growing Central Business District. This was the cities' response to the threat of the first suburban shopping malls that were built in the neighboring municipalities.

As was the case in most other European countries, the 1970s saw a policy change from urban extension to urban renewal. The old housing stock that dated back to the period before World War I and that had survived the bombing in World War II, had not been maintained, and many inner-city areas had become places of decay and social segregation where the poor and the elderly were concentrated. In 1971 a new law (Städtebauförderungsgesetz) was enacted, which introduced the first federal state subsidy program for urban renewal. This law formed the financial and legal basis for the efforts of the cities to renew and modernize the old housing stock and thus to bring higher-income households back into the inner city. This strategy has been quite successful.

In the 1980s, structural changes in industry reshaped the urban landscape. The Ruhr area and the Saar area, major urban-growth poles in the 1950s, faced a severe decline of their basic industries, particularly steel and coal mining, even though extensive subsidies were provided to cushion the process. Urban decay and stagnation with extensive areas of derelict land became and still remain a major urban planning issue in these regions. At the same time, other urban regions like Munich and Stuttgart were booming. Note that this type of situation was hardly unique to Germany. In the United States at about the same time, the Northeast and North Central regions were suffering from big job losses in automobile, steel, and other heavy industries while many parts of the sunbelt were thriving. One technique introduced in these lagging areas has been the technology park, an idea imported from the United States and Great Britain. These have had mixed results. As in the United States some of the most successful ones have been those associated with or in close proximity to universities. But, as has been the case in virtually every nation that has confronted it, the lagging-area problem has proved to be very difficult.

The 1970s and 1980s saw the emergence of two major, contradictory trends. On the one hand, there was a growing concern for the natural environment, which was reflected in new laws for the protection of soil, water, and air. This concern introduced more regulatory elements into the planning process. Along with it, a new political movement emerged, starting as a protest group against atomic energy and ending up as a new political party, the Green Party, founded at the end of the 1970s. On the other hand, there was a general trend toward a more property-led development, as noted earlier in this chapter, in connection with Great Britain, France, and Sweden. Behind the emphasis on property-led development was a basic macroeconomic condition. Germany, like many of the other nations of Western Europe, follows the European social democratic model. This trend has meant providing extensive social services, generous benefits like health care and retirement, and generally placing a very comprehensive social safety net under the individual. At the same time, job growth has been very slow, and chronic unemployment has become a major problem. So, too, has been the task of paying for the safety net. As the financial situation of the municipalities (Gemeinden) became more and more difficult, big urban projects had to be carried out largely with private capital. The pursuit of private capital has necessarily made deregulation a major issue in German planning policy.

As in Great Britain and France, the German planning scene is becoming more like the American scene in another way, too. New business parks, shopping centers, giant movie and musical theaters, and large theme parks are emerging in suburban areas near the most accessible nodes of the highway and rail systems. Something like the American edge city is beginning to appear in Germany. The situation is a little different from that of the United States in that since the late 1980s, Germany has invested heavily in a new high-speed train system, the Intercity Express (ICE). Thus in the 1990s there has been much planning for development around railway stations, many of which are in the central city.

The breakdown of communism and the fall of the iron curtain in 1989 led to the reunification of West and East Germany. Not only did this event totally change the political geography of Europe and the regional context of almost every city in Middle Europe, but it also has almost completely changed everybody's mental map in Germany. For West German citizens before reunification, the East German city of Dresden was—despite its physical proximity—psychologically much farther away from Stuttgart or any other West German city than, say, Boston or Dallas were.

The reunification of Germany was a unique historical experience. It called for policies to solve a problem for which there was little precedent: how to bring together two countries that, though they have a common language, had very different political, economic, and social structures, and different cultures and social attitudes. These questions were addressed at the political level by applying fully the West German legal, organizational, administrative, and political structures to East Germany. There has also been a tremendous investment in the former East Germany by the German government. More than 1,000 billion deutsche marks—about 600 billion U.S. dollars—of public money were spent in East Germany in the 1990 to 1998 period. Much of it was invested in the cities: urban renewal of the inner-city areas, maintainance and modernization of public housing areas (Plattensiedlungen), extension and modernizing the road network and railway system, and the like. But despite the huge effort the task of reunification is far from complete. The former East Germany remains much poorer than the rest of the nation, and its unemployment rates are much higher.

After reunification many East Germans moved to West Germany because of the better job opportunities. The urban regions in West Germany faced a new boom. Urban growth and the elimination of housing subsidies at the end of the 1980s were responsible for a dramatic new housing shortage. In the beginning of the 1990s the municipalities were again confronted with the necessity to plan and build extended urban areas in the outlying areas, even though for environmental reasons there is consensus that green areas should be preserved.

One feature of the German planning scene, which has no parallel in the United States or much of Western Europe, is the opportunity to redevelop amounts of land once in military use. The end of the Cold War and the subsequent withdrawal of the Soviet and American and Allied forces has presented many German municipalities and states with a substantial planning opportunity—the conversion of military areas to urban development. Some of the garrison towns in the former East Germany now have an abundance of abandoned military land at their disposition. Extended areas, once shut off from the public for decades, are now ready to be integrated into the existing urban pattern.

PLANNING IN EASTERN EUROPE

Eastern Europe includes an amalgam of states with different histories, cultures, economies, and political structures—a fact that makes any attempt to generalize across the region difficult. The term *Eastern Europe*, as used in this section, applies primarily to the nations that were often referred to as the Satellite Nations or the Warsaw Block during the Cold War period, and to the three Baltic nations. The former group was composed of Poland, East Germany (now reunited with the former West Germany), Czechoslovakia (now divided into the Czech Republic and Slovakia) Hungary, Bulgaria, and Rumania. This group came under Soviet domination in 1944 and 1945 as the Soviet armies pushed the Germans back in the end stages of World War II. The three Baltic nations, Lithuania, Latvia, and Estonia, were forcibly incorporated into the Soviet Union in 1940 and did not emerge as independent nations until the collapse of the Soviet Union in 1991.

The Soviet Planning Style

The Soviet planning style was highly centralized. Public participation as we know it in the West was almost nonexistent for most of the Soviet period, though there was some citizen involvement in planning initiatives in the 1980s, when most communist regimes were weaker and, arguably, more liberal. Communist planners emphasized the needs of industry, which often came at the expense of the environment. Frequently, more land than necessary was reserved for industrial facilities. This was possible because communist economies functioned under command (rather than market) principles, and the state typically owned the majority of urban land. Thus there were no cost pressures or landownership conflicts to resolve when designating land for large industrial uses. On the positive side, the command economy and state ownership of land allowed communist governments to provide their citizens with vast amounts of public space, including parks. The grand Scale—of both industrial enterprises and public facilities—was in itself a virtue for party ideologues eager to prove communism's triumph. The most telling example was perhaps in Romania, where the late dictator Ceausescu was so megalomaniacal that he built the People's Palace in Bucharest as the second largest public building in the world, smaller than only the U.S. Pentagon. This communist legacy of spatial generosity creates both problems and opportunities today. While many East European cities with postindustrial economies struggle with the liability of vast derelict industrial sites, their citizens often enjoy better access to parks and public spaces than do residents of Western cities.

The communist model of housing provision was also distinct. The state considered itself obliged to provide a decent minimum of housing to all. This commitment translated into innumerable massive state-built apartment blocks, which today form the outskirts of most large East European cities from Prague to St. Petersburg. While such spatial grandeur certainly seemed to fit the Soviet taste, some pragmatic reasons also made it more or less imperative. Specifically, the policy of rapid industrialization that marked the Soviet period demanded that extraordinary numbers of rural residents move to cities. To fulfill their commitment to the new workers and prevent mass housing crises, communist regimes had little choice but to construct new housing as efficiently, quickly, and cheaply as possible—which meant building large, uniform apartment blocks with prefabricated panels. The fact that the majority of new housing development occurred in such a manner—as opposed to the more scattered, private-sector-led fashion typical of free-market countries— led to one of the most fundamental differences between communist and many

Massiveness was one hallmark of the Soviet planning style. This is a Soviet-era housing project in the former East Berlin.

capitalist cities. While U.S. cities are typically surrounded by sprawling suburbs, communist cities were relatively compact and high density and had an urban contour clearly defined by the last towers of the communist housing districts.

Two other features distinguished communist from capitalist cities. First, because of the communist emphasis on industry, the production of commercial goods and service activies was neglected. As a result, communist cities had significantly fewer commercial spaces than capitalist cities—a difference that was strikingly visible to any visitor who compared East and West Berlin. Second, because of the lower purchasing power of communist citizens (which translated into lower car ownership, among other things), and because of the higher urban densities, communist cities functioned with very fully developed mass transit systems.

The Transition to a Market Economy

With the collapse of Soviet power the nations of Eastern Europe necessarily had to make the transition from a command to a market economy. In the first years, this transition was often painful. Output and already low living standards declined, unemployment was sometimes widespread, and the spread between the highest and lowest incomes increased greatly.[26] Recovery started in the mid-1990s for some countries and post-2000 for others. Over the last few years, most East European states have enjoyed GDP growth of 5 percent to 10 percent a year, which is much higher than the growth rates typical of Western economies.

Within a context of rapid social and political change, East European cities are undergoing substantial transformations. In short, they are gradually losing the typical features of communist spatial structure and acquiring those characteristic of capitalist structure. The increase in personal income has resulted in a major increase in automobile ownership. One result is that most large East European cities have by now developed suburban peripheries, comprising not only single-family homes but also Western-type commercial facilities like malls and hypermarkets. The proportion of commercial uses has skyrocketed, in both downtowns and the Soviet-style housing districts. While rapid commercial development has brought about economic benefits, it has also caused problems. Downtowns have lost significant portions of their residential populations. Few cities, aside from Prague, have managed to protect their historic centers from the pressure of market forces.

Part of the main square in the old center of Prague. Such areas need some protection from the free play of market forces to survive. Providing this may be a problem in parts of Eastern Europe, because half a century of Soviet domination gave all forms of planning a bad name.

With the collapse of communism and large increases in many people's incomes, there has been a wave of peripheral single-family construction in many Eastern European countries. Here, a development outside of Sofia, the capital-of Bulgaria.

Since 1990, the role of the public sector in urban development has been greatly reduced. Most new development is now initiated by private investors, in large measure because it is private developers rather than municipal governments that have the necessary funds. Large amounts of urban land, which were previously under public ownership, have been privatized. Unfortunately, this has led to great losses in public space. In the Bulgarian capital of Sofia, for example, an estimated 15 percent of public green space was lost in 15 years. The trend of privatizing urban space is also evident in neighborhood design patterns. While Soviet-style apartment blocks are located amid free-flowing greenery accessible to all citizens, new housing developments are often walled and gated.

The planning response to these dramatic urban changes has been uncertain. Doubtlessly, the planning process has experienced several positive developments, such as increased citizen participation. However, shrinking public spaces, threatened historic landmarks, and Western-type sprawl hardly provide evidence of good planning. The 1990s were difficult for planners because of the unstable economic, political, and legal conditions, and because of the legitimacy crisis that plagued the profession. This legitimacy crisis came in part from the experience of half a century of Soviet domination. Most East European governments made a sharp turn to the political right and some viewed planning as a suspicious, quasi-communist activity. As a result, enthusiasm for the sanctity of private property overshadowed concerns for advancing the overall public interest—a concern at the very foundation of planning.

The Problem of Privatization

One major problem throughout Eastern Europe and the Baltics is that of *privatization*, the return to private ownership of vast amounts of land and buildings that became public property during the period of Soviet domination. Problems of unclear titles, incomplete records, of inflicting major gains and loses upon people who may be the children or grandchildren of the original owners, and the like are very substantial. The transfer of wealth that the process of privatization inevitably involves opens up major opportunities for corruption. For example, in Russia the so-called *oligarchs*, a very small number of individuals who have become billionaires since the collapse of the Soviet union in 1991, to a very substantial degree made their fortunes by receiving industrial, commercial, and other state assets at bargain basement prices.

In all countries, one difficult puzzle has been what to do with the land under and in between the apartment blocks built during communism. Typically, this was once private agricultural land. However, it cannot simply be returned to its precommunist owners as this will lead to the loss of all green spaces between the apartment buildings. Thus in most countries this land continues to be municipal and various schemes have been devised to compensate its precommunist owners.

EU Membership and the Future of Planning in Eastern Europe

One factor favoring economic and political stabilization has been the incorporation of all of the East European and Baltic nations mentioned in the first paragraph of this section into the European Union (EU) beginning in 2004. This has integrated them into a group of nations with much more prosperous economies and older and more established political and economic institutions. As noted earlier in this section, planning in these newly admitted EU members faced a legitimacy crisis that was rooted in the bad experience that these nations had with the Soviet Union. In the EU there is much concern with egalitarianism and much willingness to restrict the market in the service of the public interest, but unlike the case in the former Soviet Union, there is also a high degree of political and personal freedom as well as a vastly higher standard of living. Perhaps the move positive experience with the EU will help to resolve the legitimacy question in planning.

PLANNING IN THE THIRD WORLD

Third World is a fuzzy term. When it came into use about 40 years ago, the term *First World* meant the westernized countries of the world. The *Second World*, a term that was never used much, signified the Soviet bloc. *Third World* signified everything else. Today, the term loosely signifies the developing world, poorer states in parts of Asia, Africa, and South and Central America. This is clearly a group of nations about which it is hard to generalize.

In some parts of the Third World, western planning influences are evident, often as elements of a colonial past. The public square in the center of many Central and South American cities is a remnant of the Spanish town-planning tradition of several centuries ago. The orderly street pattern and the public open space in New Delhi in India is a reminder of India's British colonial past. The contrast with the more densely developed and more wandering street pattern of the adjacent city of Old Delhi is striking. A few cities in Third World nations have been planned by westerners brought in by Third World governments. Islamabad, the capital of Pakistan, was planned on western lines by the Greek planner Konstantinos Doxiadis. Specifically, the most conspicuous element of the plan was the use of the superblock, a thoroughly western idea. Parts of Chandigarh in northern India were planned by Le Corbusier. Other western ideas such as beltways around cities and planned new towns are also making their appearance.

At present, western planning ideas reach the Third World by a variety of routes. International funding agencies such as the World Bank are one obvious source. Along with loans and grants also comes technical advice, and to be fundable, the project must meet the grantor's approval. Another source is education. U.S. and European planning schools now enroll large numbers of Third World students. Finally, we live in an age in which there is a large, worldwide appetite for many things western, whether they be fashions, music, technology, or abstract ideas. In a time in which the Coca Cola logo and McDonald's golden arches may be the most universally recognized commercial images on the planet, it is inevitable that western ideas about things urban will make themselves felt.

If we take a global rather than a western view of things, we see that what happens in regard to Third World cities will affect many more people than what happens in First World cities. In the United States and most of Europe, urban populations cannot grow much faster than the total population growth rate simply because so much of the population is already urbanized. The total U.S. population growth rate is now about 1 percent a year, and in most European nations, the rate is less (see the last section of this chapter).

By contrast, very large population increases are occurring in many Third World cities, and this trend will continue for many years. Then, too, many Third World nations have a huge reservoir of rural overpopulation so that their cities also grow on the strength of massive rural-to-urban migration. The average rate of urban population growth in the early 1990s across a wide range of Third World nations was about 5 percent.[27] Writing in the early 1990s, John D. Kasarda and Allan M. Parnell stated,

> Contemporary and projected aggregate increments of urban population in developing regions are nothing short of breathtaking. In 1950, only 285 million, or 16 percent of the developing world's population, resided in urban places. By 1990 this number had multiplied fivefold to 1.5 billion residents, making up 37 percent of the total population in developing countries. The United Nations (UNIDESA) projects that during the next 35 years the urban population of developing countries will triple again, reaching 4.4 billion in 2025.[28]

Though rapid population growth increases the need for planning, it also combines with other problems to make good planning much more difficult. Many Third World cities face immediate and crucial problems of providing basic urban services like water supply, solid waste disposal, and sewage treatment. Immediate problems of that sort absorb the limited funds available and necessarily take precedence over more long-run concerns. And in nations where per capita GNP is a fraction of that in the West, the supply of funds is sharply limited.

The combination of staggeringly rapid urban growth rates and problems with the most basic sorts of urban services such as water supply and sewage disposal are reminiscent of the problems faced in many western cities a century or a century-and-a-half ago. The reader may recall from

A new town about an hour's bus ride from Hyderabad, India. Note the small houses and close spacing between them. The town was designed as a bedroom community to relieve population pressure on the city.

Chapter 3 that in the United States it took a period of many decades to bring into being an effective system for dealing with such problems. In many Third World cities, the problem of contending with such rapid growth is only a few decades old, and very often, adequate institutional and administrative arrangements have not yet come into being. For example, having good maps and records on landownership is essential to planning and to the collection of property-based taxes. But in many Third World nations, that sort of administrative infrastructure is weak.

> A major reason why local administrations in most cities have not coped successfully with growth is because they do not know what is going on in their local land markets. The information base in many cities is improving, particularly with the aid of aerial photography. But most cities lack accurate, current data on land conversion patterns, number of housing units (informal and formal) built during the last year, infrastructure deployment patterns, subdivision patterns, and so forth. Often, city maps are 20 or 30 years old and lack descriptions of entire sections, particularly the burgeoning periurban areas.[29]

Planning for Housing

In many Third World cities, the most massive planning problem is housing. This includes not only the literal provision of housing but also provision of the most basic public services to support adequate housing, most notably the provision of safe drinking water and adequate sewage and waste disposal.

One ubiquitous sign of the housing problem is squatter housing. As you approach many Third World cities by road, the first sign you see of the urban area is roadside squatter housing. People migrate toward the city, get as close as they can, and then occupy whatever land they can, usually building their own housing. Most squatter-built housing is of very low quality and has a relatively short life span. Sometimes there are no contractual formalities regarding land. People simply find an unused bit of land and settle on it. In other cases, early squatters may rent sites to later squatters, so that a complex, albeit not necessarily legally sustainable, system of rights and relationships arises. At one time, many municipal governments would physically remove squatter settlements, but most now tend to be relatively tolerant of them, for in many parts of the Third World, there is simply no alternative to them.

The establishment of squatter housing tends to take planning out of the hands of municipal officials and to convert urban growth into a more haphazard, almost natural process. The squatter settlement comes into being without official sanction. Once it is there, however, it needs to be provided with at least a minimum of public services. Squatter settlements usually become permanent settlements. That is not a matter of growth following planning, but rather a minimum amount of planning and public investment following growth.

The squatter phenomenon is one factor that reverses the distance-income relationship seen in the United States. In many U.S. metropolitan areas, it is, on average, the poorer residents who live close to the center and the wealthier residents who live farther out. In many Third World cities, the situation is reversed. The area's poorest residents live in squatter settlements on the periphery.

Handling rapid urban population growth where resources are limited is not an easy task. Over the years various strategies, none entirely successful, have been tried. Several decades ago a number of nations tried to deal with the problem through the construction of public housing. But high per-unit costs and limited municipal budgets made it impossible to meet more than a minuscule proportion of the total need.[30] It was also observed that the housing was poorly cared for and deteriorated rapidly. Residents, having no ownership stake in the properties, tended not to take good care of them.

One more recent technique for dealing with the problem of housing for the urban poor has been the "sites and services" approach. This is sometimes done entirely with local funds and, in some cases, with money from both the locality and an international donor agency such as the World Bank. In either case the municipal government selects an area and provides it with minimum services. These services typically include water supply (sometimes just a common source) and sewerage, or sometimes just drainage into a nearby

A sites and services project in Madras, India. The city government provides utilities and plots of land at nominal prices. Some of the construction is with indigenous materials such as reeds, sticks, and dried mud. Other construction is with modern materials such as concrete blocks.

stream or river. It may also include electricity. The municipality then sells or leases sites at minimum cost to households, sometimes with the provision that if the household does not build within a specified time, it loses the site. This approach seems to be much more cost effective than the direct building of housing in that the per-unit cost is vastly lower. Then, too, the sites and services approach creates a better set of motivations. The resident as the owner of the plot of land and the building has a stake in maintaining them. In many sites and services projects, the original owners ultimately sell at a profit and use their capital gain to buy better housing elsewhere, to start small businesses, and the like. Finally, the sites and services approach can constitute an element of planning in that it is the municipal government that designates and develops the site and thus exerts some effect on the form of the city.

Area upgrading is another approach. Ellen M. Brennan reports that in Djakarta, Indonesia, the Kampung Improvement Program (KIP) had upgraded over five hundred poor areas in which close to 4 million people lived. Funding was partly by the municipality and partly by the World Bank.

> KIP's basic principles are to implement improvements that are simple to make, even if marginal, in the living standards of as many residents as possible. KIP funds improve public facilities—upgrading roads, canals and water supplies and building social welfare facilities and communal bathing and washing, rather than private accommodations.[31]

Like the sites and services approach, area upgrading is much less expensive on a per-unit basis than new construction, hence its attractiveness to a municipality whose means are limited and whose population is growing rapidly.

A LOOK AHEAD

For Western Europe the great migration from countryside to city is over. In all the nations of Western Europe, fertility rates are now below the replacement level of 2.1. Rates range from a low of 1.3 in Spain and Italy to a high of 1.9 for Ireland.[32] Across much of Western Europe, population is now topping out and will soon be headed down unless there is a substantial increase in birth rates, a situation that few observers expect. For these reasons, urban growth and housing the urban population is not likely to be a major problem. Then too, as in the United States, increasing personal income and very high automobile ownership rates are promoting decentralization of employment and residence. For a number of European cities, managing the consequences of population decline, not growth, may become the planners' biggest preoccupation.

In Eastern Europe, the Baltics, and much of the former Soviet Union fertility rates are low even compared with Western Europe, with many nations falling in the range of 1.1 to 1.4. There, too, planning for growth will not be the issue. The situation of low fertility—where each generation is substantially smaller than the previous one—if it continues will not only affect the concerns of planners but will also affect every aspect of society. Exactly how it will play out is hard to say, for human history offers little or no precedent for a situation in which a population voluntarily chooses not to fully reproduce itself.

In the Third World the situation is likely to be very mixed. A number of nations have experienced such rapid economic growth that their planning problems are beginning to have a very western look about them. For example, South Korea, a very poor nation several decades ago but now quite prosperous, has about 20 million motor vehicles for a population of 47 million. That ratio is roughly comparable to that of the United States at the end of World War II on the eve of the great postwar suburban housing boom. As has been true for some decades in the United States, the planners' biggest problem in Korea may be that of reconciling good urban design and near-universal automobile ownership. If anything, planning for an age of mass automobile ownership is likely to be considerably more difficult in South Korea than in the United States because the nation's population density of 1,200 per square mile makes it a dozen times as densely populated as the "lower 48" in the United States.

In China, rural-to-urban migration is now proceeding at a rate of many millions of people per year, and the huge remaining rural population almost guarantees that this phenomenon will continue at a high rate for many years. The automobile-ownership rate is still low but rising very rapidly. Given China's extremely rapid growth in per capita income and very rapid increase in industrial output, that rate is likely to continue rising rapidly for the foreseeable future. China's cities will confront both the traditional Third World problem of rural-to-urban migration and the traditional First World problem of massive automobile ownership by a growing middle class at the same time. The country will also confront major environmental problems simply because of its huge population, currently about 1.3 billion, and its rapidly growing industrial economy. For example, current plans in China call for building several hundred new coal-fired power plants in China—China has massive coal reserves but little or no petroleum—at a rate of about one per week to meet a very rapidly rising demand. Yet many Chinese cities now have severe air quality problems. The conflict between the desire to raise living standards and the need to protect the environment is likely to become even more severe.

Comparable comments might be made about India. The per capita gross national product is rising, though not as rapidly as in China, and there is a very large urban middle class that likes its automobiles and modern household appliances. At the same time, the Indian countryside still holds a huge reservoir of people to supply the rural-to-urban migration stream for many years to come. India's population, currently about 1 billion, is still growing rapidly. Though the Indian fertility rate has fallen considerably in the last several decades, it is still well above replacement level. If current projections prove to be accurate, India should surpass China as the world's most populous nation about 2030 or 2035.[33] Thus the comments about China are likely to apply as well to India, their severity perhaps compounded by the fact that India's land area is one-third that of China's.[34]

SUMMARY

The chapter began by noting some differences between the situation of planning in Western Europe and in the United States. Among these differences are the destruction of urban areas during World War II, the unification of Europe, different attitudes about the role of government, the generally greater strength of the national government vis-à-vis provincial and local governments, and, generally, a greater willingness to regulate the uses of private property.

The chapter noted the building of new towns and the creation of greenbelts in Great Britain, and the French effort to reduce the dominance of Paris and the Ile de France by supporting the development of regional centers. We noted the relatively centralized Dutch planning system and the creation of Randstat Holland. In the case of Sweden we note the use of public ownership of land and the dominant role of government in the housing market as the means by which Swedish municipal governments have shaped the pattern of development.

Throughout much of western Europe in the 1980s and 1990s, there was an increase in "property-led" (the term is explained in the chapter) development so that the European planning scene came to resemble the American scene a bit more than had previously been the case. Among the reasons for this change were a general political shift to the right, an increase in economic competition between places, and fiscal pressures that make public monies less available.

In Eastern Europe we noted the priority given the needs of industry, the construction of massive housing projects, and the relatively low emphasis on the needs of service activities during the period of Soviet domination. In the decade since the end of Soviet domination and the breakup of the Soviet Union, the planning situation has been uncertain. What sort of planning tradition will emerge is unclear. There has been some public suspicion of planning simply because the term is associated with the period of Soviet domination. Now that the nations of Eastern Europe are part of the European Union (EU) that attitude may begin to change.

In connection with planning in the Third World, we noted the extremely high rate of urban population growth and the shortage of resources for dealing with it. We described first the phenomenon of squatter settlements and then some of the approaches that have been tried in connection with housing the urban poor. These included the construction of public housing (generally not successful), then sites and services, and, finally, area upgrading.

NOTES

1. The term *spent* in this usage also includes the term *transferred*. A great deal of the one-third of GNP "spent" by government in the United States is simply money like Social Security payments that are transferred to individuals and then spent by the individual. In that sense the figures on government's share of the GNP may exaggerate the role of government in the economy.
2. J. Barry Cullingworth, *The Political Culture of Planning*, Routledge, London, 1993, p. 197.
3. Just before the start of World War II, Great Britain imported about four-fifths of all the food that it consumed. During the war, the heavy dependence on food brought in by ship was a major problem, which focused attention on the desirability of preserving as much of the nation's agricultural potential as possible.
4. For a detailed account of the evolution of British planning in the post–World War II period, see Peter Hall, *Urban and Regional Planning*, 3rd ed., Routledge, London, 1992, chap. 4. See also J. Barry Cullingworth and Vincent Nadin, *Town and Country Planning in Britain*, Routledge, London, 11th ed., 1994, and earlier editions, chap. 1.
5. Hall, *Urban and Regional Planning*, p. 81.
6. Pierre Merlin, *New Towns, Regional Planning and Development*, Methuen & Co., Ltd., 1971.
7. This idea somewhat resembles the thinking of the late-nineteenth-century American writer on economic and social issues, Henry George. He argued that increases in land value generally occurred because of forces with which the property owner had little connection and that these increases in value, which were not earned by the property owner, should be taxed away. He thus argued for a tax system that relied entirely on the value of land.
8. The Industrial Revolution is generally considered to have been well under way in Great Britain by the last decades of the eighteenth century, about 1760 to 1800 or 1780 to 1800. Germany did not reach a comparable stage until at least the middle of the nineteenth century, and Scandinavia the end of the nineteenth century. For estimates of the dates of the so-called stage of "economic takeoff" in various countries, see W. W. Rostow, *The Stages of Economic Growth: A Non-Communist Manifesto*, Cambridge University Press, England, 1971.
9. At this writing, British unemployment rates are well below those on the continent, and the British growth rate is generally higher, facts that the Conservatives are quick to attribute to the pro-market policies of Margaret Thatcher and John Major, policies generally continued under the government of Tony Blair.
10. Anthony Bianco, "Faith and Fortune," *Business Week*, January 20, 1997, pp. 55–69.
11. Hall, *Urban and Regional Planning*, p. 154.
12. Cullingworth, *Town and Country*, pp. 205–213.
13. Hall, *Urban and Regional Planning*, p. 168.
14. The term *growth pole* originated with the French economic geographer François Perroux. Though he used it to describe an industrial sector that acted as the agent for promoting national industrial development, i.e., as the leading industrial sector, rather than to describe a particular place, it quickly became used in the geographical sense. The term, in its geographical sense, was popularized in the United States by the regional economist Niles Hansen.
15. Hall, *Urban and Regional Planning*, p. 172.
16. France's high-speed passenger rail system, the *Train à Grande Vitesse* (TGV), literally Train with Great Speed, is very heavily subsidized. It provides a level of passenger service that is unmatched in the United States; in fact, the French passenger rail system apart from the TGV is far superior to that of the United States. One reason is that the French are willing to subsidize passenger rail very heavily. The U.S. reluctance to sink large amounts of subsidy money into a modern, high-quality passenger rail system has been the object of much criticism. However, the defender of the U.S. reluctance might point out that it is not entirely capricious. U.S. population density is much lower than that of France, the land-use pattern is much more dispersed, and automobile ownership rates are higher. All those factors tend to stack the deck against public

transportation and would make U.S. subsidy costs per passenger mile much higher.

17. Peter Newman and Andy Thornley, *Urban Planning in Europe*, Routledge, London and New York, 1996, chap. 7.

18. Ibid, p. 163.

19. Ibid, p. 48.

20. Hall, *Urban and Regional Planning*, pp. 197–202.

21. The idea that a small place may obtain some of the benefits or agglomeration economies of a nearby larger place has been termed "borrowed size" by the American planner William Alonso. See any standard text on urban economics, such as James Heilbrun, *Urban Economics and Public Policy*, 3rd ed., St. Martin's Press, New York, 1987.

22. Newman and Thornley, *Urban Planning*, p. 209.

23. Ibid, p. 208.

24. Author's interview with city of Helsinki Planning Dept., Spring 1994.

25. Newman and Thornley, *Urban Planning*, p. 60.

26. In the Soviet Union and in many of the satellite nations the extremes of wealth and poverty were much smaller than was later to become the case. Housing and some other necessities of life were provided at below cost and there was no unemployment. All workers were assigned to a workplace, even if there was very little for them to do there. In other words, unemployment was concealed, rather than explicit as in a capitalist society. A cynical expression for this at the time was "we pretend to work and they pretend to pay us." Though the total output of the economy was low and the society as a whole was very poor by Western standards, there was a very minimal floor under everyone.

27. David Drakakis-Smith, "Third World Cities: Sustainable Urban Development," *Urban Studies* vol. 32, May 1995, p. 659(19).

28. John D. Kasarda and Allan M. Parnell, *Third World Cities*, Sage Publications, Inc., London, 1993, p. ix.

29. Ellen M. Brennan, "Urban Land and Housing Issues," in ibid, p. 80.

30. Ibid, pp. 82–83. Also, author's observations and conversations with Indian planning officials.

31. Ibid, p. 87.

32. Fertility rates for most of the nations of the world can be found at Census.gov/ipc/www/ibdnew.html. The same site can also be found by entering *us bureau of the census, international database* on a search engine such as Google. Fertility rates for many nations can also be found in the "International Statistics" chapter of *The Statistical Abstract of the United States*. The fertility figures cited are from the year 2000.

33. China's population as of 2004 was estimated at 1.3 billion and India's at somewhat under 1.1 billion. However, India's much higher fertility rate, about 3.1 as compared with China's 1.7, suggests that India's population will catch up with China's about 2035, at which point both nations' populations will be in the 1.4 to 1.5 billion range. China's much lower fertility figure is, at least in part, a result of a vigorously enforced "one child" policy. The actual figure may be somewhat higher if, as is widely believed, some births in rural areas are not registered so as to avoid penalties for violating the policy.

34. India's population in 2004 was about 1.06 billion. With an area of about 1.15 million square miles that yields a population density of over 900 people per square mile, roughly ten times that of the lower 48 states of the United States and one of the highest in the world. At present growth rates its population will top 1,000 per square mile within less than a decade.

SELECTED BIBLIOGRAPHY

BRENNER, NEIL, AND KEIL, ROGER, eds., *The Global Cities Reader*, Routledge, New York, 2005.

CULLINGWORTH, J. BARRY, AND NADIN, VINCENT, *Town and Country Planning in Britain*, 11th ed., Routledge, London and New York, 1994.

HALL, PETER, *Urban and Regional Planning*, 3rd ed., Routledge, London and New York, 1992.

MERLIN, PIERRE (trans. MARGARET SPARKS), *New Towns, Regional Planning and Development*, Methuen and Co., Ltd., London, 1971.

NEWMAN, PETER, AND THORNLEY, ANDY, *Urban Planning in Europe*, Routledge, London and New York, 1996.

CHAPTER 19

Planning Theory

In this chapter we discuss planning theory from two perspectives: (1) theories of planning as a process, both how it ought to be done and how it is done, and (2) some ideological issues. But first, a legitimate question to ask is this: Is planning theory necessary? Cannot the planner simply apply his or her intelligence to a particular situation and proceed without theory?

IS THEORY NECESSARY?

The question of whether theory is not simply a waste of time is the question with which the "practical" person derides the philosopher. But theory cannot be avoided. We all possess theories that form the basis on which we act. Everyone has ideas about how things are and how the world works. One difference between the "practical" person and the "theorist" is that the former takes these ideas for granted, whereas the latter thinks about them consciously and makes them explicit. But when one acts, one inevitably acts on the basis of some theory about how things work. On what other basis can one act?

In 1936 John Maynard Keynes, whom some regard as the greatest economist of this century, wrote,

> . . . ideas of economists and political philosophers, both when they are right and when they are wrong, are more powerful than is commonly understood. Indeed, the world is ruled by little else. Practical men, who believe themselves to be quite exempt from intellectual influences, are usually the slave of some defunct economist. Madmen in authority, who hear voices in the air, are distilling their frenzy from some academic scribbler of a few years back.[1]

Keynes's reference to "madmen in authority" has particular reference to Europe of the 1930s—especially to Hitler, Stalin, and Mussolini. But the point that even the most powerful are themselves ruled by the ideas they hold is as valid today as then.

We noted in Chapter 6 several alternative roles the planner might play. How is a person to decide whether he or she favors an advocacy position or a neutral civil servant position, without some theories of how society works, how decisions are made, and what constitutes right and wrong? At a more concrete level, assume the city is beset with housing problems. The planner is asked to comment on whether a rent control ordinance would be a good idea. How can he or she even begin to think about the issues without some theory of how housing markets work? To the extent that controls would deliver benefits to some individuals and losses to others, how can we decide whether these effects would be good or bad unless we have some theory of what constitutes social justice? If theory is inescapable, perhaps it is best to make it explicit.

It is common to make a distinction between theory and practice, and it is easy to exaggerate this difference. To a large extent, theory is developed and tested on the basis of the experience acquired in practice. As stated, every practitioner is, to some extent, a theoretician. And, conversely, the experience of practice is likely to make the theoretician better at his or her chosen work. The theoretician who has had no contact with practice has not subjected his or her theorizing to the test and has little basis to assert its validity. Without the experience of practice, it is hard to separate good theory from bad theory and useful theory from useless theory.

A DISTINCTION BETWEEN PUBLIC AND PRIVATE PLANNING _

It is true that public planning and nonpublic planning, such as that done by corporations, have much in common. However, there is at least one important difference. Public planning is often more difficult than private planning, and its results may sometimes appear to be less rational. The reason is very simple. Public planning must usually satisfy many different ends, some of which may be in conflict with one another. Private planning, very often, is directed toward satisfying a single or a very small number of ends. It thus often admits of more coherent solutions.

Consider the builder who is formulating plans to build an apartment house. He or she is likely to have one major goal—profit.[2] No one reasonably expects a builder to consider the effect of one building on the city as a whole. Society has formulated a variety of rules regarding zoning, construction standards, taxation, and the like. Within these rules the builder is free to follow his or her own interests.

Now consider a public body that is building housing. It has cost and revenue estimates to make, as does the private builder. But it has numerous goals to consider that the private builder does not. How does the project affect community goals regarding integration? How will the project affect the process of gentrification? If the project involves demolition, where will the residents of the soon-to-be-demolished housing live? How does the rent structure of the project square with what is known about the income distribution of the city's population? And so on.

There is also the political imperative. The public body operates in the open and is accountable to the entire body politic of the city—voters, labor unions, neighborhood groups, civic groups, tenant organizations, landlord organizations, ad infinitum. The plan that the public body finally settles on must satisfy many of these groups. The plan does not have to have something for everybody, but it must have something for a number of parties if it is to have a chance of survival.

THE PROCESS OF PLANNING

Sometimes a distinction is made between "substantive" theory and "procedural" theory. Substantive theory in this usage is theory *in* planning, for example, the gravity model mentioned in connection with transportation planning. Procedural theory is theory *about* the act of planning. The various theories of planning to be discussed fall under the heading of procedural theory. Note, however, that the two types of theory are related. We have to have substantive ideas (ideas about how the world works) to form procedural theories.

Here, we address three approaches to the process of planning:

The rational model
Disjointed incrementalism
Middle-range models

The Rational Model

The rational model has been prevalent for several decades and might be considered the orthodox view.[3] It is the philosophy reflected in the comprehensive plan. Though its proponents will readily admit that in the real world it cannot be carried out precisely as described, many would argue that it still constitutes a kind of holy grail to be approached as closely as possible. The idea behind the model, as its name suggests, is to make the planning process as rational and systematic as possible. A listing of steps in the model follows. Not every writer might list exactly this sequence, but the general idea would be the same.

1. *Define the problem.* Obviously if more than one party is involved, then it is necessary to reach an agreement.
2. *Clarify values.* Suppose the problem is stated as an inadequate housing stock. Before we can formulate policy, we have to agree on how highly we value certain conditions. How important is the physical condition of housing? Is physical condition more or less important than the cost of housing? How important is it that housing be racially integrated? How important is good traffic circulation in residential areas? How important is growth in the number of housing units? Often we will find that an action that takes us toward one goal takes us away from another. Tearing down substandard units will certainly improve housing quality. But by reducing the number of units on the market, demolition will push up rents. Should we do it? We cannot answer that question unless we have our values sorted out.
3. *Select goals.* Having gone through steps 1 and 2, we are now presumably in a position to choose one or more goals relative to the problem.
4. *Formulate alternative plans or programs.*
5. *Forecast the consequences of the alternatives developed in the previous step.*
6. *Evaluate and select one or more courses of action (alternatives).*
7. *Develop detailed plans for implementing the alternatives selected.*
8. *Review and evaluate.* Once implementation has begun, it is necessary periodically to review the process and results to date with a view to decide whether the original plan should still be followed or whether—as is usually the case—changes and adjustments are necessary.

Although the steps are presented in sequence, there is a great deal of going back and forth between them. For example, if step 4 suggests that a certain goal selected in step 3 cannot be reached or can be reached only at an exorbitant price, the planners may go back to step 3 to select an alternative goal. Obviously, defining the problem and clarifying values are closely intertwined. Very often, we do not know how much we value something until we learn its price and then have to decide whether to pay it. In that case, the insights that come out of the latter steps will often carry us back to the first three steps.

Criticisms of the Rational Model.

Although the rational model seems eminently sensible, it has been subject to a great deal of criticism. Some critics assert that the steps described are simply not how things are actually planned. If the model does not describe reality at least very roughly, what good is it?

Consider the first four steps. Few real problems can be approached as if there were a clean slate in front of the planner. Legal, political, and other constraints eliminate some possibilities and necessitate others. In fact, it has been argued that the mandatory requirements and limitations that legislative bodies impose on boards, commissions, local governments, and so on are intended precisely to constrain those organizations. They are there to prevent them from going back to square one and rethinking and hence resolving the problem from the beginning.

Critics also argue that value clarification sounds logical but often cannot be done. If agreement is necessary for action and the various parties have different values, making value clarification a requisite for the next step would make further progress impossible. During World War II the United States, Great Britain, and the USSR agreed on the necessity of cooperating to defeat Germany. But their values and goals were radically different. Cooperation was achieved only by suppressing, ignoring, or denying these very deep differences. Had honest value clarification been required as a first part of the planning process, no progress would have been made.

The critic of the model might also argue that the latter steps in the process do not describe reality very well. The laying out and studying of a number of alternatives is often simply not possible because of time or resources. In many cases the planner(s) quickly arrives at a short list of alternatives and then focuses on implementation. The look-at-everything-so-as-to-make-the-optimum-choice approach is not possible.

A final point that critics make is that the goal of the rational model is optimization—making the best choice from a substantial array of possibilities. These possibilities have themselves been developed by a systematic and—as far as is possible—an all-inclusive process. It has been said that in most situations organizations do not optimize but rather "satisfice," meaning that they strive for solutions that are satisfactory or adequate.[4] Optimization is simply too difficult.

So far the arguments against the rational model are essentially arguments from practicality on values and goals. Charles Lindblom, has suggested that even in the ideal, the rational model, may not be best. He notes that it presumes that the participants in the planning process each consider the totality of goals and objectives and think of which courses of action produce the greatest good. But, he argues, this is just unrealistic. Let us admit that we live in a world of partisanship, constituencies, and special interests and therefore cannot expect the participants to act like candidates for sainthood. May we not, then, get a better result?

The argument Lindblom makes for a less highly structured and centralized approach is quite simple. Assume that the participants come into the planning process from various vantage points and that they, to some extent, represent special interests (as opposed to the public interest as a whole). Then it is doubtful that the interests of any major group in the public will be ignored.

> The virtue of such hypothetical division of labor is that every important interest or value has its watchdog. . . . In a society like that of the United States in which individuals are free to combine to pursue almost any possible common interest they might have and in which government agencies are sensitive to the pressures of these groups, the system is approximated. Almost every interest has its watchdog. Without claiming that every interest has a sufficiently powerful watchdog, it can be argued that our system often can assure

a more comprehensive regard for the values of the whole society than any attempt at intellectual comprehensiveness.[5]

In support of the "watchdog" argument, we note that it has been demonstrated beyond doubt that well-intentioned members of the majority often do not know what is important to members of minorities or how strongly members of minorities may feel. In the 1950s, how many whites knew quite how anguished blacks were about the constraints society placed on them? More recently, how many men understood how angry many women were about their limited job opportunities? How many heterosexuals perceived how frustrated gays felt about their second-class status? One can make a credible argument that no group's concerns can be completely understood by anyone other than members of the group itself. If this is true, an adversarial and a pluralistic planning process may give better results than a nonadversarial one, no matter how well intentioned. And, of course, the phrase *well intentioned* carries a heavy burden of assumption.

Lindblom's argument for an adversarial process is quite consistent with the United State's Anglo-Saxon judicial and political tradition. Our courts function on an adversarial basis. We do not expect each party's attorney to present the facts objectively. Rather, within the constraints of the law, we expect an attorney to present the strongest possible case for his or her client. We assume that truth will best emerge from this clash of adversaries, and we are extremely suspicious of judicial systems in which the roles of judge, prosecution, and defense are combined in a single individual.

Party politics as practiced in the United States and other Western democracies are clearly adversarial. We are highly dubious of any political system in which there is no real clash of adversaries, for we suspect that the outward harmony is a mask for oppression.

In Defense of the Rational Model. The defender of the rational model, of which there are many among practicing planners and planning educators, might answer some of these points as follows.

Of course values cannot always be clarified fully. But to the extent that they can be clarified, it is wise to do so. Not all parties will always be willing to reveal their real goals in the planning process, but again to the extent that goals can be clearly formulated, it is wise that this be done. We have no shortage of public programs with contradictory and unstated goals and purposes. Perhaps conscientious resort to the rational model might help.[6]

Perhaps the point about going back to square one is not such a damning criticism after all. In considering any problem of course we must always take some things for granted. How far back we go depends on the importance of the problem, the time and resources available, and other practical considerations. The rational model suggests simply going as far back to square one *as is practical.*

The argument regarding the watchdog effect of an adversarial process is not easily countered. However, the defender of the rational process might argue that the need for representation of conflicting views can, in some measure, be accommodated by requiring adequate diversity of interests in the body that does the planning. Given that the planning body is ultimately selected and empowered by the political structure of the community, that responsibility lies with the executive and legislative branches.

Disjointed Incrementalism

Having expressed strong doubts about the rational model, both in terms of feasibility and of underlying theory, its critics have suggested an alternative view of the planning process. The terms *disjointed incrementalism, muddling through,* and *successive limited comparisons* have been used for an alternative approach, of which Lindblom has been the most prominent advocate.[7]

Lindblom believes that value clarification at the outset, though it sounds attractive in principle, is usually not practical. Rather, what counts is achieving agreement on goals. Politics is, after all, "the art of compromise," not the art of optimization. He suggests that the range of possible courses of action not be the very comprehensive one suggested by the rational model. Rather, he argues, planners should quickly come down to a short list of serious possibilities and focus on these. He argues that planners and policy makers should be strongly influenced by precedent and by experience and that they should recognize the advantages of policy options that represent marginal or incremental changes from previous policies. The argument for an emphasis on marginal change is twofold. First, a policy that is simply an adjustment or fine-tuning of a previous policy is much more likely to gain acceptance than one that is a radical departure. Second, marginal or incremental adjustments require less knowledge and theory. Even if we do not really know why a policy or a program functions as it does, we can often see that if we adjusted it this way or that, it is likely to function better. In Lindblom's phrase the rational model is "greedy for facts":

> It can be constructed only through a great collection of facts. . . . In contrast, the comparative [incremental] method both economizes on the need for facts and directs the analyst's attention to just those facts which are relevant to the fine choices faced by the decision-maker.[8]

The greed for facts is not a small point. Gathering facts takes time and costs money, and sometimes the facts cannot be had no matter how much effort is expended. Similar observations can be made regarding theory. Building theory takes time and money, and sometimes when all is said and done, alternate theories will prove equally plausible. What is one to rely on then? Perhaps it is best to rely on the fine-tuning of disjointed incrementalism.

TABLE 19–1 Which Model to Use

Favors Rational Model	Favors Incremental Model
Adequate theory available	Adequate theory lacking
New question	Modification of old question
Resources generous	Resources limited
Substantial time for study	Limited time for study
Numerous relations to other policy issues	Few relations to other policy issues
Wide range of policies might be politically acceptable	Policy options highly limited by political realities

The arguments for the incremental, or muddling-through, approach are powerful, and even most advocates of the rational model will admit that there are times when incrementalism is the most practical route. But it must be said that there is one important situation in which the incremental approach is not good—the situation in which a decision to move in a new direction must be made. If the problem is new, it is hard to see how an incremental approach can work. In the 1960s the United States began to confront the problem of nuclear waste disposal. There simply was no existing program that could be incrementally adjusted to deal with a problem that had not existed a decade earlier. Perhaps the reason we have hundreds of thousands of "hot" fuel rods in temporary storage at dozens of sites around the country is precisely because we took the incremental approach.

The critic of the incremental model might also argue that excessive reliance on the incremental approach can make one excessively dependent on precedent and past experience and thus blind to worthwhile new ideas. Thus heavy reliance on incrementalism can lead one into excessive caution and missed opportunities.

To some extent the choice between the rational model and the incremental model may be an expression of one's willingness to take risks. The rational model may hold out the hope of big gains because going back to the beginning may yield a new and much superior approach. But if one goes back to the beginning and gets things all wrong, there is the possibility of big losses. The incremental approach, by holding fast to the handrail of experience and precedent, tends to reduce the chances of both big gains and big losses. Table 19–1 summarizes the circumstances in which one might favor one model or the other.

Middle-Range Models

The rational model and disjointed incrementalism represent opposite poles. Various intermediate approaches have also been proposed, perhaps the best known of which is "mixed scanning" by sociologist Amitai Etzioni.[9]

The idea is quite simple. Etzioni advocates a two-step process. First, a general scanning process is conducted to get the overall picture and to decide which elements merit more detailed examination. Etzioni uses the analogy of a weather monitoring system utilizing space satellites.

> The rationalistic approach [rational model] would seek an exhaustive survey of weather conditions . . . by scheduling reviews of the entire sky as often as possible. This would yield an avalanche of details, costly to analyze and likely to overwhelm our action capabilities.

He then goes on to contrast the rational model approach with his mixed scanning approach.

> A mixed scanning strategy would include elements of both approaches . . . a broad angle camera that would cover all parts of the sky but not in great detail and a second one which would zero in on those areas revealed by the first camera to require more examination. While mixed scanning might miss areas in which a detailed camera could reveal trouble, it is less likely than incrementalism to miss obvious trouble spots in unfamiliar areas.

Etzioni elaborates on his model by pointing out that the scanning process might actually have more than one stage. We might scan a large field quickly and then, depending on what we had learned, scan a smaller field somewhat more thoroughly. When we have located the area that deserves fine scrutiny, a systematic approach such as that of the rational model is appropriate.

Etzioni argues that his model avoids the excessive commitment to precedent and past experience inherent in the incremental model. At the same time, it is far more feasible than a doctrinaire rational model approach: "The strategy [mixed scanning] combines a detailed ('rationalistic') examination of some sectors—which, unlike the detailed examination of the entire area, is feasible—with a 'truncated' review of other sectors." Etzioni's advice resembles that given to strategic planners, sometimes summarized under the acronym SWOT, which stands for Strengths, Weaknesses, Opportunities, Threats. The advice is quickly to characterize the organization's overall position under those four general categories. When that general reconnaissance is done, then detailed planning following a structured, rational model-like approach, can begin, with less fear of being blindsided by important factors that were overlooked in a rush to premature closure.

Mixed scanning has generally received a favorable response from planners interested in how-to-plan or what-is-planning questions. It seems to describe a fair amount of what planners actually do. The working planner is likely to spend a little time looking around very broadly, narrow his or her options quickly, and focus intently on a small range of possibilities. Etzioni's synthesis appears to allow the user the strengths of both models while minimizing their weaknesses.

ADVOCACY PLANNING

The arguments described previously are about the process of planning. And the reader may recognize that they all lie along a continuum, with the rational model as the most structured and formal approach and the incremental model the least structured and most ad hoc approach. In the 1960s a rather different strand of planning theory appeared. Its focus was not on how to plan so much as for whom to plan and to whom the planner should give his or her loyalty.

The late Paul Davidoff is the founding father of advocacy planning.[10] His career in planning began in a conventional way, and for a time he was a planner for a small town in Connecticut. But he soon decided that his real loyalties lay in a different direction from serving an affluent suburban population. Much of his subsequent career was devoted to attacking what has come to be termed *exclusionary* zoning in the suburbs. He did this through a combination of speaking, writing, and litigation.

He founded and for a time ran an organization called the Suburban Action Institute (SAI), which was headquartered in White Plains, New York, and whose purpose was to bring down exclusionary zoning by means of lawsuits against suburban communities. The concept behind this was that exclusionary zoning, by limiting construction to single-family houses on large lots, a necessarily expensive housing type, promoted class and racial segregation. A metaphor he used was that of the cities, largely black and poor, surrounded by a "noose" of exclusionary zoning, beyond which were the suburbs, relatively prosperous and predominantly white.[11]

Beyond the specific issue of suburban zoning, he developed the much more general concept of advocacy planning. In this view the proper role for the planner was not to serve a general public interest but rather to serve the interests of the least fortunate or least-well-represented groups in society, which he identified as poor and minority groups.[12] He denied that planning could be value free or that it could be a primarily technical and objective process:

> The justice of the present social allocation of wealth, knowledge, skill and other social goods is clearly in debate. Solutions to questions about the share of wealth and other social commodities that should go to different classes cannot be technically derived; they must arise from social attitudes.

The Davidoffian view clearly comes from the left-hand side of the political spectrum. He is not willing to allow the distribution of wealth and privileges to be settled by the marketplace as would someone on the right. The view embodied in the language—that there are distinct classes and that which classes get what should be a matter of collective decision—is, itself, a distinctly left view. So, too, is the idea that knowledge and skills are socially allocated, rather than individually acquired.

The planner in the Davidoffian scheme would represent not a general public interest but a client, much as an attorney does. He or she takes the view that there should be a plurality of plans rather than a single plan:

> There is or should be a Republican and Democratic way of viewing city development; that there should be conservative and liberal plans, plans to support the private market and plans to support greater government control. There are many possible roads for a community to travel and many plans should show them.

Davidoff's view disturbed many planners. The notion that there was no central public interest to be served was hardly the way the profession had traditionally seen its role. What did a multiplicity of plans mean in practice? One cannot build a building or a machine from a welter of contrasting plans.

The idea of serving a client rather than the public at large also raises some issues of personal ethics. Suppose you are committed to the idea of advocacy planning but you are hired as a town planner. How much loyalty do you owe the group for whom you think you should be the advocate, and how much loyalty do you owe the taxpayers who are paying your salary? If you work for a consultant hired by a town, the question is essentially the same. How much loyalty do you owe the political body that pays your consulting fee rather than some other group or cause? If you cannot give full loyalty to the client who pays your fee, is it right that you take the fee? These are not easily answered questions.

A certain number of planners who were of the advocacy position persuasion took the view that they should be "guerrillas in the bureaucracy." One such planner noted that over the years he had never been fired for taking an advocacy stance while working for a public body, but that he had often been shunted off to the side, something he referred to as doing the "lateral arabesque."[13] Clearly, one must have a dim view of the workings of government and a strong conviction of one's own wisdom and rectitude to decide that being a "guerrilla in the bureaucracy" is both the right thing to do and a good life choice to make.

The advent of advocacy planning should be viewed in the context of the 1960s, a time when the civil rights movement was confronting America with the history of racism and the Vietnam War was splitting the nation in half. At present there are still a certain number of planners who see themselves as advocacy planners. But in this more conservative era, the movement has passed its peak.

PLANNING FROM RIGHT AND LEFT

In this section we discuss ideologically based criticisms of planning—both the idea of planning and planning as actually practiced. The reader will note that there is a certain amount of national or systemwide material in this section. This larger focus is necessary because much of the ideological debate about planning, even as practiced in small jurisdictions, is based on different views of the nation's political and economic system.

The right-wing criticism that falls on city, town, or regional planning does so largely because planning in that particular sense happens to be in the general target area. Specifically, almost any sort of public planning requires some replacement of signals from the marketplace with the calculations of planners, technicians, bureaucrats, and others. For example, we noted earlier how zoning may interfere with the workings of the market by preventing those uses that, in a pure market situation, the property owner would choose on the basis of profitability. The person on the right, almost by definition, is one who is convinced of the wisdom of markets and of the efficacy of Adam Smith's "invisible hand." He or she is likely to see the inefficiency and loss of personal freedom in centrally planned economies not as accidents but as inevitable concomitants of excessive central control and of insufficient reliance on markets. With such a general worldview, one is likely to view specific instances of planning with a degree of suspicion.

The criticism from the left, in contrast, has not been directed at the idea of planning. The replacement of market decision making by political decision making is part of the agenda of the left. A preference for planning and collective decision making as opposed to markets is one of the left's defining characteristics. Rather, the left's criticism has often been directed at municipal planning as currently practiced.

There is also another difference in the attacks from the right and the left. The criticism from the right, by and large, comes from people who are not trained as planners and who have not practiced as planners. This is hardly surprising, for if one disdains the idea of planning, one is not likely to become a planner. On the other hand, much of the criticism from the left comes from within the profession, not so much from practitioners but from planning educators—people who are trained in planning and who often have some experience as practitioners.

The View from the Right

The right-wing criticism makes two main points. First, it is argued that the marketplace does a better job of allocating resources than does planning. A modern economy involves thousands of different intermediate and final goods and, every day, millions of transactions. For this vast activity to be planned would require a degree of competence and foresight that it is unrealistic to expect from any organization. Then, too, it can be argued that performing this great task of planning would, beyond the issue of technical competence, make the virtually impossible demand that the planners know the preferences and interests of all those for whom they plan. The opponent of planning will argue that the market, because it is decentralized, requires no such knowledge of either objective facts or personal preferences. He or she would also argue that the decentralization of the marketplace permits more rapid adjustment to changes than does a centralized system. Surpluses and shortages, price rises and falls, send quick and unambiguous signals to suppliers of goods and services. Can anything unplanned provide both stability and easy adjustment to changed conditions? The free-market proponent would answer yes and might ask the doubter to consider an ecosystem such as a forest. No one planned it, yet it displays great stability over time, and should some external condition, say, the amount of rainfall, change, the ecosystem will change smoothly and quickly.

These arguments might be supplemented by comments on the administrative costs of central planning and the general slowness of bureaucratic decision making. Finally, the opponent of planning (the term here is used in its generic sense) might ask those who doubt his or her argument to consider the real world. Which economies seem to function smoothly, and which seem bedeviled with shortage and dislocations?

Perhaps more important to the proponent of the free market than efficiency is the view that economic and political freedom are inseparable. The conservative economist and Nobel Prize winner Milton Friedman argues,

> The kind of economic organization that provides economic freedom directly, namely, competitive capitalism, also promotes political freedom because it separates economic power from political power and in this way enables one to offset the other.
>
> Historical evidence speaks with a single voice on the relation between political freedom and a free market. I know of no example in time or place of a society that has been marked by a large measure of political freedom, and that has not also used something comparable to a free market to organize the bulk of economic activity.[14]

Note that Friedman's claim is a limited one. Although he states that the marketplace is necessary for political freedom, he does not state that it guarantees freedom—only that its absence guarantees the absence of freedom. Note, also, the phrase *bulk of economic activity*. He does not argue that all economic activity must be in the market sector for political freedom to prevail.

How might the planner of centrist political persuasion respond? One line of argument would be to grant the generality of the argument but point to two important caveats.

1. *Public goods.* Some goods and services must be provided outside the market because it is either impractical or impossible to create markets for them. National defense cannot be provided through market mechanisms because either everyone is defended or no one is defended. Therefore the nonpayer or "free rider" is as well served as the individual who pays. The lighthouse is often cited as a good that must be provided publicly because one is equally able to see the light whether one pays or

does not pay. Since a market cannot be created, the good or service is either provided publicly or not at all. Other goods, such as city streets, could, in principle, be provided through market mechanisms. But the difficulty of doing so renders the idea impractical.

   2. *Externalities or spillovers.* If the good or service in question visits substantial effects on parties who are not represented in the transaction, the market, even though it produces optimal results when we consider only the interests of buyer and seller, will produce suboptimal results for society as a whole. As noted earlier, third-party effects related to land use are one of the principal justifications for zoning.

   These ideas about public goods and externalities or spillovers are hardly radical and can be found in any standard economics text. They suggest that the market necessarily has its limits and thus that some degree of planning is inevitable. The issue, then, is not whether to plan or not to plan but rather how and how much to plan.

   The planner might further argue that the conservative ought to favor timely public planning efforts on the grounds that dealing with problems early will alleviate the pressure for radical change later.[15] As we shall see, some radicals have castigated planners for performing exactly that function.

   With regard to the issue of political freedom, the centrist might also grant the basic conservative argument but still raise an important caveat— that the sort of planning described in this book is hardly comparable to the sort of centralized planning that was practiced in the former Soviet Union. The difference in degree is so great as to constitute a real difference in kind. The word *planning* is applied to both, but we should not be misled by that semantic similarity.

   In summary, the centrist could argue that he or she can agree with the right in its general view of central planning and the relationship between economic and political freedom. Yet he or she can still argue that in a capitalist democracy like the United States, planning is a necessary and useful activity.

The View from the Left

In the 1970s the planning profession and planning as practiced began to come under heavy criticism from the political far left. Much of the attack came from what might loosely be called neo-Marxism. Marxist theories made a comeback in academe during the 1970s and 1980s. The radical might argue that this was due to their inherent virtue. The skeptic might respond that the cause was historical, namely, the radicalizing effect of the Vietnam War.

   The radical position was not a majority position among planning educators, but it was much more common among planning educators than among planning practitioners. One reason is that in a great many planning jobs, although not all, radicals would feel uncomfortable because they would be cooperating with a system that they did not respect and achieving ends to which they could not feel committed. That sort of psychological dissonance is not easy to live with.

What is the radical view? America's liberal capitalism, or welfare capitalism as it has been called, is regarded rather dimly (though many radicals will concede it to be more humane than the capitalism of earlier years). Radicals saw it as containing vast and inexcusable extremes of wealth and poverty and as largely dominated by and therefore run for the benefit of the capitalist class (bourgeoisie). They also believed that the working class or the "masses" accept the system largely because they have been prevented from seeing the truth by those who control the flow of information and ideas. In this view the media and the educational system disguise reality and convey a picture that is favorable to the interests of the capitalists because they are owned or controlled by or in some way beholden to the capitalists. It is thus a view that is profoundly cynical about the system as it now exists.

Norman I. Fainstein and Susan S. Fainstein, two planning educators, set forth the radical view as five propositions:[16]

1. The capitalists organize the state to serve their own interests. They quote Marx and Engels: "The state is nothing more than the form of organization the bourgeoisie necessarily adopt for internal and external purposes." In this view the state is simply the agent or "executive committee" of those who own capital.

2. "Planning is necessary to the ruling class in order to facilitate accumulation and maintain social control." The "ruling class" through its creature, the state, uses planners both to facilitate economic activity and growth and to deal with problems that, if left untended, might cause social instability, which would threaten the wealth and security of the capitalists.

3. Planners are agents of the state. Either they are directly employed by the state or if not, as in the case of consultants and the like, they still dance to a tune called by the state. (They bid for contracts let by the state, they prepare plans needed by the state, etc.)

4. "Urban planners specialize in managing the contradictions of capitalism." The term *contradiction* here does not have the meaning it has in logic, that is, a situation in which both of two statements cannot be true. Rather it is used in the Marxian sense of conflict. If *monopoly capitalism,* to use a term that appears frequently in Marxist literature, necessitates that some low-income housing needs to be leveled to make way for industrial or commercial development, the planner will help deal with the consequences for the poor and thus deflect some of their anger. This is the social control concept noted in proposition 2.

5. "Planners depoliticize." That is, they state in technical terms issues that would otherwise be cast in political terms. By so doing, they tend to legitimize much that the radical thinks is not legitimate. They wrap exploitation of one sort or another in a disguise of technical language and mathematics. For example, suppose the issue at hand is whether to spend a given sum of money available for local economic development on subsidizing the training of poor residents of a community in basic job skills or subsidizing the building of an office for a major industrial conglomerate. To the radical this looks like an issue of class conflict. The planner is likely to convert the issue to statements about numbers: so many jobs, so many tax dollars, and the like.

For the radical who sees the situation in these terms, the question is "What is a planner to do?" He or she might subscribe to the view that worse is better—the idea that the worse things are, the more chance there is for radical change. In that case there is little room for cooperation with the system. Fainstein and Fainstein take a more moderate stance, perhaps partly because of their view that the short-term prospects for radical change in the United States are extremely small. They take a "better is better" position, asserting that the radical planner can in good conscience cooperate with the system on projects that in some way help the working class even if only in small ways. They also take the view that "expansion of the state is more likely to mark a transition to socialism than its alternative." On that basis alone they tend to favor courses of action that expand the role of planned activity relative to market activity.

Like Marxism itself, the radical critics of planning have devoted more effort to discussion of the existing system than to suggesting the details of alternative policies. In general, radicals would assign a much larger role to the public sector and a correspondingly smaller role to the private sector. Issues such as where industrial plants are to be located would be decided in some collective manner rather than simply by managers and stockholders. Most radicals would favor a more equal distribution of income and wealth than now exists. Many radicals would favor a considerable public role in the setting of prices, profits, and wages. Many radicals would transfer political power downward toward neighborhoods and small groups to counterbalance the power of capital. But many others would not, for "power to the people," if that means small groups and local groups, is antithetical to the idea of planning on a large scale. In general, the radical critique is more an attack on the present than a roadmap to the future.[17]

How might the nonradical respond? He or she might begin simply by questioning the most basic assumptions of the critique. For example, the nonradical might assert the basic goodness rather than badness of the system, perhaps by comparing it with other systems. He or she might argue that the amenability of the system to a long series of reforms and ameliorative measures, from the abolition of child labor to food stamps for the poor, says something very positive about the system. If one finds the system to be good, on balance, then one should have no overarching problems of conscience in cooperating with it. Beyond this overall judgment, the nonradical might attack the radical critique by asserting the pluralism of society. Although admitting that capitalists do indeed exercise much influence over the state, the nonradical might note that other groups, including labor, academe, federal and local government workers, and so on, also exercise major influence over the actions of the state.[18] He or she might thus deny the basic Marxist postulate that the state is the "executive committee" of the bourgeoisie. If it is true that the state, by virtue of this pluralism, does not confine its services in the main to a single small class, there is little reason to be troubled about serving it.

The centrist might argue that the radical critique regarding the planner as a co-opter or a disarmer of discontent is not a very strong argument. Rather, it is an obvious truth cast in a negative way. If one satisfies grievances, whether they be about poverty, housing, or some much smaller matter such as street noise or the need for a new stoplight at the corner, of course one is reducing discontent. But what is wrong with that? Should we deny food to the hungry lest when their stomachs are full, they will lose their righteous anger about being hungry?

The centrist might also agree with the radical that the planner does indeed depoliticize and cast what could be political issues in technical terms. But does not reducing the political heat and introducing some facts and numbers increase the chances of rational solutions? In short, is not depoliticizing a good thing to do?

Finally, the centrist might note that the radical academic who takes the planning profession to task for not waging the fight for radical change is asking the working planner to take risks that he or she is not required to take. As planning educator Michael Brooks has said,

> Certainly the progressive spirit thrives more readily in the halls of academe— where there is virtually no risk attached to its espousal—than it does in the nation's city halls.[19]

The radical critique unsettled many planners, for many people go into the profession out of idealism. Thus a critique that accuses the profession of allowing itself to be used as the tool of an unjust system tends to cause some soul-searching and psychic pain. To the extent that such pain causes productive introspection, it is useful. To the extent that it demoralizes, it is not so useful. The critique just described never gained much ground with practitioners for reasons noted earlier. Its heyday among academicians is also past, though one still hears echoes of it. The tide of academic Marxism peaked sometime in the late 1970s or perhaps in the early 1980s and has receded since then. The overwhelming popular repudiation of the socialist dream in Eastern Europe during the 1980s and then the collapse of the Soviet Union in 1991 drained much conviction out of Marxism in the West.

In the United States the political pendulum has moved to the right in recent years, and so the notion of a major expansion of the role of public planning is even less likely than it was, say, two decades ago. In fact, at least some planners will be happy just to hold their ground and not lose ground to some of the recent legislation and referenda described in Chapter 5.

SUMMARY

Approaches to the act of planning are (1) the rational model, (2) incrementalism, and (3) a midlevel approach as exemplified by "mixed scanning."

The rational model prescribes a comprehensive approach, which begins with problem definition and proceeds through value clarification to selection of goals, formulation of alternative possible actions, forecasting the consequences of those actions, selection of a course of action, detailed plan formulation, and evaluation and modification. The model is comprehensive and systematic. It is designed to begin at square one and proceed to an optimum choice of actions. The model can be regarded as the orthodox view. It has been subjected to a variety of criticisms. Some have asserted that it is unrealistic and may ignore valid interests and considerations that would be taken into account in a planning process that placed less emphasis on system and optimization and more on reaching agreement among disparate and contending parties.

The incremental approach, of which Charles Lindblom is the best-known proponent, stresses reaching agreement, making incremental adjustments, and relying on precedent. For reasons discussed at length, he suggests that the use of the rational model is often neither possible nor wise.

The mixed scanning introduced by Amitai Etzioni is essentially a synthesis of these two approaches. It involves a less-than-complete scan of the situation followed by the application of a comprehensive approach to only parts of the total problem. It has been generally well received by planners, in part because it appears to describe a process that many planners actually follow.

Criticism of planning from the right has generally been based on a view that market mechanisms are more efficient allocators of resources than are administrative decisions. Some antipathy on the right also comes from the view that political freedom is most likely to flourish in an environment in which decisions about the allocation of resources are made privately rather than collectively.

Criticism of planning from the left has not been directed at planning as an idea but rather at the manner in which planning is perceived to be done in the United States. Specifically, radicals have claimed that planning as practiced supports the interest of the capitalist class (which the left sees as the dominant class) and that it papers over major injustices and disparities in wealth and power with minor reforms and palliatives.

The chapter suggested the manner in which the planner of a more or less centrist ideological persuasion might respond to criticisms from right and left. How one views planning cannot be separated from one's overall political and ideological position.

NOTES

1. John Maynard Keynes, *The General Theory of Employment, Interest and Money*, first published in 1936. The quote is from the last page of the final chapter.
2. This example is taken, with some modification, from Edward C. Banfield, "Ends and Means in Planning," in *A Reader in Planning Theory*, Andreas Faludi, ed., Pergamon Press, New York, 1973.
3. For a description of the rational model, see Martin Meyerson and Edward C. Banfield, "Supplement: Note on Conceptual Scheme," *Politics, Planning and the Public Interest*, The Free Press, Glencoe, IL, 1955, pp. 314ff.
4. The term was invented by Herbert Simon. See his *Administrative Behavior*, Macmillan & Co., New York, 1955.
5. Charles E. Lindblom, "The Science of Muddling Through," *Public Administration Review*, Spring 1959. Reprinted in Faludi, *Planning Theory*, p. 163.
6. A commonly cited example of this sort of contradiction is federal housing policy. We have, over the years, spent many billions of federal funds through Urban Renewal, Community Development, Urban Development Action Grants, housing subsidies, and the like to restore the economic vitality of central cities. We also have a federal tax code that provides very powerful incentives to the construction of suburban housing. To some degree the contradictions may exist because we do not have a unified planning process for federal urban policy. The committees that write the tax law, for example, are not the same as the committees that write the housing and economic development legislation, nor is there any statutory requirement that they consult each other.
7. Lindblom, "Muddling Through."
8. Lindblom, "Muddling Through."
9. Amitai Etzioni, "Mixed Scanning: A 'Third' Approach to Decision Making," in Faludi, *Planning Theory*, pp. 217–230.
10. Paul Davidoff, "Advocacy and Pluralism in Planning," *Journal of the American Planning Association*, vol. 31, no. 4, November 1965.
11. Davidoff, "Advocacy and Pluralism in Planning." Whether this picture made good economic sense was always open to some argument. It could have been argued that were all exclusionary zoning to disappear, the result would simply be accelerated residential construction in the suburbs permitting even faster flight of the more affluent central-city residents to the suburbs, making the city-suburb dichotomy even more pronounced. At present, some 40 years after he made this argument, we observe that the black middle class is suburbanizing quite rapidly, much as the white middle class did several decades earlier. If this "noose" is still in place, it is evidently not very effective.
12. This view is similar to that expressed by the widely cited philosopher John Rawls that how just a society is should be judged by how it treats the least fortunate of its members. See his *A Theory of Justice*, Belknap Press of Harvard University, Cambridge, MA, 1971.
13. See "Where Have All the Radicals Gone," *Planning*, October 1985, pp. 12–17.
14. Milton Friedman, *Capitalism and Freedom*, University of Chicago Press, Chicago, 1962.
15. For example, it has often been suggested that the reformist initiatives such as unemployment insurance, the right to collective bargaining, and the Social Security system during the Great Depression of the 1930s may well have prevented radical social change in the United States.
16. Norman I. Fainstein and Susan S. Fainstein, "New Debates in Urban Planning: The Impact of Marxist Theory Within the U.S.," *International Journal of Urban and Regional Research*, vol. 3, no. 3, 1979, pp. 381–402. Reprinted in *Critical Readings in Planning Theory*, Chris Paris, ed., Pergamon Press, New York, 1982, pp. 147–174.
17. For essays on what a left-wing political and social agenda might be, see Martin Carnoy and Derek Shearer, *Economic Democracy*, M. E. Sharpe, Inc., Armonk, NY, 1980. See also works by Michael Harrington, Barry

Bluestone, Bennett Harrison, and David M. Gordon.

18. For essays that discuss the rise of other centers of power in society, particularly academe and bureaucracy, see R. Bruce-Briggs, ed., *The New Class*, Transaction Books, New Brunswick, NJ, 1979.

19. Michael Brooks, "Four Critical Junctures in the History of the Urban Planning Profession," *Journal of the American Planning Association*, Spring 1988, pp. 241–248.

SELECTED BIBLIOGRAPHY

BROOKS, MICHAEL P., *Planning Theory for Practitioners*, Planners Press, American Planning Association, Chicago, 2002.

FALUDI, ANDREAS, ED., *A Reader in Planning Theory*, Pergamon Press, New York, 1973.

FRIEDMAN, JOHN, *Planning in the Public Domain*, Princeton University Press, Princeton, NJ, 1987.

MEYERSON, MARTIN, and BANFIELD, EDWARD C., *Politics, Planning and the Public Interest*, The Free Press, Glencoe, IL, 1955.

STEIN, JAY M., ED., *Classic Readings in Urban Planning: An Introduction*, McGraw-Hill, Inc., New York, 1995.

INDEX

Page numbers in *italics* indicate figures.

Abrams, Charles, 213
Advocacy planning, 101,
    411–12
"Affordable housing", 113,
    158, 220, 271, 273
aging, 121
agricultural productivity and
    employment, 23–24
AIA (American Institute of
    Architects), 109
AICP (American Institute of
    Certified Planners), 6, 102
air conditioning, 22
"airshed", 323
All-American Canal, 346
Allen, George, 255
alleys, 35, 189, 192
Amendment, 37
    (Colorado), 303–4
American Institute of
    Architects (AIA), 109
American Institute of
    Certified Planners
    (AICP), 6, 102
American League for Civic
    Improvement, 40
American Nevada
    Corporation, 115
American Planning
    Association (APA),
    5, 82, 120
American Revolution, 32
Americans with Disabilities
    Act (ADA), 97

Ammann, Othmar H., 332
Amsterdam, Netherlands,
    376, *377*
Anderson, Martin, 209
annuity serial bonds, 140
APA (American Planning
    Association), 5, 82, 120
Appalachian region, 66, 251
aquifer recharge area, 321n.27
Arab-Israeli War, 64–65, 316
architectural review, 163–64
Arcosanti (Arizona), 200
Area Redevelopment
    Administration (ARA), 251
Arizona, 86, 207
Army Corps of Engineers,
    342, 346, 348
Arrhenius, Svante, 293
assessment, 149
Atlanta Regional
    Commission, 336–38
atmospheric carbon dioxide,
    295
automobiles
    *coming to terms with the
        automobile*, 200–1
    dependence on, 188
    electric, 243, 304
    emissions standards, 286,
        303, 306
    first, 17
    fuel economy, 91
    high-occupancy vehicles
        (HOVs) lanes, 239, 240, 242

hybrids, 28, 243
intelligent vehicle
    technology, 243
numbers of, 19, 45, 225, 324,
    367, 390, 398
Smart Car, 244
sport utility vehicles
    (SUVs), 19, 225, 296–97
subsidies, 255
suburbanization and, 17

baby boom, 12, 20
Baltimore, Maryland, *211*, 216
Bassett Edward M., 46, 78
Battery Park City, 174, *175*, *179*
beltway design, *229*, 353
benefit/cost analysis, 234, 235,
    237, 246, 308
Berman v. *Parker*, 85, 207
bikeways, 317
Blair, Tony, 369
Blakely, Edward, 115
Bloomberg, Michael, 158
Board of Land and Natural
    Resources (Hawaii), 274
bond, definition of, 138
Bonneville Dam, 61, 347
"bonus" or "incentive"
    zoning, 155
bonus zoning, 155
Bosselman, Fred, 167, 274
Boston, Massachusetts, 213
Boston Metropolitan Planning
    Commission, 50

Boston Waterfront, 213, 217
Boulder, Colorado, 271–72,
    289n.9
Boulder Dam, 61, 345
Broadacre City, 193, 196, 200–1
Bronx River Parkway, 352
Brooks, Michael, 418
Brown, Gordon, 370
Brown v. *Board of Education*, 111
Brownfields program, 282,
    285, 308
Brundtland Commission, 282
    see also World Commission
    on Environment and
    Development
Buckhead, Atlanta, 194
Bucks County
    Pennsylvania, 272
Bulgaria, 387
Bureau of Land Management
    (BLM), 310, 357
Bureau of Public Roads
    (BPR), 352
Bureau of Reclamation,
    345, 346, 347–48
Burnham, Daniel, 41, 42
Bus Rapid Transit (BRT), 238
Bush, George H. W., 66, 252,
    295
Bush, George W., 66,
    252–53, 254, 300
Bush v. *Gore*, 84

Cadillac Desert (Reisner), 348
CAFE (Corporate Average
    Fuel Economy), 91, 297
CAFRA (Coastal Area Facility
    Review Act), 277
Calgary (Alberta, Canada), 183
California
    bikeways, 317
    enabling legislation, 162
    energy crisis, 300
    Proposition, 13, 66
    water supply, 346
California Coastal
    Commission, 82
California Urban Futures
    Model, 131
Callie, Fred, 167
Calthorpe, Peter, 191
Canals, historic
Canary Wharf, 370

"cap and trade" system, 298
Cape Cod, Massachusetts,
    285–86
capital budget, 132, 138, 139,
    261, 281
capital expenditures
    cost of, 132–33
    facilities, 4, 109
    financing, 138–39, 164, 182
    urban design plan,
        implementing, 182
capital improvements plan
    (CIP), 138–39
capital investment, 6, 132,
    137–40, 145, 164–65,
    264, 277
capital investment/land-use
    controls, combining,
    164–65
Carson, Rachel, 64
Carter administration,
    252, 338
CATS (Chicago Area
    Transportation Study),
    63, 231
CD (Community
    Development) funds,
    214, 219
CDBGs (Community
    Development Block
    Grants), 213, 221
central city
    beltway design, 229
    definition of, 17
    Germany, 386
    growth, 27–28
    Milton Keynes, 367
    population trends, 18
    restoring, 259, 277
    shrinkage, 18, 22–23
    Western European
        nations, 363
Central Pacific Railroad, 344
Central Park, New York, 37
CERCLA *See* Superfund
CFCs (chlorofluorocarbons),
    302
Chamber of Commerce, 105
Chandigarh, India, 54, 393
Chattahooche River
    corridor, 338
Cheney, Dick, 300
Chevrolet Volt, 243–44

Chicago, 26
Chicago Area Transportation
    Study (CATS), 63, 231
Chicago Board of Trade, 302
Chicago plan of, 42–44, 73
Chicago skyway, 242
China
    Kyoto Treaty, 296
    planning, the future of, 398
    population trends, 399,
        401n.33
chlorofluorocarbons
    (CFCs), 302
Cincinnati, Ohio, 195
CIP (capital improvements
    plan), 138–39
citizen participation, 98,
    214–15
City Beautiful movement,
    41, 42
city of the future, visions of,
    197–200
City Realty Corporation,
    60, 206–7
Civil Rights Movement, 108
Clavel, Pierre, 126
Clean Air Act, 64, 90, 297, 302
Clean Water Acts, 90, 302
Cleveland, Ohio, 118
climate change, 293, 295–301
Clinton administration, 66,
    252, 301
cluster zoning, 161
Coastal Area Facility Review
    Act (CAFRA), 277
Coastal Resources
    Management
    Council, 83
Coastal Zone Management
    Act of 1972, 302, 306
cogeneration, 318
COGs (council of govern-
    ments), 5, 326–28
cohort survival method, 128
colonial America, 32–34, 33
Colorado, 255
Colorado River, 346
Colorado River Basin
    Compact, 61, 346
Columbia, Maryland,
    54, 114, 366
Columbian Exposition (1893),
    Chicago, 41

Commoner, Barry, 64
communicable disease, 14
community development,
    213–17, 17
    Urban Renewal approach,
        versus, 215–17
Community Development Act
    (1974), 213
Community Development
    Block Grants (CDBGs),
    213, 214, 221, 252
community master planning,
    growth of, 46–48
    examples of, 47
    land-use controls, 46
    limitations of, 47
    plans, goals of, 46–47
    Radburn, New Jersey, 47, *48*
commuting, 19, 23, 249, 378
compact development, 280,
    285
comprehensive plan, 124–36
    comprehensive plans, 126–34
concurrency requirements,
    275–76
condemnation award, 74, 158
Constitution, planning, legal
    basis of, 72–74
consultants, 4, 104
Continental Congress, 342
"Contract with America", 310
Coolidge, Calvin, 35, 350
Corporate Average Fuel
    Economy (CAFE),
    91, 297
Council of Governments
    (COG), 5, 326–28
Council on Affordable
    Housing, 151
"creatures of the state",
    32, 34, 72
Créteil, France, *372*
cross-commuting, 23
curvilinear street pattern,
    38, 186
Czech Republic, 387

databases, 59, 128, 132, 231
Davidoff, Paul, 101, 411
Davis, California, 317
DCA (Department of
    Community Affairs),
    275–76

Dearborn/Fairfield Village,
    194
decentralization
    beginnings of, 14–16, *16*
    electronic communications,
        20
    technologies, effect on, 17
DeGrove, John M., 275
demand response systems, 227
Department of Community
    Affairs (DCA), 275–76
Department of Energy
    (DOE), 304
Department of Housing and
    Urban Development
    (HUD), 101
Department of Land
    Conservation and
    Development, 276
Department of Transportation
    (DOT), 236
development agreements, 162
Dial-a-Ride, 227
Dillon, John F., 72
Dillon's rule, 72–77
disjointed incrementalism, 408
Djakarta, Indonesia, 397
Doctoroff, Dan, 158
DOE (Department of Energy),
    304
Dolan v. *City of Tigard*, 83
DOT (Department of
    Transportation), 236
Doxiadis, Konstantinos, 393
Duany, Andres, 188, 190
Dulles toll road, 240
dynamic tolling, 242

easements, 140
Easley, Gail, 162
East Germany, 384, 386, 387
Eastern Europe, planning in,
    387–93
    development outside Sofia,
        capital of Bulgaria, *391*
    EU membership and future
        of planning, 392–93
    the future of, 397–98
    privatization, 392
    Soviet planning style,
        388–89, *389*
    transition to market
        economy, 389–92

EC (European Community),
    362
economic base study, 129
Economic Development
    Administration (EDA), 251
economic development
    planning
    assessment of consequences,
        263–64
    community involvement,
        258–61
    conflicts in, 254, 261
    cooperation and competition,
        261
    federal presence in, 250–54
    goals of, 124–26
    history of, 66–67, 249–50
    intermunicipal competition,
        258
    investments by higher
        levels of government,
        pursuit of, 261–62
    local programs, 257–64
    market evaluation, 263
    metropolitan areas, 257
    needs assessment, 263
    perspectives on, 250–54
    place-related programs,
        251–54
    planner and economic
        developer relationship,
        254
    social side of, 118
    state efforts, 254–57
    subsidy packages, 255–56
    systematic approach to,
        263–64
edge city, the, 193–96, 200–1, 353
Eisenhower administration,
    352
EISs (environmental impact
    statements), 304, 305
electronic communications,
    20, 22, 27
elevators, 7, 12, 201
Embarcadero Freeway, 236
eminent domain, 73–74, 75,
    85–86
Empire State Building, *199*
Empowerment Zones, 252, 370
energy costs, future of, 27–28
energy independence, 65, 316
energy planning, 291, 316–18

Enterprise Zone, 259, 369–70
environmental assessment
(EA), 304–5
Environmental Defense
Fund, 298
environmental impact
statements (EISs),
304, 305
environmental justice, 119–20
Environmental Land and
Water Management Act
(Florida), 275, 276
Environmental Lands and
Management Act, 276
environmental planning and
policy
air quality, 293, *294, 295*,
304, 306
Bush administration and,
300–01
cap and trade, 298
Clinton administration
and, 301
economic issues, 306–10
emissions-permit-trading
system, 285
emissions standards, 286,
303, 306
energy planning, 316–18
global climate changes,
293, *295, 295*–301
goals of, 291
greenhouse winners/losers,
298–300
higher-level controls over,
167–68
history of, 64–65
intergovernmental context
of, 301–6
International Earth Summit
Conference, 295–6
International Panel on
Climate Change (IPCC),
297
local, 310–13
at national level, 292–93
NEPA process, 304–6
physical environment,
analyzing, 310–13
political issues, 306–10
pollution control
expenditures, 292–93, 307

problems with, 291–92
second Bush administration,
300–1
solid waste issue of,
313–16
state-level growth
management, 274–78
Superfund, case of, 307–8
Environmental Protection
Agency (EPA), 64, 119,
297, 302, 307
environmental racism, 119
environmentalists, 236, 297,
300, 301, 304, 348, 358
"equalization rate", 169n.13
Erie Canal, 249
Estonia, 387–88
Etzioni, Amitai, 409–10
EU (European Union), 392–93
Euclid v. Ambler Realty, 362
Euclidean Zoning, 79, 156
European Community (EC),
362
European Union (EU), 392–93
Ewing, Reid, 279–80
exactions, 162–63
exclusionary zoning, 411, 420n.11
externalities, 167, 170n.27

factory production, 10
Fainstein, Norman I. and
Susan S., 416
Fair Housing Act, 151
Fairfax Center area, 273
Fairfax County, Virginia,
143–44, 273
Fannie Mae, 355
Federal Aid Road Act of 1916,
351
Federal Highway Act of 1956,
352
Federal Highway Act of 1962,
326
Federal Highway
Administration, 352
Federal Housing
Administration (FHA),
60, 355
federal land grants, 344
Federal National Mortgage
Association (FNMA), 355
Federal Register, 305

Federal Water Pollution
Control Act (FWPCA),
306
feminism and planning, 120
FHA (Federal Housing
Administration),
60, 355
FHA mortgage insurance,
60, 355
Fifth Amendment, "taking"
clause, 74, 75, 79
Finland, 383
First Pacific Railway Act
of 1862, 344
"fiscal impact analysis", 146
floor area ratio (FAR), 141,
161–62
flophouses, 117
Florida, growth management
in, 275–76
Fort Collins, Colorado,
160–61, 273–74
fossil fuels, 300, 301, 303,
304, 319
1400 Governments (Wood), 50
Fourteenth Amendment, "due
process", 74
Fourth Amendment,
"*unreasonable* search
and seizures", 74
fractional assessment, 148,
169n.13
France, planning in, 371–76
Freedom Tower, 68, 177
freeway revolt, 236
Friedan, Betty, 120
Friedman, Milton, 414
"frostbelt" to "sunbelt
movement", 20–22
fuel cell, 244
full value assessment, 148
Fuller, R. Buckminster, 197
FWPCA (Federal Water
Pollution Control
Act), 306

GALIP (Gays and Lesbians
in Planning), 120
garden cities, 52–53, *54*
Garden Cities of Tomorrow
(Howard), 52
Garreau, Joel, 194, 196, 353

gated communities, 114
Gays and Lesbians in
  Planning (GALIP), 120
gender issues, 120
general obligation (GO)
  bond, 139
general plan. See comprehensive
  planning
gentrification, 213, 222, 404
Geographic Information
  System (GIS), 128–29, 338
George Washington bridge,
  331, *334*
Germany, planning in, 383–87
  general features, 384
  Intercity Express (ICE), 386
  military areas, conversion
    of, 387
  municipalities
    (Gemeinden), 386
  post-World War II planning,
    384–87
  public housing areas
    (Plattensiedlungen), 387
  reunification, 386–87
  urban renewal
GIS (Geographic Information
  System), 128–29, 338
Glendenning, Parris, 279
Global Warming, See climate
  change
globalization, 26
Grand Central Station, 80
Grand Coulee Dam, 61, 347
Gravier, Jean Francais, 371
gravity model, 232, *233*
Great Britain, planning in
  Canary Wharf development,
    370
  Enterprise Zone, 369–70
  greenbelts, 365–66
  New Towns Act, 366
  subsidized housing, 367
  Town and Country
    Planning Act, 364, 365
  transportation system, 367
  Urban Development
    Corporation (UDC), 370
Great Depression, 19, 59–61,
  206, 346, 350, 356
"green building codes", 318
Green Hills, Ohio, 60

Green Valley, Nevada, 115
Greenbelt, Maryland, 60, 89
greenbelts, 365
Greendale, Wisconsin, 60
greenfields, 285, 308
greenhouse gases, 296,
  297–98
Greenwich Village, *153*, 154
Greer, Guy, 206
gridiron pattern, 34
growth management
  characterizations of, 266–67
  "defense of privilege" issue,
    270–71
  goals of, 266
  history of, 65
  holding-zone approach, 272
  infrastructures and, 273,
    274, 275–76
  local programs, sampling
    of, 271–74
  origins of, 267–69
  priority funding areas, 281
  pros/cons, 278–79
  state level, 274–78
  winners/losers in, 269–71
Growth Management Act,
  Florida, 275
growth management programs
  (local)
  Boulder, Colorado,
    271–72
  Bucks County,
    Pennsylvania, 272
  Fort Collins, Colorado,
    273–74
growth poles, 371, 400n.14
Guterson, David, 115

Hackensack Meadowlands, 277
Hadacheck v. *Sebastian*, 76
Hall, Peter, 366, 369, 371, 378
Hansen, Alvin, 206
HAP (Housing Assistance
  Plan), 214, 221
Haussmann, Baron, 99, 171,
  172, 173
Hawaii, *21*, 274, 275, 288, *354*
heavy rail (commuter
  railroad), 238
High Line (New York City),
  157–58, *159*

high-occupancy tax (HOT)
  lane, 242
high-occupancy vehicle
  (HOV) lane, 239, 242
Highway legislation, 230, 327
Highway Trust Fund, 227, 352
*Hills Development Co. v.
  Township of Bernards
  (Mt. Laurel III)*, 151
historic preservation, 164
"holding zone", 272
home rule legislation, 73
homelessness, 116–18
Homestead Act of 1862, 343
Hoover, Herbert, 46
Hoover Dam, 346
HOT (high-occupancy tax)
  lane, 242
housing
  comprehensive planning
    approach, 222
  federal requirements, 221
  flophouses, 117
  metropolitan planning and,
    324–28
  mobile homes, 151
  municipal policy, 117
  in neotraditional
    communities, 193
  planning, 219–22
  problems, 217–18
  public, 39, 60, 89, 109, 200
  public policy, 174, 218
  question, the, 217–19
  reform, 38–39
  rent controls, 117, 220
  row houses, 216, 219
  set-aside, 151
  Single Room Occupancy
    (SRO) hotels, 117
  "sites and services"
    approach, 396
  social issues, 109–18
  squatter housing, 395
  subsidies, 218
  tax expenditures, 218, 219
  Third World, *394*, 395–97
Third World planning,
  393–97
"town cramming" (Britain),
  365–66
Yonkers case, 110–13, 122n.5

Housing Act (1949), 60, 63, 207
Housing and Community Development Act, 213, 223
Housing and Urban Development (HUD), 5, 101, 111, 221
Housing Assistance Plan (HAP), 214, 221
Howard Ebenezer, 52–55, 367
Hungary, 387
Hurricane Katrina (2005), 69

IBM-Toshiba chip-manufacturing plant, 255–56
"ice tea", 238
Ickes, Harold, 59
Ile de France, 371
Illinois
    Saturn car offer, 255
    Sears, Roebuck, and Company, 256
Image of the City (Lynch), 180
Imperial Valley (California), 346, 349
incentive zoning, 155
inclusionary zoning, 160, 218, 287
incremental model, 409, *409*, 410, 411
"induced demand" phenomenon, 235–36
Industrial Revenue Bond (IRB), 252
industrial revolution, 368
infill development, 282, 285, 287
infrastructure, provision of, 261
integration
    public housing planning, 208, 404
    racial, 109, 115, 116, 208
    school, 97, 111
    social, 152, 191
intelligent vehicle technology, 243
Intercity Express (ICE), 386
Intermodal Surface Transportation Efficiency Act (ISTEA), 238–39, 327, 338

International Earth Summit Conference, 295–96
International Panel on Climate Change (IPCC), 297
interplace economic competition, 248
interstate highway system
    beltway pattern, *229*, 353, 354
    as completed, 353, *354*
    design and construction, 351, 353
    economic impact of, 353, 354
    federal presence in, 351–53
    fine-tuning, 239–40
    funding, 351–53
    national planning, 229
    planning/building of, *229*, 229, 351
IRB (Industrial Revenue Bonds), 252
Irvine Spectrum, 194, *195*, *196*
Isle of Dogs Enterprise Zone, 370
ISTEA (Intermodal Surface Transportation Efficiency Act), 238–39, 327, 338

Jacobs, Jane, 153, 154, 185
JAPA (The Journal of the American Planning Association), 5
Jepson, Edward J., Jr., 287
"just compensation", 74, 75

Kamen, Dean, 244, 245
Kampung Improvement Program (KIP), 397
Kasarda, John D., 394
Katrina, Hurricane (2005), 69
Kelo v. New London, 85–86, 207
Kennedy Airport, 333
Kentlands (Gaithersburg, Maryland), *192*, 193
Keynes, John Maynard, 402
Krumholz, Norman, 118
Kyoto Protocol, 296, 300

L'Enfant, Pierre, 34
La Defense, *374*
La Guardia Airport, 333
Laguna West (California), 191

Lake Ann (Reston, Virginia), *187*
Lake Havasu, 346
land banking, 260, 378
land capability analysis, 311
land grant colleges, 343
land grants, federal, 344
land ownership, federal, 358
land use allocation, *176*
land-use controls, 137–70
    architectural review, 163–64
    capital investment, combining, 164–65
    decisions, 2, 3, 79, 109–18, 264, 274, 285
    energy planning and, 319
    higher levels of, 167–68
    historic preservation, 164
    housing, planning for, 219–22
    inventory, 128
    provision of infrastructure, and use of, 260–61
    site plan review, 163
    statewide, 274
    subdivision regulations, 140–41
    techniques, 155–57, 160–63
    zoning ordinances, 141–42, *143–44*
    see also zoning
land-use planning tools, 137–70
    capital investment/ land-use controls, combining, 164–65
    land-use control, higher levels of, 167–68
    land-use controls, 140–64
    local control, forces beyond, 166–68
    public capital investment, 137–39
land value determinants of, 137–38
landfills, 313, 314
Landmarks Commission, N.Y., 164
Landmarks Preservation Committee, N.Y., 80
Largo, Florida, 161
Lasch, Christopher, 115
Le Corbusier, 197, *198*, 332, 393

League of Oregon Cities, 81
League of Women Voters, 105
leasebacks, 169n.4
light-rail systems, 237–38
light trucks, 19, 225, 296–97
limited-access highway, 19
Lincoln Center, 213
Lindblom, Charles, 406, 407, 408
"little NEPA" acts, 64, 302
"Live Near Your Work" program (Maryland), 282
local economic development programs, 257–64
  cooperation and competition, 261
  federal presence in, 250–54
  intermunicipal competition, 258
  investment by higher levels of government, 261–62
  land-use controls, 261
  larger considerations, 262–63
  motivation for, 257–58
  planners and economic developers relationship, 254
  provision of infrastructure, 261
  sales and promotion, 258
  sites/buildings, availability of, 259–60
  subsidization, 253, 258–59
  systematic approach to, 263–64
local environmental planning, 310–13
Loeks, C. David, 322
loft buildings, 11, 12, 155
long-distance commuting, 16, 366
Los Angeles, 26, 50
Louisiana Purchase, 342
Lucas v. *South Carolina Coastal Council*, 83, 307
Lynch, Kevin, 180

McCall, Thomas, 276
McHarg, Ian, 311–12
MacMansions, 220
Major, John, 369
Mall, the, Washington, D.C., 41
Mall of America, 183

Management and Control of Growth, 267
Manassas, Virginia, 255
mandates, 90–91
Manhattan
  Battery Park City, 174, *175*, *176*, 179
  Central Park, 37
  Greenwich Village, *153*, *154*, 191
  Lincoln Center, 213
  lower Manhattan, 11–12, 76, 155, 178
  Lower West Side, 11–12
  Midtown zoning, *178*
  South Street Seaport, 216, 217
  West Village, 154
  zoning, 76–78
Marine Protection, Control, and Sanctuaries Act of 1972, 302
Market Street (San Francisco), *174*
Marxism, 417, 418
Maryland, 67, *192*, 281–82, 366
Massachusetts v. *The Environmental Protection Agency (EPA)*, 297
master plan, 113–14
  see also comprehensive planning
Measures, 7, 37, 81–82
megastructures, 197, *198*, *199*, 201
métropole d' équilibre, France, 371
metropolitan area planning
  council of governments (COGs), 326–28
  history of, 324–28
  public authority, 325–26
  after World War Two, 326
Metropolitan Atlanta Rail Transit Authority (MARTA), 338
Metropolitan Council, Atlanta, 329–30
Metropolitan Planning Commission (MPC), 329
Metropolitan Planning Organization (MPO), 327
metropolitan regions, planning for

Atlanta, 336–38
Chicago, 231
history of, 231, 324–28
Minneapolis–St. Paul, 328–30
planning issues, 323–24
New York and New Jersey, 331–36
Metropolitan Washington Council of Governments (MWCOG), 327
Million Homes Programme, Sweden, 382
Milton Keynes, Great Britain, 367, *368*
Milwaukee, density of, 15, *16*
Minneapolis, Minnesota, 183
Minneapolis–St. Paul, 328–30
  skyway system, 183
"mixed scanning", 409–10
mobile homes, 151
modal split, estimating, 232
Moody's bond-rating agency, 139
Morrill Land Grant Act, 343
mortgage insurance, 60, 355
Moses, Robert, 98–99
Mount Laurel, 150–51
MPC (Metropolitan Planning Commission), 329
MPO (Metropolitan Planning Organization), 327
muddling through, 408
Mugler v. *Kansas*, 76
Mumford, Lewis, 52–53
Municipal Art Movement, The, 40–41, *42*

National Ambient Air Quality Standards (NAAQSs), 303
National Association for the Advancement of Colored People (NAACP), 111
National Association of Regional Councils, 326–27
National Defense Highway Act, 19, 61, 63, 230
National Environmental Policy Act (NEPA), 64, 302
  see also NEPA process
National Forest Service, 358
National League of Improvement Associations, 39

National Municipal
League, 337
National Park System, 358
National Parks Service, 358
National Recreation Area, 338
National Resources Planning
Board (NRPB), 61, 341
natural catastrophe, 69–70
neighborhood concept,
185–88, *186*, *187*
neo-Marxism, 415
neotraditional design,
55, 188–89, 191–93
neotraditionalists, 188–89,
191–93
NEPA (National
Environmental Policy
Act), 64, 302, 304–306
Netherlands, planning in,
376–78
"new community"
provision, 275
New England Regional
Commission, 61
New Jersey, 150
New Jersey Turnpike, *334*
New Orleans, 69
New Source Review (NSR), 301
New Towns Act, Great
Britain, 366
new urbanism, see neotraditional design
New York City
Landmarks Commission, 164
as port city, 333
population trends
public transportation, 226
regional planning, 50, *51*
Richmond Parkway, 312–13
Staten Island, 312, 333, 335
Tenement House
Commission, 38–39
Westway, 236, 306
World Trade Center
rebuilding plan, 177–78
zoning ordinance, 45, 46
Nicollet Mall, *184*
NIMBY (Not in My Back
Yard), 281, 314
nineteenth-century city,
40, 52, 173
Nixon, Richard, 302
no growth, 267

Nolen, John, 49
*Nollan v. California Coastal
Council*, 82–83
nonattainment areas, 239
nonmetropolitan population
(U.S.), 27
Norris, George, 350
Northern Pacific Railroad, 344
Northwest Ordinance of 1785,
358
Northwest Territory, 342
NSR (New Source Review), 301

Office of Management &
Budget (OMB), 356
Oglethorpe, James, 32, *33*
oil prices, 64, 65, 316, 319
Olmsted, Frederick Law, 37, 38
Olmsted, Frederick Law Jr., 41
Olympia and York,
development firm, 370
1000 Friends of Oregon, 277
open spaces, 35, 37, 213
opportunity zones, 253–54
Ordinance of 1785, 342–43
Oregon, *21*, 81, 82, 276
Oregon Compromise, 342
Oregonians in Action, 81
Osborn, F. J., 53

Pacific Northwest Regional
Planning Commission, 61
Palazzolo v. Rhode Island, 83–84
paratransit, 227
Paris et le désert Francais
(Gravier), 371
Parker Dam, 346
parks, 37, 40, 46–47, 186,
214, 323
parkways, 19, 50, 352
Parliament, 363–64, 365, 366
Parnell, Allan M., 394
PAS (Planning Advisory
Service), 5
PATH (Port Authority
Trans-Hudson) tubes, 177
patient's rights movement, 116
pedestrian pocket
developments, 191
Penn, William, *33*, 35
*Penn Central Transportation
Company v. New York
City*, 80

Pennsylvania (Volkswagen
subsidy), 255
Pennsylvania Turnpike, 352
performance zoning,
161–62
Perry, Clarence, 186
Philadelphia, Pennsylvania,
33, 35
pilote, 198
plan formulation, 127, 131,
135, 264
planned community, 366
planned unit development
(PUD), 160–61
planners
as advocate, 101
as agent of radical change,
101–2
description of, 4–5
economic developers,
relationship between, 254
as entrepreneur, 100–1
and power, 95–96
professional organizations
of, 5–6
"planners depoliticize", 417
planning
aging and, 121
definition of, 59
feminism and, 120
history of, 31–71
local, federal presence in,
89–91
master planning, 46, 56
models, 197, 409–10
and politics, 93–107
research in, 127–30
styles of, 99–102
planning, legal basis of,
72–92
constitutional framework,
72–74
eminent domain, fight over,
85–86
federal role, 89–91
mandated responsibilities,
90–91
powers and limitations,
73–74
public control over private
property, 74–84
state-enabling legislation,
87–88

state planning, legal link
to, 88
Supreme Court and "taking"
issue, 82–84
Planning Advisory Service
(PAS), 5
planning agencies
community, links to, 104–5
organization of, 102–4
planning consultants, 104
planning and politics
connections between,
93–94
planners and power, 95–96
planning agencies, how
organized, 102–5
planning, styles of, 99–102
power, fragmentation
of, 96–99
planning commission,
44, 46, 87
planning consultants, 5, 46,
104
planning degree programs, 5
Planning District
Commissions, 327
Planning (magazine), 191,
193, 237
planning research, 127–30
planning schools, 119, 248,
393
planning theory
advocacy planning,
411–12
disjointed incrementalism,
408–9
incremental model, 409,
410, 411
left-wing views of, 415–19
middle-range models,
409–10
rational model, 404–8
plug-in hybrid, 243–44
pod and collector plan,
190–91
police power, 75, 76, 140
population
central-city, 17
coastward movement of, 22
congestion, 14
decentralization, 14–16, 16,
17, 20
densities, 11, 12, 15, *16*

farm, 23–24
forecasting, 127–28
growth, 10–11
1990s trends, 24–25
projections, 26–28
redistribution, 17
regional trends, 20–22, *21*
rural-to-urban migration,
23–24
shrinkage, in central cities,
18, 22–23
suburbanization, 17, 19
Third World Countries, 398
Port Authority of New York
and New Jersey, 50, 177,
325, 331–36
Port of New Orleans, 69
Portland, Oregon, 237, 280, *354*
poverty, 66, 214, 251, 257, 350
"prior appropriation", 348
priority funding areas, 281
private communities, 113–16
private property, public
control of, 44–48, 74–84
private property rights,
34, 85–86
professional organizations,
of planners, 5–6
proffers, 273
"property led" development,
370, 373
Property Rights movement, 80
property tax relief, 66
property taxes
collection of, 2, 146, *148–49*
deducibility of, 356
intermunicipal cooperation,
329
planning questions, 94, 125
subsidization, 258–59
suburbanization and, 356
tax expenditures and, 218
tool of land-use planning,
141
and zoning, *148–49*,
290n.19
Proposition, 13California, 66
Proposition, 49 (Oregon), 82
Prospect Park, Brooklyn,
N.Y., 37
Pruitt-Igoe public housing
project, 109
public authority, 325–26

public capital investment,
137–39
Public Choice, 89
public goods, 414–15
"public purpose", 85
public safety, 67–69
public transportation,
planning for, 225–7, 237–8
"public welfare", 76
PUD (planned unit
development), 160–61
Putrajaya, Malaysia, 55

racial integration, 208
Radburn, New Jersey,
48, 54, 201
Radiant City, the, 47, 197
radio, 19
railroad flat, 12
railroads
establishment of U.S.
systems, 343–45
in France, 371, 400n.16
high-speed train system
(Germany), 386
Ramapo, New York, 268–69
Randstad Holland, 378, *379*
rational model, 404–8, *409*
criticisms of, 405–7
in defense of, 407–8,
420n.6
Reagan administration,
66, 215, 252
Reclamation Act of 1902, 345,
359n.10
Reclamation Service, 345
recreation studies, 130
Reed, Thomas, 337
reform politics, 96
Regional Contribution
Agreement (RCA), 152
Regional Plan Association
(RPA), 49, 324
regional planning, emergence
of, 49–50
Reilly, William, 309
Reilly's Law of Retail
Gravitation, 232
Reisner, Marc, 348
remediation, Superfund and,
307
rent controls, 117, 220
rent/income ratios, 60

Resettlement
  Administration, 60
Resource Conservation and
  Recovery Act, 302
Reston, Virginia, 54, 114, *187,*
  188, 366
retirement communities,
  114, 179
revenue bonds, 139, 242
Rhode Island, *21,* 32, 281
Richmond Parkway,
  New York City, 312
ring road, 367
  see also beltway
Riverside (Chicago suburb), *38*
road building, on federally
  owned land, 301
Roanoke, Virginia, 216
Roosevelt, Franklin D., 59, 350
Roosevelt, Theodore, 347
Rouse Corporation, 211, 366
row houses, 216, 219
RPA, See Regional Plan
  Association
Rumania, 387
Rural Heritage program,
  281–82
rural-to-urban migration,
  Third World, 394
Russell Sage Foundation, 49

Sacramento River, 347
Safe, Accountable, Flexible,
  Efficient Transportation
  Equity Act: A Legacy for
  Users, 239, 242, 327
Safe Drinking Water Act
  of 1974, 302
"Sagebrush Rebellion",
  310, 358
SAI (Suburban Action
  Institute), 411
St. Louis, Missouri, 22, 109,
  237, 255, *354*
San Francisco, 163, *174*
Sand, Leonard B., 111, 112
sanitary reform, 35–36
sanitation and integrated
  design, 37
Savannah, Georgia, 32, *33,* 34
Scandinavia, planning in, 299,
  363, 368, 378–83
Schaumburg, Illinois, 194

schools, 3, 88, 125, 138, 140, 180
Schumacher, Ernest F., 268
Schumpeter, Joseph, 213
scoping process, 305
"scrubbers", 292
Sears, Roebuck, and
  Company, 256
Segway, 244–45
SEM (*Société d' Économie
  Mixte*), 197, 373
September 11, 2001, 68
sequestration, of carbon
  dioxide, 304
set-aside, 151
sewers, 36, 37, 88, 323, 395
"shell building", 260
Sierra Club, 97, 271
Silent Spring (Carson), 64
Silverstein, Larry, 177
Single Room Occupancy
  (SRO) hotels, 117
sinking fund, 169n.5
SIPs (state implementation
  plans), 90, 302–3
site plan review, 163
"sites and services" approach,
  396, 396–97
skyscrapers, 78
skyways, 183, *184*
slums, 16, 208
Small is Beautiful
  (Schumacher), 268
Smart Car, 244
Smart Growth, 67, 279–82
smart highway, 243
Smith, Adam, 413
Smith, Alfred E., 331
"social democratic" model, 382
"social housing", 362
social planning, 122
Social Security, 22
socialism, 362
Société d' Économie Mixte
  (SEM), 373
soil characteristics, study
  of, 129
Soleri, Paolo, *198,* 199–200, 201
solid waste disposal, 214,
  323, 394
South Coast Air Quality
  Management District
  (AQMD), 303
South Korea, 398

*Southern Burlington County
  NAACP* v. *Township of
  Mount Laurel,* 150
Soviet planning style,
  388–89, *389*
Soviet Union, 58, 67, 388, 392,
  397–98
sport utility vehicles (SUVs),
  296–97
sprawl, 67, 276, 278, 279,
  280, 288
squatter housing, 395–96
SRO (Single Room
  Occupancy) hotels, 117
Stamford, Connecticut, *212*
Stamford/Greenwich area, 194
Standard and Poor's
  bond-rating agency, 139
Standard Enabling Act, 46
state economic development
  efforts, 254–57
state-enabling legislation,
  87–88
state implementation plans
  (SIPs), 90, 302–3
State Land Use Commission
  (Hawaii), 274
state-level growth
  management
  Florida, 275–76
  Hawaii, 274
  New Jersey, 277–78
  Oregon, 276–77
state planning, 50–51, 65–66
Staten Island, 312
steel-frame construction, 12, 76
stepped-back configuration,
  old-style office building,
  77, 78
Stockbridge, Massachusetts, 39
Stockholm, 382–83
street patterns, 3, 34, 46, 186,
  212, 393
Streetcar Suburbs (Warner), 14
streetcars, 14–15
"strict constructionism", 59
structural unemployment, 66,
  250–51
subdivision regulations, 140–41
subsidization, 258–59
"substantive" theory and
  "procedural" theory,
  distinction between, 404

Suburban Action Institute
(SAI), 411
suburbanization, 15, 17, 19, 23,
28, 355–57
and tax policy, 356–57
and planning, 188–89,
191–93
successive limited comparisons,
408
Suffolk County, New York,
142
Sunbelt, growth of, 20–21,
23, 354
sunshine laws, 315
superblock, 393
Superfund, 302, 307–8
Supreme Court, 111
"taking" issue, 76, 79, 80,
82–84
Supreme Court of New Jersey,
150, 151
Supreme Court of
Pennsylvania, 150
sustainable development
defined, 282
economic development, 283
environmental requirement,
282
local plan, implementing,
284–86
planning for, 282–86
planning techniques,
287–88
social equity, 283
sweat equity, 216
Sweden, planning in, 378, *380*,
381, 382–83
systematic regional planning,
349–51

*Tahoe-Sierra Preservation
Council et al. v. Tahoe
Regional Planning
Agency et al.*, 84
"taking" issue, 74, 75, 82–84
Tallahassee, Florida, 162
Tapiola, Finland, 383
tax expenditures, 218
Tax Reform Act of 1986, 357
taxes
excise, 227, 352
gasoline, 227, 316
levying of, 73, 96–97

local, 66, 148, 357
planning questions, link
between, 94
property taxes. *See* property
taxes
sales, 131, 259
Third World, 395
Taxpayer Relief Act of 1997,
356–57
tear downs, 220
technology parks, 385
telecommuting, 239, 240
Tenement House Act (1901),
38, 39
Tenement House
Commission, 38–39
tenements, *13*
Tennessee Valley Authority
(TVA), 61, 349, 350–51
terrorism, 68
Thames embankment
(London), 40
Thatcher, Margaret, 364, 369
The Closing Circle
(Commoner), 64
*The Death and Life of Great
American Cities*
(Jacobs), 185
"the export of pollution",
320n.19
The Feminine Mystique, 120
The Image of the City (Lynch),
180
*The Journal of the American
Planning Association
(JAPA)*, 5
*The Social Life of Small Urban
Spaces* (Whyte), 183, 185
theme parks, 386
Third World planning, 31–32,
393–97
Thomas, Craig, 358
Thompson, James R., 256
Thornley, Andy, 376
3M (Minnesota Mining and
Manufacturing), 330
TOD (*transit-oriented
development*), 191
tolls and privatization, 240, 242
top-down planning system,
Netherlands, 341
Town and Country Planning
Act, 364, 365

"town cramming", 365
Toxic Substances Control Act
of 1976, 64, 302
traffic metering techniques, 239
Train à Grande Vitesse (TGV),
400n.16
transfer of development
rights (TDR), 155–57,
157–58
transit, 225–26
transit-oriented development
(TOD), 191
Transportation Concurrency
Exemption Areas
(TCEAs), 276
Transportation Equity Act for
the Twenty First Century
(TEA-21), 239
transportation planning
approach to, 237–38
benefit/cost analysis, 234–35
CAFE, 91, 297
citizen involvement/
opposition, 235–36
concurrency problem, 276
European, 367, *368*, *375*,
376, 378
federal role in, 238–39
fine-tuning, 239–40
growth management,
276, 284, 288
HOV lanes, 242
"induced demand"
phenomenon, 235–36
intelligent vehicle
technology, 243
land use, 228–29
light-rail systems, 237, 238
mass transit, 231–32, 238
metropolitan planning,
230–34
modeling, metropolitan
area, 230–34
paying for, 227–28
pedestrian considerations,
237, 245
plug-in hybrid, 243–44
policy decisions, 234–37
public transportation,
237–38
Segway, 244–45
smart highway, 243
social implications, 118–19

transportation planning
  (*continued*)
  tolls and privatization,
    240, 242
  traffic flow studies, 129
  transportation system
    management (TSM),
    239–40, *241*
  travel demand management
    (TDM), 240
  travel movements,
    four-step procedure
    for estimating, 231
  urban trends, 225–27
  vehicular circulation, *175*
Tri-State District plan for the
  Philadelphia area, 50
Triborough Bridge and
  Tunnel Authority (TBTA),
  333
trucks, 17, 63, *227*, 331, 354
tuberculosis, 14
Tucker, William, 117
Tugwell, Rexford, 59, 61
TVA (Tennessee Valley
  Authority), 61, 349,
  350–51
Tyndall, John, 293
Tyson's Corner, Virginia,
  54, 194

Ulm, Germany, 39
Union Pacific Railroad, 344
Union Station, Chicago, 43
United Airlines, 255
United Nations, 296, 394
United States, national
  planning
  financing the suburbs,
    355–57
  interstate highway system,
    351–55
  land acquisitions, 342
  land management, 357–58
  land settlement, pattern of,
    342–43
  national plan, lack of, 341–42
  rail network, establishing,
    343–45
  systematic regional
    planning, 349–51
  water and the west, 345–49
urban design, 171–203

automobile, coming to
  terms with, 200–1
explained, 173–74, 179
future visions, 197–200
good, 182–88
neighborhood concept,
  185–88, *186*, *187*
process of, 180–82
success factors, 185
urban design process
  analysis, 180–81
  evaluation, 182
  implementation, 182
  synthesis, 181–82
urban designers, 171
Urban Development Action
  Grants (UDAGs), 101–2,
  215, 252
Urban Development
  Corporation (UDC), 370
"urban growth area", 273
Urban Growth Boundaries
  (UGBs), 276–77
urban homesteading, 215–16
Urban Mass Transit Act of
  1964, 237, 326
urban open space, 37–38
urban parkland, 37
urban regions, 15
Urban Renewal
  community development,
    213–17
  displacement, 222
  economic effect, 100–1
  gentrification, 213
  housing, 217–22
  origins of, 60, 62–63, 206–7
  overview, 205–6
  in retrospect, 210–13
  side effects of, 209–10
  termination of, 210
urban sprawl, 15
urban transportation, recent
  trends, 225–27
"urban underclass", 109
urbanization
  central-city shrinkage, age
    of, *18*, 22–23
  city poverty, 23–24
  concentration and density,
    11–12, *13*, 14
  decentralization, beginnings
    of, 14–16, *16*

forces behind, 10–11
future outlook, 26–28
nineteenth century, 9–16
1990s, 24–25
post-Civil War, 12, 14
rapidly growing regions,
  trends in, 26
regional trends, 20–22
suburbanization, 19–20
Third World, 394–95
U.S. Bureau of the Census,
  28, 221
U.S. Constitution, 34
U.S. Department of
  Commerce, 46
U.S. Senate, 296, 297, 300
U.S. Supreme Court of
  Appeals for the Second
  Circuit, 111

Vaux, Calvin, 37, *38*
VDOT (Virginia Department
  of Transportation), 166
vehicular circulation, *175*
Veiller, Lawrence, 39
Verrazano Bridge, 333, 335
"vest-pocket" park, 155
Veterans Administration
  (VA), 356
*Village of Euclid v Ambler
  Realty*, 79
Ville Radieuse, 197
Virginia, state-enabling
  legislation, 87–88
Virginia Department of
  Transportation (VDOT),
  166
visual survey, 180–81
"Voisin" plan, 198, 201

"walking city", 15
Wallace, Henry, 59
"war on terror", 58, 68
Washington, D.C., 34, 41
Washington Monument, 41, 68
waste disposal, planning for, 36
wastesheds, 315
"water carriage" sewer, 36
Water Resources
  Development Act
  (WRDA), 10, 348
Waterfront (Boston),
  213, 217

watersheds, 49, 338
Weber, Adna, 10, 12, 14
Wells, H. G., 15, 278
Welwyn Garden City
    (London), 53
Westchester County, New
    York, 50, 164–65
Westway, 236, 306
wetlands, 348
White Plains, New York, 164,
    210, 216
Whyte, William, 183
Willamette Valley,
    Oregon, 276
"Wise Use" movement, 310
Wood, Robert, 50
World Bank, 393, 396, 397
World Commission on
    Environment and
    Development, 282
World Court, 378
World Trade Center, 68, 179
World Trade Center site,
    rebuilding, 177–78
World War II, regional
    planning after, 326

WRDA (Water Resources
    Development Act),
    10, 348
Wright, Frank Lloyd,
    193, 196, 197
Wrigley, Robert L., Jr., 44

Yonkers, New York, 110–13,
    112, 154

zero population growth
    (ZPG), 65, 268
zoning
    bonus or incentive, 155
    cluster, 161
    constitutionality of, 75
    courts and, 149–52
    density bonuses, 220
    development agreements,
        162
    effectiveness of, 145
    exactions, 162–63
    exclusionary, 411, 420n.11
    fiscal, 125–26
    flexibility, 155–57, 160–63
    growth management, 272–73

    incentive, 155, 287
    inclusionary, 160
    limitations of, 145–47, 149
    ordinances, 141–42, *143–44*
    overzoning for commerce,
        45–46
    performance, 161–62
    planned unit development
        (PUD), 160–61
    police power, 75
    popularity of, 142, 144
    private property, public
        control over, 44–48
    process of, 45
    property taxes and,
        148–49
    recent developments in,
        152, 154–55
    rush to, 45–46
    "saturation" studies,
        152, 154
    transfer of development
        rights (TDR), 155–57,
        157–58
Zoning Board of Appeals,
    142